Consumer Behaviour

The Marketing Series is one of the most comprehensive collections of books in marketing and sales available from the UK today.

Published by Butterworth-Heinemann on behalf of The Chartered Institute of Marketing, the series is divided into three distinct groups: *Student* (fulfilling the needs of those taking the Institute's certificate and diploma qualifications; *Professional Development* (for those on formal or self-study vocational training programmes); and *Practitioner* (presented in a more informal, motivating and highly practical manner for the busy marketer).

Formed in 1911, The Chartered Institute of Marketing is now the largest professional marketing management body in Europe with over 24,000 members and 28,000 students located worldwide. Its primary objectives are focused on the development of awareness and understanding of marketing throughout UK industry and commerce and in the raising of standards of professionalism in the education, training and practice of this key business discipline.

Titles in the series

Business Law
R. G. Lawson and D. Smith

Cases in Marketing Financial Services
Edited by Chris Ennew, Trevor Watkins and Mike Wright

Consumer Behaviour
Chris Rice

Economic Theory and Marketing Practice
Angela Hatton and Mike Oldroyd

Effective Sales Management
John Strafford and Colin Grant

Financial Aspects of Marketing
Keith Ward

The Fundamentals of Advertising
John Wilmshurst

The Fundamentals and Practice of Marketing
John Wilmshurst

International Marketing
Stanley J. Paliwoda

Marketing Communications
C. L. Coulson-Thomas

Marketing Financial Services
Edited by Chris Ennew, Trevor Watkins and Mike Wright

Mini Cases in Marketing
Lester Massingham and Geoffrey Lancaster

The Principles and Practice of Selling
A. Gillam

Strategic Marketing Management
R. M. S. Wilson and C. T. Gilligan with D. Pearson

Consumer Behaviour

Behavioural aspects of marketing

Chris Rice

Published on behalf of
The Chartered Institute of Marketing

Butterworth-Heinemann Ltd
Linacre House, Jordan Hill, Oxford OX2 8DP

$\mathcal{R}$ A member of the Reed Elsevier plc group

OXFORD   LONDON   BOSTON
MUNICH   NEW DELHI   SINGAPORE   SYDNEY
TOKYO   TORONTO   WELLINGTON

First published 1993
Reprinted 1994, 1995

British Library Cataloguing in Publication Data
Rice, Chris
   Consumer Behaviour: Behavioural aspects
   of marketing. – (CIM Student Series)
   I. Title II. Series
   306.3

ISBN 0 7506 0549 9

Typeset by TecSet Ltd, Wallington, Surrey
Printed and bound in Great Britain by Clays Ltd,
St Ives plc

Contents

Preface

The subject of consumer behaviour is relatively new – books with such words in the title have only been appearing for twenty-five years or so – but it has its roots in more well-established behavioural sciences.

It is a fascinating subject area, and one in which every individual has a vested interest as the field is both expanding and changing rapidly. We now have television programmes which create great joy and mirth by showing early commercials. We all laugh at the naivety of many of the messages – but it may well be a laugh with an undercurrent of embarrassment as we remember actually being impressed by them when we first saw them. At the same time we have shows which focus on current advertisements, but which come from other cultures. We find them funny, but one might question the effect that they have of our stereotypes of other cultures.

Other changes have involved the use of influencing techniques well beyond the area of 'shopping'. Vast efforts are now expended to convince us of the need to vote in favour of particular political parties, to conserve the environment, to support charities and other, similar, 'non-commercial' ideals. The basic element of influencing other people remains at the core, however, and it is this process which forms the main thread of the ideas within this text.

The book has been designed to meet the requirements of the Chartered Institute of Marketing professional education scheme, but will also be of immediate relevance to undergraduate and Higher National business studies courses. In a field which has such a rapid rate of change it was decided, as a matter of policy, to encourage the reader to look around and find current examples. This has the advantage that reading newspapers and watching television may now be counted as 'coursework'!

My objective in writing this book has been to produce something which is 'user-friendly'. The aim was to attempt to reproduce the processes which make a 'good' class when teaching – involvement of teacher and students, exchange of ideas, activity, thought and, above all, fun.

To this end the text has deliberately been broken up with 'Think' exercises. Some readers may find this a distraction, but a large majority of the people on whom sections have been tried out say that it *has* made them stop and think. Encouragingly they have also said that they have understood, remembered material and enjoyed the process of learning as a result.

In other places, I have referred to 'the loneliness of the long-distance learner' – the problems experienced by the solitary student (whether as a long-term experience or because of missing a session at college). It is hoped that, by emphasising some of the discussion points in this way, some of the difficulties may be reduced. For those who are studying in a group, the 'think' exercises have no 'right' answers, so comparisons of opinions and subsequent arguments are not only common, but are to be welcomed.

End-of-chapter exercises have been included. One set refer to applying the material from the chapter to the marketing of a wide range of different 'products' (attempting to get the reader to think beyond their own work situation) and the second seeks to encourage the reader to apply the material to their own work and organization. As the world of education moves towards measures of competence – it is hoped that the student who has addressed each of the end-of-chapter exercises would have developed the framework for an impressive and relevant portfolio presentation.

A final note of thanks to my family for tolerating my distraction during the production of this manuscript, to Ted Johns for his encouragement at the start of the project and his unerring eye at the end, to my colleagues Lynette Harris – who helped make some space, and John Stewart – who listened and supported far beyond the call of friendship. Lastly, my thanks to all the students who have been the experimental proving ground for so much of my work and enjoyment.

Chris Rice

Part One   Social Sciences

1 There's nowt so strange as folk

The behavioural sciences – practice and problems

This chapter sets the scene for the behavioural sciences – defining them and looking at the problems associated with them (especially as compared with the physical sciences).

Learning objectives

At the end of the chapter students should be fully familiar with the following concepts and *should be able to relate them to marketing situations*:

- Range and focus of various behavioural sciences
- The scientific method:
  - Hypotheses
  - Theories
  - Laws
- Experimental design and control groups.
- Types of data.
- Methods of data collection.
- Problems of measurement.
- Uses of behavioural sciences:
  - Description
  - Explanation
  - Prediction
  - Control
- Ethical issues surrounding behavioural research.

The behavioural sciences are about people. This makes the course you are starting both the easiest and most interesting that you will tackle and also the most difficult.

The subject is 'easy' in as much as it is about life and our experience. At one level it should pose few problems as it could be argued that we are all expert practical psychologists – we live in a complex world and cope with it successfully – so the main problem may be in understanding the ideas, language and mystique that surrounds the subject.

On the other hand 'there's nowt so strange as folk'. People come in an infinite variety and are continually surprising. So the subject is very difficult in as much as it is very hard to know that you are right in the same way you can have confidence in having done a calculation correctly.

Another difficulty is the range of subjects that become relevant to marketing, syllabi for consumer behaviour courses and this book. The behavioural sciences include:

1 *Psychology* is the study of human and animal behaviour and usually centres on the individual. Its aim is to predict behaviour by reference to the nature of the individual. So psychology examines the individual differences (e.g. intelligence, personality, attitudes) and the processes (e.g. motivation, perception, decision making) which help to explain different responses by different people to similar situations. In addition, there are a number of sub-disciplines such as social psychology which extends the knowledge of individual differences and processes into a study of their significance in social (one-to-one and group) settings. Organizational psychologists focus their investigations on the workplace.

2 *Sociology* is a much less 'individual centred' discipline. It develops theories to explain and make predictions about social groupings and more wide-ranging social processes. So it is the study of collective behaviour of people in groups, and seeks to describe and explain phenomena such as social change, values in society and patterns of family life. It focuses not on the differences between individuals but on the differences between 'groupings' or 'collections' of individuals. Thus sociology will seek to compare people by social class, religious belief, occupational grouping etc. The size of the groupings can expand up to the consideration of whole cultures so sociology finds it difficult to go into a laboratory setting and determine the relative weight or importance of various causal factors in explaining behaviour. Thus it is often better at describing and explaining than at predicting.

3 *Psychiatry* is defined by the *Concise Oxford Dictionary* as 'the study of mental disease' and is very much an individually centred area of study. At first there may be questions as to the relevance of this as a basis for looking at the broad mass of the population. However, such a focus may give us useful insights into important everyday issues such as personality, coping, defences, frustration and communication.

4 *Anthropology* is one of the earliest of the behavioural sciences, traditionally centred on the study of whole communities and societies. In its early days there was considerable emphasis on 'primitive' societies – these have the advantage of being relatively small and simple which allows the study of the functions and interdependence of complete units within the society. While much contemporary anthropology still focuses on simple societies some researchers are developing models to describe and explain groupings at the industry or even the firm level.

5 *Economics* is the study of the allocation of scarce resources to unlimited wants. It may be either micro or macro (individual or governmental) and is generally based on logic and the assumption of humans being 'rational–economic' creatures. Such ideas, particularly those which pay attention to the decision making processes, may well have application to the marketing situation where we are seeking to influence the consumer in making economic decisions in favour of our product.

The idea of the different subject areas concentrating on different levels of human activity may be useful in introducing the disciplines and the extent to which they are separate or overlapping.

Some texts also include Geography and History in the list of social sciences – but in this course we will be concentrating primarily on Psychology and Sociology with a sprinkling of Psychiatric ideas thrown in. These are set out in tabular form in Figure 1.1.

The alert reader will realize that degree courses could be followed in each of these disciplines – so this text is, in effect, edited highlights from those areas which will help to illuminate our understanding of the marketing process.

Level	Elements	Typical category	Discipline
Society	A system of institutions and their relationships	Great Britain, EC	Anthropology and sociology
Institution	A system of organizations and their relationships	The public sector	
Organization	A system of groups and their relationships	CIM, Joe Bloggs and Co	
Group	A system of roles and their relationship	CIM Branch, Managers at Joe Bloggs & Co	Economics
Role	A system of expectations regarding behaviour	Marketing Manager	Social psychology
Personality	A system of characteristics, abilities, experience, attributes and dispositions	Person 'types'	Psychiatry and psychology
Organism	A system of organs	The human body	

Figure 1.1 Adapted from Drake and Smith *Behavioural Science in Industry* (McGraw-Hill, 1973)

This field of study is also a living area so there is plenty of ancillary work to be done. In addition to this text there are marketing examples all around us – advertisements, government statements, messages about healthy living, television, radio, newspapers, experiences of friends and colleagues, etc. The reader should be aware that the examples are all around us and should be continually updated.

The behavioural sciences, as we have observed, are full of problem areas. In order to explore some of the difficulties and issues involved try the following exercise.

Think – Imagine that you are asked to evaluate formally the effectiveness of the course of study you are currently undertaking.

- How you would set about such a task?

- Define the procedures, measures and timescales necessary to fulfil the request.

Write down your thoughts on how you would tackle the assignment and keep the document handy as we will refer to it later.

Acquiring knowledge

There are a variety of ways in which we, as human beings, acquire knowledge – 'experts' pontificate; preachers preach; teachers teach! We read newspapers, listen to gossip, and generally learn by our own experience of life. Helmstadter (1970) formalized and described a number of processes which may be relevant to our course of study:

1 *Tenacity* – or the persistence of a belief. Here we are concerned with the beliefs which we hold on to and react to as if they were facts.

Think – What beliefs do you hold?
   – How do they affect your behaviour?

---

2 *Intuition* – the process of coming to knowledge without reasoning or inferring. There is currently a lot of speculation about intuition stemming from the right hemisphere of the brain while logical thinking occurs in the left. There is interesting work going on regarding relaxation, releasing the power of intuition and of increased learning power.

Think – What experience have you had of Intuition?
   – How reliable has it been?

---

3 *Authority* – the acquisition of knowledge by accepting information because it comes from a respected source. This is rather different to taking expert advice – here the essence is the required acceptance. In this

sense it can encompass religious absolutes (and also superstitions if the receiver believes them).

> **Think** – What strong beliefs (authorities) do you accept?
> – How do these affect the way you see the world?

4 *Rationalism* – the development of knowledge through reasoning. It assumes that 'good' knowledge is acquired if the correct process of reasoning has been followed. This can have unfortunate consequences if the initial assumptions are not valid. The current computer expression GIGO (garbage in – garbage out) might be an example of the inadequacy of logically processing inadequate data. This is not to belittle the use of reasoning – indeed it is a crucial part of the scientific method – reasoning is used to arrive at hypotheses.

> **Think** – What experiences have you had where reasoning has 'come unstuck'?

5 *Empiricism* – this approach focuses on our experiences. In effect it says 'if I have experienced something, then it is valid and true'. So 'facts' that agree with our experience are true and those that do not are rejected. When we come to examine perception and the phenomena in that area we may well come to doubt the reliability of our own experiences. Once again, this is not to denigrate empiricism – it is a vital part of our intellectual armoury – but to counsel caution in unquestioning belief in our experiences.

> **Think** – What experiences have you had which look different with hindsight?

Each of these approaches is 'real', but each has its difficulties as the basis for systematically acquiring knowledge about our world. The notion of belief or superstition is a reality for many people – 'lucky' mascots and rituals are common for many of us. As one acquaintance says 'I'm not superstitious – I just don't take chances walking under ladders'. Clearly an awareness of superstition is relevant to our studies but it is unacceptable as the basis for professional study in this area.

Similarly, intuition, authority, rationalism and empiricism all have limitations of greater or lesser importance when we are seeking to learn about people and their behaviour. Intuition is important but we would be unwise to base our preparation for the examinations purely on 'I've got a feeling ...' without any other back-up. Authority in the form of deeply held religious beliefs exist, but we may need to be aware that there are different (sometimes contradictory) beliefs which co-exist within our society. If we are to progress our studies, rational thought might be a requirement – but in our incomplete state of knowledge it might be unwise to deny other people's intuitions and apparent oddities. Lastly our own experiences are a valuable source of input for our learning processes, but we have to face up to the question of how typical are we, and how typical was our experience?

In our society and in this particular programme of study the preferred method of acquiring knowledge is:

6 *The scientific method* – This represents a logic or method of enquiry and is concerned with establishing general principles. Natural sciences (chemistry, physics etc.) are based on direct observation, consistent relationships, experiments to test hypotheses and mathematical reasoning. Generally the following pattern is followed:

> *Idea* about things or relationships
> *Hypothesis* a researchable statement to be supported or refuted by facts
> *Facts* to test hypothesis
> *Theory* tested again to determine when true/ when not
> *Law* 'a statement of invariable sequence between specified conditions and phenomena'

This is shown diagrammatically in Figure 1.2.

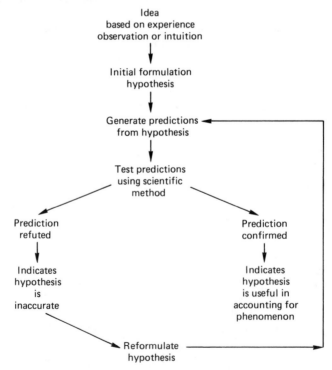

Figure 1.2   The scientific method

Clearly this could also be represented as a circular diagram, but we then realize that we do not return to exactly the same point as the one from which we started. Our investigation allows us to hold our prediction with greater or lesser confidence – so we have moved on slightly with regard to our acquisition of knowledge. Thus it might be more realistic to think of this process as a *'spiral of knowledge'*.

The behavioural sciences and the scientific method

The physical sciences utilize this method of investigation. Most of us remember physics experiments at school and are familiar with following the laid down procedures and (hopefully) getting the 'right' results (some of us can remember *not* getting the right results and deciding that it was less hassle to copy someone else's results knowing that there *was* a right answer).

There are significant problems, however, when we come on to look at the behavioural sciences. Human beings are not identical. Indeed it is a truism that every individual is unique. We also cannot subject humans to processes and experiences in the same way as we can deal with inert chemicals or materials. We have difficulty in 'repeating' experiments on people – they are clearly *not* the same the second time around, having already experienced the experiment – i.e. they can easily become 'contaminated'. Additionally, people are seldom subject to just one single influence at a time.

So if we are to understand behaviour we will need to conduct research in order to find and test relationships between a stimulus and a response, a given set of circumstances and an outcome etc. We therefore need to spend a little time examining the problems associated with the design of our experiments.

Experimental design

This stage requires a great deal of preparation, thought and planning. We need to ensure that the hypotheses stated are those we actually test. We must control extraneous variables, we need to separate the experimental variable as well as the response variable.

Two important concepts need clarifying at this point

1 *internal validity* is concerned with answering the question as to whether the stimulus had any effect in the response and
2 *external validity* which refers to confidence with which we can generalize the outcome, or how much a result is peculiar to the subjects used, or the circumstances surrounding the experiment.

In order to protect internal validity we may need to guard against time as a variable. We could get different results from a survey today than we would have got six months ago – e.g. opinion polls are carried out regularly as we expect political feelings and intentions to change. If we are aiming to measure change we will have to use the same measure before and after – but the act of measuring before may give participants an idea of what it is you are interested in – so they may change their attitudes or behaviour in order to 'help' the experimenter. We have problems of who we choose to take part in the experiment – volunteers might well be untypical! What do we do about those who drop out? – their stories/views might be more significant than those who do not.

External validity is also prone to difficulties – the time factor comes up again – by the time you have come to some conclusions the situation in the world at large might have changed so your results become irrelevant. The process of measuring may make subjects untypical in itself.

Most of these difficulties will be known to those working in marketing because market research activities are subject to very similar problems and constraints.

Experimental format

There are a number of different experimental forms that have differing strengths and limitations. We can set these out diagramatically where:

X = event in which we are interested, T_n = test or measurement

1 Case study or survey

$$\boxed{\quad X \quad T \quad}$$

Figure 1.3

Think – The 'Walkman' personal stereo is an example of a successful innovation.
– Why was it successful?
– What can we learn which will ensure our product innovation is also a success?

In the instance of the 'Walkman' a situation/company/product is being analysed retrospectively. This may provide useful suggestions for future actions (or hypotheses for testing) but care must be taken to ensure that future situations are comparable to the original case. Problems of '20/20 hindsight' abound as we have no measure of the situation before the event.

2 One group pre-test/post-test design

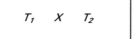

Figure 1.4

> **Think** – Imagine that you have a steady level of sales of product X. You change your advertising agency, develop new advertisements, and sales rise.
> – Is this because of the new advertising campaign?

We must address the problem of whether it was the stimulus that led to a change by measuring before and after. In the example above, we could discover that the increase in sales was due to some other factor. If, for instance, we were selling do-it-yourself products, the upturn in sales could be due to economic recession and unemployment leading more people, literally, to do it themselves. We still have enormous problems of external validity, i.e. how typical was it? can any lessons be learned and transferred to other situations?

3 Time-series design or survey

Figure 1.5

In a time-series survey, measures or tests are applied to the respondents over a period of time. Examples of this approach are opinion polls when the effect on attitudes of a particular event are assessed, or product panels which monitor reactions by checking how those reactions to a product change over a period of time. Here the issues of sample size and of picking respondents who are typical of the group you are seeking to study become important.

4 Non-equivalent control group design

Experimental group	T_1	X	T_2
Control group	T_1		T_2

Figure 1.6

Think – Imagine that you have a sales force of twenty representatives and they are all on a fixed salary. A consultant has suggested that you consider a bonus scheme, whereby their pay will be related to the level of sales that each rep attains. You decide to try this, but before adopting it for the whole department, you decide to conduct an experiment. You pick the ten best salespersons and put them on the new bonus scheme. The remainder stay on their original salaries. The sales figures of the 'bonus group' increase over the previous level. The ten who stay on the old pay scheme show no change in their sales performance.
– Does this prove that the bonus scheme improves sales performance?

It is a major step forward to have the idea of a control group emerging. This is a group who are subject to the same measures or tests but who are not exposed to the stimulus. Thus they can act as a check as to whether it *was* the stimulus that gave rise to the response – if the change is due to an extraneous factor then both groups would show the same change and we would not be able to support our hypothesis that it was the stimulus that caused the change. Despite this being an improvement on earlier efforts there are still significant potential problems surrounding the choice and representativeness of the two groups (i.e. are they actually the same or are they different – in the latter case, as in the example, it could be *these* differences that are being measured by any comparison, i.e. the fact of choosing the best ten for the bonus scheme may mean that it only works for good salespersons).

5 Classic experiment design

Experimental group (random)	T_1	X	T_2
Control group (random)	T_1		T_2

Figure 1.7

In Figure 1.7 the subjects are randomly allocated to the experimental and control groups and the measures are applied to both. This is the format which overcomes the majority of problems in terms of the scientific method.

> **Think** – In the previous 'Think' exercise, would offering the bonus to ten salespersons chosen at random and comparing their performance improvement to the ten in the control group (also chosen randomly) have improved the confidence with which you assess the effectiveness of the bonus scheme?

None of these designs is without its limitations, however. Even with the classic experimental design we commonly have the practical difficulty of access to suitable numbers of random subjects willing to take part in the study. We may also have 'unnatural' behaviour exhibited due to people knowing that they are part of an experiment.

The use of logic and reasoning

Earlier we referred to the use of reasoning as a method of acquiring knowledge, and much of the foregoing section involves the use of reasoning or logic. A central problem that is faced in the behavioural sciences lies in deciding what we can accept as 'evidence'.

> **Old Joke** – A behavioural scientist was travelling with a friend and on the journey they saw a flock of sheep in a field.
> 'They've been sheared' said the friend.
> 'They seem to have been, on this side' replied the scientist.

As we have seen, a second problem is the interpretation of the evidence, and the confidence we can have in that interpretation (which encompasses the internal/external validity issues discussed above).

Basically the chain of reasoning can go one of two ways:

1 *Inductive thinking* – the inferring of a general law from particular instances, and
2 *Deductive thinking* – the inferring of particular instances from general laws.

Generally, as we have seen, the behavioural sciences are not strong on general laws, so deductive thinking is somewhat less common than in the physical sciences. The danger being that deductions are made from theories, hypotheses or hunches rather than true laws.

In contrast, inductive thinking is relatively common. The temptation is often to infer a general law from a single case study. The section on experimental method emphasizes the need for careful design to increase the confidence we might have in any conclusions. The case study approach is very common:

XYZ plc 'did it by the book' and succeeded,

but before we believe what is basically an anecdote we might like to examine:

Firms who 'did it by the book' but who did not succeed,
Firms who 'did it all wrong' and succeeded
Firms who 'did it wrong' and failed

only then may we have the basis of a sound conclusion.

In dealing with the 'real world', it is sometimes difficult to set up rigorous experimental designs, so research is sometimes conducted 'after the event'. Data is collected and different aspects compared in order to develop hypotheses. It sometimes occurs that high positive correlations are obtained between separate sets of information, but great care must be taken to test whether:

A has led to B,
B has led to A,
a separate factor entirely has caused both, or
it is just a statistical oddity.

This is the point at which sound experiments need to be conducted in order to test the various hypotheses and identify the proven from the disproven, unproven or random chance occurrence.

Description, explanation, prediction and control in the behavioural sciences

The scientific method has a number of aims which we can imagine as being at different levels.

- Firstly it seeks to *describe* the event
- Secondly it seeks to *explain* what has happened
- Next it moves on to *predict* the happening in advance, and
- Ultimately it seeks to *control* the phenomenon

The physical sciences give us good examples of this process. Returning to our memories of science classes at school or college, many of us will remember doing experiments which illustrate this method quite well – investigations of gravity, evaporation, expansion all spring to the author's mind. Each followed the process closely and resulted in describing, explaining, predicting and controlling – and all had to be written up in the standard form.

The predictability of these natural phenomena allow us to exercise control over processes which enable us to develop many of the machines which are so much part of our life.

But we need to face up to the problem that these activities may be different in the behavioural sciences. We will now go on to examine each level in turn.

Description

The first objective/level of scientific enquiry is that of description – the portayal of a situation or phenomenon accurately. This stage also seeks to identify the variables that exist and the extent to which they exist.

In the behavioural sciences we do face specific problems in attempting description. Some behaviour is ambiguous. Some of the variables are invisible. Some behaviours are difficult/impossible to observe and describe – an example might be learning. We cannot find physiological changes – but we can measure your knowledge at the end of a course (a problem then arises whether the knowledge might have been there before the start of the course ...). The process becomes even more difficult, however, when we have to rely on individuals' accounts of what they are doing – they may lie, they may tell us what they think we want to hear, or they may not know!

This focuses our attention on the problem of the reliability of the data and we have three broad approaches we can follow in collecting data.

1 Observation

1 *Non-participant observation* – here we have the researcher watching the subjects. This looks quite good until we realize that the act of observing people may cause them to behave 'abnormally' (we see this later in the 'Hawthorne Effect'). We might therefore decide to go for 'hidden' observation, but even this has its problems. Observing pedestrian flow in a city centre from a hidden position does not appear too controversial, but other observations could seem to be a serious violation of privacy (e.g. Christensen (1988) reports a study which used hidden periscopes in a public lavatory!).
2 *Participant observation* – in this case the researchers 'disguise' themselves as ordinary group members/punters and observe what goes on 'from the inside'. Here we have problems regarding the influence of the investigator on what occurs – he or she could be the cause of the effect they describe, thus invalidating many of the conclusions. There are also some interesting and difficult ethical issues. The UK legal system rejects *agents provocateurs* – why should marketing investigations be subject to less stringent controls?

Both of these approaches to observation are also subject to difficulties about whether the observer is describing or interpreting. The element of subjectivity has to be guarded against when recording events.

3 *Unobtrusive measures* – this is where we look at outputs rather than asking opinions – classic methods are recording which books are brought or taken out of libraries rather than asking people what they read (few people 'admit' to reading Mills & Boon – but the evidence that they do is overwhelming!); similarly carpet wear can suggest that the reality of what exhibits are most popular at an art exhibition differs from the results of an exit survey!

2 *Analysing documents*

Diaries, letters, minutes, accounts, policy statements, customer records, productivity measures, etc. may provide apparently 'neutral' data and facts. However, we must always be wary of the circumstances under which they are produced and the reasons for them.

3 *Asking questions*

1 *One to one interview* – may be either structured or unstructured. The unstructured interview is the very straightforward meeting of the researcher and the subject where questions are asked and answers recorded. The structured interview gives manageable data with the ability to follow interesting or unexpected avenues that might arise from an answer. However some people criticize the structure as defining an agenda which is the researcher's rather than the respondent's – e.g. if asked whether you are finding the course useful or not you are likely to answer 'yes' or 'no'. Given a free choice, however, you might prefer to describe it in terms of interesting/boring, relevant/irrelevant or any other construct which is relevant and meaningful *to you*.
2 *Questionnaires* – commonly used, but they are really only highly structured interviews, so the key is asking the right questions first time! This needs careful development and pilot testing to avoid mistakes.

Explanation

At this level we are seeking the cause of a given phenomenon. We must, however, ensure that we get cause and effect in the right order as we saw earlier when the processes of logic, inductive and deductive thinking were introduced in the section on rationality. An example of such a problem might be that race and criminality are claimed by some to be linked – but 'the facts' may not support the *causal* relationship – i.e. it may not be that black people are more criminally inclined, it could be that police officers are more likely to arrest members of the black community.

The laws of natural science are inviolate but human laws are things we can choose to disobey or amend. Many of our rules of behaviour will only apply in one society rather than be universal. Some of our behaviour will only be tolerated within certain social groups. On the other hand the social sciences have the advantage that they can ask people why they do things – I can ask students how they feel about the course so far, whereas I tend to get no answer if I ask my bicycle why it is rusty!

The difficulty of explanation is compounded by the fact that people appear to behave in accordance with *their own* theories of how the world works. The nature of our society is such that we will tend to share these 'rules' with others in our groups (even anarchists share a belief in the absence of rules) – but we must also accept that we live with multiple realities (trade unionists and management may view industrial relations legislation very differently, similarly marketing personnel and consumers have varying views of the concept of 'profit'). We will see that many of these theories have been handed down through family links and standards, while others come from membership of certain groups or classes.

Another increasing problem is the use of 'technical' behavioural science language in everyday life. The colour supplements happily use words such as 'neurotic', 'intelligent', 'pathological' so that we get used to them. We may have to check that such technical jargon is being used with the correct technical meaning.

Prediction

In the behavioural sciences prediction is usually probabilistic rather than absolute – we can predict future labour turnover by cause but we cannot determine exactly who will get an offer they can't refuse, have a heart attack, get pregnant etc. There is also the danger of the self-fulfilling prophecy – you read something, believe it, act on it and it becomes true! Predictions depend on the rules but these are social phenomena and, as noted above, we can choose to disobey.

Control

Because of the choice element and cultural variations social scientists can be critical of what they observe (unlike the natural scientist). Our judgements are based on the perceived evidence and our own values. Thus we become involved in the process – we cannot step outside as the natural scientist can.

Most management activity may be viewed as being concerned with coping with, and controlling, an uncertain environment. The basic ideas of control theory come from engineering and centre on the concept known as feedback. This may best be described diagrammatically, as in Figure 1.8.

This cycle is perhaps most easily explained by using an example such as a refrigerator. Here the situation to be controlled is the temperature of the container. The output is temperature and the machine must be able to detect this output. We will also need to measure the level of the temperature and this can then be compared with the standard that we have set via the 'warmest/coldest' dial. This comparison tells us whether we are on target or

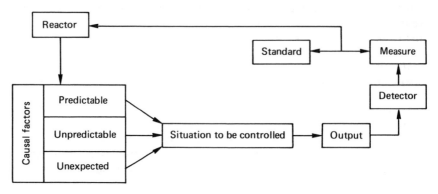

Figure 1.8   The control cycle

whether it is necessary for the system to react in some way in order to achieve the standard desired. Reaction will be through what we are calling 'causal factors'. In the fridge the motor is triggered when the temperature rises above the desired limit and its action causes the temperature to be reduced. When the lower level is reached the motor reacts by switching off so that the container slowly warms up. In this way we control the temperature inside the machine within the limits set.

1 *Causal factors* are any factors which affect the situation to be controlled and fall into the three categories set out above.
2 *Predictable factors* are those which affect the situation and whose effects can be accurately and consistently predicted – many of the physical laws fall into this category e.g. materials expand by predictable amounts with rises in temperature and water boils at 100°C.
3 *Unpredictable factors* are those things that we know have an effect on the situation but these effects cannot be accurately or consistently predicted – having a puncture will affect the performance of my bicycle, but the detailed effect is likely to be a function of a lot of other things such as whether it is in the front or back tyre, whether I am moving fast or slowly, whether it is a slow puncture overnight and what road conditions obtain at the particular point in time.
4 *Unexpected factors* are those factors that you have not thought of – generally these are occurrences which have not yet happened, once they have happened they will no longer be unexpected and will therefore be reclassified as predictable or unpredictable.

At the risk of appearing sexist, the traditional view of management is that it is the manipulation of the five 'M's in the interests of the objectives of the organization. The five 'M's being money, materials, machines, men and markets.

If these are the basic elements of the managerial situation it follows that we could examine them as causal factors to the situation to be controlled (the enterprise).

1 *Money* is not predictable – future interest rates, exchange rates, credit worthiness etc. are all clearly open to question, so we must consider it to be an unpredictable factor.
2 *Materials* run into similar problems – is quality what we require? will they arrive on schedule? will they arrive at all? So again it looks as if materials will have to be considered as an unpredictable factor.
3 *Machines* look rather better at first sight – but then we look at breakdowns – they do happen, usually at the worst possible time, so once again it looks like an unpredictable factor.
4 *Men (including women)* are perhaps the most erratic resource of them all – they are the ones with minds of their own – the resource that can vote with its feet, work to rule, come up with productivity enhancing suggestions, buy competitors' products – at best they are unpredictable at worst unexpected!!
5 *Markets* are also made up of people, so they share all of the problems identified above – but in addition they are prone to interference by external factors such as the level of unemployment, interest rates, wars and so on.

At first it may appear that we have showed that management is impossible! The reality is that management is about coping with unpredictable factors in an uncertain world. It is difficult – this is what makes it rewarding and well paid. If the factors were not unpredictable we would not need managers only planners and doers – i.e. in a 'better' world my cat could manage ICI!

Rather that prove that management is impossible I think we have explained the phenomenon sometimes known as Sod's Law (also attributed to Murphy on occasion). This is not a true law, but a joke which has enough truth in it to make it funny. Sod's Law comes in many forms but at its most general it claims that:

If something can go wrong, it will – but only at the most inconvenient and unexpected times.

Thus it is often used to explain why buttered bread falls butter side down (except when we are conducting an experiment to prove Sod's Law!). Another formulation of the same idea emerges as:

When you have found the answer, they change the question.

Its applicability comes from the fact that we tend to notice things that go wrong more than we recognize that something has gone to plan.

It is quite possible to perceive management as activities designed to minimize the effect of Sod's Law – in fact much managerial activity is devoted to making the various factors more predictable.

Money is made more predictable by establishing borrowing capacity in advance of need, borrowing at fixed rates of interest and above all by budgeting for income and expenditure.

Materials are subjected to goods inwards inspection to ensure that sub-standard materials are not allowed into the system which can lead to enormous expense if work is carried out only to be scrapped subsequently. Carrying adequate stocks of necessary materials is one way of minimizing the risks associated with running short of crucial inputs to the organization.

Machines are made more predictable through maintenance – this extends the time that they work effectively, but may still leave us with a problem of sudden breakdown. This can be minimized by preventative maintenance where items are replaced before they are able to affect the whole machine. Predictability of machine systems may also be improved by avoiding dependence on single units.

The human factor is made more predictable by a series of devices associated with the personnel function – manpower planning, recruiting and selecting, reward systems, training, rules, appraisal, job descriptions.

Markets are made more predictable through the activity of advertising after suitable market research. The aim is to create and control demand for our product.

This view is therefore a useful focus for our study of the behavioural aspects of marketing – i.e. how does what we are doing illuminate or assist us in this central problem of controlling that prime aspect of the organization – its market, both existing and potential?

Think – How do you feel regarding the manipulation of the behaviour of staff, colleagues and the public?

Ethical considerations

This last exercise leads us on to discuss some of the ethical considerations. There are three main categories to think about.

1 Relationship between society and science

This concerns the extent to which society and its cultural values should intervene in the process of experimentation and the acquisition of knowledge.

'He who pays the piper calls the tune' is a well-worn cliché, possibly because it is so often true – funding sources may define the focus of investigation and the development of knowledge.

> **Think** – You discover an addictive (but not banned) substance which is tasteless and appears to have no side effects. You manufacture instant coffee and realize that adding a little of ingredient *X* could ensure product loyalty.
>   a) Is it ethical to do it?
>   b) If you manufactured pet food would it be any more acceptable/less acceptable/different?

2 Professional issues

This concerns the potential for faking in research. The scandal surrounding Sir Cyril Burt, the British psychologist, who was knighted for his work on heredity and intelligence and who, it was alleged, faked some of his results, shocked the scientific world. The impact of the allegations was compounded by the claim that his work directly affected Government policy in the field of education and segregating children at eleven plus. The assertions discredited all his work (but it has never been shown that he faked results in all his studies) – so we lose what might be valuable knowledge.

The pressure to give the client (paymasters as in (1) above) what they wish to hear can be very great.

There can be no justification for altering or faking scientific data.

3 Treatment of subjects

This concerns the potential in the behavioural sciences for harming (either physically or psychologically) the subjects who take part in the studies.

> **Think** – Imagine you wish to find out more about the characteristics of people who buy your product. You watch outlets, spot purchasers, follow them to their homes, and, at a later date call on them posing as health researchers conducting a random sample survey and ask detailed personal questions about their lifestyle.
>   a) Is this ethical?
>   b) If not, which are the unethical aspects
>   – observing them,
>   – following them,
>   – questionning them on personal matters,
>   – posing as a researcher with a different objective?

There are common ethical dilemmas for researchers when a judgement has to be made as to whether the potential benefits of a piece of research outweigh the possible difficulties for the participants.

The researchers concerned should not make this judgement as they may not be impartial. They should involve other, independent behavioural scientists in the decision to ensure the protection of the basic human rights of participants.

Deception poses problems for the dignity of subjects – yet often it is important to the very integrity of the investigation that the subjects remain unaware that they are taking part in 'an experiment'. Television shows such as *Candid Camera* trade on the embarrassment of people being 'set up' in order to generate laughs at their expense. The problem centres on how we decide what is an acceptable joke/jape/trick and at what point the treatment becomes unacceptable.

Teachers may experiment with classes as a matter of course development – what rights have students in controlling the extent to which they are being 'experimented' upon? Teachers may be unwilling to admit that this is the first time they have tried a particular approach to teaching a subject – it can also be argued that if they announce that 'this is an experiment' the students may react unnaturally – thus invalidating any judgement as to the effectiveness of that particular approach.

Confidentiality of data is another issue that can become difficult in some situations.

Marketing itself can be problematic:

Think – You are the marketing manager for a firm who distributes 'health foods'. Recent research has cast doubt on the safety of one of the products you handle – 'Steroidal' – a preparation for body builders. The Government have just announced a ban on its sale in the UK. The firm holds considerable stocks of the preparation and your managing director asks you to explore the possibility of selling the stock abroad to a country which does not ban the substance.
   a) What would you do?
   b) Is it different if you are offered a sizeable bonus for disposing of the preparations?
   c) Is it different if failure to do so could result in the closure of the company with the loss of 50 jobs?

Evaluation issues

Let us go back and consider the design for evaluating your course (or this book) that you produced at the beginning of the chapter. In the light of this discussion how well did you do?

Clearly for a sound experiment or evaluation you should have included:

1 measures of achievement, behaviour or knowledge both before and after the training event.
2 a control group

The reality is that evaluating training is very difficult to do.

Bloom (1956) observed that people are 'apparently so constituted that they cannot refrain from evaluating, judging, appraising or valuing almost everything that comes within their purview'.

There seems to be a paradox in that it is both difficult and we do it all the time. Imagine two people settling down to an evening in front of the television – one chooses a documentary because (s)he is interested in the topic, the other chooses a comedy show seeking entertainment. Assuming both shows lived up to expectations both individuals would rate their decision as 'right', thus highlighting the importance of:

1 *Criteria* – the obvious criterion for judgement is 'did it achieve its objective?'

> **Think** – In your evaluation of the course
> - What criteria did you use?
> - Is it likely that students will all have the same objectives?
> - Are they the same as others in your group?
> - Are they the same as your tutor's objective?
> - Are they the same as the college's objective?
> - Are they the same as the Institute's objective?

Some of you will have focused on outcomes (e.g. passing), others on process (e.g. enjoyment). Other issues that often emerge from this exercise are:

a When did you intend to evaluate? During the course or after it has finished?

b Do we look for unexpected outcomes or learning? Here we may have someone who came on the course to complete the C.I.M. Certificate programme – but the prime learning might be that they discover that they are grossly underpaid relative to other course members doing similar jobs!!

c At what level do we evaluate:
  i Reaction (like/dislike)
  ii Learning (it would need a pre-test to measure the start point)
  iii Behaviour (does it show?)
  iv Results (does it pay off? and for whom?)

d Who will conduct the evaluation? and for whom?

There are many weak links in the chain – a major one being the issue of transferability of the learning from the classroon to the workplace. Other difficulties include inadequate analysis of the need leading to unsuitable training design, using measure which show training success but which may not reflect job performance, using measures which show job success but which are unrelated to training, using measures because we have them rather than because of their relevance. Thus we may have a situation which could be described by Figure 1.9.

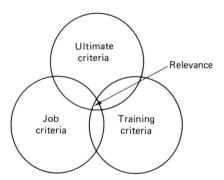

Figure 1.9   Evaluation criteria

As with any test the criteria (measures) must be valid, reliable and relevant. The sources of unreliability are numerous – the sample size may be inadequate, the range of behaviours of the group may be too great, the instructions to the test may be ambiguous, conditions during measurement may not be consistent, or the instrument itself may 'help' the participant.

The problems increase still further if rating methods are used. Here the competence of the judges may be a problem, difficulties can arise with complex or simple behaviours, sometimes the behaviour is not overt, or observers may have difficulty in observing. Reality poses even more problems – acceptability of the measures to both the organization and the participants, in terms of cost, time and inconvenience.

Generally evaluators seek to find a single measure that will pin down the behaviours required – but it is reasonable to assume that behaviour is affected by a number of factors such as motivation, satisfaction, values, and expectancy, so the logic is that we may well need a variety of criteria against which to judge the effectiveness of our training. The chances of positive outcomes against all of these criteria may be remote and perhaps unattainable.

Throughout there are significant numbers of choices to be made, objectives, criteria, designs etc. which will define the confidence with which you can draw conclusions as to the value of the training. While the exercise was chosen as being possibly the only common experience for all readers of this book, the parallels with marketing exercises that you might be asked to undertake are striking – in fact if you were the publishers of the volume you might make this request of your marketing staff.

On a lighter note:

An alternative view of the scientific method

In response to an examination question which concerned the explanation of 'theory/hypothesis, stimulus/response/intervening variables, experimental/control groups', illustrating each with examples from behaviour studies ...' one student came up with the following answer:

Theory/hypothesis
The critical difference between a theory and an hypothesis is one of evidence or experimentation.

One may have an *hypothesis* that, when poked in the eye, a person would say 'ouch'. However it cannot be said to be a *theory* until it has been tested and there is evidence to support it.

So, you go out and poke some people in the eye – let us take a sample of ten people. The first four people that you poke did, indeed, say 'ouch'; the other six, however, poked you back!

Having conducted this experiment you would then be able to say that although your original hypothesis had been disproven, you have arrived at a new theory – that, generally, when poked in the eye, people will poke back.

In a marketing context this would come into play when planning a new product launch. Any statements regarding the product or its likely take up, would merely be hypotheses until some evidence had been gathered in the market.

You may well say 'What if an existing theory has been used, or a proven model of consumer behaviour?' The problem here is that such theories and models may only hold good for the precise circumstances in which they were created. They can be used to help arrive at a new hypothesis, but should never be taken as gospel.

Stimulus/response/intervening variables
Going back to our eye poking example. In this experiment the original poke was the *stimulus*, and the victim's cry or counter-attack was the *response*.

However, the response was not simply caused by the original stimulus. It is affected by the *intervening variables* that are responsible for shaping the precise form of reaction.

So, if the victim of the original attack was a pacifist, their response might be different from that of a member of the SAS. Similarly, if the original victim was a small and thoughtful person his (or her) response would be different from that of a six-foot, sixteen-stone professional wrestler.

In the real world and in a marketing context, intervening variables include social class, peer pressure, affluence, education, political opinion, etc.

These are all elements that people pick up (or are subjected to) throughout their lives. Their response to various stimuli depends largely on this sort of factor.

For instance, a marketer may use a politician to endorse a product in an advertisement (probably not a good idea in the real world). A consumer response to that advert will be determined by their attitude to politicians in general, their politics in particular and any preconceived ideas about the personality concerned.

Obviously, this is a very simplistic view of the subject. In reality the consumer's response would be affected by a great number of other factors as well – but it helps to understand the problem if one isolates the various components.

Experimental/control groups

When we were busy poking people in the eye and developing theories, we forgot to take into account one vital thing – what would be the response of the 'victims' had we not poked them in the eye?

In order to enhance the accuracy of any experimentation, but particularly in the case of behaviour, one must also set up a *'control' group*. That is a group who are observed but who receive no stimulus.

If, in our control group, six people still poke us back unprovoked, and four say 'ouch' apparently without reason, we must abandon our old theory, develop new hypotheses and conduct new experiments since it is clearly *not* the poke in the eye that caused the response.

Such control groups are particularly helpful to those studying advertising and its effectiveness.

One group of people can be exposed to the campaign (the *experimental group*) while another group (the *control group*) are kept isolated from it. By observing the subsequent actions of the two groups (whether or not they buy the products concerned, etc.) a theory about the advertisement and its effectiveness can be built up.

This level of originality is very unusual under examination conditions – the candidate did get bonus points for making the examiner laugh while demonstrating a sound grasp of the issues involved! I would happily acknowledge the authorship if I knew who the examinee was – in the event I was marking 'blind' – only an examination number to go on, but thank you 'anon from North London'!

Some 'typical' examination questions – behavioural sciences

A Below are listed some of the principal methods of data collection typically used by behavioural scientists.

- Surveys
- Observation
- Experimentation

Using examples to illustrate your material, show how each of these methods can be employed by marketers. What are the typical problems associated with each of these techniques of information gathering and how can they be overcome?

B Behavioural scientists typically obtain information by analysis of existing data, by surveys, by observation and by experimentation. Comment upon the problems of gathering reliable and valid information about human behaviour from each of these sources and show how the problems can be overcome.

C Explain the meaning of the following terms connected with research into human behaviour and illustrate each concept with examples taken from behavioural studies relevant to the marketing process.

- A theory and an hypothesis
- Stimulus, response and intervening variables
- Experimental and control groups

D What are the problems associated with the collection of information on buyer behaviour? How might these difficulties be overcome?

E What do you believe are the ethical limitations that should apply to marketers seeking information on the behaviour, motivation and emotions of the population?

Sources

Bloom, B. S. (1956) *Taxonomy of Educational Objectives. Handbook 1: The Cognitive Domain*, Longmans Green.

Buchanan, D. A. and Huczynski A. A. (1985) *Organisational Behaviour*, Prentice-Hall.

Christensen, L. B. (1988) *Experimental Methodology* (4th edn.) Allyn & Bacon.

de Bono, E. (1967) *The Five-day Course in Thinking*, Penguin.

Drake R. I. and Smith P. J. (1973) *Behavioural Science in Industry*, McGraw-Hill.

Helmstadter, G. C. (1970) *Research Concepts in Human Behaviour*, Appleton-Century-Crofts.

Maxwell, A. E. (1970) *Basic Statistics in Behavioural Research*, Penguin.

Reeves T. K., and Harper, D. (1981) *Surveys at Work: a Practitioner's Guide*, McGraw-Hill.

Robson C. (1973) *Experiment, Design and Statistics in Psychology*, Penguin.

Thouless R. H. (1953) *Straight and Crooked Thinking*, English Universities Press.

Part Two   People as Individuals

Areas of difference

2 'All the world is strange – except you and me ...'

Individual differences – intelligence, aptitudes and mental processes

Introduction

This chapter introduces some of the basic ideas of psychology and highlights some of the ways in which people are different from one another. It is of interest because, in dealing with mental processes and intellectual styles, it covers some of the concepts that influence people both as consumers and as students.

At the end of this chapter readers should be comfortable with the following concepts, the associated language, and, where appropriate, their application to marketing situations:

- Intelligence,
- Abilities and aptitudes,
- Cognitive style,
- Creativity.

Intelligence

Intelligence has many synonyms – Roget's Thesaurus gives us well over 100, from astuteness to wisdom. It is a concept which has important social value and vocational significance. It is therefore not surprising that it has received much study and attention from educationalists, selectors and even politicians.

> **Think** – What do *you* understand by the word 'intelligence'?

The problem of defining intelligence is more difficult than appears at first sight. It is a word that most of us use in our everyday conversation but when challenged most of us find it difficult to define in a way that is acceptable to other people. If you compare notes with others who have defined it you may well discover that you are describing subtly different characteristics, or alternatively different aspects of what might be the same thing. It is either reassuring or disturbing to find that psychologists have similar problems of definition!

In 1923 a psychologist with the delightful name of Boring proposed that 'intelligence is what intelligence tests measure', a definition that is still widely accepted. This approach is less silly that appears at first sight, as most tests of general intelligence are constructed to measure the ability of people to carry out certain specific mental operations. This leads us on to the next problem of whether the mental processes measured are the same ones we recognize in other people and describe as symptoms of 'intelligence'.

One useful view is that 'pure' intelligence is something to do with an ability to see relationships, and the capacity to use that ability to solve problems. The main difficulty seems to centre on the fact that, in casual interaction, we use the word to mean something which is a mixture of 'pure' intelligence and acquired or taught knowledge.

Historically, an important stage in the study of intelligence was the work of two French psychologists, Binet and Simon*, who were asked in 1905 to examine ways of identifying children who were too 'feeble minded' for education in normal schools. They developed a series of simple verbal and practical problems designed to test abilities in the areas of understanding, reasoning, making judgements and adaptation. They identified those problems which could be tackled by older children better than by younger, and by 'brighter' children better than those classed as 'duller' ('brighter' and 'duller' as assessed by their teachers). Binet standardized the scoring procedure so that each child's mark could be compared to the norm for their age.

This gave rise to the concept of each child having a *'mental age'* – the chronological age at which most children scored similarly to his or her own score. So an eight-year-old child who obtains a score normally achieved by ten-year-olds has a mental age of ten; and a ten-year-old who obtains a score normally achieved by eight-year-olds has a mental age of eight.

In 1916 the American, Terman, developed this concept further into what is now called the 'intelligence quotient' or IQ. This is calculated by taking the ratio of the child's mental age to its chronological age and multiplying by 100. So the first child in the previous paragraph (aged eight, mental age ten) has an IQ calculated:

$$\frac{10}{8} \times 100 = 125$$

The second child (aged ten, mental age eight) has an IQ calculated:

$$\frac{8}{10} \times 100 = 80$$

One particular advantage of this calculation is that the average child of whatever age has, by definition, an IQ of 100; thus it enables instant

*Reviewed in Gregory, 1987; Reber, 1985; and Robertson and Cooper, 1983.

comparison of any child with the intelligence levels of its chronological cohort.

While IQ tests have gone through a number of developments over succeeding years, the principles originated by the Binet–Simon studies remains basically unchanged.

There are, however, a number of difficulties with IQ measurement. One is the assumption that intelligence is normally distributed within the population. In the design phase of tests the items are adjusted, if necessary, to produce a normal distribution. While it is attractive to make such an assumption and assume that intelligence falls into a similar patterns as, for example, height and weight, it appears to be unproven. Another potential problem is that such measures may be culturally biased, and a third problem may centre on the reality that the tasks which are set may not adequately distinguish between the 'pure' intelligence and the acquired or taught knowledge that we referred to above.

Another common experience is that we know people who are clearly highly intelligent but who are better at some mental activities than others – the copywriter who is good at writing, spelling and doing crosswords, but who has difficulty in completing a mileage claim involving numbers, or the engineer who has the opposite profile of talents. At first sight such a statement contains unreasonable stereotypes of copywriters and engineers, but the different ability profiles that people have appear to be an important determinant of their job choice. Complete the exercise in Figure 2.1.

Having completed the ratings, you might like to consider how much these variations in your ability profile have affected your choices of job, courses undertaken, hobbies and interests. It seems likely that most people will make choices which will play to their strengths – thus poorly co-ordinated children will tend to avoid ball games in the playground, persons who find reading difficult tend not to be very interested in books and so on. An interesting corollary to this is that people, in playing to their strengths, will tend to get more practice at those activities and so improve their performance even further.

One advantage of working with abilities or aptitudes of this sort is that it becomes easier to understand what we are doing. It is also more straightforward to design tests to measure the specific ability in which we are interested. Items from such tests are shown in Figures 2.2, 2.3, 2.4 and 2.5.

These questions are clearly attempting to measure ability in different aspects of mental processing. The first part of the numerical ability section deals with numbers, but concentrates on the capacity to manipulate them via addition, multiplication, subtraction and division – the kind of activities that many readers will recognize as mental arithmetic from their school days. The second part of the numerical section – finding the missing number in a sequence – tests the reader's capacity to apply logical thinking to a problem which is expressed in numerical terms. Thus it is, in many ways, a more complex process than the first part of the section.

Similarly, the verbal section starts with problems focused on the meanings of words while the second part demands the identification of patterns and

Think   – How good are you at different mental activities?
        – Rate yourself on the following scales:

I am:

bad					average					good
0	1	2	3	4	5	6	7	8	9	10

at using words, writing essays, spelling, crosswords.

• • •

I am:

bad					average					good
0	1	2	3	4	5	6	7	8	9	10

at using numbers, doing mental arithmetic.

• • •

I am:

bad					average					good
0	1	2	3	4	5	6	7	8	9	10

at dealing with patterns, shapes, maps, drawings.

• • •

I am:

bad					average					good
0	1	2	3	4	5	6	7	8	9	10

at dealing with mechanical things, either practically or understanding them.

• • •

I am:

bad					average					good
0	1	2	3	4	5	6	7	8	9	10

at assessing other people.

Figure 2.1

groupings before the solution can be found. So this again attempts to measure the capacity to use logic and problem solving processes in situations which are defined by words.

The perceptual problems are of the logic type, but this time using patterns and shapes as the medium for defining the problem, while the mechanical set are concerned with the understanding and application of mechanical principles.

Are the following sums right? Y = yes; N = no (underline your answer)

352	185	723	268	497
123	456	101	345	294
218+	109+	166+	222+	131+
693	750	990	835	922
Y N	Y N	Y N	Y N	Y N

77	93	83	69	57
46 ×	39 ×	37 ×	58 ×	39 ×
3542	3627	3071	4002	2223
Y N	Y N	Y N	Y N	Y N

542	721	550	183	334
175 −	498 −	469 −	176 −	255 −
367	223	81	7	79
Y N	Y N	Y N	Y N	Y N

1287/9=143	7707/3=2569	7784÷8=973	5238÷6=873	6573÷7=939
Y N	Y N	Y N	Y N	Y N

Here is a sequence of numbers but with one number missing. Work out the missing number. Circle the correct answer from the options on the right.

1	2	4	8	16		28	32	24	36
1	3	9	27	81		243	245	168	249
1	4	9	16	25		24	30	36	41
1	2	3	5	8		12	15	17	13
0	3	8	15	24		35	37	41	33
3	9	6	15	9		17	15	13	21
2	5	11	23	47		83	95	92	105

Figure 2.2   Numerical ability

Here are some pairs of words – do they mean the same (S) or the opposite (O)? Underline the answer you think is right.

begin	S	O	start
brave	S	O	timid
alive	S	O	dead
clean	S	O	sordid
quick	S	O	speedy
scatter	S	O	disperse
tardy	S	O	slow
attractive	S	O	repugnant
order	S	O	chaos
resonant	S	O	sonorous
serious	S	O	frivolous
cosmetic	S	O	fundamental
chagrin	S	O	mortification
compromise	S	O	insist
trifle	S	O	bagatelle
shallow	S	O	profound
burgeon	S	O	stunt
valedictory	S	O	welcome

Here are groups of six words – four have something in common – *find the two that do not belong* (spot the oddities!) Underline the two you choose.

autumn	leaves	summer	holiday	spring	winter
hot	tepid	cold	warm	meal	dish
dog	stone	cat	rock	mouse	elephant
dirty	clothes	washing	scruffy	messy	grimy
war	combat	battle	army	ship	conflict
trumpet	violin	drum	horn	trombone	euphonium
walk	train	car	bicycle	sledge	bus
pink	dress	green	leaf	red	blue
safe	bank	secure	key	sound	protected
potato	apple	turnip	leek	cherry	carrot
senior	old	citizen	elderly	pension	aged

Figure 2.3   Verbal ability

Here are a row of symbols. Work out which of the following figures

a = □   b = ■   c = ○   d = •   e = △   f = ▲

g = ☐   h = ◼   i = ◯   j = ⬤   k = △   l = ▲

completes the sequence. Write the answers in the spaces provided.

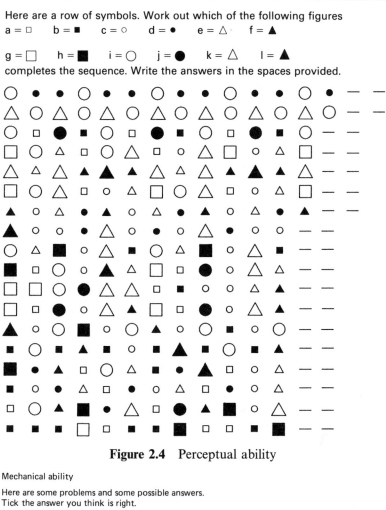

Figure 2.4   Perceptual ability

Mechanical ability

Here are some problems and some possible answers.
Tick the answer you think is right.

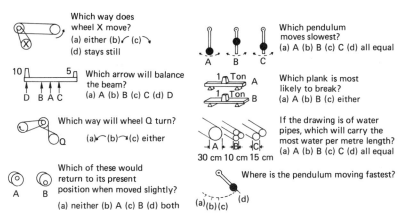

Figure 2.5   Mechanical ability

> **Think** – Which of the test items did you find easiest – Verbal, Numerical, Perceptual or Mechanical?
> – Does this coincide with your earlier rating of your relative strengths in Figure 2.1?

Some organizations use tests of this sort as part of their selection process – the advantages seem fairly obvious – if they are seeking a school leaver to train as an engineer, it would seem sensible to choose candidates with relatively strong mechanical and numerical abilities.

> **Think** – What ability profile would you expect for
>   a librarian?
>   a sales representative?
>   a market researcher?
>   a marketing manager?

At the same time as the Binet–Simon work described above, Spearman put forward what has become known as the *two-factor theory* of intelligence. This proposed that an underlying factor of general intelligence – *g* – was helpful in performance in all areas of human ability. The existence of such an underlying factor would help to explain why there is a persistent positive correlation between test scores covering a wide area of different abilities. Spearman suggested that, in addition to the general factor *g*, there are a series of *s* factors that are specific to given abilities.

When the data obtained from large numbers of test results are examined using mathematical techniques such as factor analysis, there is evidence to support the idea that there may be two significant subgroups of abilities which appear to centre around verbal and spatial skills respectively.

Vernon proposed a hierarchical model of intelligence, which encompasses many of these ideas (see Figure 2.6).

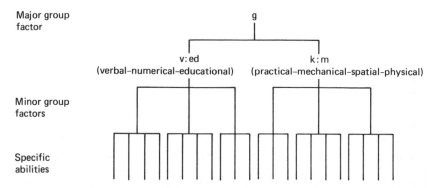

Figure 2.6   Hierarchical structure of human abilities (after Vernon, 1969)

6 Evaluation	– the ability to make judgements using explicit and coherent criteria. These criteria may be either derived from the work of others or be devised by the individual.
5 Synthesis	– the ability to assemble data into new and meaningful relationships, thus forming a new whole.
4 Analysis	– the ability to break material down into its component parts and to see the relationships that exist between them.
3 Application	– the ability to apply knowledge, understanding and comprehension to new, concrete and real life situations.
2 Comprehension	– the ability to understand the meaning of knowledge from level 1.
1 Knowledge	– the simple knowledge of facts, terminology, theories, etc. commonly learned by rote.

Figure 2.7   Bloom's taxonomy of cognitive processes

Intelligence and cognitive style

Bloom (1956) identified six categories in what he called the cognitive domain. The suggestion is that these are arranged as a taxonomy – in some sort of hierarchy but without having equal gaps between the stages. The categories identified are set out in Figure 2.7.

This work suggests that we can consider mental activity as being in one of these categories.

Think – What examples can you find of advertising messages utilizing the different levels of Bloom's taxonomy?

Creativity

Once again we are faced with a concept which is both very familiar and yet difficult to pin down. Most of us will claim to be able to recognize creativity in others (and sometimes in ourselves); on the other hand we are also likely to have difficulty in defining it satisfactorily.

Think – What do you understand by the word 'creativity'?
  – How do you recognize it in other people?
  – How do you recognize it in yourself?
  – Does a creative individual show this talent in different situations (e.g. at work, at home, in hobbies)?

Edward de Bono, the guru of 'Lateral Thinking' argues that in general our mental tools for judging and processing and analysing are very good, but we are much less successful at generating new ideas and hypotheses because we fail to realize that in a patterning system provocative methods are required. The contrasting mental processes are often referred to as *convergent and divergent thinking*.

In convergent thinking individuals are said to converge upon the single acceptable solution to a problem (such as the one set in Figure 2.8), while divergent thinking is described as the ability to generate a range of possible solutions to a given problem for which there is no unique right answer (like 'how many uses can you think of for a brick?'). Clearly such an ability is likely to be part of the creative act as the creator will most probably need to evaluate a number of possible approaches to solving the problem. Divergent thinking and creativity are sometimes used interchangeably, but it seems likely that divergent thinking alone is not sufficient for true creativity. There is evidence to suggest that knowledge and reasoning, as well as divergent thinking, are used in combination during the creative process (Entwistle, 1981).

Stages in creative thinking

Perkins identifies four stages that are typically involved in the creative act:

1 Preparation

Preparation is primarily concerned with recognizing that a particular problem is worthy of study or thought. The statement of the problem is often a crucial stage and may well help or hinder solution. All too often we define problems in highly personal and behavioural terms – 'the problem is that you have got to stop smoking'. This may be confusing problems with symptoms, and in this example the solution has been predetermined by the statement. The highly creative person is often the one who recognizes the significance of something that has been under the noses of other people (often for a long time), but which has been disregarded by them. This is the element that leaves us thinking 'why didn't *I* think of that?'.

> **Think** – What ideas have made *you* think 'why didn't *I* think of that?'?

A marvellous example of 'why didn't I think of that?' comes from my friend and colleague, Dr Ted Johns who, in a consultancy situation, observed a group of senior marketing persons gathered round a table to brainstorm ways of selling more toothpaste. During an interval the coffee was brought in by one of the catering staff, who saw what they were doing and said, 'It's obvious, all you have to do is make the nozzle bigger on the end of the tube . . .'

2 Incubation

This incubation stage is the 'mulling over' phase, which commonly seems to occur at a subconscious level. The putting aside of a problem (which is sometimes confused with procrastination) or the statement 'let me sleep on it' presupposes a relatively lengthy incubation period. However, in real life, we often do not have time – journalists and copywriters have deadlines to meet so the luxury of sleeping on it is not always possible. The idea of such activity continuing in our subconscious mind is attractive as it could explain the originality of some ideas as being the result of not being subject to rational, conscious logic (a significant barrier to creativity as discussed below).

3 Inspiration

Inspiration is when the possible solution to the problem, or a flood of ideas, come abruptly and suddenly into the conscious mind.

> **Think** – What experience have you had of 'inspiration'?
> – Under what circumstances did it occur?
> – Can you be inspired to order?

Most people report that the moments of illumination rarely come 'to order'. Ideas seem to spring unbidden in the most unusual and unlikely situations, in the bath, while taking exercise or even in dreams. Indeed, it sometimes seems that it is the very absence of conscious thought which generates the magical insight.

4 Verification

When the solution or idea is tried out in practice, verification is the point at which the 'goodness' of the solution is determined. My world is littered with good ideas that didn't work.

This schema of the creative process is interesting as many people see creativity solely in terms of stage 3 – inspiration. The understanding that the other stages carry equal or even greater weight is particularly useful.

It also concentrates on creativity as being about the production of highly original solutions. From a practical viewpoint it might be useful to consider a continuum of creativity which would stretch from the truly inspired, through an adaptive creativity (taking someone else's idea and improving it, or adapting it to new situations), and a willingness to try other people's ideas, to the other end of the scale which cannot tolerate any change or perceive any problem.

Barriers to creativity

1 The fallacy of 'one right answer'

We seem to devote much of our waking lives to establishing patterns and relationships that help to explain our world. Much effort goes into finding the 'right' answer to problems. There may be situations, however, where there is not a single right answer. One favourite example is illustrated by Figure 2.8.

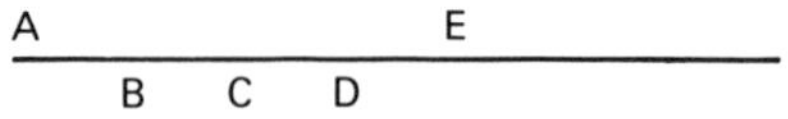

A _____ E
    B   C   D

Figure 2.8

Where does *F* go? – above or below the line?

Here we can have two, equally logical solutions – *F* can be placed below the line on the grounds that it is not a vowel (*A,E,I,O* or *U*), or alternatively it can be placed above the line because the letter itself is made using only straight lines.

Think – Which solution did you come up with?
       – Did you 'see' the alternative?

All too often we perceive a solution to a problem and then stop thinking. What we do not realize is that the first solution may not be the best.

2 The self imposed limitation

We may fail to explore all the possibilities through processes which are limited by our own thinking. One popular example to illustrate this is shown in Figure 2.9.
The task is to join all the dots with four straight lines, without taking your pencil from the paper.

It is usual to begin by drawing three lines round the outer dots and it then comes as a surprise to discover that that the final line misses out one dot (Figure 2.10).

It can be a shock to find that the solution is quite simple and the main barrier was inside your head. Breaking out of the self-imposed limitation is an important step towards creativity (see Figure 2.11).

A similar, perhaps even older, problem is to take six matchsticks and arrange them to make four identical triangles. Here the problem is made simple by breaking through the self-imposed barrier of assuming the

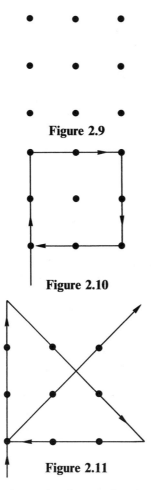

Figure 2.9

Figure 2.10

Figure 2.11

triangles must all be horizontal – by moving into three dimensions and building a pyramid.

Think – Now you can join the nine dots with four straight lines, can you do it with three?
– When you have done that, think of how you can do it with a single line*

---

3 Settling for what is expected

We tend to exert mental effort until we think we have done enough. Here is another old chestnut: how many squares can you see in Figure 2.12?

* see page 406

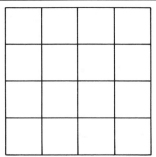

Figure 2.12

Here the first reaction is usually '16' – but it is usually followed by the thought that there must be more to it than that, especially after reading the last few pages, so we look for more. How many did you get to? 17? 22? 23? 31?

Did you then relax and think 'that will do'? If you really work at it, ignore self-imposed barriers and forget the idea of a right answer, you may be surprised at how many you can identify.

4 Evaluating too early

All too often we have an idea, but fail to express it on the grounds that we instantly evaluate it as being unworkable. This is often closely linked to the next barrier.

5 Failing to challenge the obvious

Asking the question 'Why not?'. De Bono argues that in order to generate creative lateral thinking, we need to 'provoke' thought by challenging the obvious and approaching a problem from a different angle. He uses the delightful example of a toddler upsetting granny's knitting by playing with the ball of wool. One suggestion (the obvious one) is to put the child into the playpen, the lateral thinker considers leaving the child outside and putting granny into the playpen!

> **Problem** – You have been asked to organize a table tennis tournament. You have twenty-nine entrants for the singles competition – how many matches will you have to schedule?

6 Fear of looking stupid

We generally try to avoid losing face by only putting forward ideas that we think others will see as sensible, sound suggestions. Here the environment may be an important factor – the child who is told 'don't be stupid' by its parents when it came up with an original idea may grow up being particularly careful to avoid repetition as an adult. Similarly organizations have different cultures regarding their tolerance of originality. Working with managers, the author is often amused by their claims to welcome originality amongst their subordinates, but their behaviour denies this to such an extent that anyone wishing to survive and progress will dare to do nothing but 'toe the line'.

Solution to the previous problem
– The correct answer is that you will need to schedule twenty-eight games.
– Did you get it right?
– Did you tackle it by starting with the first round matches and working towards the final? or
– Did you start at the final and work back to the earlier rounds (rather easier)
– The best approach I have found, however, is to look at it in these terms – you will have one winner and twenty-eight losers. Each loser needs to lose one (and only one) game!

Another problem – You have been asked to organize another tournament. This time you have only seventeen entrants for the singles competition – how many matches will you need to schedule this time?

Think – Did you get the solution quicker this time?
– Why?

Creativity is an important element in marketing. It occurs at a number of locations within the function:

1 *Copywriting* – is perhaps the most obvious area being concerned with the *creation* of novel advertising messages.
2 *Product innovation* – the field of devising products or services which consumers have not yet realized they 'need' – examples could include the development of the Sony Walkman personal stereo system, round tea bags as promoted by Tetley, and Energy Return Systems as the selling point of Reebok training shoes.
3 *Product name* – the need for originality is, in many cases, self-evident. Names such as 'British Telecom', 'Mercury' or 'Rabbit' for telephone systems, have all been *created*. Some of the implications in terms of emotional loading of names will be considered later in the chapters on perception and communication processes.

Whether creativity is an essential for all marketing specialists may be open to question, however. It could be argued that creativity can be bought from specialists such as advertising agencies or consultants who will develop appropriate and original product names for an organization. Some writers such as Argyle and Sidney have suggested that, within organizations, an ability to accept other people's creativity may be as important as having the original idea. The idea of an enterprise which is full of highly creative individuals is likely to pose significant managerial problems. So it could be argued that the key skill for marketing is the ability to recognize the 'good' new idea.

Other cognitive styles

There are a number of other aspects which may be of significance to marketing. These are included here despite being on the interface between mental characteristics and personality which is discussed later.

Pask (1976) has worked on the strategies adopted when people are faced with learning new material or solving complex problems. He draws a distinction between:

1 *Holists* who approach the material in a very broad, divergent manner and who tend to examine many aspects of a problem more or less simultaneously, and
2 *Serialists* who adopt a more step-by-step approach, which might even be described as narrow in comparison with holists.

> **Think** – To what extent are you primarily a holist or a serialist?
> – How do you think this will affect your course of study?

Witkin *et al.* (1977) identified differences in the way people analyse incoming information. Again we have two broad categories:

1 *Field independent* individuals take an analytical, structured approach to material while
2 *Field dependent* people take a less analytical approach and tend to perceive things in a more global fashion.

> **Think** – To what extent are you primarily field dependent or independent?

Another cognitive style dimension is that of *reflective-impulsive decision making*. Kagan *et al.* (1964) showed that there was a consistent tendency for individuals towards either fast or slow decision times when faced with problems with high response uncertainty. Some people, the *impulsive* ones, report the first hypothesis that occurs to them (often producing incorrect answers); while others, the *reflective* ones, delay before responding (and get right answers more often). The reflective style attempts to consider the validity of all the different answers and tends to be more persistent. The impulsive style values quick response and reflects lack of concern with mistakes.

Think – To what extent are you primarily reflective or impulsive?
– How does this affect your buying behaviour?

The study of *risk taking* is another aspect of mental processing which has received attention from psychologists, and may be regarded as an extension of the reflective/impulsive continuum. Here the evidence suggests that some consumers, often the ones with low boredom thresholds, seek stimulation and excitement. Some marketing specialists have dubbed these types as 'thrillseekers' or 'Type *T*' persons with additional subsets of '*T*+' for those who seek positive thrills and '*T* –' for those who look for thrills that are negative and destructive. *T*+ types appear to list success and competence as life goals, whereas risk avoiders rate happiness as their first choice. Risk takers appear more likely to end up with health hazards such as drugs, alcohol and reckless driving, but are more likely to be self-motivated and well adjusted.

Think – What advertisements can you identify that are aimed at the risk taker?
– What advertisements can you identify that are aimed at the risk avoiders?

There is an excellent book by George Wright called *Behavioural Decision Theory* which explores individual optimism and pessimism when faced with uncertainty. It includes some very interesting questionnaires which enable readers to calibrate their own style when faced with ambiguity. The author's own limited research with CIM students indicates that they are, on the whole, remarkably optimistic. Perhaps this is a characteristic that is necessary for the marketing role!

Engel and colleagues highlight another element of our mental make-up which they call the *need for cognition (N_{cog})*. This is a measure of an individual's tendency to enjoy thinking. The evidence suggests that people who are high in N_{cog} are more influenced by the quality of the arguments put forward, while individuals low in N_{cog} are more influenced by peripheral advertising stimuli such as endorser attractiveness, and may need more repetitions for an advertisement to be effective. The high N_{cog} is more likely to continue thinking about the message (therefore giving the advertiser 'free' repeats of the advertisement) but may need longer messages containing more information. It is also speculated that high N_{cog} individuals might best be impressed by written material while the low N_{cog} person could be more influenced by film or television adverts. This concept is very similar to the process of *elaboration* which is becoming significant in the study of learning and attitude change.

Examples of N_{cog} type advertising could include the use of anagrams (e.g. Holsten Pils), verbal puns (Players cigarettes uses variations on back/black in a series of adverts on the 'black to the future' basis) and the famous series of Benson and Hedges 'surrealist' image making.

Think – What other examples can you find of advertisers seeking to involve the consumers' cognitive processes?

Chapter summary exercises

Think – How can the material in this chapter be applied to the marketing of:
camcorders
the social policy of a political party
skis
holidays
soft drinks
instant coffee
sports shoes (trainers)
razors
hair colourant
toothpaste
shampoo
motor cars
low-fat/low cholesterol/low salt spread
sanitary protection
kitchen equipment
spirits and liqueurs
low-alcohol wine
a restaurant
newspapers
toilet tissue
bicycles

Think – How *has* my organization recognized and used individual differences?

Think – How *could* my organization utilize individual differences?

> **Think** – How have *I* used individual differences?

Some 'typical' examination questions – Individual Differences

A The intelligence and cognitive style of the target market segment are crucial factors for the marketer to consider when designing marketing messages. Discuss.

B Outline the main stages of the creative process. Illustrate your answer with examples and explain some of the main barriers to creativity in practice.

C Engel, Blackwell and Miniard emphasize an element of our mental make-up they call the need for cognition (N_{cog}). Explain what they mean by N_{cog} and give examples of how this need can be satisfied in advertisements.

D 'Ability profiles vary from individual to individual'. Explain the importance of such an observation to the marketer – with particular reference to the ways in which advertisements may need to be framed and presented

Sources

Bloom, B. S. (1956) *Taxonomy of Educational Objectives. Handbook 1: The Cognitive Domain,* Longmans Green.

Boring, E. G. (1923) 'Intelligence as the tests test it', *New Republic,* 35.

de Bono, E. (1967) *The Five-day Course in Thinking*, Penguin.

Engel, J. F., Blackwell, R. D. and Miniard P. W. (1990) *Consumer Behaviour* (6th edn.), Dryden.

Entwistle, N. J. (1981) *Styles of Learning and Teaching,* Wiley.

Gregory, R. L. (ed) (1987) *The Oxford Companion to the Mind*, Oxford University Press

Kagan, *et. al.* (1964) 'Information Processing: Significance of Analytical and Reflective Attitudes', *Psychological Monographs,* No. 1.

Pask, G. (1976) 'Styles and strategies of learning', *British Journal of Educational Psychology.*

Reber, A. S. (1985) *Dictionary of Psychology*, Penguin.

Robertson, I. T. and Cooper, C. L. (1983) *Human Behaviour in Organisations,* MacDonald and Evans.

Vernon, P. E. (1956) *The Measurement of Abilities*, University of London Press.

Vernon, P.E. (1979) *Intelligence: Heredity and Environment*, Freeman.

Witkin, *et. al.* (1977) 'Field Dependent and Field Independent Cognitive Styles and their Educational Implications', *Review of Educational Research.*

Wright, G. (1984) *Behavioural Decision Theory*, Penguin.

3 '... and even you are a little strange!'

Individual differences – personality

Introduction

This chapter continues our look at some of the basic ideas of psychology and focuses on some of the ways in which people's personalities are different from one another. As in the previous chapter, it deals with some of the concepts that influence people as consumers and as students.

At the end of this chapter readers should be comfortable with the following concepts, the associated language, and, where appropriate, their application to marketing situations:

- Psychoanalytical theories
- Trait approaches
- Behaviourist theories
- Self-concept theories
- Defence mechanisms
- Personal learning style

Personality

This is another idea which has wide usage but little agreement on what is being described. As long ago as 1927 Gordon Allport, the American psychologist, identified over fifty different definitions of personality. His work showed that there was little common agreement as to its use or meaning. If the work were to be repeated now the number of definitions would be spectacularly larger – with, perhaps, even less agreement. Currently there is a significant debate as to whether intelligence is a part of personality, or whether it is a separate, independent characteristic.

It is, however, an important concept in both the subject we are studying and in everyday life, so it may be helpful to look at some of the issues involved.

Personality is a part of the way in which we perceive other people.

Exercise – How would you describe the Prime Minister to me?
– Jot down some of that person's characteristics on a piece of paper.

In doing this you will have used some dimensions of personality according to your view of character or temperament.

Think – Which characteristics did you use?
– How many did you use?

In everyday usage we commonly describe people using a single characteristic e.g. 'an outgoing person', 'a blunt individual', 'an aggressive so-and-so'. This is an interesting example of selectivity, as we choose to use only a limited number of the facets that make up the person. Even if we are looking at the same person we may choose different aspects to emphasize – you may pick out their honesty while I might highlight their cheerfulness. We have potential problems with the process called 'stereotyping' – generalizing and simplifying characteristics to make a tidy 'package' we can handle. In the exercise above a person who you are unlikely to know personally was chosen. This highlights the fact that we can make judgements based on very little first hand knowledge, using evidence from the media, much of which may have been carefully rehearsed and edited. In real life we seem to have no problems in 'summing up' a person within seconds of meeting them. It is something that we all do every time we meet someone new as the assessment is important in determining how we respond.

Think – What example have you of situations where your first impressions of a person were proved right?
– What examples do you have where they were wrong?

We often use a single characteristic and build a complete personality around that solitary element. However, people are much more complicated than that and examples abound of charming criminals, morose comedians and so forth. It is claimed that Hitler loved both Mozart and dogs, both characteristics of 'good' people according to many.

If this is true, and we are all prone to make false assumptions about other people, our social interactions should be chaotic! Fortunately the situation is helped by the fact that our behaviour is, to a greater or lesser extent, limited by the roles we are playing and the situation in which we find ourselves.

Think – What is your 'personality' when you are at work?
with your parents?
with your grandparents?
out with your friends?
at college?

Whatever our response to these questions it implies that there is a certain consistency or stability in our behaviour. We recognize in ourselves and in others the tendency to behave in particular ways in given situations. It is this distinctive tendency which we commonly identify as the personality of an individual.

A model which may help clarify some of the issues and this is shown in Figure 3.1. According to this model the psychological core is a central feature of what we may call personality while accepting the *interactive* nature of behaviour with respect to the person, the role, the environment and some concept such as the 'real' self.

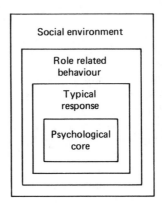

Figure 3.1

We can identify a number of different aspects of personality:

- *External aspect* – typical behaviours and the way they affect others.
- *Internal aspect* – the psychological core – values, attitudes, belief systems which it may only be possible to infer from behaviour.
- *Dynamic aspect* – the adaptation to a changing environment.
- *Consistent aspect* – the stable cognitive processes that give rise to what we might recognize as a characteristic style for the individual.
- *Role aspect* – the behaviours that are associated with specific roles or interactions.
- *Stereotypes* and selective perception also pose potential problems in that they create assumptions such as 'all students are lazy' or 'all red-haired people are short-tempered' which are unlikely to be universally true.

Think – What personality types feature in advertisements for:
    Banks?
    Political parties?
    Male deodorants?

Personality theories

1 *Type theories* – this approach goes back thousands of years to Hippocrates who suggested that there are four basic temperaments – choleric, sanguine, melancholic and phlegmatic. The basic assumption is that each individual is a unique balance of these elements. The assumption still holds good today, the main difference being that different theorists have put forward different elements. Typical examples include the work of Marston who identified four scales – dominance, influencing others, steadiness and conformity. This approach has been adopted by several purveyors of personality measures for use in selection.

2 *Psychoanalytic theories* – Freud was the father-figure of the study of personality giving us the notion of a *subconscious* element to our makeup. He proposed a tripartite set-up with the *Id* being the wholly subconscious, intuitive bit of us – working on the pleasure principle, dominated by sexual drives, and being subjective and gratification seeking. The *Ego* is wholly conscious and deals with reality and is the bit that helps us develop interactive skills. It is the element that includes our self-image. The *Super-Ego* deals with morality and corresponds roughly to the idea of a conscience acting as the umpire between the pleasure seeking id and the reality based ego.

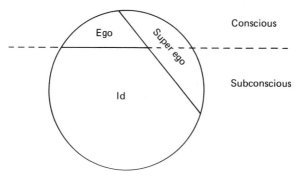

Figure 3.2

One of the central ideas in this theoretical framework is that the eventual goal of all human behaviour is pleasure and that the id is the basic source of energy, drive and motivation. As this source is subconscious, it has led to the activities called motivational research which seek to determine the underlying perceptions of products and needs.

Freud was also the originator of the idea that early experiences cause later behaviour. He suggested that people develop through a number of stages:

1 *Oral stage.* Dominated by sucking in the earliest stages of life, the mouth becomes the dominant organ. It provides the source of food, reassurance and pleasure to the infant.

2 *Anal phase*. Here the main source of pleasure becomes the process of bowel evacuation. The socialization process insists on toilet training which commonly induces some form of crisis (the infant learns that bowel control can be a 'weapon' to use against its parents).

3 *Phallic phase*. Here the child discovers its own sexuality and may enjoy self-directed sexual experiences. Freud also suggested that this stage would include the emergence of some sexual desires with regard to the parents (particularly those of the opposite gender). This causes another crisis area as society does not tolerate such feelings – and the ways in which such events are resolved are thought to exert strong influence on the development of personality and the capacity for forming relationships later in life (this stage is the potential source of the 'Oedipus' and 'Electra' complexes).

4 *Latent phase*. Freud hypothesized that this lasted from the age of about five years to the beginning of adolescence and was a quiescent period during which few significant changes in personality occurred.

5 *Genital phase*. This is characterized by the re-emergence of sexuality, but this time interest is focused outside of the self and the parents. Adolescence and the processes of adjusting to adulthood are a well recognized period of potential crisis. Again the ability to resolve the difficulties allows the individual to progress to the final stage.

6 *Maturity*.

Along with this theory of phase development, Freud introduced the notion of *regression* where an individual, faced with a threatening environment may regress to behaviours from an earlier stage of development where satisfaction was obtained. These basic ideas have been some of the most influential within our society and pervade nearly all thinking on the subject.

In advertising terms Freud provides fruitful grounds for image making which may suggest that product use will make the individual more popular, interesting or sexually attractive.

Think – Which current advertisements imply enhanced sexuality?

Freud, in identifying the importance of the super-ego or conscience, has a part to play in making some of the more extreme images socially acceptable. Many people might find the idea of enhanced sexuality uncomfortable to cope with and this could cause the message to be rejected. In one famous advertisement for condoms a couple were pictured at a party, the sexual attraction was clearly portrayed, they rush from the party to consummate their lust . . . The punch line comes with the realization that they are married. In this way the use of condoms is made acceptable by presenting it as being responsible rather than an incitement to immorality. In Freudian terms the id is stimulated by the implied sexuality, while the super-ego is satisfied by the couple being married.

It links in closely with the work of Berne who viewed personality as being made up of three elements – Parent, Adult and Child ego states. These are usually displayed as in Figure 3.3.

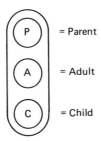

Figure 3.3

The ego states are summarized in Figure 3.4.

The similarity between these ideas and those of Freud is clear. Berne has utilized some of Freud's language (as in ego state) and the parallels between the two views seem fairly self evident:

Freud		Berne
id	being the equivalent of	Child
ego	being the equivalent of	Adult
super-ego	being the equivalent of	Parent

Berne also introduced the notion of 'games' – repeated behaviours which allow the individual to 'win' by recreating a desired situation e.g. children who are told regularly by their parents that they are 'hopeless' may grow up to engineer situations in which they appear 'hopeless' thus reinforcing their own assumptions about themselves imprinted at an earlier stage of their development.

Rotter suggests that people may be distinguished by their locus of control – internal or external. Are they 'doers' or 'done unto's', 'originators' or 'pawns'? He used a scale which asked questions aimed at determining the extent to which an individual believed in 'fate' or 'luck' as opposed to the notion of persons determining, and being responsible for, what occurs in their lives.

Parent	Verbal clues	Non-verbal clues
'Learned' behaviour from one's own parents or parent figures gives rise to attitudes and beliefs (just like real parents this ego state can be either critical or supportive).	objections... maxims.... 'you ought...'	frowning belligerent posture impatience
The 'parent': Defines, takes care of, sets limits, gives advice, disciplines, guides, protects, nurtures, supports, teaches, instructs, makes rules, keeps traditions, judges and criticizes.	'you should....' categorizing injunctions	finger shaking clenched fist doting smile
Adult	Verbal clues	Non-verbal clues
The 'computer' bit of us collecting and processing data not much to do with feelings emotions or attitudes.	when? where? who?	active listening attention eye contact
The 'adult': Gathers data on the current state of the parent and the child, on previous experience, and external situation. Analyses best alternatives, plans, makes decisions	which? what? why? how?	erect posture thoughtful
Child	Verbal clues	Non-verbal clues
Mostly concerned with emotions and feelings, may be either 'natural' or 'adapted'.	I wish.... I like....	laughter tears
The 'child' can be: angry, rebellious, scared, conforming, creative, loving, spontaneous, fun-loving, exciting, adventurous, trusting, joyful, etc.	I want.... May I....?	anger defensiveness shrugging sulking

Figure 3.4

Critique

Psychoanalytical theories of human personality such as Freud's are often criticized for

1 subjectivity and a lack of scientific rigour,
2 their lack of satisfactory definitions of important concepts and
3 the fact that, being based on an assumption that the root of most behaviour is subconscious, there is a lack of testable predictions and measurable, objective data.

Psychologists such as Eysenck have been particularly hard on the psychoanalytical approaches and have argued that the popularity and wide acceptance of the ideas does not constitute proof. Eysenck points out that there was a time when it was universally accepted that the world was flat! Further criticism has stemmed from what many people see as an over-emphasis on sexual motivation – although Freudian psychologists might argue that this is evidence of defence mechanisms at work.

On the other hand Freud's ideas reflect many people's experience and offer explanation of some well recognized life crises. The acceptance of the subconscious nature of many motives is of great importance to the development of marketing, and there is some face validity in the notion that purchasing behaviour may be an extension of personality.

Think – How good an explanation of human personality do you think psychoanalytic theories offer?
– Why?

Trait approaches

Traits are characteristics which are common to many but the strength of any characteristic will vary between individuals; hence a person can be defined by the profile of their traits. Traits are relatively stable, are assumed to influence behaviour and are therefore able to be inferred from consistencies observed in the behaviour of individuals.

Cattell is perhaps the best known of the supporters of the Trait approach to personality. He used the technique of factor analysis to identify what he believed to be the principal factors of personality as set out in Figure. 3.5.

Cool	A	Warm
Concrete-thinking	B	Abstract-thinking
Affected by feelings	C	Emotionally stable
Submissive	E	Dominant
Sober	F	Enthusiastic
Expedient	G	Conscientious
Shy	H	Bold
Tough-minded	I	Tender-minded
Trusting	L	Suspicious
Practical	M	Imaginative
Forthright	N	Shrewd
Self-assured	O	Apprehensive
Conservative	Q_1	Experimenting
Group-oriented	Q_2	Self-sufficient
Undisciplined self-conflict	Q_3	Controlled
Relaxed	Q_4	Tense

Figure 3.5 Cattell's 16 principal factors (16PF)

In addition a number of second order or composite factors are identified which include:

- *Extroversion* – the extent to which an individual is socially outgoing.
- *Anxiety* – the extent to which an individual is habitually anxious.
- *Tough Poise* – the extent to which an individual is more influenced by facts than by feelings.
- *Independence* – the extent to which the individual is aggressive, independent, daring and incisive.
- *Superego/control* – the extent to which an individual tends to conform to the rules and expectations associated with their roles in life.
- *Neuroticism* – the extent to which an individual is apprehensive and emotionally reactive.
- *Leadership* – the extent to which an individual appears to have the traits that are commonly associated with leadership potential – sociable, relaxed, assertive and self-assured.
- *Creativity* – the extent to which an individual is imaginative and experimenting.

Cattell uses sixteen traits in the standard 16PF measure while Eysenck generates personality characteristics which cluster into two main dimensions – the Extroversion/Introversion scale and the Stable/Unstable continuum as displayed in Figure 3.6.

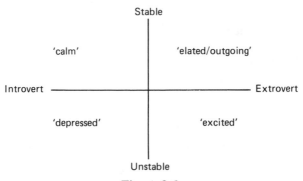

Figure 3.6

Critique

Trait theories perhaps come close to describing the structure of personality in the way that we use the term in everyday language. It uses words such as shy, tense, controlled, anxious, extrovert which we can recognize and use to describe persons we know. However, it does assume that these traits represent predispositions to behave in particular ways, in a wide variety of situations. Both Cattell and Eysenck share the belief that stable, underlying personality traits can be used to explain people's behaviour. Both focus on the role of internal person variables in determining behaviour. On the other hand some people believe that personality may be more situational than trait theorists propose. It is also worth examining the basis of the Cattell/Eysenck approach. Subjects are asked to complete extensive questionnaires and the responses are subjected to powerful mathematical analysis but, inevitably, there is a degree of subjectivity in question formation and interpretation. Hypothetical yes/no questions or the 'would you rather be a musician or a gardener?' type pose potential problems of interpretation (especially if there is little interest in either). There is a tendency to answer questions either as the respondent thinks a 'normal' person would, or as the respondents wish themselves to be. At an even deeper philosophical level there is a problem of whether the way individuals see themselves is the same as others see them. The linkage to behaviour is important and problematic – if a person is seen to keep themselves to themselves they are rated as introvert – but is this inference from observation or explanation i.e. they keep themselves to themselves *because* they are introvert?

At the level of face validity it seems highly plausible that personality traits should have some effect on purchasing behaviour.

Think – How useful is the trait approach to understanding personality?
– Why?

Some alternative approaches to personality

Behaviourist theories

These are based on the assumption that situational factors may well determine personality. Behaviourist ideas are discussed in more detail in Chapter 5 where we look at learning processes. The most influential of the exponents of behaviourist thinking is Skinner who rejects the idea that behaviour is shaped and determined by internal personality factors such as those outlined above. He suggests that each person's behaviour can be explained entirely by reference to the individual's reinforcement history and specific behaviour that has been rewarded or punished. Thus the proposal is that our personalities are formed by the process of operant conditioning. Freudian and Behaviourist approaches are commonly held to be opposite views of personality development, but it is interesting to note that the Behaviourists, in common with Freud, suggest that people's personalities are determined by past experience and also that people seek to maximize pleasure.

Think – To what extent do you think your personality has been determined by conditioning?

Personal construct theory

Another approach which deserves mention is personal construct theory, which is built on the work of George Kelly and assumes that our personality is determined by our personal construct system. This is described in more detail in Chapter 4 where it is considered in the light of our perceptual processes. Again it seems plausible to suggest that the personality is a function of the way in which individuals perceive their worlds. As we will comment in the perception chapter, this approach seems to be highly relevant; it suffers, however, from the very uniqueness that it identifies. Unless we could identify significant sections of the population as sharing the same personal construct systems, it would seem to have limited use for marketers in segmenting a market.

Exercise – Make a note to refer back to this section after you have attempted the repertory grid exercise described on page 98.
– What does this tell you about your personality?

Clearly, one significant part of our personal construct system is the way in which we see ourselves. This is the basis of self concept theories, the subject of the next section.

Self concept theories

Freud's notion of the ego as the conscious part of us which deals with reality implies that each individual has some concept of who he or she is, and Kelly's emphasis on perception suggests that our perception of ourselves may be a key element of our personality.

Mead argues that the self has two elements which are in a way the private and public faces of the personality. He identifies:

- *The 'I' component* – unique, individual, conscious and impulsive aspect (the personal, private, individual 'I') and,
- *The 'ME' component* – internalized, learned and accepted norms and values (the socially acceptable 'ME').

Rogers makes a similar distinction between the way 'I' see myself and the way others see 'ME'. Newcomb takes these ideas and has started an interesting approach based on the idea of self-concept as a major determinant of behaviour and hence personality.

In marketing terms the self-concept approach to personality has a number of attractions. Firstly it can be hypothesized that people will purchase products that are compatible with their self-concept and they may be particularly attracted to products which enhance their 'ideal-self' image.

Additionally they may be specifically drawn to products which will confirm and support their longer term 'aspirational' image of themselves.

Thus marketers may have a powerful tool for identifying their products with personality characteristics which are considered to be desirable by the consumers. However, the notion of 'the ideal' may be influenced by social factors. Advertisers' continuing emphasis on slim females causes distress to some observers who claim that it may lead to the development of unreasonable 'ideal selves' and expectations for impressionable young women who aspire to a shape they can never physically attain. The plus side is that the 'ideal' may be amenable to change which will allow still further 'aspirational' imagery.

This approach suggests that characteristics are not directly comparable, that we are all socially conscious, we all have our own self-image, and, as learning organisms, we can learn and modify our personality.

As stated earlier, this ideographic approach links closely to Freud's concept of the ego. Indeed, we often use the word in everyday language to describe our self image. However, there is little reason to assume that (a) the way people see themselves; (b) the way others see them and; (c) the way they would like to be should be the same.

Luft and Ingham developed an interesting model of interpersonal perception known as the Johari Window. This focuses on the differences between our self perceptions and others' perceptions of us. It is usually displayed in the form shown in Figure 3.7.

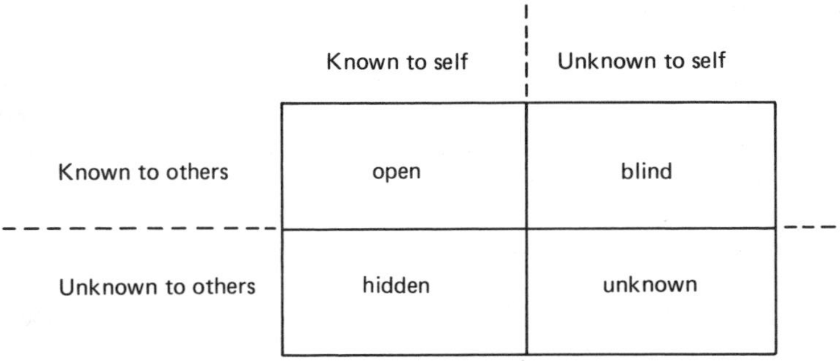

	Known to self	Unknown to self
Known to others	open	blind
Unknown to others	hidden	unknown

Figure 3.7

The *Open* quadrant illustrates the facets of ourselves (attitudes, behaviour and personality) which are known to us and which are also apparent to others. The *Hidden* area represents those elements which we keep to ourselves and do not disclose to others. These two are centred on those parts of our personality of which we are aware – that are part of our consciousness – and so they would seem to relate to the Freudian notion of the Ego.

The *Unknown* describes those parts of us which are unknown to both ourselves and to others, but which do influence our behaviour. The *Blind* quadrant encompasses those aspects which are evident to other people of which we are unaware. This pair centre on those parts of our personality of which we are unaware – they are part of our subconscious and the Unknown quadrant in particular would seem to correspond to Freud's idea of the Id. The Blind quadrant is interesting in that it contains things unknown to me but known to others. This could incorporate two well recognizable states:

1 *paranoia* – the delusion that we are more unpopular than we really are, and
2 *pronoia* – the delusion of popularity stemming from an ignorance of what people really think about us.

Think – How do you see yourself?
– How would you like to be?
– How do others see you?
– How do you know?
– How much agreement is there between the three views?
– How does this self-concept affect your buying behaviour?

From personal experience, it would seem to be a characteristic of being human that the three different aspects of self image (how we see ourselves, how others see us and how we would like to be) differ to a greater or lesser extent. Individuals also vary in the robustness of their characters – some are more confident than others. This idea of self-esteem is an interesting one in terms of interpersonal perception – too little and we perceive a person who 'does themselves down' and who is commonly depressive; too much self-esteem and we see someone who is conceited, 'big headed' and in need of being brought down a peg or two.

It can also be argued that the degree to which the three self-concepts agree or overlap gives a working measure of what we commonly call 'adjustment'. We normally behave in ways that are consistent with our self image, but, inevitably, from time to time life does not pan out in the way we would wish. Things go wrong. We experience feelings that are not consistent with our image of ourselves. Sometimes our actions are misinterpreted. Freud suggested that in such circumstances our self concept (ego) is threatened and, *subconsciously*, we will adopt various stratagems to relieve the dissonance. He described these behaviours as *ego defence mechanisms*. There are a number which he described and here are pen pictures of some of the best known:

1 *Repression* is the mental process used to protect the individual from memories, ideas and impulses which would produce emotional discomfort in the sense of apprehension, anxiety or guilt. The notion is that we supress, censor and exclude disturbing thoughts from our conscious mind.

2 *Rationalization* is the application of logic to a situation primarily to avoid facing up to the true motivation for one's actions. In other words it is

rather like a subconscious version of the more conscious process of 'making excuses' – 'I've been too busy at work to revise adequately for this examination'.

3 *Projection* refers to the process whereby we will sometimes ascribe our own emotions and motivations to other people. It is normally associated with the individuals denying their own feelings or tendencies and may often be linked with criticizing those characteristics in others – it is sometimes suggested that those students who worry most about others cheating in examinations are the ones who have been tempted themselves.

4 *Sublimation* is the term used to describe the process whereby people will sometimes redirect energy from the socially unacceptable (often libidinous and sexually driven) to the socially acceptable. It can also refer to displacing personally undesirable behaviour by less threatening activities – students often 'revise' what they already know rather than face up to the reality of the inadequacy of their knowledge in other areas.

5 *Identification* is the process we may adopt in attributing to ourselves, either consciously or unconsciously, the characteristics of another person or group. This is clearly used in many marketing situations where it is hoped that the endorsement of a product by a successful personality will enhance the chances of the consumer identifying with that personality and hence using the product. Obviously the identification process will vary from individual to individual and will cause great effort to be expended to find the 'right' personality to promote any given product. This is considered in a little more detail in Chapter 7 where the process of attitude change is considered.

6 *Fantasy* can sometimes be used as a pleasant escape from reality. Most of us have had the experience of day-dreaming during boring classes or suffering from attacks of 'mind wandering' when revising!

The notion of '*displacement*', '*fight or flight*', *aggression* (both positive and negative) as coping devices all fit more or less comfortably into this section.

Think – Which of these defence mechanisms can you recognize in your own behaviour?

Defence mechanisms and 'game playing' as described by Berne have a number of common characteristics. They are both subconscious processes and both are mechanisms to provide desired outcomes for the individual – primarily the reduction of dissonance between our self image and the feedback from life.

Personality and predicting consumer behaviour

We have mentioned above on a number of occasions that it seems plausible to suppose that there is a link between personality and buying behaviour. However the evidence to support this view is less than convincing. Evans' famous attempt to determine the personality characteristics of Ford and Chevrolet owners in 1959 found few statistically significant differences. In fact the study was only able to predict ownership in 63 per cent of cases, which, given there was only two choices, is little better than the 50 per cent that could be expected from random chance. Evans' conclusion was that personality was of relatively little value in predicting brand ownership of cars. Several other studies at that time found equally inconclusive results.

The problem may lie in our initial assumption that personality should be a prime factor in determining brand choice. Engel *et al.* point out that personality is only one variable in the process of consumer decision making and that intention might be a better correlate. They continue their argument by proposing that if personality traits were found to be valid predictors of intentions (or even behaviour), they would only be useful as a means of market segmentation if:

1 People with common personality traits are similar in terms of demographic factors such as age, income and locality. This is necessary if they are to be reached economically through the mass media. If they do not have these common demographic characteristics there will be no practical means of reaching them as a unique market segment.
2 The personality measures used are demonstrably reliable and valid.
3 The differences identified reflect clear-cut variations in buyer activity and preferences. If this is not true then consumers can show different personality profiles while preferring essentially the same product attributes.
4 Any grouping identified is of sufficient size to make a marketing initiative worthwhile. The recognition that 'every individual is unique' is not helpful in terms of market segmentation.

The evidence to date does not support the notion that personality is linked to demographics because:

1 personality measurement has numerous problems of reliability and validity as described above,
2 personality is not a significant factor in most consumer decisions, and
3 the creation of larger groupings tends to dilute the clarity of market segments.

It is therefore not surprising that Engel *et al.*, conclude that 'the evidence to date falls short of these criteria, and personality has not been demonstrated convincingly as a useful means of market segmentation'.

The relative failure of personality measures in predicting consumer behaviour has led to the development of alternative approaches in more recent times. The first is the exploration of the notion of brand personality, examined in the following section.

Brand personality

Peter and Olson suggest that we can look at a brand as a series of 'bundles' – they recognize that consumers will see a product as a bundle of *attributes* (physical characteristics which could be abstract concepts such as 'quality' or more concrete and tangible aspects), a bundle of *benefits* (these could be functional benefits or social/psychological pay-offs) and a bundle of *value satisfactions* (possibly short-term instrumental values or longer time-scale terminal values). This gives rise to the interesting notion of the product or brand possessing a personality. One can think of examples where specific personalities have been created for products – the perfume which is young, fun-loving and a bit rebellious compared to the perfume which has the image of being more mature, sophisticated and upper-class.

> **Think** – What is the brand personality of
> Levi jeans?
> Coca Cola?
> BMW cars?
> Swatch watches?
> Carling Black Label?

In the USA Anheuser-Busch created four separate 'personalities' for four new brands of beer. They developed commercials for each brand aimed at different 'drinker personalities' – e.g. one commercial portrayed a 'social drinker' (characterized in one account as a typical campus guzzler), another as an 'indulgent drinker' (a male who perceives himself as a total failure), yet another showed a 'reparative drinker' (middle-aged) and one who had made sacrifices of personal objectives to help others – drink was the reward!

Two hundred and fifty beer drinkers watched the commercials and sampled all four beers. They were then asked to state their preferences and to complete a questionnaire which measured their own 'drinker personality'. The results indicated that a majority of the respondents preferred the brand that matched their own reported drinker personality. Most consumers also felt strongly enough to respond that at least one brand of beer was not fit to drink.

Unknown to the 250 respondents, all four brands were the same beer!

This evidence links well with the self-concept approaches to personality described above. However it might be useful to reflect that while consumers are likely to be attracted to a product personality which enhances or matches up with their 'ideal self', this may be subject to all the reservation we have expressed regarding personality measurement in general. Thus it may be more prudent to suggest that the brand personality may complement, rather than match, that of the consumer.

Having examined some of the ideas surrounding intelligence, abilities, creativity and personality, There is one final element which we will consider and that is the idea that we may each have our own individual learning style. While learning is the subject of a later chapter, this approach links well with ideas such as cognitive style and personality and so is introduced here.

Experiential learning – the work of David Kolb

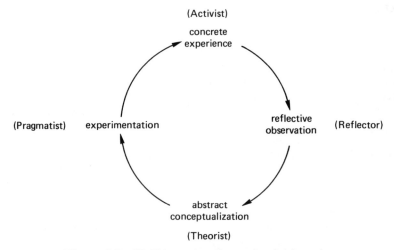

Figure 3.8   Kolb's cycle of experiential learning

Kolb's view of the learning process is that human beings learn by experience. In the first stage we experience something. The second stage is the observation of what happens and the reflection on the experience. Thirdly comes the conceptualization and generalization of the event. The final stage is when we test out our ideas and theories. This, in turn gives us another experience to reflect upon, theorize about and test. So the process of learning can be seen as a 'spiral' of developing understanding of our world, exactly similar to that described in Chapter 1.

More significantly, at this stage, the ideas of Kolb have been developed by the work of Peter Honey and Alan Mumford who believe that each of us, as individuals, will have developed a *preferred learning style*. This is the sum of our learning habits that we have acquired over the years and the Honey and Mumford styles match up with the stages in Kolb's learning cycle as shown in the outer circle of the diagram in Figure 3.8.

Thus, they suggest that some people prefer the concrete experience (Activists), others are happier observing and thinking (Reflectors), some enjoy the process of conceptualizing (Theorists), while others are concerned primarily with trying out the ideas and making things work (Pragmatists).

Clearly, it is unlikely that people will fall neatly into one category to the total exclusion of the others. Try this activity:

Exercise – Read through the following descriptions of the four learning styles.
– Give each one a score out of 20 to represent how much like *you* that description is (20/20 = exactly like you; 0/20 = nothing like you)

Activists

Activists involve themselves fully and uninhibitedly in new situations. They enjoy the 'here and now' and are happy to be dominated by immediate experiences. They are open-minded, not sceptical, and this tends to make them enthusiastic about anything new. Their philosophy is 'I'll try anything once'. They dash in where angels fear to tread. They tend to throw caution to the wind. Their days are filled with activity. They revel in short-term crisis fire fighting. They tackle problems by brainstorming. As soon as the excitement from one activity has died down they are busy looking for the next. They tend to thrive on the challenge of new experiences, but are bored by implementation and longer term consolidation. They are gregarious people constantly involving themselves with others but in doing so, they hog the limelight. They are the life and soul of the party and seek to centre all activities around themselves.

My score for Activist ☐

Reflectors

Reflectors like to stand back to ponder experiences and observe them from many different perspectives. They collect data, both first hand and from others, and prefer to chew it over thoroughly before coming to any conclusion. The thorough collection and analysis of data about experiences and events is what counts – so they tend to postpone definitive conclusions for as long as possible. Their philosophy is to be cautious, to leave no stone unturned. 'Look before you leap' and 'sleep on it' are two common maxims for the reflector. They are thoughtful people who like to consider all possible angles and implications before making a move. They prefer to take a back seat in meetings and discussions. They enjoy observing other people in action. They listen to others and get the drift of the discussion before making their own points. They tend to adopt a low profile and have a slightly distant, tolerant, unruffled air about them. When they act it is part of a wide picture which includes the past as well as the present and others' observations as well as their own.

My score for Reflector ☐

Theorists

Theorists adapt and integrate observations into complex but logically sound theories. They think problems through in a vertical, step-by-step, logical way. They assimilate disparate facts into coherent theories. They like to analyse and synthesize. They are keen on basic assumptions, principles, theories, models and systems thinking. Their philosophy prizes rationality and logic. 'If it is logical, it is good'. Questions they frequently ask are 'Does it make sense?', 'How does this fit with that?', 'What are the basic assumptions?'. They tend to be detached, analytical and dedicated to rational objectivity rather than anything subjective or ambiguous. Their approach to problems is consistently logical. This is their mental set and they rigidly reject anything that does not fit in with it. They prefer to maximize certainty and feel uncomfortable with subjective judgements, lateral thinking and anything flippant.

My score for Theorist ☐

Pragmatists

Pragmatists are keen on trying out ideas, theories and techniques to see if they work in practice. They positively search out new ideas and take the first opportunity to experiment with applications. They are the sort of people who return from management courses brimming with new ideas that they want to try out in practice. They like to get on with things and act quickly and confidently on ideas that attract them. They don't like 'beating about the bush' and tend to be impatient with ruminating and open-ended discussions. They are essentially practical, down-to-earth people who like making practical decisions and solving problems. They respond to problems and opportunities as 'a challenge'. Their philosophy is 'There is always a better way' and 'if it works, it's good'.

My score for Pragmatist ☐

Finally, plot what you believe to be your learning style on the scales in Figure 3.9.

The significance of this exercise so early in the book is that your learning style is likely to directly influence your experience of the text and the benefits you are likely to gain from it.

Activists tend to be doers – they are likely to get bored just sitting and reading a textbook, so they may need to think more about ideas that are being put forward (reflection); reviewing the evidence and ideas in the light of their own experience and develop their own modifications and reservations regarding the theories being discussed. Finally they may need to think consciously about the application of these ideas in 'real life'.

Reflectors, in contrast, are relatively happy reading and thinking about the material being presented. Their main task is likely to be questioning theories, testing practicalities and getting involved in activities.

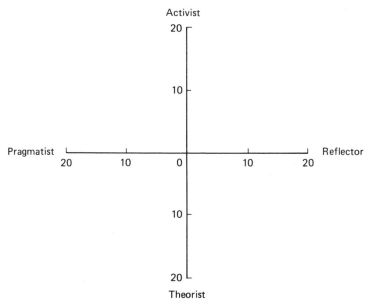

Figure 3.9

The theorists are likely to need to reflect more and also to go beyond the theory to the application to marketing situations.

The pragmatists, being concerned with whether things work will need to consciously put effort into understanding and learning the theories, and reflecting on their experience of the marketing world.

Remember, few are likely to be equally strong on all four activities, if Kolb is to be believed then it is necessary to go through all four stages of the learning cycle. Don't take short cuts, use the insight given by the Learning Style Questionnaire to strengthen your own learning patterns.

True story – The author was meeting a group of managers for the first time. They were following a course for an external examination. As a first exercise each was asked to think about their own personality, character and ways of tackling learning situations. Following discussion of the experiential learning theory their preferred learning styles were identified and collected. While the managers had a break the author spotted that there were roughly equal numbers of activists, reflectors, theorists and pragmatists and so, after coffee, the managers were split into those four groups (but without telling them how the groups had been identified). The groups were then set the task of discussing how they wanted the course to run and were given twenty minutes for the exercise.

The activists had a very noisy and combative discussion, the reflectors were very quiet, the theorists had a good debate and the pragmatists went for another cup of coffee.

At the playback the activists reported that they had enjoyed themselves but failed to reach any conclusion; the reflectors said they needed more time to think about it; the theorists said they thought I had asked the wrong question; and the pragmatists said that they didn't mind how the course was run so long as they all passed!

Chapter summary exercises

Think – How can the material in this chapter be applied to the marketing of:

camcorders
the social policy of a political party
skis
holidays
soft drinks
instant coffee
sports shoes (trainers)
razors
hair colourant
toothpaste
shampoo
motor cars
low-fat/low cholesterol/low salt spread
sanitary protection
kitchen equipment
spirits and liqueurs
low-alcohol wine
a restaurant
newspapers
toilet tissue
bicycles

Think – How *has* my organization recognized and used individual differences?

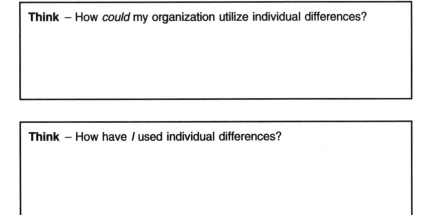

Think – How *could* my organization utilize individual differences?

Think – How have *I* used individual differences?

Some 'typical' questions – personality

A   What is meant by the term 'personality'? Compare and contrast any two theories of personality with which you are familiar, and demonstrate how such theories can be valuable to marketers in such areas as advertising and product positioning.

B   To what extent should marketers take any notice of Freud's work?

C   Compare and contrast *any two* of the following three theories of personality, with special reference to the application of these theories to marketing:

- Freudian theory
- Trait theory
- Self-concept theory

D   What do you understand by the term 'defence mechanisms'. Explain how a knowledge of such mechanisms might be of use in a marketing situation.

Sources

Bannister, D. and Fransella, F. (1977) *Inquiring Man*, Penguin.

Buchanan, D. A. and Huczynski, A. A. (1985) *Organisational Behaviour*, Prentice-Hall.

Cattell, H. B. (1989) *The 16 PF: Personality in Depth*, IPAT.

Cattell, R. B., Eber, H. W. and Tatsuoka, M. M. (1988) *Handbook for the 16 PF*, IPAT.

Engel J. F., Blackwell R. D. and Miniard P. W. (1990) *Consumer Behaviour* (6th edn.), Dryden.

Engler, B. (1985) *Personality Theories* (2nd edn.), Houghton Mifflin.

Eysenck, H. J. (1964) *Uses and Abuses of Psychology*, Penguin.

Eysenck, H. J. (1970) *The Structure of Human Personality*, Methuen.

Eysenck, H. J. and Wilson, G. (1978) *Know Your Own Personality*, Pelican.

Gregory, R. L. (ed.) (1987) *The Oxford Companion to the Mind*, Oxford University Press.

Kakabadse, A., Ludlow, R. and Vinnicombe, S. (1987) *Working in Organisations*, Penguin.

Kolb, D. A. *et al.* (1971) *Organisational Psychology: An Experiential Approach*, Prentice-Hall.

Luft, J. and Ingham, H. (1955) *The Johari Window: A Graphic Model of Interpersonal Awareness*, UCLA.

Mehrabian, A. (1968) *An Analysis of Personality Theories*, Prentice-Hall.

Peter, J. P. and Olson, J. C. (1990) *Consumer Behaviour and Marketing Strategy* (2nd edn), Irwin.

Reber, A. S. (1985) *Dictionary of Psychology*, Penguin.

Williams, K. C. (1981) *Behavioural Aspects of Marketing*, Heinemann.

Part Three   People as Individuals

Cognitive processes

4 'There's more to this than meets the eye!'

Perception

Introduction

This is an important chapter and makes a very useful start to the study of the behavioural sciences by examining the phenomenon known as perception. It looks at the processes of perception, which is a topic that crops up throughout the whole field of study.

At the end of this chapter students should be fully familiar with the following concepts (and the associated language) and *should be able to relate them to marketing and organizational (work) situations*:

- The senses, sensation, awareness, thresholds.
- Weber's Law.
- Selectivity of perception:
    External Factors:
    – Intensity and size
    – Position
    – Contrast
    – Novelty
    – Repetition
    – Movement
    Internal Factors:
    – Interests
    – Needs
    – Motives
    – Expectation
- Habituation.
- Awareness, evoked, inert and inept sets.
- Organization of perception:
    – Figure/ground
    – Grouping
    – Closure
    – Contour
- Repertory Grid Technique.
- Communication:

  – One way/Two way
  – Facts and emotions in language
  – Addressing different audiences

Perception

Perception is the term used to cover those processes which give coherence, unity and meaning to a person's sensory input. It involves all those processes we use to select, sort, organize and interpret sensory data to make a meaningful and coherent picture of 'our world'.

Here is a very old sensory input:

Do you see a woman's face?
Is she young or old?
Can you see both?

Figure 4.1

This immediately raises an important point. Although subject to the same sensory input, different people may perceive quite different things.

As individuals we are continually subject to stimuli from our environment. These stimuli impinge on us via our senses, and it is the way that we interpret these sensory signals that determines the way we see our world. It is generally accepted that our perception of the world is not an absolute, determined by the physical stimulation received, but is both organized and dependent on a variety of other factors.

Clearly, we need to consider the sensory channels as they are the source of perception. We are all aware of the five senses:

- Hearing
- Sight
- Smell
- Taste
- Touch

However, it is usual for physiologists to point out that we do, in fact, possess a number of other senses with pain being an obvious one, while other internal senses identify variations in temperature and the state of some of our internal organs (e.g. heartbeat). Additionally there is the kinesthetic sense which reports on our physical attitude and the position of our limbs – this seems to be linked to what we sometimes call co-ordination, the ability to catch a ball, operate the clutch on a car and so forth. Another is our sense of balance, which is sometimes refered to as the vestibular sense stemming from the position of the head and determined by the operation of the inner ear.

Marketers will often attempt to involve all of the five primary senses in order to influence consumer behaviour. Supermarkets commonly put vegetables just inside the entrance. Here the aim is to get the customer actively involved in the buying process by touching, picking up and choosing produce right at the beginning of the shopping visit. Products are displayed in attractive packaging designed to catch the eye, so they utilize sight. Tempo-controlled music is sometimes played – interspersed with announcements drawing the customer's attention to special offers or groups of products (hearing is thus involved). Taste can be brought into play by offering customers 'tasters' of food products, while smell has proved a most potent weapon since the development of in-store bakeries. There would seem to be considerable potential for further expansion using smells such as fresh coffee in appropriate areas of the store.

There is a need for the consumer to be aware of a stimulus. This involves the notion of *sensory thresholds*. Psychologists draw a distinction between different types of threshold:

1 The absolute threshold. This is the level of stimulation at which the individual begins to experience sensation – i.e. it is the lowest level of stimulus that can be detected.
2 The differential threshold. This is the point at which the magnitude of the difference between two stimuli is sufficient for the individual to perceive that the two are, in fact, different – i.e. it is the lowest level of *difference* between stimuli that can be detected.
3 Dual thresholds. This term refers to the fact that some senses appear to have two separate thresholds. An example is that people can commonly identify the presence of an odour at one threshold, but have a second, higher threshold at which they can identify what the smell is.

One obvious problem for the marketer is that the efficiency of people's senses may vary widely. We are all aware of people with hearing difficulties and of those who need glasses or contact lenses to see adequately. It therefore becomes clear that the same stimulus will be received differently by different individuals, thus leading to different perceptions, even before we consider the internal processing of the signals received.

Sensation may also be relative. When at junior school you may have done the experiment where you have three bowls of water. One bowl contains hot water (hand-hot, not scalding), the second contains cold water, while the third has a tepid mixture half-way between. You place one hand in the hot water and the other in the cold and leave them there for thirty seconds or so – time enough for you to adjust. Both hands are then placed in the tepid water. If you have not done this, do try it because the experience is fascinating – the tepid water feels hot to the hand that was in the cold water and cold to the hand that had been placed in the hot. So we have 'first hand' evidence that the same stimulus can feel different to different parts of our own body.

On the other hand people have the ability to 'adjust' their perception to produce the phenomenon called 'constancy'. This refers to the tendency for our perceptual world to remain 'the same' despite significant alterations in the sensory input – e.g. a saucer or plate seen from any angle (other than directly above or below) is still perceived as being round, although the image received by the eye is an ellipse. This, of course, raises the issue of how much of perception is innate and how much is learned through experience. The opposite situation is also of some significance – the extent to which learning can function to modify our perceptions and this will be discussed later.

One interesting aspect of our senses is the way in which high intensity inputs appear to dull the senses (reduce our sensitivity), while low levels of input may increase our sensitivity. Actors (and sometimes teachers) say that one way to get people's attention is to speak more softly – it makes them concentrate and gets them 'on the edge of their seats'. Another, more extreme example, is the way in which persons who suffer from (e.g.) impaired sight will often seem to compensate for this by developing other senses, e.g. hearing, to high levels of sensitivity.

Another complicating factor is that we seem to respond best to changes in our environment. We can 'get used to' noises such as the flow of water through a radiator or the ticking of a clock.

> **Exercise** – stop reading and sit silently for a minute. Close your eyes and concentrate on the sounds in the room.
> – what can you hear?
> – what sounds were you unaware of before you did this exercise?

This exercise illustrates the phenomenon of *habituation*. There are some sounds which we filter out of our consciousness. Not all of them are quiet, like the clock ticking. It is possible to work in very noisy environments and 'not hear' the noise most of the time.

On a quiet night we can hear clearly sound which would be lost during the noisier daylight hours, if we are away from our usual home base we sometimes claim that these sounds keep us awake at night. Similarly, the absence of the sounds to which we are habituated can disturb our sleeping routines.

Another example of habituation is the hot bath – getting in can be quite a painful experience, yet after only a short while all feelings of discomfort can vanish as we get used to the temperature of the water.

> **Think** – Habituation can mean that consumers get used to our advertising and cease to be aware of it – how can we combat this tendency?

An important contribution to our understanding of sensation is Weber's Law. This was developed by the German physiologist Ernst Weber (1795–1878) and concerns a phenomenon called the 'just noticeable difference'. Formally it states that the just noticeable differences in stimuli are proportional to the magnitude of the original stimulus. In mathematical terms:

$$\frac{\Delta I}{I} = k$$

where ΔI is the increment in intensity that is just detectable, I is the intensity of the comparison stimulus and k is a constant.

Weber's Law is of interest to marketers when they seek to establish their product as being 'different' from either the competition or an earlier version. The ideas of 'new, improved' products imply and demand that the consumer can detect the difference from the old product. Weber's Law points out that the notion of 'noticeable difference' is proportional. The addition of a small amount of salt will be noticeable in a bland, unseasoned soup; but that same amount of salt would go unnoticed if added to a highly spiced and already well salted dish. Similarly we will notice the difference if we upgrade the lightbulb in our lamp from 30 to 60 watts. What we notice is the *doubling* of the light power rather than the addition of 30 watts. If we have a 100 watt bulb in the lamp, we would need to go to 200 watts to get the same effect – moving to 130 watts would have a lot less impact.

It is likely that consumers will see price increases in much the same way – a 10p increase in the price of a packet of cigarettes may be seen as much more significant than putting the price of a car up by £100.

Thus marketers may be concerned to initiate changes which are above the just noticeable difference in some circumstances and just below that level in others.

> **Think** – What is the just noticeable difference for products you are concerned with?
> – What other examples can you identify of marketers using this idea?

Selectivity of perception

Before we can perceive an event or object, it is necessary that it attracts our attention, that we notice it. A problem that we then run into is that attention is selective – attending to one stimulus (awareness, focusing, processing) tends to reduce the attention paid to others. Generally selectivity functions so that, at any instant, a person focuses on certain features of their environment to the (relative) exclusion of other features.

> **Exercise** – 1 Find someone who wears an analogue wristwatch (one with a dial and hands rather than a digital read-out).
> 2 Ask them what form the figure '6' takes on their watch dial – *without looking.*
> 3 Having got an answer, invite them to check whether they are correct or not.
> 4 Then say 'Without looking at your watch again, what is the time?'

When trying this out in practice we find the majority of people cannot say what the time is, despite having just looked at their watch! They have clearly looked at the watch dial, they must have observed the position of the hands, but because they were not looking for that information they did not 'see' it.

Attention may be conscious (we make a conscious decision to concentrate on one element of the total input); alternatively, and quite commonly, it is unconscious in that something 'catches our attention' and we find ourselves attending to it although we are not explicitly aware of the factors which caused us to perceive only that small part of the total stimulus array. One interesting phenomenon is sometimes called the 'cocktail party effect' where most people find it possible to concentrate on (or attend selectively to) one person's speech when surrounded by the competing speech of many others. At the same time we appear to be able to monitor other incoming messages so that our attention can switch to another topic or person almost instantly. We can therefore focus on one activity at any given moment, but that may, in turn, become peripheral in the next moment. This gives rise to the notion of attention span. Attention span has two meanings:

1 in the technical sense it is the number of objects or separate stimulus elements that can be perceived in a single, short presentation – but in common usage it means
2 the amount of time that a person can continue to attend to one type of input.

The evidence suggests that the attention span of students in lectures is very short! However, individuals can develop longer attention spans when they practise some activity in which they are interested. An example might be listening to music, where there seems to be a need to develop listening skills in order to attend longer pieces of music. Advertisements are short partly because of cost, but also because there is a fear of boring the receiver – a fact noted by many politicians who practise shortening their messages to create short, sharp soundbites.

Marketers are very concerned that their messages attract the attention of potential consumers. Initially their targets may not be aware of the product or the message so the factors which direct our attention is of obvious importance. The broad classifications are of external and internal elements; external factors relate to the physical characteristics of the stimulus; internal factors relate to our feelings, motives, interests and expectations.

External factors influencing attention

Size

Generally we notice larger, rather than smaller, stimuli. The size element suggests that the sensory input to the system is proportional to the size, although it is possible to imagine situations where a small, bright object is highlighted against a large, dull background, and is by far the more eye-catching. Increasing the size of an advertisement will increase the chances of it being noticed. Similar relationships appear to hold good for the size of the illustrations or pictures within an advertisement.

Intensity

Perhaps even more significant, as pointed out above, is the idea that the intensity of a stimulus may be the very facet that catches the attention. Bright primary colours can be dominant features of packaging or visual advertising material. An interesting 'new' development has been the emergence of advertisements which feature sounds which have been 'over recorded', with the natural sound boosted and intensified. Lucozade used this idea when the opening of a can in the grandstand was enough to cause a false start in an athletics race.

Position

Stimuli may be more noticeable simply because of their location. Supermarkets place products they especially wish to sell at eye-level on their shelves – the so-called 'hot spot'. Similarly, impulse items such as sweets and chocolate are often placed next to the checkout. In print media

(a)

there has been work to indicate that right hand rather than left hand pages get more attention as do the covers both inside and out. The same work suggested that the front of the magazine is the best part of the journal in which to place material, but it would seem that this must be a function of the ways and patterns adopted by readers when flipping through the magazine. Depending on the target population, placing material amongst the sports pages is likely to attract the attention of a different set of readers to those advertisements positioned among the arts pages. Similarly the choice of which slots in the midst of which television programmes will determine who sees your advertisement.

Contrast

As noted above, much of our attention is relative to norms or standards. The phenomenon of habituation has been discussed. Our attention is grabbed by *changes* in the stimulus. Thus our attention can be attracted as much by a sudden silence as by a sharp, unexpected noise. Black and white pictures can stand out when surrounded by colour (and vice versa). Main points and headings are picked out in this text by making them look different – **heavier type**, *different typeface*, <u>underlining</u> or ***all three***!

In effect, contrast is a form of perceptual judo as it can create apparent intensity of stimulus without utilizing size, loudness or colour. The contrast can be thought of in two dimensions – firstly it needs to be different from its specific context. Hence the idea of styles, whether of advertisement, or packaging, or product, passing through phases of unusual, fashionable, standard, old-fashioned and ready to be overtaken by the next wave. Secondly there is a need for advertisements, packaging or products to offer a contrast to their competitors – thus giving an identity and, hopefully, a competitive edge. The presentation of stimuli that are inconsistent or contrast with one another creates a perceptual conflict that attracts attention.

(b)

Novelty

The unusual or unexpected attracts attention. Here the problem centres on who's view of unusual is taken, and for how long does a stimulus remain unexpected. In this sense it is very similar to the contrast element discussed above. There is also some sort of parallel with jokes in that there is nothing so attractive as a new joke, and nothing quite so boring as the joke you have already heard!

Repetition

As mentioned earlier, our attention continually switches from one stimulus to another and it seems logical to assume that a stimulus that is repeated has an improved chance of catching our attention. This does need some words of warning, however, as repetition is the route to habituation and loss of attention. The art is to get enough repetition to reinforce the message but not so much as to switch off the receivers.

Movement

Stimuli in motion attract greater attention than static stimuli. Skilful artwork which gives the illusion of movement may enhance the awareness factor of stationary material. The developmemt of billboards which 'roll over' to display a sequence of different posters is an example of how eye-catching movement can be. Sometimes watching the advertisements *change* can be more interesting that the football match which is supposed to be the focus of our attention when watching television!

Learned attention-inducing stimuli – there are some stimuli that we have been taught to attend to. Telephones and doorbells are typical examples of stimuli that we have been conditioned to respond to immediately. The inclusion of such sounds in radio and TV advertisements could have the negative effect of making the receiver leave the room!

(c)

> **Think** – List some current advertising campaigns.
> – What external factors do they employ to attract our attention?#

Internal factors influencing attention

There are internal factors which affect our awareness of stimuli.

Motivation

Hungry persons are commonly more aware of food stimuli – the moral being to eat before you visit the supermarket for your groceries! Similarly the motivation associated with undertaking this course of study is likely to increase your awareness of advertising messages and media.

Interest

We tend to be more aware of things in which we are interested. The soccer fan can tell you which clubs play in which colours, the film buff can recite appearances by actors, the keen cook can remember recipes apparently without effort.

Need

If we need to replace our trainers we may well become much more aware of sports shoe shops and what others are wearing.

> **Think** – using your list of current advertising campaigns, what internal factors do they employ to attract our attention?

(d)

Awareness set

Howard and Sheth (1969) point out that consumers can only select products from those of which they are aware. So they draw a distinction between those brands within a market that the consumer is aware of. This they call the *awareness set*. They call the remainder of the available brands the *unawareness set*. They argue that consumers, in order to simplify the process of choice, will make their final choice from a limited range of brands drawn from the awareness set. These are the brands about which the consumer has positive feelings. This group is called the *evoked set*. The important fact is that for a product to be chosen, it is not enough for the consumers to be aware of it, they must think well enough of it to place it in their evoked set.

These ideas were further developed by Narayana and Markin (1975) who suggested that those brands which did not feature in a consumer's evoked set could be subdivided into an *inert set* (those the consumer was aware of but where their feelings for the brands were neutral – neither positive nor negative) and an *inept set* (those the consumer was aware of but where

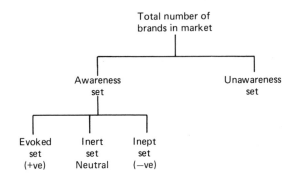

Figure 4.2

(e)

feelings for these brands was negative). This is commonly represented diagrammatically as in Fig. 4.02.

The message for marketers from these ideas may be highly significant as it can help determine the advertising objectives and strategy that should be adopted. Should market research indicate that the brand is in the unawareness set for a large proportion of the population then the task is to raise awareness in order to get it into the awareness set. Thus widespread media campaigns are indicated with the aim of getting the brand known. An example might be Cornhill Insurance raising their profile by sponsoring Test cricket.

If the brand is found to be in the evoked set, the promotional strategy would be defensive reinforcement. Whereas should it appear in the inert or inept sets positive attempts will be made to change consumers' perceptions and attitudes towards the brand.

Think – What advertising/promotion examples can you think of for each of these awareness set situations?

Earlier we explored some of the factors, both internal and external, that influence selective attention. One hazard in the path of the marketer who is seeking to design strategies for advertising and promotion is that consumers may not select his or her message to attend to. The other side of this coin is the idea of *selective exposure*. Here we will seek out inputs which we find rewarding/interesting/satisfying and avoid those which are the opposite. The soccer fan purchases and reads the sports pages of the daily newspapers, the theatre buffs are likely to read the programmes of the shows they attend, while the keen cook may choose to switch on the television to watch a cookery programme.

(f)

Think – What newspapers do you read?
– Why do you choose them as opposed to others?
– How does this choice affect the stimuli to which you are subjected?

This is an obvious way to target specific market segments. If you have a clear idea of the people you are trying to reach with your advertising message, the special interest publication, programme or medium is likely to be a useful way of getting your message across. However, to some extent this approach is preaching to the converted, and there may be even more problems emerging as the habits of 'zapping' (changing channels during advertisements in the midst of television programmes) and 'zipping' (fast-forwarding through the advertisements on a recording of a television show) become ever more established and possible with the advent of the remote control device for television sets. These habits reduce or even eliminate the advertising process so carefully and expensively developed by the marketer.

An even more interesting challenge is how we might attract new customers. Here we may look to what Peter and Olson (1990) have christened 'accidental exposure'. This refers to the advertisements on such things as posters, buses and tube trains. Here the target is not selected by some process of segmentation, the advertisement is offered up to the population at large, and so may attract the attention of those who would not normally select such a stimulus for themselves.

Expectation is another crucial determinant of what we perceive. Indeed it may not be unreasonable to claim that people often perceive what they *expect* to perceive rather than the message that they *do* receive. Figure 4.4 is a well worn example.

Most people coming across this for the first time read it as 'Paris in the spring' rather than what is actually printed – 'Paris in the the spring'. Here

(g)

A B C D E F

Figure 4.3

Figure 4.4

the human brain seems to process the stimulus and jump to the wrong conclusion – thus it may be an accelerated form of closure.

Jokes are another example of expectation

> **Joke** – Q. Why do surgeons wear masks when they are operating?
> – A. So if anything goes wrong, the patient won't know who did it!

and

> **Joke** – Q. Have you heard the one about the terrorists who tried to blow up a car?
> – A. They burned their lips on the exhaust pipe!

(h)

In both of these examples the reader's expectations are formed by the initial statement – and the punchline alters that perception by changing the situation or the meaning of a word. Some psychologists have suggested that laughter is a form of release from the 'shock' of such sudden changes in our perceptions.

There has recently been a growth in amusing books which purport to 'teach' readers the way to speak in accents or dialect. Here the sounds of the accented speech are 'translated' into standard English words – but the words do not have the meaning we expect. The trick is to say what is written and listen to the sounds. Here are some examples:

Joke – Can you translate the following into 'English'?:
    (a) Write and cider ode
    (b) Count's louse
    (c) Grape written

For those who have had trouble (a) approximates to the statement 'right hand side of the road'; while (b) reproduces quite closely the sound which we make when we say the words 'council house'; and (c) is a version of 'Great Britain'.

Exercise – A number of drawings have been reproduced on the bottom of the foregoing pages – they are not all the same, changes have been incorporated as they progress.
    – Have you noticed the changes?
    – At what point in the sequence did the image change?
    – Look back at the drawings again and see when the change occurs this time.

Most people see the kneeling woman much earlier in the sequence when they look a second time. When asked they often reply 'because I knew what I was looking for'.

Il I2 I3 I4 I5

Figure 4.5

Exercise – Look back at Figures 4.3 and 4.5.

Here we have a similar example in 'the ambiguous B'. In Figure 4.3 (second image in the sequence) we see the letter 'B'. It is identical to the third image in Figure 4.5, but this time the context of the message has led the reader to perceive 13. Thus we have some further, first-hand evidence of perception being a function of both context and expectation.

The phenomenon seems to be quite widespread in everyday life. It seems that many of us will sit down to watch a comedy programme on TV, and expect to laugh. The stars of such shows have won more than half the battle before they even start, because we are looking for them to be funny!

Think – How do your expectations affect the way you watch party political broadcasts?

Subliminal perception

This expression is something of an anomaly as 'subliminal' means below the threshold for perception. So this area refers, not to perception in the way we have been discussing it above, but to the effects of below-threshold stimuli upon an individual's behaviour. In other words we are concerned with the effects of stimuli which are too weak to be consciously heard, seen, tasted, smelled or felt.

This notion of perception without awareness has given rise to a great deal of controversy within the behavioural sciences, both regarding the validity/reliability of the evidence and ethical issues raised by the possibility of using such techniques to influence behaviour (not least amongst consumers).

Physiologists have been able to identify electrical activity in the brain of subjects, given levels of stimulus below that which they could sense – so there is evidence that inputs may be received without the individual being aware of it.

In one of the most famous cases, messages such as 'drink Coca-cola' and 'eat popcorn' were flashed on to the screen during film shows at an American drive-in cinema. The messages were only a single frame of the film, films run at 24 frames per second, so the stimulus was only on the screen for less than 1/24th of a second and so were 'undetectable' by the cinema goers. The cinema reported increased sales of both products during the six-week test.

This gave rise to a great deal of interest and anxiety but it proved difficult to reproduce the results in other settings. Reber quotes the American psychologist J. V. McConnell who reviewed the evidence and came to the conclusion that 'all things considered, secret attempts to manipulate people's minds have yielded results as subliminal as the stimuli used'.

Despite this lack of convincing evidence that subliminal advertising has any effect, there is still interest in the notion of 'hidden' images in advertisements, and recent American court cases have alleged subliminal messages hidden on heavy metal rock records. Similarly there is a growing interest in behaviour shaping via relaxation and 'self-hypnosis' techniques in such areas as giving up smoking, slimming, and coping with stress.

Organization of perception

Continuation

We tend to 'follow the line' when looking at visual stimuli, we have little problem in following a graph which is drawn – even if it is drawn on squared graph paper. Another example is in Figure 4.6.

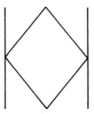

Figure 4.6

We 'follow the line' and tend to see a diamond between two uprights rather than a 'W' on top of an 'M'.

Similarity

We tend to group stimuli that are similar to each other and different from other stimuli – so Figure 4.7 is seen as two columns of one kind of dot and two of another.

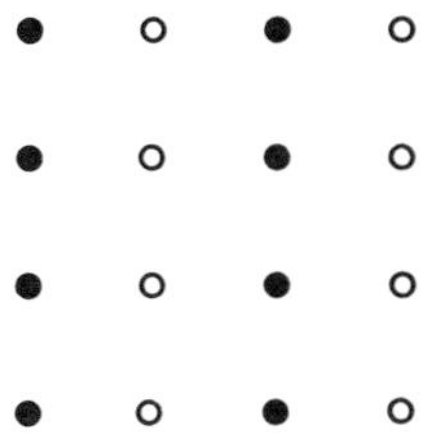

```
●   o   ●   o

●   o   ●   o

●   o   ●   o

●   o   ●   o
```

Figure 4.7

However, we also group symbols to aid our recognition. The act of reading is helped by breaking up the input into recognizable groups of letters that we can identify as words. An example of the difficulties that occur when this convention is not followed may be illustrated by Figure 4.8.

Once again the significant omission might be said to be 'nothing' (i.e. spaces) but it does make the message noticeably more difficult to decipher.

Figure 4.8

Proximity

We tend to group together stimuli that are close to each other. So Figure 4.9 is seen as three groups of two lines.

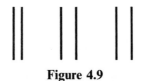

Figure 4.9

Closure

The tendency of people to perceive incomplete objects as complete, to close up or fill in gaps in sensory inputs and to view asymmetric and unbalanced stimuli as symmetric and balanced. In Figure 4.10, most people see (a) as being a square, (b) as being a circle and, most interesting of all, (c) as a triangle.

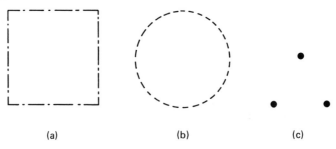

Figure 4.10

Another fascinating aspect of perception is the way in which many people can 'see' things which are not there. A classic example is Figure 4.11, where we construct the triangle from startlingly little information.

Figure 4.11

Another element of closure is the context within which the stimulus is received. In the context of this book most readers should be able to 'read' the stimulus in Figure 4.12 even though half of the image has been removed. It is likely that a stimulus less related to Consumer Behaviour might prove more difficult to read.

ιVIAΚΚͼ ι ιιVG

Figure 4.12

Marketers have used the idea of closure in such classic advertising messages as 'Schh . . . You know who' which has worked well for the Schweppes organization for many years. The observer completes the message on behalf of the advertiser, thus involving mental processing or elaboration which in turn is likely to imprint the message.

In this area come some interesting advertisements for the Heinz company where the cans are presented side on. Figure 4.13 illustrates what the observer sees of the label, but few people seem to have any problem in identifying the product.

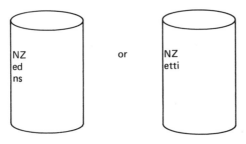

Figure 4.13

Another example of closure which saves the advertiser money is the short version of the longer advertisement on television. Here we seem to relish the process of spotting the advert on minimal input – *and then completing it in our own minds*! Very economical given the cost of TV slots!

Distortion

This is another variable which can be triggered by strong emotional feelings, drugs, lack of sleep, sensory deprivation or sensory overload (including emotional stress). This is a potentially interesting phenomenon as the misperception/distortion arises 'inside the head of the perceiver' rather than from the environment.

Ambiguous stimuli/illusions

Ambiguous stimuli or illusions are a fascinating field of study. We started this chapter with a very ancient example – the old/young woman, but there are many other examples. Many of these figures have been around for some time, but they give graphic illustration to the old axiom (and title of the chapter) that 'there is more to perception than meets the eye'!

In Figure 4.14 the two vertical lines are of equal length – check them with a ruler if you have doubts. The imposition of the horizontal V gives the illusion that the left hand vertical is longer than the right-hand one.

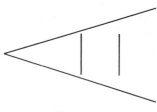

Figure 4.14

In Figure 4.15 the two equal parts of the horizontal line appear to be different in length. The fishtails are believed to be interpreted by the brain as elements of perspective, implying important messages as to the distance the line is from the eye. Our brains seem to compensate for this 'different' distance so that the lengths are seen as unequal.

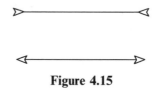

Figure 4.15

In the example in Figure 4.16 the horizontal line appears to be curved – check it with a ruler!

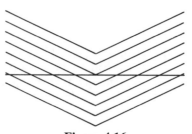

Figure 4.16

Figure-ground

The classic example of this effect is Figure 4.17.

Figure 4.17

In this case we see two faces if we make the black area the figures and the white the background – in contrast, we see a vase, goblet or candlestick if we make the white area the figure and the black portion the background.

By now the reader will have entered into the spirit of this section and will possibly be looking for alternate images. When you see a vase or candlestick, the black printing is the figure and the white area is called the ground (as in background). However the image of two faces looking inward reverses this with the white elements becoming the figure(s) and the black the ground.

A similar effect can be obtained with the Necker Cube shown in Figure 4.18. Can you make the 'box' switch from coming towards you to going away from you?

We started this chapter with the observation that different persons, viewing the same stimulus, might 'see' different things. Clearly this idea could be of crucial importance to marketers – if people see your marketing messages differently to the way in which you had intended them, you could

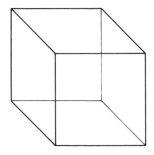

Figure 4.18

have severe problems. We will now look at an interesting way of assessing people's perceptions.

Personal construct theory – the work of George Kelly

The American psychologist George Kelly published a book in 1955 called *The Psychology of Personal Constructs* in which he proposed a useful way of considering both psychology and the processes of perception.

His starting point is that people are fundamentally inquisitive and wish to make sense of their world. He suggests that we all conduct our lives rather like scientists – exploring, hypothesizing, experimenting, explaining our experiences and predicting the future via developing strategies and procedures. The term that Kelly uses to describe the units of meaning we develop in order to make sense of the world is *personal constructs*. He suggests that we have personal constructs about all aspects of our lives (including ourselves). These constructs essentially define and make sense of our existence and, once formed, they will be the basis on which we interpret events, experiences and future possibilities.

His theory has a basic assumption which is that people determine actions on the basis of their *perception* of what *is* going on, what *has* gone on and their *predictions* of what *will* go on in future situations and happenings.

The basic insight to emerge from this approach is that no people ever share an identical construct, and so their experiences of 'reality' will be unique and separate. For example, if I use the word 'father', this will immediately trigger the reader's unique personal construct of 'father', a construct that will have been formed over a long period of time, based on the reader's experience of fathers. If they had a good, positive relationship with their own parents their construct would be very different to that of a person who had been regularly beaten and abused by their father, which in turn may be very different from that of a person who was orphaned at an early age. In other words your construct of 'father' is uniquely your own, and this will influence the perceptions, reactions and responses every time that word is used.

Kelly allowed that there are different types of constructs. For example there are:

1 *core constructs* are the one which refer to ourselves, and are crucial to our identity and self-concept – e.g. 'I am a good student'.
2 broad constructs are those which are applied very widely – e.g. 'all teachers are ignorant of the real world'.
3 *tight constructs* have a specific application and which become useless if found faulty – e.g. scientific laws.
4 *loose constructs* can vary according to the circumstances – e.g. 'some chapters of this book are fascinating, others are boring'.
5 *constricted constructs* have very narrow application – e.g. 'the only reason for getting a qualification is to move job'.

Clearly the more a person can develop positive constructs about their work or their course of study, the more effectively they are likely to perform. Similarly, the more a person can develop positive constructs about our products, services or ideas, the more likely they are to 'buy' them.

To explore constructs, Kelly devised what is called the *Repertory Grid Technique*. In the original format he would make a series of cards which related to (e.g.) occupations known to the subject (elements) – so there would be cards with job titles written on them such as Barperson, Teacher, Accountant, Doctor, Librarian, and so forth. The experimenter would choose three of these at random, show them to the subject and ask 'which one is different?'. When the subject had identified the 'different' one, the next question was 'in what way is that occupation different to the other two?' – thus eliciting a personal construct about occupations. The full set of element cards was then shown to the subject and all the other jobs which also had that quality (i.e. shared the construct) were picked out. Next, another three cards were chosen at random and the process repeated with the sole proviso that the same construct could not be used a second time – in other words an alternative way of recognizing 'differences' between jobs had to be found.

In this way a grid can be developed which allows examination of the ways in which constructs relate or overlap, or of the similarities and differences in perceptions between elements.

Clearly such a technique could be used to establish the dimensions (constructs) which consumers use to differentiate between products and the

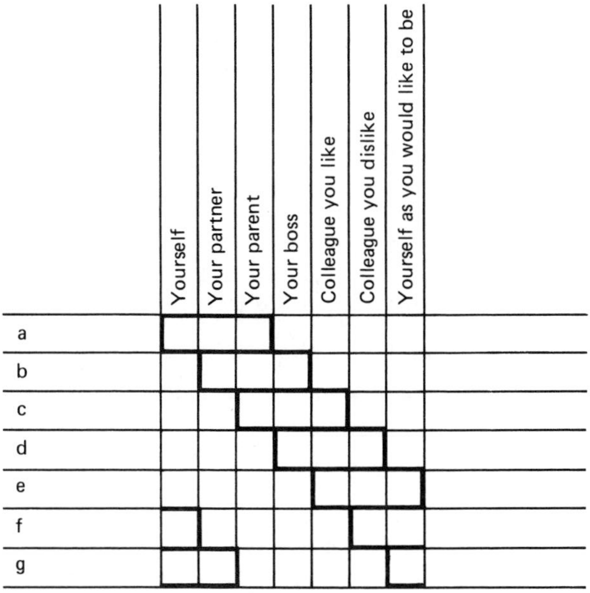

Figure 4.19a

extent to which competing brands are similar or different. This approach is revisited in Chapter 7 when we consider the problems of measuring attitudes.

Try this exercise to look at your own constructs regarding different people.

Exercise

1 Across the top of the grid in Figure 4.19a you see a number of 'people-types' set out at the top of the columns – yourself, your partner, your parent, your boss, a colleague you like, a colleague you dislike, yourself as you would like to be. Pencil in the space provided the names of the real people who fit those descriptions in your life (do it in pencil so that you can rub the names out when you have finished).

2 You will see that three boxes have been picked out in heavier print in the first horizontal row – corresponding to the characters 'yourself', 'your partner', 'your parent'.

3 Think of the three people you have identified – which one is different?

4 Place a tick in the box of the one you have chosen.

5 Write in the right hand column the characteristic that makes that person different from the other two.

6 Write in the left-hand space what you perceive as being the opposite of that characteristic. It will help if you avoid using 'closed' constructs such as male, female, bald, etc. wherever possible and use more open, personality type adjectives.

7 Now work along the remainder of the row, consider each of the persons you have identified and put a tick in the appropriate box for any of those persons who also share the characteristic you listed in the right-hand column.

8 Complete the rest of the grid, row by row, following the same procedure – the only limitation is that you should not use the same construct more than once.

You should now have a grid that looks something like this:

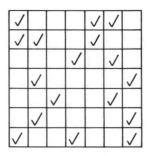

Figure 4.19b

9 To score the grid we need a measure of how similar or different two rows are. Let us imagine that the first two rows are:

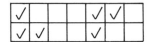

Figure 4.20

We count a point for each pair that match – i.e. whenever there is a tick in both rows we score a point; and whenever there is a tick in neither row we also score a point. So the example above would get a matching score of:

1 + 0 + 1 + 1 + 1 + 0 + 1

Figure 4.21

= 5 for the comparison score for rows 1 and 2.

As you can see the scores will always lie between 0 and 7.

10 Repeat stage 9 for rows 1 and 3, 1 and 4, 1 and 5, 1 and 6, 1 and 7.

11 Then work out the scores for rows 2 and 3, 2 and 4, and so on to 2 and 7.

12 Complete the remainder of the comparisons – 3 and 4, 3 and 5, 3 and 6, 3 and 7, 4 and 5, 4 and 6, 4 and 7, 5 and 6, 5 and 7, 6 and 7.

13 Put the values into the appropriate 'holes' in the diagram.

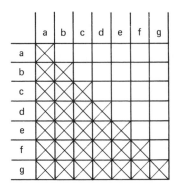

Figure 4.22

14 As mentioned above the scores can vary from 0 to 7. The higher the score, the more similar the two constructs are until we reach a score of 7 when it might suggest that the two constructs are identical. Similarly scores of 0 or 1 suggest the constructs may be opposites.

15 In our example grid above the comparisons scores might produce a grid that looks like this:

	a	b	c	d	e	f	g
a		5	2	6	5	2	1
b			2	4	5	2	1
c				3	4	7	6
d					4	3	2
e						4	3
f							6

Figure 4.23

Interpretation of this data would suggest that constructs (a) and (d) are similar and constructs (c), (f) and (g) form another, separate cluster of constructs which are similar. Construct (g) seems to be nearly opposite to both (a) and (b).

Think – What do the relationships look like in *your* grid?
– What does that tell you about the way you perceive other people?

Communication

While we are considering the problems and issues surrounding perception it is useful to look briefly at the process of communication. We may define this as the process whereby ideas, information and instructions are transmitted from one brain to another. Figure 4.24 gives a representation of the channels which might be followed when one person is talking to another.

Firstly there is a clear implication that there will be a message of some sort. This will be transmitted by the sender (*A*) and taken in by the receiver (*B*) (stage 2). However, in order for the communication to be effective, we

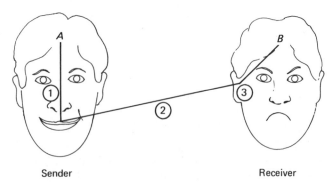

Sender   Receiver

Figure 4.24

must also consider the stages at which *A* decides what sounds to make and which words to use (stage 1), and the sense that *B* makes of the message that has been received (stage 3).

So we can say that the communication process has three basic stages:

$$Encoding \rightarrow Transmission \rightarrow Decoding$$

Once this sequence has been understood, it becomes clear that the effectiveness of communication can only be measured at the receiver's end of the process. In other words effective communication depends on the perceptions of the message received being the same as the perceptions of what the sender thought was sent.

Once the idea of coding and decoding messages has been absorbed, we can see the importance of language. Clearly it is necessary for both the sender and the receiver to be using the same code, language or system.

If I send you the following message:

yjod dysyr,rmy od om vpfr

you will find it difficult to read unless you understand the code which has been used (in this case the message was typed shifting one letter to the right of the 'true' message on my typewriter keyboard). Given this information, a typewriter and sufficient interest and motivation, it is possible to decode it as:

this statement is in code

(was it worth the effort?) You may have used codes as a child to pass messages to a friend in what you hoped was complete secrecy.

An interesting aspect of communication is that if you *do* receive a message such as:

yjod dysyr,rmy od om vpfr

the readers are likely to realize that they do not understand the message and may therefore decide to take further action to clarify what was meant.

Perhaps a more difficult situation arises when I send a message such as:

you are requested to scan the contents of this book.

Think – What are you going to do?

The answer that you give to that question is likely to depend on your decoding of the verb 'scan'. Many people (certainly most managers and students) decode it to mean 'have a quick look through', 'cast an eye over the main headings', or 'get a rough idea of what it is about'.

However, the *Concise Oxford Dictionary* defines the verb 'to scan' as 'look intently at all parts successively' (amongst other meanings), so if the sender intends the message to mean 'study carefully' and the receiver interprets the message as 'cast a quick eye over' (or vice versa) we have poor communication in the sense that the perceptions of the sender and the receiver do not coincide. Perhaps the most important aspect of this example is that in this case *the receiver did not realize that there was a misunderstanding.*

This brings us on to the idea of words, perhaps the most common medium of communication in our society. The key point to realize is that the meaning of a word is relatively arbitrary – if we move to another country we rapidly discover that common objects are called by different words. We may also discover that even within our own country local words exist for objects which are not understood in other localities. Even more odd is the occurrence of the same word being applied to different objects in different places. The author has been told, apparently in all good faith, that the word 'moggie' is used in parts of Scotland to mean a mouse, in other parts of the UK it commonly means a cat, while still others claim it is the word used for a Morris Minor car!

One interesting aspect of this is that words mean what people and society decide they mean. Despite complaints from those who wish to 'prove' that standards of English are declining, it must be realized that language is a developing entity. If people in general use the word 'scan' to mean 'cast a quick eye over something', then the dictionary definition will have to change.

Emotional meanings. As well as the dictionary definition it is useful to examine the emotional or affective associations of words:

Request   Ask   Demand

are all verbs meaning similar things.

Think – Which is the most aggressive?
   – Which is the most neutral?
   – Which is the most gentle?

It takes little analysis to understand that while the cognitive definition might be similar, the emotional meaning is clearly different. Thus an important part of any message may be the affective content of the words and the emotional perceptions which are created in the receiver.

As an aside, it is an interesting piece of social conditioning that in the field of industrial relations, trade unions make 'demands' while managements make 'offers', an emotional distinction that seems rather loaded.

Similarly, advertisers will be careful to create the emotional overtones they feel are appropriate for their product. Many washing powders use words such as 'soft', 'gentle' and 'delicate' in their copy, usually accompanying pastel shaded images. In contrast, Radion used very strong 'dayglo' colours and slogans such as 'Radion dismantles dirt' (this last with a very powerful visual image of a spanner clamping on to the 'd' in the word 'dirt').

Think – Motor manufacturers spend a great deal of money on selecting the names for their products. What are the emotional overtones of:
    'Fiesta'?
    'Cavalier'?
    '480 ES'?

Other products use words such as 'natural', 'fresh', countryside' alongside rural visual images to create the emotional message they are seeking to transmit.

Think – What other 'emotional' messages can you think of in current advertisements?

Propaganda

This, in itself, is an interesting word as, when it is looked up in the dictionary, one finds it defined as:

'Association, organized scheme, for propagation of a doctrine or practice; doctrines, information, etc. thus propagated; efforts, schemes, principles, of propagation' (*Concise Oxford Dictionary*)

while in the writer's mind there was a much more ominous definition, with heavy undesirable emotional overtones. A definition closer to 'normal' use is:

any attempt to manipulate opinion . . . a message will be regarded as propaganda only if it (a) represents a conscious, systematic and organised effort, (b) conceals the true nature of the debate by presenting only one side of the issues and (c) is characterised by an attempt to disguise the fact that it is, indeed, propaganda (Reber, 1985).

Think – How much of marketing falls within this definition of propaganda?

The Guardian newspaper published a summary of the language used by the media during the reporting of the Gulf War (Figure 4.25).

Think – To what extent does the language in Figure 4.25 constitute propaganda on the part of the press?
– To what extent do we all do this anyway?

Mad dogs and Englishmen

We have	They have
Army, Navy and Air Force	A war machine
Reporting guidelines	Censorship
Press briefings	Propaganda

We	They
Take out	Destroy
Suppress	Destroy
Eliminate	Kill
Neutralise or decapitate	Kill
Decapitate	Kill
Dig in	Cower in their foxholes

We launch	They launch
First strikes	Sneak missile attacks
Pre-emptively	Without provocation

Our men are . . .	Their men are . . .
Boys	Troops
Lads	Hordes

Our boys are . . .	Theirs are . . .
Professional	Brainwashed
Lion-hearts	Paper tigers
Cautious	Cowardly
Confident	Desperate
Heroes	Cornered
Dare-devils	Cannon fodder
Young knights of the skies	Bastards of Baghdad
Loyal	Blindly obedient
Desert rats	Mad dogs
Resolute	Ruthless
Brave	Fanatical

Our boys are motivated by	Their boys are motivated by
An old fashioned sense of duty	Fear of Saddam

Our boys	Their boys
Fly into the jaws of hell	Cower in concrete bunkers

Our ships are . . .	Iraq ships are . . .
An armada	A navy

Israeli non-retaliation is	Iraqi non-retaliation is
An act of great statesmanship	Blundering/Cowardly

The Belgians are . . .	The Belgians are also . . .
Yellow	Two-faced

Our missiles are . . .	Their missiles are . . .
Like Luke Skywalker zapping Darth Vader	Ageing duds (rhymes with Scuds)

Our missiles cause . . .	Their missiles cause . . .
Collateral damage	Civilian casualties

We . . .	They . . .
Precision bomb	Fire wildly at anything in the skies

Our PoWs are . . .	Their PoWs are . . .
Gallant boys	Overgrown schoolchildren

George Bush is . . .	Saddam Hussein is . . .
At peace with himself	Demented
Resolute	Defiant
Statesmanlike	An evil tyrant
Assured	A crackpot monster

Our planes . . .	Their planes . . .
Suffer a high rate of attrition	Are shot out of the sky
Fail to return from missions	Are Zapped

● *All the expressions above have been used by the British press in the past week*

Figure 4.25

We have already mentioned the use of colour in advertisements to create appropriate atmosphere and it is perhaps worth mentioning the increasing use of music to form associations and set 'moods' for products. Much use is currently made of music which has 'transferred' from other areas, most notably pop music. At present, some advertisers are using classical themes (*Carmina Burana* for aftershave) while many others are utilizing pop classics from some years ago (jeans, building societies). Here the thinking may be to recreate the feelings and wants of youth in the minds of people who are both older and better off in material terms, and thus better able to afford the product. These ideas are explored in more detail when we consider attitudes and attitude change.

One-way and two-way communication systems

It is possible to look at the communication process and distinguish two significantly different patterns.

1 *One-way* communication is where there is no immediate feedback from the receiver to the sender. It therefore encompasses media such as radio, television, newspapers, magazines, letters, memoranda.

Sender → Receiver

2 Two-way communication, on the other hand exists when there is immediate feedback. So this includes most face-to-face encounters, meetings, interviews, conversations, telephone calls.

Sender ⇆ Receiver

> **Think** – How is your current course of study conducted – using one-way or two-way communication?

If you have a group of people on whom you can try it out, there is a well known exercise you can run to investigate the characteristics of the two systems.

> **Exercise** – Participants will require pencil and paper.
>
> 1 Choose a 'sender' whose task is to transmit the patterns shown on page 406, *in words*, to the remainder of the group as quickly and as accurately as possible.
> 2 Create a 'one-way' communication situation by having the sender position him/herself so that the remainder of the group cannot be seen.
> 3 Remainder of the group stay totally quiet, making no sound at all, and resisting all temptation to giving feedback by laughing, sighing or snapping pencils!

4 The 'sender' describes pattern *A*, *in words*, as swiftly as he/she is able and the 'receivers' draw the pattern as accurately as they can.

5 The length of time taken for the communication process is noted.

6 Next create a 'two-way' communication situation by allowing the 'sender' to see the 'receivers' and allowing them to interrupt and ask any questions they want to at any time they wish.

7 The 'sender' describes pattern B, *in words*, as swiftly as he/she is able and the 'receivers' draw the pattern as accurately as they can.

8 The length of time taken for the communication process is again noted.

9 The accuracy of the communication is checked by allowing the receivers to see the original patterns. They can then allocate themselves a mark out of seven for the accuracy of their drawing (7 = identical to the original, 6 if they have got one of the oblongs 'wrong' and so forth down to a zero if there is no resemblance at all between the two patterns.

10 Compare the two systems.

Normally we find that:

a one-way communication is faster;
b two-way communication is more accurate;
c the receivers are more sure of themselves in the two-way system and make more correct judgements;
d the sender often feels under attack in the two-way system, especially when the receivers ask questions which point out the inadequacy of the message they are receiving;
e the two-way method is relatively noisy and, on occasion, can appear chaotic. In contrast the one-way method looks neat and efficient to an observer.

Think – How similar were your findings?
– What signs of emotion emerged?

It is not unusual for the sender to have quite a rough time, especially if the receivers are taking the exercise seriously. On some occasions the lack of competence of the sender has been mentioned along with their absence of intelligence! On another memorable occasion, the sender lost his temper after answering the same question a number of times and reversed the process!

The exercise, which the author first found in Harold J. Leavitt's 'Managerial Psychology', has worked consistently over the years and highlights the point that the two communication systems are, in fact, different and have quite different characteristics. (Note: the results seem not to be affected by having the two-way communication before the one-way, or by swapping the patterns for the different communications.)

Think – Under what circumstances would you wish to use one-way communication?
– Under what circumstances would you wish to use two-way communication?

As marketers communication is our business and the majority of the media we use is one-way. This suggests that we may be opting for the quick, cheap but inaccurate message.

Think – How can we improve the efficiency of our communication?

A key concept in communication studies is that messages need to be tailored to the audience to which they are addressed. Marketing messages are no different as a single department may need to communicate with:

- potential customers
- existing customers
- wholesalers
- retailers
- competitors
- suppliers
- government
- shareholders
- employees
- the public at large

Think – In what ways might messages need to be tailored for each of these groups of receivers?

Transactional analysis

In the previous chapter we looked at some ideas of the structure of personality and the work of Eric Berne. His idea of each individual having Parent, Adult and Child ego states offers an interesting way of analysing communication.

As we saw:

- The Parent ego state is opinionated, knowledgable, rule making.
- The Adult ego state is enquiring, data collecting.
- The Child ego state is emotional and fun-loving.

Using these ideas Berne created the approach to examining communication known as 'Transactional Analysis'. Here we can chart which ego state of the sender is addressing which ego state of the receiver. Berne argues that communication is only effective when there is a parallel or matched transaction and that communication breakdown is imminent when we get a crossed transaction.

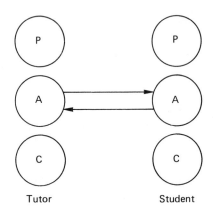

Figure 4.26

Dialogue:
Tutor: Have you finished your group discussion?
Student: Yes, we are ready to report back.

This constitutes a parallel or matched transaction.

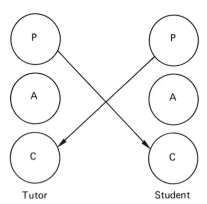

Figure 4.27

Dialogue:
Tutor: Don't you dare come into my class late again.
Student: I pay my course fees and I'll come in when I want to.

This is an example of a crossed transaction.

> **Think** – What example of Parent ego states can you think of in current advertisements?
> – What example of Adult ego states can you think of in current advertisements?
> – What example of Child ego states can you think of in current advertisements?

Other ideas concerning marketing communication and the specific problems of attitude change, and diffusion of ideas are dealt with in Chapters 7, 8 and 9.

Chapter summary exercises

> **Think** – How can the material in this chapter be applied to the marketing of:
> camcorders
> the social policy of a political party
> skis
> holidays
> soft drinks
> instant coffee
> sports shoes (trainers)
> razors
> hair colourant
> toothpaste
> shampoo
> motor cars
> low-fat/low cholesterol/low salt spread
> sanitary protection
> kitchen equipment
> spirits and liqueurs
> low-alcohol wine
> a restaurant
> newspapers
> toilet tissue
> bicycles

> **Think** – How *has* my organization used the processes of perception?

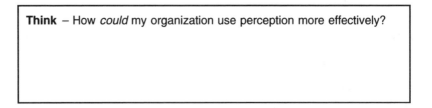

Some 'typical' questions – Perception

A 'Individuals act and react on the basis of their perceptions, not on the basis of objective reality . . . Thus, consumers' perceptions, are much more important to the marketer than is their knowledge of objective reality' (Schiffman and Kanuk, *Consumer Behaviour*). Why is it, in fact, that a person's perception of reality can often be different from the objective nature of that reality? How do marketers typically take advantage of the process of selectivity in perception?

B   Write notes on the relevance of each of the following to marketers:

a Subliminal perception
b Appeals to fear in advertising
c The concepts of the evoked set, the inert set, and the inept set in consumer evaluation of competing products.

C   Why do we perceive some things and not others? How can marketers make use of this 'selective perception' process in order to increase the likelihood that their products or services will be recognized and remembered?

D   What are the external factors influencing perception? How can these factors be utilized by advertisers in promoting (for example) new models of motor cars, cigarettes and tea?

E   Examine the relevance of each of the following concepts to the objectives of an advertiser trying to gain audience attention during TV commercials for products such as washing powder, car tyres, and a new brand of confectionery.

● Habituation,
● The interests, needs and motives of the viewers.

- Cognitive consistency.
- Closure.

F 'Perception is not solely influenced by the direct input of immediate sensory data, but is conditioned by the manner in which stimuli are presented, and by other cognitive influences such as past experiences and learning' (Williams). Discuss.

G Why is it that we perceive some things and not others?
How can marketers make use of this conscious and unconscious selectivity?

Sources

Bannister, D. and Fransella, F. (1977) *Inquiring Man*, Penguin.

Buchanan, D. A. and Huczynski, A. A. (1985) *Organisational Behaviour*, Prentice-Hall.

Engel, J. F., Blackwell, R. D. and Miniard, P. W. (1990) *Consumer Behaviour*, (6th edn.), Dryden.

Gregory, R. L. (ed.) (1987) *The Oxford Companion to the Mind*, Oxford University Press.

Hawkins, D. I., Best, R. J. and Coney, K. A. (1989) *Consumer Behaviour: Implications for Marketing Strategy* (4th edn.), Irwin.

Howard, J. A. and Sheth, J. N. (1969) *The Theory of Buyer Behaviour*, Wiley.

Kakabadse, A., Ludlow, R. and Vinnicombe, S. (1987) *Working in Organisations*, \Penguin.

Kelly, G. A. (1955) *The Psychology of Personal Constructs*, vols 1 and 2, Norton.

Leavitt, H. J. (1964) *Managerial Psychology*, University of Chicago Press.

Narayana, C. L. and Markin, R. J. (1975) 'Consumer behaviour and product performance: an alternative conceptualisation', *Journal of Marketing*, 39.

Peter, J. P. and Olson, J. C. (1990) *Consumer Behaviour and Marketing Strategy* (2nd edn.), Irwin.

Reber, A. S. (1985) *Dictionary of Psychology*, Penguin.

5 'To hell with school – I went to the University of Life!'

Learning – processes and theories

Introduction

This is an important topic. We are concerned with 'teaching' the consumer about our product – the consumers learn from their experiences. Our ultimate aim is for them to 'learn' brand loyalty.

This chapter is structured to allow us to define learning, to review theories of learning and to look at their application to marketing situations. Some of the language may seem difficult at first – but it is an area of which we have all had experience – so an important task is to understand the concepts and learn the appropriate labels.

This is an area which is very popular with examiners as it offers a clear basis of theory on which to base our marketing activity. As marketing specialists, focus on what is important for your professional development. Do not get misled into 'over-learning' this material – we are concerned with the general theories and their applications, not the detail of what Pavlov gave his dogs for breakfast!

At the end of this section the reader should be fully familiar with the following concepts and *should be able to relate them to marketing situations*:

General principles of learning

- Association
- Reinforcement (positive and negative)
- Motivation

Connectionist learning theories (S–R)

- Classical Conditioning – Pavlov
- Operant Conditioning – Skinner
- Stimulus Generalization

- Primary and Secondary Reinforcement
- Continuous and intermittent reinforcement

Cognitive learning theories (S–O–R)

- Insight Learning – Kohler
- Latent Learning – Tolman

Other learning theories

- Vicarious learning – Bandura
- Experiential learning – Kolb
- Information processing theories – Norman

Memory

- Receiving – encoding – storage – decoding – retrieval model
- Short term memory
- Long term memory

Forgetting

- Retroactive inhibition
- Proactive inhibition
- Emotional factors
- Repression

Associated processes

- Rehearsal
- Elaboration

As with most areas of consumer behaviour, learning does not stand alone. The material from the chapters on perception and motivation is very relevant and our study of learning will also lead on to activities such as the changing of attitudes.

Learning

Defining learning is somewhat difficult as we have at least two contrasting views of what learning is.

1 *Behaviourist approaches* are solely concerned with observable behaviours. Behaviourists argue that mental processes are unobservable and must therefore be inferred. They believe that learning is shown by changes in behaviour which have their roots in the associations developed between stimuli and the resulting responses. They focus on learning resulting in *behaviour change* e.g. 'the process of acquiring, through experience, knowledge which leads to changed behaviour' (BPP).

2 *Cognitive approaches* emphasize the changes in knowledge and focus on the processes by which people learn information. In this last sentence 'learn' is used to imply that the changed knowledge has been stored in long term memory. An example of this approach is given by Hawkins, Best and Coney who define learning as 'any change in the content or organisation of long term memory'

Engel and colleagues attempt to encompass these two contrasting views by defining it as 'the process by which experience leads to changes in knowledge, attitudes and/or behaviour'.

However, as we will see, not all learning is 'used' immediately. Knowledge may lie dormant for long periods before a situation arises in which it is useful; so an even more all-encompassing definition might be that learning is:

A relatively permanent change in potential response which occurs as the result of reinforced practice.

This definition has a number of significant components:

1 The notion of 'relatively permanent' change eliminates from our consideration changes in behaviour which may be due to other factors such as fatigue, illness or the influence of drugs or alcohol.
2 The idea of 'potential response' is included as it accepts the possibility that learning may not be immediately observable in changed behaviour. This allows for the inclusion of ideas such as 'latent learning' and 'incidental learning', discussed later in the chapter.
3 'Reinforced' emphasizes the importance of the concept of reward and/or consequences following behaviour. This is the basis of behaviourist theories and approaches to the learning process.
4 The word 'practice' implies that, even if learning has occurred at a purely cognitive level, eventually the learning will be emitted as behaviour and will then be reinforced leading to enhanced learning or extinction.
5 There is nothing in the definition that implies that learning must be a conscious activity. A great deal of learning appears to occur without overt awareness on the part of the subject.

Behaviourist approaches

Thorndike in the early part of the twentieth century, examined *trial-and-error learning* – the trying of different responses in a problem-solving situation until a response which is effective in solving the problem is hit upon.

He observed cats attempting to escape from a box (witnessed nowadays by anyone taking a cat to the vets in a catbox) and was struck by the vigour with which they would seek to escape. The animal clawed and bit at the bars of the box, thrusting its paws out though any opening, striking anything which appeared loose or shaky. The box was designed so that a door would open when a string (or loop, or button) was clawed. Eventually the animal would claw the string, loop or button; the door would open and the cat escape. Repeating the exercise resulted in improvements in the 'escape time' as gradually the other non-successful behaviours were stamped out and the particular behaviour leading to the successful act was stamped in by what Thorndike called the 'resulting pleasure' of escape from the box. Eventually the cat, when put in the box, immediately clawed the button or string in the required manner.

Figure 5.1

Given this evidence Thorndike noted that the time it took to solve the problem systematically decreased as the number of trials increased, i.e. the more opportunities the animal had, the faster it solved the problem. He concluded that learning was *incremental*, that it occurs in very small systematic steps rather than in huge jumps.

He was also convinced that the learning had come from direct experience and not mediated by any processes of thinking or reasoning. He believed that this learning process applied to all mammals, including humans, which was a view that upset many people at the time it was put forward.

> **Think** – Do *you* think all human learning is incremental?
> – To what extent do you think that consumer behaviour is a series of trial-and-error experiments?

Pavlov was working on learning processes at roughly the same time. He was an eminent Russian scientist who had already won the Nobel Prize in 1904 for his work on the physiology of digestion before the work which brought him universal fame. His interest in learning did not emerge until the turn of the century when he was measuring the stomach secretions as the response of dogs to such things as meat powder. He noticed, that after the dogs had been in his laboratory for a period of time, that the mere sight of food, or even the sound of the attendant's footsteps bringing the food, caused the dog to salivate. He proceeded to set up a series of classic experiments which investigated the phenomenon we now know as the *conditioned reflex*. He arranged for the amount of saliva produced by the dogs to be measured. Then he sounded a bell slightly before food was placed in the animals' mouths. After a number of repetitions it was found that the bell by itself would produce salivation and therefore the dogs had been *conditioned* to respond to the bell.

Pavlov's view of learning is called *Classical Conditioning* and in its general form it involves four elements:

1 an *unconditioned stimulus* (UCS) such as the food which produces
2 an *unconditioned response* (UCR) such as salivation, which is the natural and automatic response to the UCS.

that is: $UCS \rightarrow UCR$

Conditioning occurs when the unconditioned stimulus becomes associated with the

3 *conditioned stimulus* (CS), in this case the bell, which is a neutral stimulus in that it does not elicit an automatic and natural response from the subject. The result is that the CS brings about the
4 *conditioned response* (CR), salivation, which is the same as the unconditioned response (UCR).

that is: $CS \rightarrow CR \ (= UCR)$

In order for the conditioned response (CR) to be produced, the conditioned stimulus (CS) and the unconditioned stimulus (UCS) must be paired a number of times. First the CS is presented and then the UCS (note that the order of presentation is very significant). Each time a UCS occurs, a UCR occurs. Eventually the CS can be presented alone and it will elicit a response similar to the UCR. When this happens a conditioned response has been created.

In other words the response has been transferred from the UCS to the CS and in this way the subject may be considered to have learned.

A conditioned response depends upon an unconditioned stimulus for its very existence – this is why the UCS (food) is referred to as *reinforcement* – as without it a CS would never develop the capability of generating a CR.

Pavlov showed that the strength of the conditioned response increased with successive pairings of the conditioned and unconditioned stimuli as illustrated in Figure 5.2.

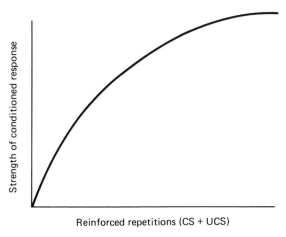

Figure 5.2

This is sometimes called the *Pavlovian* or *Classical learning curve*.

Extinction

He also explored the opposite effect – what happens when reinforcement is removed. Not unexpectedly, he found that in the absence of reinforcement the conditioned response gradually disappears. When the CS no longer elicits a CR, *experimental extinction* is said to have occurred.

Spontaneous recovery

After a period of time following extinction, if the CS is again presented to the animal, the CR will temporarily reappear. The CR has spontaneously recovered despite there being no further pairings for reinforcement.

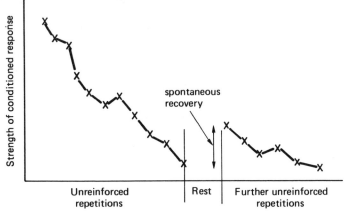

Figure 5.3

These phenomena are shown in Figure 5.3.

Higher order conditioning

Once a conditioned stimulus has been paired with an unconditioned stimulus and suitably reinforced, it can, in turn, be used in much the same way as an unconditioned stimulus. In other words, it is quite possible to 'attach' a new conditioned stimulus to bring about the same conditioned response.

In our example of the dog learning to associate the sound of the bell with food, it would be possible to pair the sound with another stimulus such as blinking a light just before the bell is rung. After suitable repetition and reinforcement the dog would salivate at the blinking of the light alone. This is called second order conditioning, and it is possible to imagine that linked chains of responses could be created. The evidence, however, suggests that successive higher order conditioning inevitably weakens the strength of the conditioned response and that the construction of long, linked chains of response may rapidly become unreliable.

Generalization

Pavlov and others discovered that a subject who had been conditioned to respond to a specific stimulus, such as a buzzer pitched at a specific frequency, would respond at the sound of a buzzer operating at a different frequency. The further away from the original frequency, the weaker the conditioned response. Similarly there would be some response to other sound stimuli such as bells, metronomes and rattles. Once again the more like the original stimulus, the stronger the response.

This phenomenon is called generalization, and appears to depend on similarity. Thus subjects may respond to new situations and stimuli in ways which have been learned in *similar* situations.

Discrimination

This is the opposite effect to generalization and refers to the tendency to respond to a very restricted range of stimuli (or only the one used during training). One of the key factors appears to be the length of training time. The work to date suggests that if the minimum number of pairings between the CS and UCS necessary to develop a CR is used, there is a relatively strong tendency towards generalization. However, if the training is prolonged, there is less tendency to generalization. The greater the training, the less generalization and the greater the discrimination.

A second approach to limiting generalization is through differential reinforcement. Here the procedure would be to present (for example) sounds at a number of different frequencies, but only reinforcing the desired one. In this way discrimination between stimuli may be 'taught'.

Skinner was one of the most influential behaviourist psychologists of the twentieth century. He drew a distinction between respondent behaviour and operant behaviour. Respondent behaviour is similar to that described and defined in classical Pavlovian conditioning when a stimulus triggers a 'natural' reaction such as dogs salivating in the presence of food and other similar reflex actions.

Operant behaviour is that which operates on the environment and is not the result of simple, automatic responses. In reality, most human behaviour, e.g. going to work, playing games, going shopping, is operant under this analysis. According to Skinner, such behaviour is learned and strengthened by the process of *operant conditioning*.

Again the major elements involved are the stimulus, the reinforcement and the response. In operant conditioning the emphasis is very much on the response as opposed to classical conditioning where the emphasis is on the stimulus. Indeed, Skinner himself coined the expressions Type *S* conditioning (the Stimulus elicts the desired response) for classical Pavlovian conditioning; and Type *R* conditioning (the Response elicits the reinforcement) for operant conditioning.

Again, much of the work on operant conditioning has been carried out with laboratory animals such as rats and pigeons. In some of his most famous experiments Skinner was able to show that by giving reinforcement, usually in the form of food, immediately following particular actions, the animals became more likely to repeat those actions. They could also be 'taught' to exhibit a wide range of behaviours.

The device most commonly associated with these techniques is called a 'Skinner Box'. Reinforcement is usually when the animal in the box exhibits certain behaviours such as pressing a lever, or pecking a specified area of the box. The reinforcement may also be either positive (e.g. food) or negative (e.g. mild electric shock) – behaviours which are negatively reinforced tend to be repeated less often.

These techniques have allowed experimenters to teach their subjects behaviours which are not 'normal' – for example, there are accounts of pigeons being taught to 'play' table tennis.

There are two principles which underpin operant conditioning:

1 any response that is followed by a reinforcing stimulus tends to be repeated, and
2 a reinforcing stimulus is anything that increases the rate at which an operant response occurs (or a reinforcer is anything that increases the probability of a response recurring).

Thus operant conditioning is different from classical conditioning in a number of ways:

1 Operant is essentially *voluntary* on the part of the subject whereas classical deals with involuntary behaviour.
2 In operant conditioning the subject is *active* as opposed to the passive role of the subject in classical.
3 Reinforcement strengthens responses selectively in operant conditioning while it is a neutral concept strengthening the association between behaviour and response in Pavlovian terms.
4 In classical conditioning the subject's response is *triggered* by a reinforcer, in contrast to operant conditioning where the response *triggers* the reinforcement.

The two approaches are similar in that:

1 they both accept and agree that *motivation, association* and *reinforcement* are key concepts;
2 they share phenomena such as extinction, spontaneous recovery, generalization and discrimination;
3 they both suggest that behaviour is solely a result of conditioning and subscribe to Thorndike's view that learning comes from direct experience and is not mediated by any processes of thinking or reasoning.

For this reason this behaviourist approach to learning is often called *Connectionist* or *S–R* (*Stimulus–Response*) learning.

Reinforcement schedules

In most of the foregoing work the reinforcement took place continuously i.e. the subject was reinforced *every time* the required response was made. However, in some situations reinforcement only occurs intermittently. This is particularly true of activities which involve gambling.

> **Think** – Why do people continue to do the pools, 'spot the ball'
> competitions, play bingo and back horses when their behaviour
> is rarely reinforced?

Cognitive approaches

Cognition is a word which means mental activity. There is a form of learning which is purely mental and which is called *iconic rote learning* (see also Bloom's Taxonomy of mental activities in Chapter 2). Technically this is a process whereby two concepts are associated in the absence of conditioning – an example might be in the way in which many of us learned our multiplication tables. Eventually we learn to associate the statement 'four fours are . . .' with the appropriate end to the statement which is 'sixteen'. However, there are other approaches to learning which also imply cognition, and which are rather more complex.

In Chapter 4, when looking at perception, the Gestalt school of psychology was mentioned. This was a group of German psychologists who focused less on the behavioural and reductionist view of learning and more on holistic and cognitive processes. The start of the movement is claimed to be when the founder of the group, Wertheimer, had the insight that if two lights blink on and off at a certain rate, they give the impression of one light moving back and forth. This apparent motion was called the 'phi phenomenon' and emphasized what was to become the Gestalt psychologists' theme – 'the whole is greater than the sum of the parts' (an alternative statement is 'to dissect is to distort'). In the context of learning and perception they believed that the phenomenological experience (e.g. the apparent movement of the lights) resulted from sensory experience (e.g. the flashing of the pair of lights), but could not be understood by analysing the components because *the experience as a whole is different from its components parts*. This view, of course, is entirely consistent with the discussions in Chapter 4 on issues such as closure, perceptual constancy and the other elements of the organization of perception.

Köhler conducted some of the most famous experiments of learning done by the Gestalt psychologists and published in the 1920s. As a group they believe that learning is a cognitive process – the individual 'comes to see' the solution to a problem after a period of pondering.

Köhler set up a number of experiments primarily using apes as the subjects. The most relevant to our study of marketing were those which centred on problem solving. He devised experiments in which the solution to the problem lay in the animal using implements of various kinds. In one case food was placed just out of reach of the ape so that it needed to use a stick to reach it. In another it was necessary for the ape to fit two sticks together so that they were long enough to reach the banana. In other cases the subjects built up stacks of boxes to reach food that was set high above the floor, and in yet other scenarios the apes used combinations of previous solutions by utilizing poles while balancing on top of constructed 'towers' of boxes. In all instances the subjects had all the ingredients required for a solution to the problem – it was 'just' a case of putting them together in the 'right' way.

Observation of the animals led Köhler to the conclusion that the problem-solving sequence involved a lengthy *pre-solution period* in which the subjects appeared to run through a number of 'hypotheses' as to the effective ways of solving the problem. At first sight this may seem to be similar to Thorndike's trial-and-error learning, but the Gestalt school would claim that this trial-and-error is *cognitive* – i.e. the animal *thinks* about the different possibilities until it hits upon one that works. It then carries out the solution.

This discovery of the 'right' solution is called *insight*. The magic of insight is usually accompanied by some sort of release of tension in which we make sounds of satisfaction and show signs of excitement when 'the penny drops'. This phenomenon is also called the 'aha' or 'ooh-aah' reaction.

Think – Did you experience the 'aha' reaction when examining some of the ambiguous stimuli in Chapter 4?

The process of insight learning is said to have a number of characteristics, one of which is that there is a clear difference between the pre-solution and the post-insight stages of dealing with the problem. Indeed, it is possible to imagine that, given the assumptions of insight learning, Figure 5.1, describing the Thorndike's cat escaping from its box, should resemble Figure 5.4 more.

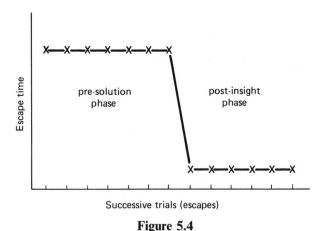

Figure 5.4

Think – How might you reconcile these two, apparently opposed, views?

One explanation offered is that Thorndike's cat, unlike Köhler's ape, was not exposed to all the elements of the problem and its solution. The Gestalt psychologists suggest that Thorndike's cat exhibited what appeared to be incremental learning because important elements of the problem were hidden from the animal, thus inhibiting insight learning.

Other characteristics of insight learning are:

1 the transition from presolution to solution is sudden and complete – in linguistic terms we use the expression 'a flash of insight',
2 performance based on a solution found by insight is usually smooth and free from errors,
3 a solution to a problem gained by insight is usually retained for a considerable length of time; and,
4 a principle obtained by insight is easily applied to other problems.

Transposition

When characteristic (4) above is invoked and a principle learned in one problem solving situation is used in the solution of a different problem, the process is called *transposition*. Köhler set up an interesting experiment as follows.

Chickens were trained to approach one of two shades of grey paper by always feeding them on a dark shade of grey paper, but not on a lighter one. After such training, when given a choice, the animal would approach the darker one. This tends to confirm behaviourist theories. However, after this early training, the animal was given a choice between the dark grey paper on which it had been trained and an even darker sheet.

Think – Which sheet of paper do you think the chicken will approach?

Behavioural principles suggest that it should approach the original (now lighter) grey paper on the grounds that this was the exact shade that had been reinforced in the first stage of the experiment. Gestaltists, however, do not see learning as a simple S–R connection and they suggested that what had been learned was the *principle* of approaching *the darker of the two papers*. The Gestaltist would therefore predict that the chicken would approach the new darkest paper in phase 2, despite being reinforced for the other paper in phase 1. Generally speaking the prediction of the Gestalt psychologists turns out to be the accurate one.

This has also given rise to the notion that behaviourism could be viewed as an *absolute theory* as opposed to the Gestalt view which is that it is a *relational theory*.

Tolman was an American psychologist who was by nature a rebel. Part of his rebellion was to work on cognitive processes at a time when behaviourism was at its height in the USA (i.e. during the 1930s and 1940s). He believed that behaviour was *purposive* and always directed towards some goal. He never argued that behaviour could not be split down into ever smaller units for study as in behaviourist techniques, but he felt that the meaning of the whole pattern would be lost if such an elementistic path was followed. He called these large patterns of behaviour *molar behaviours* which, he believed, constituted a Gestalt that was greater than the elements that made it up.

His view was that learning was essentially a process of discovering what leads to what in the environment, thus following some of the Gestalt school's interest in problem solving in the real world. Tolman thought that in everyday language what was learned was what we often call 'the lie of the land'. He believed that the subject gradually develops a picture of its environment that it uses to get around in it. He called this picture a *cognitive map*. His idea was that the organism, having developed its cognitive map, can reach a goal from any number of directions. If one commonly used route is blocked, then an alternative one is taken. He suggested that the subject will always choose the shortest route or the one requiring the least expenditure of energy. This he called the *principle of least effort*. For Tolman the idea of reinforcement as defined by other investigators was less important. He argued that the *confirmation* of a hypothesis was the real reinforcement – and only confirmed hypotheses were retained in the cognitive map.

This notion of confirmed hypotheses leads on to the idea of *expectancies*. This has already been touched on in Chapter 4 and will also be discussed in later chapters. Confirmed expectancies are what is commonly referred to as beliefs. Tolman's views also suggest that learning is a continuous process and one in which it is not necessary to 'motivate' the subject (e.g. by hunger) as a prerequisite to learning.

When working with rats in a maze, Tolman observed that the animal would often pause at a point where a choice was possible and look around as if it were considering the alternatives open to it. The pausing at a choice-point he called *vicarious trial-and-error*. In Thorndike's trial-and-error the cat acted out the options behaviourally – Tolman's rat seemed to test the different approaches cognitively. An important assumption lies within this statement and that is that learning can take place but not necessarily be acted out behaviourally. Up until this point most of the theory has only accepted behaviour as evidence of learning.

Hergenhahn (1988) summarizes some of Tolman's conclusions as follows:

1 The organism brings to a problem-solving situation various hypotheses that it may utilise in attempting to solve the problem. These hypotheses are based largely on prior experience. . . .
2 The hypotheses which survive are those that correspond best with reality; that is, those that result in goal achievement.
3 After a while a clearly established cognitive map develops which can be used under altered conditions. For instance, when an organism's preferred path is blocked, it simply chooses, in accordance with the principle of least effort, an alternative path from its cognitive map.
4 When there is some sort of demand or motive to be satisfied, the organism will make use of the information in its cognitive map. The fact that information can exist but only be utilised under certain conditions is the basis for the very important distinction between learning and performance (p. 296).

This leads on to the important concept of latent learning. Tolman set up a further series of experiments with rats learning mazes. His conclusions suggested that the rats could *learn* the maze even when they were not reinforced by rewards of food. Furthermore, they appeared to be able to store this unreinforced knowledge until placed in a situation where it was necessary to know the maze in order to obtain food. He took these results as evidence to support his contention that reinforcement is a variable affecting performance rather learning.

The cognitive approaches to learning admit that there may be intervening variables and processes operating between the stimulus and the response. These have been called *organizing forces* by some and this has given rise to the idea that such theories of learning be known as S–O–R (Stimulus – Organizing force – Response).

The foregoing sections have attempted to summarize some of the important ideas that have influenced our view of the learning process. In following the accounts the reader may have noticed that the experiments described have largely been conducted with animals – cats, dogs, rats, pigeons and so forth.

The question may need to be posed:

> **Think** – How useful do you think that findings based on animal behaviour
>   are for predicting human behaviour?
> – If you feel that animals are *not* suitable models for human
>   behaviour, what do you think are the characteristics that make
>   human learning different?

There are no simple answers to these questions. Humans possess advanced cognitive processing skills which seem not to have been developed by most animals (see some of our earlier discussion in Chapter 3). Language development is further advanced. Human beings have also generated views on philosophical issues such as 'right and wrong' and have whole belief systems which are built on the notion of individual responsibility and the ability to control our own destiny and affect our own world.

On the other hand, few of us will be unable to recognize conditioned responses – answering a ringing telephone, lighting a cigarette before commencing to write a letter, the ritual behaviours we indulge in which preceed a good night's sleep, and so forth.

> **Think** – What conditioned responses will you admit to?

Cognitive theories appear to be more attractive in the sense that they propose a rational, planned puposeful approach to life – something to which, I am sure, most people would aspire. Many of our life experiences reflect insight learning and much of our education is inevitably likely to depend on latent principles.

> **Think** – What cognitive learning can you identify in your life?

The likelihood is that we learn in both of these dominant fashions. It may be fruitful to consider what sort of things you learn on an S–R basis and which on S–O–R principles.

> **Think** – What sort of learning has governed your study so far on this course?

Before we go on to examine some alternative views of the learning process we will recapituate some of the key issues in the field of learning, and their application to human behaviour.

1 *Association* – Fundamental to all connectionist theory is the notion that the organism must make the association between a stimulus or cue and the response. The author, after many years of being called 'Chris', suffers a momentary onset of fear when he is referred to as 'Christopher' – this appears to be associated in his mind with being in trouble as a child!
2 *Reinforcement* – The notion of a pay-off, either positive or negative which confirms the association that has been made. *Positive reinforcement* is something which is perceived as a reward and which seeks to confirm a positive linkage between stimulus and response. *Negative reinforcement* may be regarded as some sort of punishment. The result of negative reinforcement should be to lead the subject to avoid situations where such a response may be forthcoming. *Primary reinforcement* is aimed at satisfying a basic need such as food or water. We no longer live in a society where withholding such basic elements is acceptable, so it is more common to use *secondary reinforcement* which depends on such things as social approval which we generally assume is desired by people.

Another interesting area of research is the effects of *partial or intermittent reinforcement*. Earlier in the chapter you were asked to think about why people continued to indulge in gambling – a behaviour in which reinforcement is usually very rare! Here, the subject is not reinforced every time, and in this way is very like real life, i.e. good work is not always recognized by teachers and, on occasion, people do not laugh at our jokes. The evidence is somewhat surprising. Learning using partial or intermittent reinforcement is rather slower, but the learning is less prone to extinction. Indeed, such learning is more likely to persist when all reinforcement is removed. In one experiment (Lewis and Duncan 1956) people were asked to gamble on fruit machines. The machines had been 'fixed' so that some paid out every play, while others paid out on a partial reinforcement schedule (just like 'real' unrigged fruit machines). In the second part of the experiment all of the subjects played on machines that were rigged so that they would *never* pay out. Subjects who had been trained on partial schedules were much more resistant to extinction and kept playing much longer than those who had been trained on a continuous reinforcement basis. The evidence suggests that the lower the percentage of responses rewarded, the more resistant to extinction the behaviour and learning becomes.

It must be stressed, however, that positive and negative used in the context of reinforcement is very much a matter of the perception of the individual. Offering meat to a vegetarian will be a negative reinforcement, while the same offer would be a reward to others.

3 *Motivation* –The reader will have noticed that the primary motivation throughout most of the experiments described in this chapter has been hunger. As mentioned above, such crude methods are rarely appropriate or acceptable when we are dealing with people. Much of the thinking on the place of motivation in the learning process seems to tie in closely with our examination in Chapter 4 of the internal factors affecting attention and perception. Tolman's argument that the need to explore the environment is enough to 'cause' learning may just be another statement of motivation – i.e. he assumes that individuals are motivated to explore and understand their environment. A fuller range of motivations is discussed in the next chapter which is devoted to the subject.

Bandura working more recently (in the 1970s and 1980s) conducted experiments which confirmed many of Tolman's findings. He also clarified the notion of *observational learning*. This is the process, widely accepted for many years within our society, whereby people are believed to learn from observing other people and to imitate many of the observed behaviours. Thorndike (amongst others) had conducted extensions of his learning experiments to include an investigation of observational learning by allowing other animals to observe the activities of those which were in their boxes, mazes or cages. When these 'observers' were put into the experimental situation they behaved exactly as if their had been no previous learning.

Bandura suggested that observational learning may be a human rather than an animal characteristic, dependent on cognitive processes such as language, morality, thinking and the notion of self regulation of behaviour. Observed learning or imitation falls into three categories:

1 same behaviour – two or more individuals respond to the same situation in exactly the same way – for instance, we applaud at the end of a play in the theatre or stop at red lights.
2 copying behaviour – an example might be learning to swim – one person's behaviour is guided by another and rewards are given when things are done 'right' therefore reinforcing the behaviour. Much teaching in schools falls into this category.
3 matched-dependent behaviour – where an observer is reinforced for blindly repeating the actions of a model. One way of coping in unfamiliar situations is to look round and observe what others are doing – and then

copy it! Examples could include being in a foreign country for the first time or eating in company with unfamiliar cutlery.

> **Think** – What experiences have you had where you have learned by imitation?

It does seem likely, however, that there is more to vicarious learning than pure imitation.

> **Think** – Imagine you are walking down a freezing road in winter. You observe the behaviour of the person walking ahead of you and see them slip and fall on a patch of ice.
> – Do you then imitate their behaviour?
> – Or are you more likely to take *extra* care?

Bandura highlights a number of variables which may affect observational learning – the ability to produce behaviours being one obvious limitation. By observation of birds it is possible to understand the nature of flight – but the human observer is physically incapable of translating this knowledge into flying behaviour due to the lack of the necessary physical equipment. Memory (discussed later) is another important factor – it is clear that faulty memory will cause problems in the modelling process. The selectivity of attention has been mentioned in Chapter 4. This phenomenon will clearly affect what is perceived, what is observed and hence, what is vicariously learned. Hergenhahn (1988) quotes the following from Craighead, Kazdin and Mahoney (1976) to make this point:

Suppose you are holding a 4-year-old child on your lap while two other 4-year-olds play on separate areas of your living room floor and that, as child A gently pets your English sheepdog, child B inserts a butter knife into an electrical outlet. Everyone would learn something from this incident. Because it was directly associated with severe, unexpected pain and accompanying autonomic arousal, child B would learn to avoid using wall sockets as knife holders, and possibly, to stay away from electrical outlets altogether. Child A might learn, or at least begin to learn, to avoid the sheepdog, or dogs in general. When child B suddenly screamed and cried, it startled child A, and since the occurrence of any strong, sudden, unexpected, and novel stimulus produces autonomic arousal, the harmless dog was associated with a strong, unconditioned response to a stressful stimulus. Depending on the focus of his or her attention at the time, the child on your lap might later display avoidance of wall sockets (if he/she was watching child B), of dogs (if he/she was watching child A), or of you. Incidentally, since many of the principles of learning apply to both humans and animals, it is also possible that this sheepdog may subsequently try to avoid children (p.188).

This notion of the role model is one which is important to marketing and one to which we will return later. At this stage it is worth noting that considerable publicity has been given to the idea of vicarious learning and the suggestion that what is observed will influence our subsequent behaviour. The debates about the influence of television violence on the behaviour of young people is an example, the arguments as to the influence of 'page three pin-ups' on the behaviour of men towards women is another. At the present time the evidence is not convincing either way – but the notion of such learning seems highly plausible and may have an impact on marketing and advertising styles as we shall see later.

Kolb's experiential learning

This approach to learning was described in Chapter 3 when the idea of learning style was explored as an aspect of personality and in the context of studying. As it was designed specifically to describe the learning processes of adult humans it does not suffer from any apparent lack of relevance in general terms. Its main application to date has been in the fields of education and training so it is worth spending a few moments to examine whether the idea might have an application beyond the book/course/examination.

> **Think** – What other examples, outside of education and training, can you identify where Kolb's cycle of learning has applied to you?

Some recent work by Norman has focused on learning as an aspect of information processing psychology. He has formulated three laws of learning which are:

1 *The law of causal relationship* – For an organism to learn the relationship between a specific action and an outcome, there must be an apparent causal relation between them.

2 *The law of causal learning* – For desirable outcomes: the organism attempts to repeat those particular actions that have an apparent causal relationship to the desired outcome. For undesirable outcomes: the organism attempts to avoid those actions that have an apparent causal relation to the undesirable outcome.

3 *The law of information feedback* – The outcome of an event serves as information about that event.

The word apparent is used here to emphasize the importance of the perception of the subject. As we have already met the phenomenon of differing perceptions in Chapter 4, this seems a suitable footnote on which to end this review of learning theories.

Memory

There is an obvious link between learning and memory. Most authorities draw a distinction between short-term memory (STM) and long-term memory (LTM). This is an area of interest to both the marketing specialist and students. Marketers want their product to remain in the consumers' memory while the students are concerned with their ability to recall learned material under examination conditions.

A common representation of the memory process makes an analogy with computer systems and is illustrated in Figure 5.5.

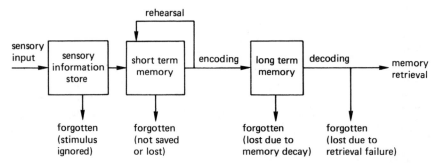

Figure 5.5

The *sensory store* or *sensory information store* (SIS) is believed to be a memory system of extremely short duration. Immediately after the removal of a stimulus input, there appears to be a sensory representation of the stimulus which is held in the mind for a brief time – perhaps one or two seconds only. The capacity of this sensory information store is limited to that which the individual is aware of. Thus our earlier references to attention and sensory input under the heading of perception become significant once more. Material is assumed to be 'lost' from this part of the system by a process of decay which occurs very rapidly unless the information is processed to the next stage of memory.

Short term memory

Short term memory (STM) appears to be a limited capacity storage system that is capable of holding only a small amount of information for a short time. To keep information in the STM it is necessary to concentrate hard on the material continually, often repeating it over and over in our mind. This is the effect that can be observed when, in a group, you offer to buy a round of drinks – each member of the group is asked what they want, the list is compiled and is then often muttered continually until the order can be placed. It is then a relief to be able to 'forget' the order as the brain has moved on to other concerns. In this sense it is possible to consider STM as our 'working memory' with items being held and retained solely for the task in hand and being replaced as soon as the activity changes.

Evidence suggests that the STM storage capacity of most people is about seven items or pieces of information.

Exercise – try to memorize the following words.

considerable	are
studying	gained
to	there
people	be
behaviour	benefits
from	consumer

How did you get on? Generally people find such an exercise difficult as you were asked to memorize twelve items of information i.e. twelve unrelated words. However if we rearrange the same twelve words to make our old friend – 'there are considerable benefits to be gained from people studying consumer behaviour' – we generally find the task much simpler. It would seem that we have craftily changed the twelve disparate items into one item (the recognizable sentence). This process is sometimes called 'chunking' information.

Think – How do you 'chunk' your telephone number?

Another good example of STM as our 'working memory' lies in looking up a telephone number, retaining it long enough to dial (often rehearsing it by silent repetition), and then forgetting it.

The next stage from our diagram is *encoding*. While we are actively rehearsing the information we will assign the information symbols that will represent the data in the memory store. Once again, the work we tackled earlier in the perception chapter is likely to be of relevance, as what is coded will be a function of perceptual selectivity and will depend on our awareness, motivation and predispositions. Additionally, many symbols carry a great deal of coded information. The symbol or code may be figural (a pictorial image), semantic (words) or numeric (numbers). We may also code sounds, smells, tastes and so forth.

One point does need to be made at this juncture – the human brain is not an empty computer disc waiting to receive input. It already stores masses of information and will also hold its own internal programmes for processing data. Psychologists sometimes refer to these knowledge structures as *schema* or *schemata*. The reader will be using a linguistic schema in the process of understanding this sentence. The assumption is that they are mental programmes which serve as guides for interpreting information and solving problems.

These schemata are also structures within which new information can be recorded, so our new input is stored and filed *in relation to existing data*. The emerging belief is that we find things easier to encode (and hence retrieve) if it is a good 'fit' with existing information. Our earlier examples of 'chunking' are instances of this. There is evidence to suggest that learners recall more efficiently information which has been processed according to classifications devised by themselves than data which has been presented in a predetermined sequence that the learner has had to comprehend and follow. So our existing memories and classifications may be an important element in the coding process.

Long term memory

Long term memory (LTM) is exactly what the name implies. We normally do not say that something has been learned until the material can be recalled at will after a period of days, weeks or months. When this occurs, it is clear that the material has been retrieved from our LTM. The LTM has a much larger capacity than the STM and is able to store very large amounts of material. It is widely believed that STM is translated into LTM through a process which is called *consolidation*.

The mechanisms of memory are not clearly understood – but an analogy is often made with the computer. The STM is the equivalent of the on-screen data input which is then saved on disc (roughly equivalent to the LTM). Perhaps the area which is least understood is the process by which we decide which items to transfer from STM to LTM and the mechanism by which this happens.

There are some reservations about the computer analogy, however, as the human memory system appears to operate a form of database which is far in advance of anything which computer specialists have yet developed. As human beings we possess the wonderful capacity of recognizing the required information when it is found *even when we did not know the significance of the information in the first place.* An example might be trying to remember the name of a person met at a party or a meeting – the memory retrieves the name William Shakespeare – but we reject this on the grounds that it is the wrong answer.

> **Think** – How do we know that is wrong when the whole point of the exercise is that we do not know the name we are looking for?

We also seem to have the ability to find the information necessary to answer a question, even when the question was not known (or anticipated) at the point at which the information was obtained/memorized.

This leads us on to the next element in the diagram, *decoding*. This is the other end of the process and may be one of the most crucial in terms of making our memories work effectively. It is a common experience to have a memory failure ('I know it, I know it, it's on the tip of my tongue . . .') which is rectified at some later point in time, often when you are not consciously making an effort to recall the data. This experience suggests that the brain *continues subconsciously* to process information and seek solutions to problems *even when the problem has been 'dropped' by our conscious brain.* All too often it seems that there is little doubt that you have the information – the real trick is to extract it from the long-term store on demand. Once again the code used for storage is likely to be significant as the associations with existing information are important to the whole retrieval process. Organizing cues for retrieval is important for students. Mnemonic devices are very popular as examinations approach.

> **Think** – What are the colours of the rainbow?
> – How do you remember that?

'Richard of York gave battle in vain' is one common way of remembering this. The author has to admit to only being able to recall the colours in the right order by singing a song learned as a child!

Rehearsal

Rehearsal seems to be an important element – the repetition or playing with the idea or information appears to help imprint the material in the LTM. In this way we might explain why some material seems to 'stick' without effort, while others seem to need a great deal of work. Things in which we are interested may be rehearsed many times because we are already mentally involved, and do not perceive this rehearsal as memorizing in a formal sense. We also rehearse by linking the information to other items. This has the advantage of 'protecting' it against other, competing incoming data.

> **Think** – Can you remember the twelve words set as the memory test on page 131?

The rehearsal and chunking exercise we went through may well have allowed you to recall the words – even though it is unlikely that you were able to remember them when they were randomized and jumbled.

Elaboration

Another aspect of the memory and rehearsal processes is elaboration, where we use comparisons with previous experiences, values, attitudes and beliefs to evaluate information in our working (short term) memory. It is also the process by which we add to relevant previously stored information. Elaborative activities such as rehearsal serve also to redefine or add new elements to memory. The greater the amount of elaboration or mental processing that is involved, the greater the number of linkages that are forged with existing knowledge. This increases the number of avenues or paths by which the information can be retrieved. Many of the popular 'memory systems' are based on this principle – the classic party trick of memorizing random information is often achieved by processing or elaborating it, to make associations with existing knowledge (or surreal links are forged between the items) to aid recall.

Forgetting

Forgetting is important as it highlights the fact that for all the miracles of the human brain the processes of memory are far from perfect. Our initial diagram suggests that forgetting may occur at any of four stages in the overall process.

The first stage is where the incoming stimulus is unattended. The assumption is that received inputs enter the SIS but that only some are focused upon or noticed. The remainder appear to be forgotten very quickly. It is generally assumed that this form of forgetting is an example of decay. This view is that memory traces are laid down in the brain when we allocate attention to any perceptual event. With the passage of time (in this first stage we are talking in terms of a second or so, in the later stages such as LTM the timescale is very much longer) the trace, and hence our memory of the event, decays. This concept has high acceptance by most people who have read of the loss of brain cells day-by-day so often reported in the popular press.

Although decay theories have a common-sense attraction, an alternative view is that of *interference theory*. This suggests that our ability to retrieve information is less than perfect because things which we have learned, both before and after a specific event, will interfere with our capacity to recall the event. Some early experiments showed that when a period of sleep came between learning and recall, the results were much better than when a period of activity intervened. Here the implication is that it is not so much the period of time which elapses but it is more likely to be the intervening activities which influence recall. It seems plausible that the relative inactivity of sleep provides less interference to the process of memory than a period of mental activity.

The interference can take two main forms: *retroactive inhibition* or interference occurs when material that has been learned *later* prevents the recall of the target material.

Think – Can you remember your telephone extension in your *previous* office?
    – The registration number of your *previous* car?
    – The postcode of your *previous* address?

If you have difficulty in remembering any of these things it is likely that it is because the new information has taken precedence over the old.

Proactive inhibition or interference is when prior learning hinders the learning and retrieval of new information i.e. this is the opposite phenomenon to retroactive inhibition. In this case the existence of the old material prevents the learning of the new information.

Think – Have you ever had the embarrassment of referring to the partner of a friend by the name of their previous partner?
  – Have you had trouble recalling your new phone number after moving?
  – Or registration number of a new vehicle?

These experiences stem from existing information inhibiting the recall of new data. Other factors that reduce our capacity for recall fall into the broad category of personality inhibitions.

Emotion

Emotion can cause problems for the memory process. Indeed, it could easily be classified under the previous interference heading. It is, however, slightly more complex in that strong positive emotions may aid retrieval by creating the phenomenon sometimes called 'total recall'. More commonly we find that heightened anxiety or other negative emotions cause interference and inhibit recall and memory. It is depressing to realize that we commonly measure recall in examination situations where the level of anxiety is often very high.

Hint – Before an examination practise relaxation exercises such as deep breathing and avoid contact with other class members who are likely to induce hysteria by talking about how well/badly their revision has gone!

Repression

One of the defence mechanisms described in Chapter 3, repression, can also interfere with the process of recall. As you will remember it occurs where people subconsciously avoid retrieving material that they may find disturbing or threatening. The extreme form is sometimes called amnesia where a loss of memory follows a traumatic experience. While not a common phenomenon it has formed the basis for many a film and television thriller.

Marketing implications

To complete this chapter we will consider the application of learning theory and its associated ideas in marketing situations.

Trial and error learning

This was one of the earliest theories to have been put forward, and while we can see it applying to certain situations, its application to marketing is relatively limited. Few consumers find themselves in situations where their behaviour is completely undirected and unprogrammed. The basic principles however, apply to most S–R learning and the notion of trial and error is developed much more by Skinner's ideas which are discussed below under the heading of operant conditioning.

Classical conditioning

This is of more direct interest. Many advertisements create associations between the product and desirable outcomes – Bounty chocolate bars seem an obvious example of this concept of linking the product to an image of paradise. Another example may be of shoppers in a supermarket following a standard route around the store and filling their baskets with a standard range of goods while 'shopping on autopilot'. One reason for changing store layout from time to time is to ensure that shoppers get to see ranges that they may miss due to habituation.

The notion of *familiarity* has already been discussed when we looked at habituation in the chapter on perception. It is also of interest in this context as there is evidence that prior experience of a stimulus can, in some cases, undermine the conditioning process. Some have suggested, for instance, that a tune created specifically for a product is more effective than a well known song. However, many products are now linked with classic pop music tunes of years gone by, most notably jeans. Here there may well be more potent and significant associations with happier times past when the consumers were both younger and more carefree.

> **Think** – What associations do these songs have for you?

Operant conditioning

This has fairly obvious and strong links with consumer behaviour. The assumption of an active subject who is rewarded according to behaviour fits well with the marketer–consumer relationship. The aim is to get the consumer to purchase your product and to ensure that the purchase results in positive reinforcement or reward. The reinforcement should lie in satisfaction with the product so the implications for marketers are that quality is a key determinant of satisfaction and so should be high on the organization's agenda. Secondly the concept of the perceived value of the product is important and thirdly it does not pay in the long run to claim benefits in advertisements that the product cannot deliver.

Shaping

This expression is used by some psychologists to describe the reinforcement of successive behaviours which ultimately lead to the desired response. In many of the animal experiments the researcher would have had to wait a very long time before the animal produced the desired complex behaviour unaided. So animals are often taught by rewarding increments of behaviour. Similarly it is possible to break down the desired consumer behaviour into a number of stages – and reward each successively. So we may realize that people are unlikely to purchase if they do not visit our store – we could therefore decide to reward attendance through rewards such as door prizes or loss leaders. Another example is the practice of some motor manufacturers and garages of offering a prize for undertaking a test drive in a car. Thus shaping encourages the marketer to examine the behaviours which must precede purchase and to consider ways in which those prerequisite behaviours can be encouraged via appropriate reinforcement.

Generalization

The phenomenon of Pavlov's dogs responding to stimuli that were similar to the original has significant echoes in the field of marketing. Some organizations make use of generalization through using family branding – the labelling of all company products with the same name or logo so that the positive associations with one product will spill over to others. BMW use the tag 'the ultimate driving machine' to cover all of their range of cars from the largest to the most compact. Many companies will introduce a new product as a product line extension rather than developing separate brand identities – 'Crest Tartar Control' was presumably named to build on the existing positive ratings of Crest toothpaste; the advertising for Saab cars emphasizes the organization's links with high technology by using the Saab fighter plane as a counterpoint image to the car; the name Rolls-Royce covers both cars and aero engines and has become a generalized synonym for excellence.

However, there are some potential limitations to family branding especially where a company wishes to market products at different ends of the quality range. Additional problems can occur when competitors have company or brand names which are similar to market leaders. It is for this reason that legal action is often taken to prevent the use of confusing titles.

Another aspect of generalization that can also result in litigation is what is sometimes called the 'me-too product'. Here some manufacturers seek to encourage sales by using packaging that is very similar to that used by a leading competitor. The producers of such goods are seeking to evoke the same positive response that the competitor has spent a great deal of time and effort generating.

Generalization is therefore something of a two-edged sword for the marketer – highly desirable in some circumstances, and highly undesirable in others. An example of this was the famous series of advertisements for vermouth which were made by Joan Collins and the late Leonard Rossiter. They became a cult, watched by millions and loved by all. Unfortunately few of the consumers were clear as to whether the advertisements were for Cinzano or Martini. The net result was that sales for both brands went up. Whether or not you think generalization is a good thing or not may well depend on whether you are paying the bill!

Discrimination

Here we have the converse of generalization – the process where a subject learns to exhibit a response to one stimulus, but avoids making the same response to similar stimuli. It is important because, in many circumstances, marketers want consumers to differentiate their products clearly from those of their competitors. Discrimination is usually achieved by emphasizing the unique qualities, benefits or features of a product. In blind taste tests it has commonly been found that consumers cannot distinguish between different beers, cigarettes and spirits – so marketers often have to create distinctive 'personalities' for such products to make them distinctive.

Another approach to making your product 'different' is the use of what is sometimes called 'knocking copy' – criticizing competitors' products. This occurs fairly often with motor car advertising, but one of the classic examples is Qualcast's advertising of their lawnmowers as being 'much less bovver than a hover'. 'Knocking' was also a feature of the 1992 General Election in the UK where both of the larger parties devoted most of their advertising effort to discrediting the others. So Conservative party political broadcasts and posters talked almost entirely about Labour and vice versa. The dangers of such an approach may be highlighted by the fact that the Liberal Democrats were the party which made the most significant gains in terms of influencing public opinion.

Repetition

A key concept in conditioning theory, and significant to advertisers, is repetition. Experiments measuring recall of advertising messages show that the average recall rises when commercials are repeated – the exact improvement varies from study to study but figures in the range of 60 per cent increase in recall for a message repeated four times as opposed to a single showing. Our earlier consideration of awareness in Chapter 2 suggests that repetition could backfire if receivers either get annoyed or bored by the repetition. Too much repetition could cause receivers to actively shut out the message, pay no attention, or evaluate it negatively. Thus advertisers need to get the balance of repetition right in order to maximize the impact of their messages.

Another aspect of repetition of interest to the marketer is the *frequency* with which a message should be delivered. Here the key is the objective of the programme – if you are seeking to develop positive long-term images of the store/organization/product it would seem sensible to space out the messages. Conversely political parties who seek to influence voters on a specific date tend to bunch their communications and aim for a 'media blitz' immediately prior to polling day

This leads us on to consider *extinction*. If repetition or reinforcement is removed, then people are likely to forget the product or message. If we overdo it then people get bored or otherwise alienated from the product. However, the advantage from the point of view of the advertiser is that not advertising does not involve direct costs and the evidence of spontaneous recovery suggests that what has been lost may be quickly recovered.

The rate of extinction appears to be inversely related to the strength of the original learning. In other words, the more repetition, the stronger the imagery, the more reinforcement, the more important the content, the more resistant is the learning to extinction. So the marketer has another balancing act to perform – early strong learning followed by occasional top-up versus a steady medium level of input.

Think – What examples can you identify of campaigns which have gone for 'strong' learning followed by lower levels of top-up advertising?
– What examples can you identify of steady, medium level campaigns?

Higher order conditioning

This effect centred on getting Pavlov's dogs to associate the reward of food with stimuli such as showing a card, prior to sounding the buzzer prior to the reinforcement. It gives rise to the notion of a chain of associations which may be quite extensive. In marketing terms the associations may be between the product and desirable social status – convenience foods are shown being consumed in luxury surroundings, cars pull up in front of desirable Georgian houses, instant coffee passing muster in an expensive restaurant. The examples are many and various but, none the less important as they enable the product to be linked to potent subjective (and possibly subconscious) desirable outcomes.

Elaboration

Earlier we commented that the more mental processing that was gone through, the greater was the learning. This is an aspect that is receiving increasing attention from marketers. If we can get the individual 'hooked' on our message, the process of elaboration seems likely to produce repetitions within the person's mind for which we do not pay. Hence its attraction to advertisers. For some years the John Player cigarette company ran a series of advertisements which played word games based on their distinctive black packaging. Puns such as 'Black to the future', 'Black to front', etc. involved the observer in the decoding of the message and, in many cases, actually caused people to start making up their own slogans – very efficient marketing!

The phenomenon of *closure* discussed under the heading of perception falls into a similar category with people becoming actively involved in spotting the Benson and Hedges gold cigarette packet or recognizing the latest Silk Cut advertisement.

The wordplay approach emerged again recently with Holsten Pils running a series of advertisements which were based on anagrams of the letters making up the product name. Once the consumer is seduced into playing such games the imprinting of the product becomes very much stronger.

Peugeot cars recently produced a campaign with several linked characteristics – they ran an advertising article about the advantages of diesel engines and Peugeot developments. In the same magazine they had a separate free draw in which a 405 diesel was the prize. To enter the draw the reader had to answer a number of questions, the answers to which were in the article. Finally an 'I would go for diesel because . . .' tiebreaker was to be completed. This multi level approach demanded considerable elaboration – and all for partial/intermittent reinforcement!

Vicarious learning

This comes from Bandura's observational learning and suggests that we can learn at second hand by observing what happens to other people. Here the examples might be negative reinforcement – people will be offended and cause you to be ostracized if you suffer from unpleasant body odour. The solution (which encompasses a degree of *insight learning*) is to use the advertised deodorant. Similarly soft drinks are sometimes portrayed as making the consumer more socially popular.

Latent learning

This applies to many of the advertisements which appeal to the more expensive, one-off purchases. It is unlikely that readers will rush out and refit their kitchens because thay have seen an advertisement. Here the aim is to lodge the product in the consumers' cognitive map/awareness set so that the product is positively viewed at the time that kitchen refurbishment is being considered.

Our review of memory needs little linking to marketing activities as the need for the consumer to remember the product name, personality and characteristics is, hopefully, self-evident. It is perhaps worth commenting about the possible marketing applications of forgetting.

> **Think** – Under what conditions might you wish consumers to forget?

It is possible to imagine that your product has received some undesirable publicity – the contamination of Perrier would be a classic example. Here the problem is to speed the forgetting of the bad news and the reintroduction of positive images.

> **Think** – Given the information we have reviewed so far, how would you tackle such a problem?

Experiential learning, the Kolb cycle of activity, reflection, theorizing and testing fit in well with any of our sampling approaches to marketing and, to some extent, subsumes many of the principles of operant, insight and latent learning. Offering free cheese or pâté 'tasters' as customers come into the supermarket, test drives for potential car buyers and free samples pushed through letter-boxes all allow the potential consumer to try out the product or service and hence build brand awareness.

Involvement

Involvement is a concept which covers several of the ideas expressed above. It seems sensible to differentiate between consumer decisions which are of low significance and those which may hold high importance for the individual. In other words it is not unreasonable to think that buying a tin of beans is of less significance than purchasing a new hi-fi system and that the mental processing and learning is therefore likely to be different. Cost is likely to be a major factor, but even here we are not able to analyse this in absolute terms – buying a car may be one of the biggest purchasing decisions of our lives for the majority of the population, but for others it is purely a pipe dream, while for the very rich it may be far less significant.

This concept, which is closely related to elaboration and cognitive (S–O–R) processes, provides a useful way to illustrate some of the major theories discussed in this chapter and this approach is summarized in Table 5.1.

Table 5.1   Learning theories, marketing and involvement

Theory	Examples of low involvement	Examples of high involvement
trial and error learning	Free sample of hair shampoo delivered through front door and stored in bathroom. When usual shampoo runs out, trial pack is used, found acceptable and purchased (or not).	Faced with mounting debts, individual responds to advertisement offering to solve the problems with a single loan. Learns the costs of borrowing from loan sharks.
classical conditioning	A positive emotional response is generated by the use of a particular pop tune. This becomes associated with a product, even though the person does not consciously pay attention to the advertising.	The generation of higher-order conditioning allows the customer to have positive feelings about a product which may be more expensive than alternatives e.g. luxury goods.
operant conditioning	A common brand of baked bean is purchased. They taste 'OK'. The consumer continues to purchase that brand.	Clothes purchased and worn give rise to numerous compliments. Further clothes of the same label are bought.
iconic rote learning	An individual learns that Amstrad make personal computers without ever consciously focusing on PCs or Amstrad advertisements.	Keen cooks learn about various makes of kitchen knives by careful reading of advertisements which they find enjoyable.
insight learning	'The Guardian' unavailable at newsagents when on holiday. Customer buys 'The Independent' instead.	Commuter, distressed by daily difficulties with parking, decides to purchase mountain bike to solve the problem.
latent learning	Consumer spots 'low salt, low sugar' beans on the supermarket shelf. Remembers healthy eating advertisements and purchases a tin.	Consumers as a family, having won the pools, decide that they can now afford their 'dream car'. Choose the model they have always wanted.
vicarious learning	A child learns parental roles by observation – but without really 'thinking' about it.	Individual observes reaction to a friend's new style suit before deciding to purchase.
experiential learning	Commuter finds level of smoke pollution on upper deck of bus too offensive to tolerate and decides to travel on the lower deck.	Car taken to garage for service. Customer offered new higher powered model to use for the day. Impressed by the car, the consumer decides to move up the range when the time comes to change car.

Review Exercise

What examples in current advertising/marketing campaigns can you find of the following:

General principles of learning
- Association...
- Positive reinforcement...
- Negative reinforcement..
- Motivation...

Connectionist learning theories (S–R)
- Classical conditioning...
- Operant conditioning...
- Stimulus generalization...
- Higher order conditioning..
- Intermittent reinforcement...

Cognitive learning theories (S–O–R)
- Insight learning..
- Latent learning...

Other learning theories
- Vicarious learning...
- Experiential learning..
- Information processing theories..

Memory
- Short-term memory...
- Long-term memory...

Forgetting
- Retroactive inhibition...
- Proactive inhibition..
- Emotional factors...
- Repression..

Associated processes
- Rehearsal..
- Elaboration...

Think – Which of these elements have been used in this chapter?

Chapter summary exercises

Think – How can the material in this chapter be applied to the marketing of:
  camcorders
  the social policy of a political party
  skis
  holidays
  soft drinks
  instant coffee
  sports shoes (trainers)
  razors
  hair colourant
  toothpaste
  shampoo
  motor cars
  low-fat/low cholesterol/low salt spread
  sanitary protection
  kitchen equipment
  spirits and liqueurs
  low-alcohol wine
  a restaurant
  newspapers
  toilet tissue
  bicycles

Think – How *has* my organization used learning theory?

Think – How *could* my organization use learning theory more effectively?

Think – How have *I* used learning theory?

Some 'typical' questions – Learning

A Clarify each of the following concepts associated with learning theory, and show how each can be applied to the marketing process:

- Classical conditioning
- Stimulus generalization
- Higher-order conditioning
- Positive and negative reinforcement.

B Outline the essential differences between operant conditioning and classical conditioning. In what ways can understanding of the conditioning process (in either of its forms) be helpful to marketers?

C Write short notes on the following in order to demonstrate their potential applications in marketing:

a The causes of 'forgetting': (e.g. retroactive inhibition, proactive inhibition, emotion and repression).

b The main stages in the processes associated with memory.

D 'In every simple learning situation there are three factors that can be identified as being important. These are association, reinforcement (or reward), and motivation'. Discuss this statement, with special reference to its relevance for the marketing of one of the following: financial services, public transport, or consumer durables.

E Demonstrate the ways in which marketers can make use of these features of the learning process:

- Positive and negative reinforcement
- Primary and secondary reinforcement.

To what extent is it necessary for marketers to pay heed to any other theories of learning?

F Examine the usefulness and relevance of Stimulus–Response theories of learning to the marketing of washing powder, newspapers and washing machines. What other approaches to learning might be more applicable?

G What do you understand by the term 'vicarious learning'? How can this be applied to marketing situations?

H 'S–O–R' theories of learning are much more appropriate than simple S–R approaches in high involvement purchasing decisions'. Discuss.

Sources

BPP (1991) *Behavioural Aspects of Marketing*, BPP.
Buchanan, D. A. and Huczynski, A. A. (1985) *Organisational Behaviour*, Prentice-Hall.
Engel, J. F., Blackwell, R. D. and Miniard, P. W. (1990) *Consumer Behaviour*, (6th edn), Dryden.

Gregory R. L. (ed.) (1987) *The Oxford Companion to the Mind*, Oxford University Press.

Hawkins, D. I., Best R. J. and Coney K. A. (1989) *Consumer Behaviour: Implications for Marketing Strategy* (4th edn.), Irwin.

Hergenhahn, B. R. (1988) *An Introduction to Theories of Learning* (3rd edn.), Prentice-Hall.

Kakabadse, A., Ludlow, R. and Vinnicombe, S. (1987) *Working in Organisations*, Penguin.

Kolb, D. A. *et. al.* (1971) *Organisational Psychology: An Experiential Approach*, Prentice-Hall.

Lewis, D. J. and Duncan, C. P. (1956) 'Effect of different percentages of money reward on extinction of a lever pulling response,' *Journal of Experimental Psychology*, SR.

Peter, J. P. and Olson, J. C. (1990) *Consumer Behaviour and Marketing Strategy* (2nd edn.), Irwin.

Reber, A. S. (1985) *Dictionary of Psychology*, Penguin.

Robertson, I. T. and Cooper, C. L. (1983) *Human Behaviour in Organisations*, Macdonald and Evans.

Williams, K. C. (1981) *Behavioural Aspects of Marketing*, Heinemann.

6 What makes people tick?

The relevance of motivation in consumer behaviour

This chapter covers a crucial area in the study of behaviour. It can be seen as being of triple importance as it crops up in three separate parts of the syllabus – we need to know about motivation in order to understand the behaviour of consumers – but we also need to look at people's motivation to understand their behaviour in their roles as employees. Additionally we will look at the area of motivational research – the techniques which help us to determine the most effective advertising strategies.

Learning objectives

At the end of this section students should be fully familiar with the following concepts (and the associated language) and *should be able to relate them to marketing and organizational (work) situations*:

General principles of motivation

- Primary or unlearned motives.
- Secondary or learned motives.
- Positive and negative motives.
- Causality, directedness, need satisfaction.

Theories of motivation

- Economic (Taylor).
- Social (Mayo).
- Self-Actualisation (Maslow).
- Two Factor (Herzberg).
- Expectancy (Vroom).
- Equity (Adams).

- Achievement (McClelland).
- Complex (Schein).

Motivation Research

- Utilitarian and Hedonic benefits of products.
- Depth interview.
- Group discussion.
- Projective techniques – Thematic Apperception Test (TAT), Rorsach Test, Word Association Test, Psychodrama.

Exercise – What is your purpose in undertaking this course of study?
– Jot down your answer as fully as possible and keep it for later.

Many people see the study of motivation as being of prime importance to understanding behaviour. Certainly it has become a key and central plank of many management courses. The ideas and assumptions stemming from this chapter will influence many of the practical marketing applications we will look at later. In order to understand the emphasis which is placed on the subject it is worthwhile trying to define some of the terms that are in use and the way in which the basic ideas interact.

Motivation is the mixture of wants, needs and drives within the individual which seek gratification through the acquisition of some experience or object. In many cases the goal or outcome sought will be less important in absolute terms, but will be valued for the reward or satisfaction with which it is associated or, alternatively, for the release from the tension of being in a wanting state (our ultimate aim could be to be unmotivated!). In fact the prime objective of the marketer might be said to persuade or convince consumers that the use of their product will satisfy a specific need or group of needs.

This seems fairly straightforward until we realize that motives may be unconscious and multiple. Life would be much easier if our wants, needs and drives came one at a time! And easier still if we were fully aware of each. The word 'fully' is used here because often our motives are more complex than we appreciate. A person may state with all honesty 'I am buying this car because it is economical and its carrying capacity suits my needs' but without doubt there will have been other motives that will have influenced the choice, some of which the person might partially recognize, others might be completely unconscious. Here we have another example of the difficulties in the behavioural sciences (mentioned earlier in Chapter 1) where respondents may be unaware of their true motivations and reasons for their behaviour – on the other hand few of us are willing to admit that we do not know why we do things, so we must treat with some caution the accounts that people give us of their motivation.

At a very crude level Figure 6.1 proposes a simple cycle governing behaviour. An example could be where Need = thirst; Action = get glass of water; Satisfaction = no thirst.

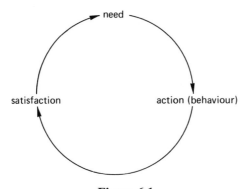

Figure 6.1

This may hold the key to the popularity of motivation as an area of study for both managers and marketing specialists.

IF we can determine the needs that people have, and

IF we can set up a situation where the only way in which they can satisfy that need is controlled by us,

THEN we may well be able to control their behaviour!

In some circumstances this cycle has remarkable similarities to what is called extortion!

In a less extreme setting we can see the importance of this to marketing specialists – if we can identify (or create) the need then we can offer our product as the satisfaction of that need.

Similarly, one popular, if trite, definition of a manager is 'a person who obtains results through the actions of others'. While this is a simplistic definition, it does highlight the importance of the human resource to most managerial activities. It also explains some of the management strategies that are adopted – we assume people need money, so we devise systems where money can only be obtained by certain behaviours approved of by the organization – systems such as bonuses or commission.

But, as we have observed, *every individual is unique* and this raises a major problem; if we accept the uniqueness proposition at face value the process of managing or marketing becomes totally individualistic. Thus it will be of value to examine areas of similarity and attempt to develop ideas about some of the ways in which individuals' motivations are alike.

There is a consensus forming amongst psychologists that there are a number of ideas which are implicitly common to the many current theories of motivation:

1 *Causality* – the idea that human behaviour is caused, just as the behaviour of physical objects is caused, by forces that act on them. Causality is implicit in the beliefs that environment and heredity affect behaviour and that what is outside influences what is inside.

2 *Directedness* – the idea that human behaviour is not only caused but also directed towards something – i.e. behaviour is goal-directed, people want things.

3 *Motivation* – the idea that underlying behaviour one finds a push, a want, a need or a drive.

These three ideas can provide the beginning of a system for conceptualizing behaviour in a slightly enlarged version of our earlier diagram as shown in Figure 6.2.

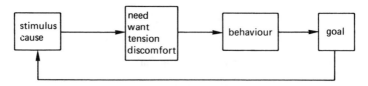

Figure 6.2

The closed-circuit conception perhaps needs a little explanation. Arrival at a goal eliminates the cause, which eliminates the motive, which eliminates the behaviour. A typical example might be feeling hungry. However, not all of our goals will be physical. Many 'psychological' goals will not be finite and specific, e.g. can one consume a given amount of 'affection' and know that you will be sated? Love, affection, prestige and other psychological goals seem to be ephemeral and boundless. Some individuals may never obtain enough of these emotional satisfactions to inactivate the causes and hence the motivation and the behaviour.

Managers are very much concerned with the behaviour of superiors, colleagues and particularly subordinates. Marketers are concerned with the behaviour of existing and potential customers and clients. As explained above, both seek to control these behaviours in an attempt to achieve their own goals.

The notion of controlling behaviour through some sort of 'blackmail' is generally not simple in the management or marketing context because:

1 all staff, customers and clients will be unique as mentioned above,
2 managers and marketers have to work with 'used', not new, humans
3 managers and marketers are themselves 'used' humans.

By the word 'used' we acknowledge that other outside, and perhaps historical, influences have 'got at' people – forming their attitudes, beliefs, perceptions, personalities and expectations. Also these variables become facts in the real-life situation. While such thinking has only become explicit in the relatively recent past, assumptions about motivation (or 'what makes people tick') have been implicit in the major schools of thought about management during the last century.

All of this may appear fairly daunting – posh words (causality, drive, etc.) and complicated ideas – but have faith, I believe that thinking about motivation is something that we all do regularly. We say, for instance: Why is he buying rat poison? – perhaps he's thinking of doing away with his wife, but probably he needs it to get rid of rats. Why did the chicken cross the road? – to get to the food on the other side. Why is she so grumpy this morning? – I don't know, but something must have gone wrong at home. We seem to spend most of our time ascribing purpose or motives to people in order to explain their actions.

Needs or motives can be either *unlearned (primary)* or *learned (secondary)*. They can also be *positive* or *negative*.

Unlearned or *primary motivation* comprises the basic physiological drives for survival of the organism – hunger, thirst, sleep, etc. It seems that the body has an in-built capacity for recognizing imbalance and for automatic response to restore the required balance. One example might be temperature control – if we overheat the body sweats, the evaporation cools the surface and balance is restored. Similarly if we are cold our body hair stands erect, goose-pimples are formed, the flow of air across the surface of the skin is reduced and with it heat loss, so we warm up. This self balancing process is sometimes called *homeostasis*.

The sex drive appears to be an unlearned motivation in all of the animal kingdom (humans included) and is a very powerful and potent motivator. There are also primary drives which involve a curiosity about the environment – a need to explore and be active, and a need for physical contact.

The exploration drive can be seen in both rodents and small babies – a hamster, on being released, will immediately explore the limits of the space by running around the walls while babies are interested in their environment and respond to it from an early age. Babies also need physical contact with either other persons or with tactile substances (comforters). These basic needs coincide with what we will later call lower-level needs when we look at formal theories of motivation such as the Maslow Hierarchy of Needs.

Learned motives are many and various – in many ways this whole book is about the wide variety of learned drives. We learn how to gain approval of others; we are are taught acceptable behaviour by family, school and friends; we learn to value certain rewards that society prizes and we learn to avoid behaviour that will cause people close to us to withdraw affection. We learn to obey the laws of the land and to sublimate or redirect antisocial tendencies (often associated with the unlearned, primary motives) into behaviours that our society accepts.

Motivation may also be viewed as being *positive* or *negative* (similar in concept to the notions of positive and negative reinforcement). Positive motives are those we seek to satisfy while the negatives are those we seek to avoid. Much of motivation theory is expressed in positive terms but I suspect that much of our behaviour will, at root, be negatively motivated – i.e. our behaviour will be directed towards avoidance of something we perceive as unpleasant.

The idea of behaviour being goal directed identifies further facets of motivation. Our goals may be *general* or *specific* – we may have a general need to keep healthy and extend our life expectancy or we may have a specific need for a drink of water.

We may also reflect on the fact that our goals may be a function of the way we see ourselves and the way we would like to be, this idea of *aspiration* is of great significance in the marketing field as it is likely to form the basis of many of our advertising messages. This emphasizes the importance of perception in our study of motivation, and the fact that many of our motivations may be both learned and dependent on our culture, class and upbringing.

So, in terms of our earlier discussion, we need frameworks to describe, explain, predict and control behaviour – and motivation is a key element in that process. The whole area of human motivation is so complex that we do not have a single unified theoretical framework to work with. The ideas are fragmented and incomplete. They are also better at describing and explaining than they are at predicting or controlling. So it is of importance to review theories sceptically – think about the extent to which they fit *your* experience, the extent to which they adequately explain the phenomenon they claim, and whether they can be used to predict human behaviour.

In view of the need to examine both the motivation of people as consumers and also people as employees we will now consider various theories of motivation. This section will be split into theories which are of a general and marketing interest and a second category which are more centred on work motivation.

A General and marketing orientated theories

Hierarchy of needs – the work of Maslow

Maslow, starting from our initial assumption that a person's behaviour is directed to satisfying needs, groups these needs into broad categories, arranges them into a hierarchy of prepotency, and theorizes on their relationships. The notion of prepotency implies 'over-riding force' and proposes that some groups of needs will take precedence over others when the individual is faced with choices as to which needs to satisfy. The hierarchy is commonly displayed as a pyramid or triangle, but an alternative is a 'stepped' model as shown in Figure 6.3.

Maslow's hypothesis is that a satisfied need is no longer a motivator and that the hierarchy operates such that a person's behaviour will tend to be

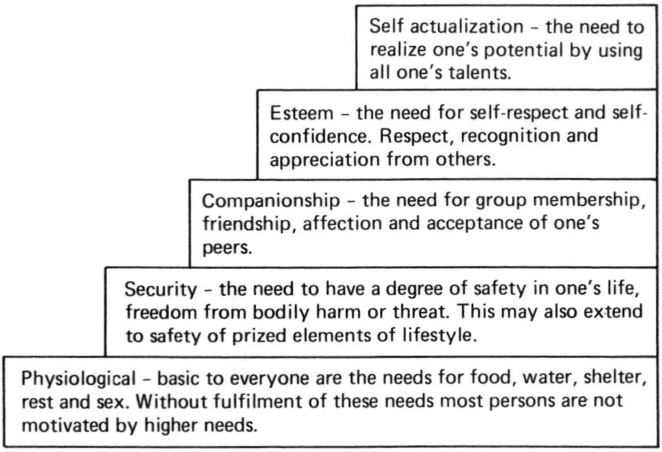

Self actualization - the need to realize one's potential by using all one's talents.

Esteem - the need for self-respect and self-confidence. Respect, recognition and appreciation from others.

Companionship - the need for group membership, friendship, affection and acceptance of one's peers.

Security - the need to have a degree of safety in one's life, freedom from bodily harm or threat. This may also extend to safety of prized elements of lifestyle.

Physiological - basic to everyone are the needs for food, water, shelter, rest and sex. Without fulfilment of these needs most persons are not motivated by higher needs.

Figure 6.3

dominated by trying to satisfy the lowest unsatisfied need i.e physiological needs will tend to take precedence over security, companionship or esteem needs; companionship will tend to take precedence over esteem or self-actualization needs and so forth.

The notion is one of a needs ascending process, sequential in nature, whereby one particular class of needs must reach a sufficient level of satisfaction before the next needs level becomes operational. The emphasis is on sufficiency – each successive level must be relatively satisfied before the next level of need becomes more important in motivating behaviour. Thus the steps might be better represented by a more rounded, wavy line.

It has also been speculated that additional levels of need might be applicable – the freedom of inquiry and expression is sometimes quoted, referring to a need for social conditions which permit free speech and which encourage values such as honesty, justice and fairness.

Another high level need that is sometimes proposed is that of knowledge and understanding. This suggests a need to explore and experiment in order to learn about, and understand, our environment.

Another view of the prepotency approach is that an individual is continually responding to the 'lowest' unsatisfied need. In reality the different categories of needs may operate on very different timescales. Food needs could be defined in terms of calories per day whilst self-actualization may be a lifetime target measured in years. This has given rise to the observation that for many people life is a struggle to achieve higher level satisfactions against the 'obstacles' of lower-level needs. This has become known to some of my students as 'Rice's yo-yo' as they picture life whizzing up and down the hierarchy trying to satisfy very different needs!

Maslow's theory is perhaps the most all-embracing and influential theory in common currency. In a way this is both its strength and its weakness. We have a useful device for the description and explanation phase – but it is significantly weaker at prediction. Many discussions of its application rapidly become arguments on semantics with more energy spent on defining words than on validating the model – this seems to reflect the importance of individual perceptions of what constitutes the needs in each broad category.

Other problems with the theory centre on:

- a lack of empirical evidence to support it. Physiological and safety needs are not always the predominant factor in determining behaviour – examples of heroism are sometimes recognizable and notable for apparently emphasizing the precedence of 'higher' needs over the individual's physiological and safety needs.

- the absence of money from the list of needs worries some people. Here the answer would seem to lie in the argument that money is the means to an end. In motivational terms we may be more concerned with *what* a person chooses to expend money on – it could be to buy food, security, status or satisfy any number of needs.

- self-actualization and esteem needs are likely to be a function of each individual's self-perception. This in turn may be socially conditioned. Thus we may question whether we are describing an innate need or something which may be defined by family, gender, culture and class.

It does, however, give us an interesting notion that 'behavioural efficiency' can be obtained by actions that satisfy more than one need at the same time.

> **Think** – Which category of needs is your prime motivator?
> – To what extent does this theory reflect white, male, middle class western values?

Marketing implications

Given its all-embracing scope it is not surprising that marketers have found Maslow's ideas useful. Clearly we can associate certain products with appropriate levels of the hierarchy and so *segment* the market into large target populations – Low fat margarine with Physiological, Insurance with Security, etc. It also offers the marketer the opportunity to offer the product as a solution to a problem or the satisfier of a need. The notion of 'behavioural efficiency' mentioned above, can also be utilized – one television advertisement for fitting a particular brand of security lock did it spectacularly well. Doing-It-Yourself clearly saves money and satisfies an economic need; locks satisfy the security need; the male doing the fixing was depicted as enjoying the companionship of his family; the looks given him by his children boosted his esteem while the glance from the wife figure would seem to confirm his high status in the eyes of his partner. One could hypothesize that self-actualization could stem from the achievement and use of his talents to solve a significant problem.

Organizational implications

Being so broad, the theory also has implications for the explanation of work behaviour. The levels of the hierarchy can be associated with work-based concerns:

- *Physiological* needs are likely to reflect an interest in working conditions;
- *Security* becomes important when jobs are threatened;
- *Companionship* is concerned with the creation of compatible work groups;
- *Esteem* is likely to emerge as a concern for job titles and status symbols;
- *Self-actualization* could be related to the need for a demanding job.

The overriding implication of this theory is that employees are more than 'human machines' and their interests and motivation may be determined by their overall position on the hierarchy. Thus we can organize to satisfy the appropriate unsatisfied need. For many organizations in our society this will subsume the ideas of social theory (encompassed by the companionship level of the hierarchy) and will be focusing on the esteem level which may involve designing jobs with greater autonomy, moving towards participative decision making, having more flexible structures and more two-way communication (see also Chapter 11 for an expansion of some of these ideas – Maslow translates most easily in organization terms into McGregor's Theory *Y* approaches to management).

ERG – the work of Clayton Alderfer

A similar approach to Maslow's has more recently been suggested by Alderfer. He has developed a hierarchical, three factor theory of needs known as ERG – Existence, Relatedness and Growth. Existence is similar to Maslow's physiological and security needs, relatedness is similar to Maslow's companionship need, and growth is similar to Maslow's esteem and self-actualization needs. He suggests that

1 the less a need is satisfied, the more important it becomes,

2 the more a lower level need is satisfied, the greater the importance of the next higher level need, and

3 the less the higher level need is satisfied, the greater the importance the lower need assumes.

This suggests that if individuals cannot get what they want, they will demand more of what they *can* get. This corresponds closely to what is called 'displacement behaviour' in other contexts. Alderfer also accepts the idea of different needs coexisting. This is sometimes displayed as overlapping waves.

> **Think** – What examples from your own experience can you find to
> support Alderfer's ideas?

Marketing implications

Given the similarities between the theories, it is not surprising that much of
the comment on Maslow's approach will apply in this case. Alderfer does
raise the notion of the possibility of 'displacing' frustration into the
purchase of your product. If you cannot afford a Ferrari you may be
pursuaded to 'personalize' your Ford to satisfy 'status' needs.

Organizational implications

Again, the implications are very similar to those outlined above when
reviewing the Hierarchy of Needs. Perhaps one additional insight is gained
from Alderfer's views on relative importance of needs depending on the
relative satisfactions. One example might be in the industrial relations field
where employees sometimes demand more money when what they really
seek is more interesting and worthwhile work.

Achievement – the work of David McClelland

McClelland argues that many needs are not as universal as Maslow
proposes. He believes that some needs are socially acquired and picks out
specifically the need for achievement, the need for affiliation and the need
for power. The need for achievement reflects the desire to meet task goals;
the need for affiliation reflects the desire to develop good interpersonal
relationships; the need for power reflects the desire to influence and control
other people.

He proposes a profile of needs – some people being high on achievement
needs (high and visible performance targets), some high on power needs (in
charge of a department or section), others high on affiliation needs (project
or team work).

> **Think** – Which is your principal need?
> – What other examples can you think of?

Marketing implications

It is suggested that people with high power needs will be attracted to
products which imply superiority – fast cars, 'power' clothing fashions and
so forth. In contrast, those high in affiliation needs are likely to conform to
group norms and select products that will be approved of by their friends
and social contacts. They are also more likely to respond well to friendly and
non-pressure sales techniques. Achievers will seek products which enhance

their esteem and self-actualization needs, particularly those which indicate personal attainment.

Using such a framework we can both segment a market and shape appropriate marketing messages. The product could be portrayed as helping people achieve their objectives (computers, filofax, etc.) or suggest power (pinstripe business suits, large cars). It would also be possible to use similar ideas to reinforce a belief that the product will make the purchaser more socially desirable.

Organizational implications

McClelland himself has argued that organizations need to select managers who are high achievers, who like a challenge and who have, historically, hit their targets. This might also be the blueprint for the successful marketer/ salesperson. It also implies that we may need to design jobs that enable staff to satisfy their achievement needs (as well as their affiliation and power needs) at the workplace. This usually means some scheme of joint target setting along with a sound appraisal or feedback system.

Expectancy – the work of Vroom

Vroom is the main name associated with 'Expectancy Theory'. Under this approach individuals are assumed to make rational decisions based on the importance of the outcome to them and their perception of the likelihood of that outcome arising from an action. Vroom puts forward four premises:

1 People have preferences (valences) for various outcomes or incentives that are available to them.

2 People hold expectations about the probability that an action or effort on their part will lead to the intended outcome or objective.

3 People understand that certain behaviours will be followed by desirable outcomes or incentive rewards, e.g. a pay rise or increased status.

4 The action a person chooses to take is determined by the expectancies and preferences (valences) that the person has at the time.

The relationship is commonly presented as:

$$F = E \times V$$

where F = motivation to behave,

E = expectation that the behaviour will be followed by a particular outcome (subjective probability),

V = valence of the outcome.

Normally a number of different outcomes will be associated with a particular behaviour. The expectancy equation has to be summed across all of these outcomes so the formula becomes:

$$F = \Sigma \, (E \times V)$$

The hypothesis is that we will behave in the way which we believe will give the most desired outcomes overall.

Exercise – Buchanan and Huczinski, in their book *Organisational Behaviour*, present the following activity:

First: List the outcomes that you expect will result from working hard for your 'Behavioural Aspects of Marketing' course, such as:

   1   High exam marks
   2   Bare pass
   3   Sleepless nights
   4   No social life
   5   ?
   6   ? etc., etc.

Second: Rate the value that you place on each of these outcomes giving those you like +1, those you dislike −1, and those for which you are neutral O. These are your '*V*' values.

Third: Estimate the probability of attaining each of these outcomes, giving those that are certain the value 1, those that are most unlikely the value 0, and those for which there is an even chance the value 0.5. Estimate other probabilities as you perceive them at other values between 0 and 1. These are your '*E*' values.

Fourth: Now put your E and V values into the expectancy equation

$$F = \Sigma \, (E \times V)$$

and add up the result

Fifth: Compare your F score with the scores of your colleagues. We predict that:
   • those with higher scores are the course 'swots';
   • those with the higher scores will get higher exam marks.

Think – Do we actually do this (without pencil and paper) for all behaviours?
   – Are we really as rational as this theory supposes?

Marketing implications

Here there seems to be a clear parallel to the work of Fishbein on attitudes (which we shall come to in the next chapter). If we accept the expectancy equation it follows that we can attack the marketing problem in three ways:

1 we aim to increase the perceived value of our product
2 we aim to raise the expectancy of satisfaction
3 we do both 1 and 2.

This might account for some otherwise 'irrational' behaviour such as doing the football pools. As a relatively numerate person I am aware that my chances of winning the 'Treble Chance' are infinitesimal – but the value I place on winning a very large sum of money makes it worth trying! Marketers must, of course, take great care not to raise consumers' expectations of a product beyond the level that it can satisfy. A very quick way to achieve a poor reputation is to promise things you cannot deliver. These ideas are developed further in the PV/PPS model of consumer behaviour put forward in Chapter 10.

Organizational implications

This view of how people make behavioural decisions is a useful one. It also places great emphasis on people's perceptions as being important in determining the way they behave. A diagrammatic version of expectancy theory at work is shown in Figure 6.4. It offers no tidy simple solutions, but may have significant implications for who we select for certain tasks and what rewards we will offer. Clearly is gives little motivation to someone who wants time off to be with their family if they are offered extra overtime as a motivator! The notion of expectancy also means that individuals will have learned from their previous experience – which may have major implications for consistency and honesty on the part of management. If we are to take this idea to its fullest extent it follows that management may need to start

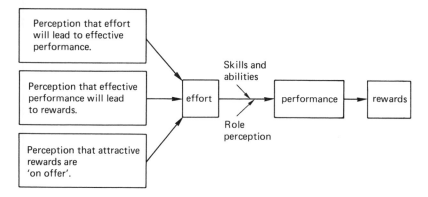

Figure 6.4

paying attention to the values and expectations of employees and may need to put as much effort into influencing them as they do in influencing their customers – a kind of internal marketing of the organization to itself.

B Work orientated theories

Economic – the work of Taylor

Taylor's work was conducted at the turn of the century and resulted in the movement known as 'Scientific Management'. His contribution to motivation theory centres on the work which developed time study and piecework systems.

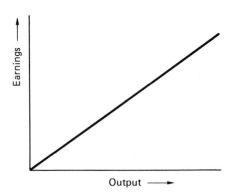

Figure 6.5

The assumption underlying his approach is that workers are rational, economic creatures who will modify their behaviour to maximize the financial/economic return. The outcome of such a theory (commonly called the 'economic man' theory of motivation) is the practice called piecework where each worker is paid strictly in accordance with the amount he/she has produced. The earnings curve is a straight line through the origin (as shown in Figure 6.5) and the implications of the graph is that money motivation is both continuous and constant.

Think – Is that true?
       – Is your desire for more money constant?
       – When does it change?

Taylor's aim in all this was to create a 'mental revolution' so that both management and employees would gain their satisfactions (money) in achieving the goals of the organization as shown in Figure 6.6. Such a model

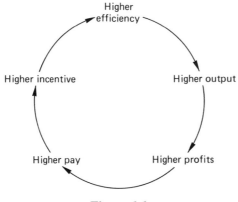

Figure 6.6

of behaviour is attractive in its simplicity, but we may need to question how widely the assumptions hold in real life.

> **Think** – How important is money to you?
> – Why is it important to you?
> – What do you want the money for?
> – What would you *not* do for money?
> – Why not?

Clearly money is important to most people. It is the means by which we purchase goods (and many satisfactions) within our society and is the essential requirement for many people's survival.

What becomes interesting, however, is the assumption built into this theory (and into the piecework graph) that our motivation for money is both continuous and constant. However, many people report that this is not so – there seems to be a point at which the desire for a rest overcomes the desire for additional money. This concept is sometimes called the marginal utility of labour. It also seems logical to surmise that this point may vary for the same individual at different times – e.g. saving up for a holiday may raise the level of income desired, but following the holiday the 'need' for money may decline to its original level.

Organizational implications
If we accept this theory we will tend to design jobs that are simple, repetitive, and with a clearly measurable output that can be related to money. We will reward staff with piecework, incentives, bonuses and performance related pay. Management style is likely to be autocratic as supervisors will use the economic threat ('do what you are told or else . . .') to ensure procedures and systems are adhered to. The organization structure is likely to be hierarchical, formal and bureaucratic.

Marketing implications
For the marketer the principal message from a belief in this theory is to place prime emphasis on the concept of 'value' expressed in economic terms. So followers of this approach will offer low prices, discounts; or alternatively, more for the same price.

We might therefore conclude that the economic theory of motivation is highly relevant to an explanation of behaviour, but that it has significant limitations in its ability to account for many observed behaviour patterns.

Social – the work of Mayo

Mayo conducted the famous Hawthorne Experiments in the late 1920s (see Chapter 8 for a more detailed account). They highlighted the importance of the primary workgroup and the overriding influence of social factors on workplace behaviour. This triggered a great interest in group behaviour and the results of the many research studies suggest that:

1 Groups serve the needs of both the organization and the individual.
2 Most groups have both formal and informal functions.
3 The importance of groups within the organization focuses on their ability to unite their members against management and to frustrate the 'official' policy.
4 The informal standards and roles may run counter to the formal organization's standards and roles and are highly influential.
5 The satisfactions an individual can obtain from membership of a group may be more potent than the rewards offered by management.
6 Individuals may therefore be caught between conflicting motivational forces.
7 Group unity and solidarity become a means to force management to improve a group's rewards, status or professional standing.

This approach to motivation (often referred to as the 'social' theory) suggests that an individual's behaviour is largely determined by the social groups belonged to.

> **Think** – What groups affect your behaviour?
>   – How?

The influence of groups on our behaviour and our needs for social contact and approval seem to be well established and are discussed in much more detail in the chapter devoted to people in groups. The ideas underlying social theories of motivation are interesting in as much as they suggest that we may each be made up of a number of 'different' people who exist in different social settings. The problems associated with this multi-role experience and the resolution of the inevitable conflicts that arise are of great interest to the social scientist.

Organizational implications

In organizational terms this theory emphasizes the importance of the social group – both formal and informal – as a key determinant of work behaviour. Jobs will be designed to encompass group interaction and identity, communication will be encouraged, and management style is likely to be consultative.

Marketing implications

Here we may decide to emphasize social acceptance as a benefit of using our product. Some may even offer fear of isolation as a threat for *not* using it! Positive images of consumers in group situations will become common. As we will see in later chapters, the media and advertising exert considerable influence on the way in which we define roles in society – so the marketing process itself may also help determine what is expected of certain roles.

Two factor – the work of Herzberg

Herzberg asked a sample of professionals about circumstances affecting their satisfaction/happiness at work. From the responses he developed the well-known 'two-factor' theory of motivation. In this a distinction is drawn between:

1 'satisfaction' in the sense of a positive, conscious state of elation and
2 'satisfaction' as a neutral state reflecting an absence of negative sensations.

Many of us take good health for granted and therefore are satisfied until we become ill. Teeth are a classic example of things we take for granted – until we get a toothache!

Herzberg classified the positive satisfiers as 'motivators' while the neutral version (or potential dissatisfiers) he refers to as 'maintenance' or 'hygiene' factors. His studies suggested the following:

Hygiene/maintenance factors	Motivators
Company policy and administration	Achievement
Supervision	Recognition
Salary	Work itself
Interpersonal relations	Responsibility
Physical working conditions	Advancement

The theory suggests that the presence of dissatisfiers causes low work performance, so the maintenance/hygiene factors must be put right. However this does not lead to motivation, only to the 'no dissatisfaction' type of 'satisfaction'. Motivation (and hence high work performance) is generated by the motivators.

It can be seen that the maintenance factors are commonly extrinsic to the job and the motivators intrinsic. The work can be criticized on a number of grounds, not least that it was based on a relatively small sample of engineers and accountants in Pittsburg – but it has had wide acceptance in the organizational setting.

> **Think** – Herzberg does not list money as a motivator – do you agree?

Organizational implications

This work has direct applicability to work design as it focuses specifically on motivation in the work situation. The prime implications are:

1 to ensure that the hygiene/maintenance factors are satisfactory and
2 to redesign jobs to include the motivators – commonly called job enrichment.

Marketing implications

These are relatively limited, but the emphasis on responsibility, achievement and interesting activity relate fairly closely to Maslow's higher level needs. They may however give an insight into industrial/organizational product marketing and the use of promotional (in the marketing sense) tools as motivators or badges of achievement (e.g. offering incentives such as 'achieve your sales target for a period and win a trip to exotic places').

Equity – the work of Adams

Another approach which centres on the individual's perceptions is commonly called 'Equity Theory'. Here it is assumed that the individual assesses their internal 'balance sheet' and will choose behaviours for which a fair exchange exists. The inputs are the costs incurred (effort, fatigue, anxiety, etc.). The outcomes are any events that contribute to need gratification. Comparison Level is any standard used to assess the 'fairness' of a particular exchange.

If we assess our inputs as being fairly rewarded then all is fine. If we perceive that we are under-rewarded we can reduce our inputs, seek to increase our outcomes or change the comparison level. Similarly if we perceive a situation where we are over-rewarded we may increase input, decrease outcome or change comparison level.

> **Think** – How fair do you think your reward package is?
> – How does that affect your work behaviour?

Table 6.1 Summary of motivation theories

Theory	Name/ Originator	Assumption	Implications Organizational	Implications Marketing
Self-actualization	Maslow	Hierarchy of Needs	Determine level on the hierarchy and respond appropriately More autonomy etc.	Aim product at the appropriate need satisfaction
ERG	Alderfer	Existence Relatedness and Growth needs	As Maslow, but aware of 'displacement'	As Maslow Use 'displacement'
Achievement	McClelland	Achievement Affiliation and Power needs	Setting appropriate targets for staff	Identify product with satisfaction of these needs
Expectancy	Vroom	Motivation = Valence × Expectation	Link effort, reward and expectation	Raise perceived value and expectation of product satisfaction
Economic	Taylor	Maximization of financial return	Job simplification Piecework, payment by results, commission. Formal, authoritarian management style	Emphasis on 'value' cut price promotions × % extra free!
Social	Mayo	Behaviour affected by social group including informal groups	Work groups planned. More open communication Consultative style	Emphasis on social acceptance Fear of isolation
Two factor	Herzberg	Maintenance/ Hygiene factors Motivators	Get hygiene factors right Job enrichment	Limited to emphasis on motivators
Equity	Adams	Effort/Reward balance	Influence perceptions	Influence perceptions
Complex	Schein	None/all	Diagnose	Diagnose

Organizational implications

Here the emphasis is on a concept sometimes referred to as 'felt fair' – the actual concept of fairness is extremely hard to define other than in terms of it being what the people concerned *feel* to be fair. So the implications for management may be similar to those suggested under expectancy theory – they may need to work harder at influencing the perception of their own staff.

Marketing implications

Here we may be looking at attaining a balance between what a consumer pays and what they get in return – the idea of enhancing perceived value is not new in marketing terms and has resonances with other parts of the CIM course of study. Both expectancy and equity approaches stress the consumers' perceptions and there is a possible application of both theories in reassuring consumers who have bought the product that they have made a sound choice while, at the same time, boosting expectations. 'Aren't you glad you bought . . .' style advertising falls into this category and is an example of Festinger's Cognitive Dissonance theory which is discussed in the following chapter.

Exercise – Look back at your statement from the beginning of this chapter.
– Which theory looks a 'best fit' for you as
a consumer?
an employee?
an employer/manager?
– Which theory do you think provides the best model for other people's behaviour overall?

There is one final contribution to our review of motivation theories.

Complex – the work of Edgar Schein

Schein, having reviewed the evolution of behavioural assumptions in our organizational systems, concludes that managers are far too susceptible to 'the bandwagon'. He points out that all of the theories are in part 'right'; but none of them are adequate to explain organizational behaviour on their own. He goes on to propose the idea of 'Complex Man' – subsuming all the above theories – but believing none to the exclusion of others. He suggests a diagnostic approach to management, identifying probable problem variables and applying appropriate remedies. This should be followed by analysis of outcomes and reappraisal of the underlying assumptions if necessary.

This approach is compatible with that of my colleague Tony Watson who has suggested that the best analogy for the motivation theories is that of waves breaking against the shore – one dominates temporarily but rapidly mixes with the waves that have preceded it.

Organizational and marketing implications
As the essence of Schein's contribution is the denial of a single universal theory, the implications may be dealt with jointly as they can apply to both marketing and managing. We should reject a single assumption, analyse the situation, apply the most probable solution, monitor, measure and assess. If we are not successful we can only assume an inaccurate diagnosis – so back to the drawing board!

The acceptance of Schein's view also implies that new ideas, hypotheses and theories of behaviour may emerge in the future and will join the existing canon of motivation theory for consideration in the same way – the obligation on us all as both marketers and managers will be to keep abreast of developments in the field.

Motivation research

As early as 1924 Copeland introduced a framework for marketing decisions that drew a distinction between rational and emotional motives. Notions of value for money, efficiency and utility would fall into the former category. However, it is now widely accepted that products have symbolic values that go way beyond these rational factors. Engel, Blackwell and Miniard use this format when discussing motivation to buy, but use the terminology of 'Utilitarian' (objective product attributes) and 'Hedonic' (subjective/emotional) benefits.

Motivation research is the area of activity that seeks to find the underlying 'why?' of our behaviour and, in particular, 'why?' we purchase one product in preference to another. It focuses very strongly on the hedonistic benefits encompassing emotional responses, sensory pleasures and other aesthetic considerations. If we can identify common perceptions and motivations associated with our product, we can use the information, emotions and symbols to promote it further. Motivation research seeks to identify the attitudes, beliefs, motives, and other pressures that affect our purchasing decisions. In marketing terms this theory came of age in the 1950s when researchers such as Ernest Dichter used Freudian psycho-analytical ideas to explain behaviour on the basis of unconscious motivation. Statements such as 'women bake cakes because of an unconscious desire to give birth' gave rise to Pillsbury's slogan 'Nothing says lovin' like something from the oven'. In other words motivational research concentrates very much on the emotional and symbolic values of products.

Packard produced his classic, and best selling *Hidden Persuaders* in 1957 and in that book reports the problems of the Ronson lighter company in determining its advertising strategy. Motivation research suggested that the key characteristic of the product was the flame, which was seen as having phallic symbolism. Eventually the company advertised without showing a lighter at all – only the flame and the logo 'Ronson'. Sales rocketed! Similarly, the Mary Baker Cake mix had poor response in the marketplace despite being a product that seemed destined for success. Perfect cakes and all you had to do was add water. Motivation research suggested that some women felt that it had made the process of cooking too easy! As a result the company modified the mix so that the cook had to add an egg and beat the mixture. The claim was that this would enable the 'mothers' to fulfil their roles concerning a need to be actively involved in making a contribution to caring for their families. Again sales rose dramatically.

Motivation research methods

There are a number of techniques associated with motivation research and, as mentioned above, they come primarily from the field of clinical psychology.

1   Depth interview

Normally this lasts for an hour or more and consists of a one-to-one interview which is relatively unstructured. The pattern is commonly to explore the 'why?' questions in depth. Attempts are made to get the subject to talk about the product rather than answer predetermined questions. The aim is to probe below the surface to uncover and expose the underlying motivational influences. Commonly the interview starts at a relatively broad and shallow level but becomes more detailed and focused on the key topics as it progresses. This is sometimes done by coming back to 'why?'. Those readers who have been questioned by small children using this technique will know how quickly it is possible to reach a position where you really have to think about the answer!

2   Group discussion or focus group

The aim of such a group (usually numbering no more than ten persons) is the same as the in-depth interview, but here the respondents are invited to discuss their motivations in a relaxed, informal setting. There is usually a skilled group leader to guide the discussion in such a way as to ensure the relevant issues are aired, but without pre-empting or determining the outcomes. The belief is that such a setting provides an opportunity for people to interact and to allow the thoughts of one person to stimulate others. The theory is that people will talk more freely in such a setting and the process will yield much richer information than is possible from more structured and sterile questionnaire techniques.

Clearly there are some subjects that respondents may find too personal or embarrassing to discuss or admit amongst a group of strangers so group methods are not universally applied. The role of the discussion leader (or interviewer) is also crucial and one which requires a very high level of skill. Groups can have the additional weakness of being 'hijacked' by a strong personality or the discovery of an 'opinion leader' (see Chapter 9) within the group.

The development of tape and video techniques for recording group processes has given the researcher a useful tool to help overcome bias in the observer, allowing a group session to be replayed to a panel of specialists who can compare and agree ratings.

3 Projective techniques

There are a number of these methods which come primarily from clinical psychology where they are used to examine aspects of personality and perception. In the marketing sphere it is possible to alter the focus of the process slightly to encompass the product we are considering.

1 *Thematic apperception test* (TAT): here the respondent is shown a picture, drawing or photograph which is suitably ambiguous and which could be interpreted in a number of ways. They are then asked questions such as 'what story does the picture tell?', 'what led up to the events in the picture?', 'what is happening?', 'how are things going to work out?' etc. Many respondents identify with the characters in the pictures and reveal feelings, motives, emotions and desires associated with the situation shown. It is thought that by putting things into the third person and telling stories about imaginary people it may allow them to reveal things they would be unwilling to admit to themselves (or of which they may be genuinely unaware). A similar technique involves respondents filling in 'balloons' or captions on a cartoon. This again allows the subject to express perhaps deep feeling but in the third person without having to 'own up' to them.

2 *Word association tests*: this involves the researcher presenting a word to the subject who has to respond with the first word which enters their head. Many of the stimulus words used are neutral 'dummies', but interspersed with these are a number of 'test' words – the reaction to which we are particularly interested in. The responses to these test words may give us insights into the perceptions and feelings the respondent has towards the product concerned. There is a significant problem in such approaches i.e. the assumption that words have the same meaning (both in facts and emotions) to all respondents.

3 *Rorschach test*: this consists of a random inkblot, presented to the subject who is then asked what it represents to them. As the pattern is random it is suggested that any perceptions must be from the respondent's

subconscious and hence, analysis of responses may give insights into personality and perceptions. While this test is a staple of the psychiatrist it does seem to have limited use in the field of marketing due to the difficulty of introducing specific products or product types into the process to analyse.

4 *Psychodrama*: in this technique respondents are asked to improvise mini plays about situations, products, etc. Again the assumption is that in getting people to act out (for example) a pain killer dealing with a headache the researchers can gain valuable information about the way the process is seen – in our example the pain killer could be viewed as 'fighting off' the evil pain or alternatively comforting the sufferer.

> **Think** – Can you identify analgesics using these different perceptions and marketing messages?

Some researchers are using a development of this approach by inviting subjects to relax and make clay models that represent the product, service or organization. They claim that analysis of the outcomes sheds light on the respondent's inner feelings.

Motivation research is big business. Advertisers seek the maximum return from their investment so considerable effort is put into discovering the underlying motives of consumers. But it is not without its problems. If we go back to our introductory chapter on the scientific method we can see that the approaches described suffer from significant flaws. Firstly we have difficulty with the process of interpretation of evidence. In all of the techniques the researcher's interpretation is crucial – but, more importantly, the interpretation is rarely standardized, thus we are open to researcher bias.

> **Very old joke** – Researcher administering Rorschach Test : What do you see in this inkblot?
> – Subject : Two people having sex
> – Researcher offering next inkblot : And what in this one?
> – Subject : Another couple having sex
> – Researcher turning to next inkblot : And this one?
> – Subject : More sex
> – Researcher : My diagnosis is that you are what we psychiatrists call a 'sex maniac'
> – Subject : Me? a sex maniac? you're the one who's been showing all the dirty pictures

We also have difficulties with both internal and external validity. Internal validity is at risk due to the inadequacy of the experimental method and the subjectivity of the interpretation as highlighted in the very old joke. To this day there is a lack of convincing proof of many psychiatric assumptions. That they work in many instances is not denied, but this may be as a result of the processes involved rather than the truth of the underlying assumptions. Similarly external validity is suspect if the numbers of respondents is not large (and commonly it is not, due to the costs involved in one-to-one testing) as we are then faced with the problem of how typical respondents are of the population at large. We may have a difficulty in as much as it could be hypothesized that people who willingly subject themselves to this kind of exposure might not be 'normal'!

A clinically trained researcher contended that people in one European country disdain consumption of fluid milk because of unfavourable childhood imagery. The proposed solution, supposedly based on depth interviews, was to associate milk with motherhood. This was accomplished by naturelike packaging and advertising imagery, complete with rolling hills, suggesting a most obvious part of the female anatomy as viewed at the time of birth. Plausible? Well sales *did* increase.

Perhaps a more logical explanation is that greatly increased advertising enhanced name recognition.

Source: Engel, Blackwell and Miniard, *Consumer Behaviour* (Dryden, 1990).

Chapter summary exercises

Think – How can the material in this chapter be applied to the marketing of:
  camcorders
  the social policy of a political party
  skis
  holidays
  soft drinks
  instant coffee
  sports shoes (trainers)
  razors
  hair colourant
  toothpaste
  shampoo
  motor cars
  low-fat/low cholesterol/low salt spread
  sanitary protection
  kitchen equipment
  spirits and liqueurs
  low-alcohol wine
  a restaurant
  newspapers
  toilet tissue
  bicycles

Think – How *has* my organization used motivation theory?

Think – How *could* my organization use motivation theory?

Think – How have *I* used motivation theory?

Some 'typical' examination questions – Motivation

1 Motivating consumers

A Examine the applications for marketers (in both the marketing process and in the organization of work within a marketing department) of *any two* of the following theories of motivation:

- Maslow's theory of self-actualization.
- McClelland's theory of need achievement.
- Herzberg's two-factor theory.
- Expectancy theory.
- Equity theory.

B To what extent is Maslow's hierarchy of needs a useful tool for marketers who are looking for new ways to enhance the sales of (a) soft drinks, (b) do-it-yourself tools and accessories, and (c) safari holidays in Africa?

2 Motivating people at work

C There is an ongoing debate about the extent to which compensation, especially pay, is a salesforce motivator. One view, mostly associated with Herzberg, is that earnings do not cause motivation but do cause dissatisfaction if not adequately provided. How far do you agree with this view? What methods would you use in order to obtain optimum performance from a salesforce, and how would these methods be related to specific theories of motivation?

D Describe the Hawthorne experiments. What is their significance for our understanding of behaviour in organizations in the 1990s and beyond?

E To what extent can it be argued that money is the principal (if not the sole) motivating factor determining the work behaviour of (a) sales/ marketing managers and (b) sales representatives?
What other considerations help to explain the motivation of these particular types of employee?

3 Motivation research

F Comment on the view that the problem with projective techniques is that convincing proof of their validity is lacking and too much depends on the interpretation given by the researcher. To the extent that the criticism is valid, how might it be overcome?

G Why is it so difficult to find out the reasons and motives behind consumer purchasing decisions? Outline some of the methods used by marketers in an attempt to overcome these difficulties.

4 Motivation (general)

H In the film *Wall Street*, Gordon Gekko, an unscrupulous corporate raider, asserts that 'greed, for lack of a better word, is good. Greed is right. Greed works . . . Greed in all its forms: greed for life, for money, for love, knowledge, has marked the upward surge of mankind.' How far do you think that Gekko has captured the essence of human motivation, and how do his views compare with the observations of the major motivation theorists?

I Discuss the extent to which Maslow's hierarchy of needs can be used in practice (a) as a tool for motivating employees in a marketing department, and (b) as a tool for marketing analysis and planning.

Sources

Bartol, K. M. and Martin, D. C. (1991) *Management*, McGraw-Hill.
BPP (1991) *Behavioural Aspects of Marketing*, BPP.
Buchanan, D. A. and Huczynski, A. A. (1985) *Organisational Behaviour*, Prentice-Hall.
Engel, J. F., Blackwell, R. D. and Miniard, P. W. (1990) *Consumer Behaviour* (6th edn.), Dryden.
Hawkins, D. I., Best, R. J. and Coney, K. A. (1989). *Consumer Behaviour: Implications for Marketing Strategy* (4th edn.), Irwin.

Herzberg, F., Mausner, B. and Snyderman, B. B. (1959) *The Motivation to Work*, Wiley.

Kakabadse, A., Ludlow, R. and Vinnicombe, S. (1987) *Working in Organizations*, Penguin.

Peter, J. P. and Olson, J. C. (1990) *Consumer Behaviour and Marketing Strategy* (2nd edn.), Irwin.

Packard, V. (1957) *The Hidden Persuaders*, Penguin.

Turton, R. (1991) *Behaviour in a Business Context*, Chapman & Hall.

Watson, T. J. (1986) *Management, Organisation and Employment Strategy*, Routledge & Kegan Paul.

Williams, K. C. (1981) *Behavioural Aspects of Marketing*, Heinemann.

7 And how it shows

Attitudes and marketing – what they are, how we measure them and how they may be changed

Introduction

This is an important area of study for marketers – mainly because of the assumed link between attitudes and behaviour. The chapter has three subsections. It deals firstly with a general view of attitudes and some of the theories associated with them. Next it looks at the problems and techniques of measuring attitudes. Lastly it focuses on the central problem of how we may change or influence attitudes.

Learning objectives

At the end of this chapter the reader should be clear about, and able to relate to, examples from the marketing field ideas such as:

Theories of Attitudes

$$\text{Attitudes} \rightleftharpoons \text{Behaviour}$$

$$\text{Attitude} = \text{Belief} \times \text{Value}$$

The three elements of attitudes – *Cognitive, Affective and Conative.*
The four functions of attitudes – *instrumental, ego-defensive, value-expressive, knowledge.*
Links to our earlier work on perception, selectivity and expectancy.

- *Balance Theory* – Heider.
- *Congruity Theory* – Osgood and Tannenbaum.
- *Cognitive Dissonance* – Festinger.
- *Fishbein's Theory* – note similarity to expectancy theories of motivation.

Attitude measurement

Awareness, utility and limitations of:

- *Thurstone scale* – ponderous, not much used.
- *Likert scale* – common and relatively easy to design.
- *Osgood Semantic Differential scale* – relatively easy to design and use.
- *Kelly's Repertory Grid* – potentially the most useful

Changing attitudes

Problems of existing attitudes.
Significance of the stage of the product's life cycle.

- *Source factors* – personal attributes, similarity, intentions.
- *Message factors* – discrepancy, half-sided, repetition, fear.
- *Channel factors* – status, reliability
- *Receiver factors* – self-esteem, intelligence, sex.

Throughout this chapter it will be useful to think about current advertising campaigns, many of which will be attempting to change attitudes – think particularly of campaigns which aim solely at attitude change – political parties, green movement, Aids, Channel Tunnel, etc.

Attitudes

A mental and neural state of readiness, organized through experience, exerting a directive or dynamic influence on the individual's response to all objects and situations with which it is related (Allport).

An enduring organization of motivational, emotional, perceptual, and cognitive processes with respect to some aspect of the individual's world (Krech and Crutchfield, 1948).

Certain regularities of an individual's feelings thoughts and predispositions to act toward some aspect of his environment (Secord and Backman, 1969).

An overall evaluation that enables one to respond in a consistently favourable or unfavourable manner with respect to a given object or alternative (Engel *et al.*, 1990).

All the above definitions highlight the fact that attitudes relate to persons, objects or behaviours that are part of the individual's perceptual world. They represent our basic orientation towards the given stimulus and as such form an important part of the way in which people perceive and react to their environments. We have seen earlier (in the chapter on perception) that individuals may *select* what they perceive from the environment. Thus attitudes influence, and are influenced, by our goals, perceptions and motivations.

At an intuitive level the importance of attitudes in marketing seems obvious – if we believe that a product has certain desirable characteristics, it seems probable that we will like the product, and, should the appropriate situation arise, we would purchase the product.

All things being equal, people generally behave in a manner consistent with their attitudes and intentions, certainly, in everyday life we assume that that there is a positive relationship between attitudes and behaviour – we attempt to 'change people's minds' about issues we care about on the assumption that this will result in the behaviour we desire. It is commonly held that attitudes are 'leading variables' to behaviour i.e. attitude change predates and predicts behaviour so we might suggest a relationship such as:

$$\text{Attitude} \rightarrow \text{Behaviour}$$

On the other hand we have all had the experience of indulging in a particular behaviour which has led to outcomes which have formed our attitudes. This suggests that we may also have a relationship:

$$\text{Behaviour} \rightarrow \text{Attitude}$$

The combination is usually represented by the symbol:

$$\text{Attitude} \rightleftharpoons \text{Behaviour}$$

This emphasizes that our attitudes may influence our behaviour, but our behaviour may also, in turn, affect our attitudes, either by changing them or by confirming them. In this sense it is very similar to connectionist learning theory (see Chapter 5) and generally it is agreed that attitudes are learned and are relatively enduring – they do change, but usually only slowly. They imply evaluation and feeling.

Attitudes have three components:

Affective – emotional element may be positive or negative.
Cognitive – knowledge element concerning belief/disbelief.
Conative – predisposition or behaviour tendency element.

Earlier on this page we used the phrase 'if we believe that a product has certain desirable characteristics' – representing the cognitive element of our attitude; we continued 'it seems probable that we will like the product' – representing the affective part; and concluded 'should the appropriate situation arise, we would purchase the product' – representing the conative component.

Think – Identify the cognitive, affective and conative elements of your attitude towards studying behavioural aspects of marketing.

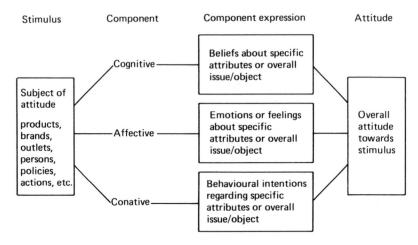

Figure 7.1

We could represent this as shown in Figure 7.2.

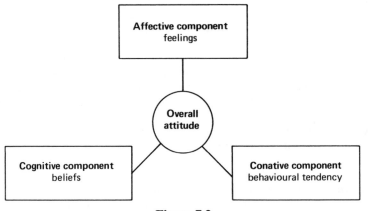

Figure 7.2

An attitude must have all three components and it is this fact that distinguishes it from opinions and beliefs which have no affective or feeling component.

Others have highlighted the importance of the three components by defining an attitude by the expression:

$$\text{Attitude} = \text{Belief} \times \text{Value}$$

This approach (expanded later) bears a marked similarity to expectancy theories of motivation discussed earlier and also the rational model of decision making.

Katz identified four functions underlying the motivational basis of attitudes:

1 *Instrumental or adjustive function* – this is the tendency of people to acquire attitudes which they perceive as being helpful in achieving desired goals, or conversely, avoiding undesired outcomes. Thus they will direct people towards rewarding objects and away from those which are viewed as undesirable.

2 *Ego-defensive function* – this allows people to avoid admitting their inadequacies to themselves in very much the same way as ego-defence mechanisms discussed in Chapter 3. Holding attitudes emphasizing the bad points of another group may enable the individuals to raise their own self-esteem and their perceived status (similar to the Sherif experiments described in Chapter 8).

3 *Value-expressive function* – this allows individuals to express attitudes which are central to their self-concept – the expression of centrally held values which are important to the expression of the individual's personality – in many ways the very opposite of the ego-defensive function.

4 *Knowledge function* – this aspect, Katz claims, allows individuals to use cognitive processes in order to make sense of their world.

All writers are agreed on the conative element (see above) this is sometimes developed as saying that attitudes are leading variables to behaviour. As both managers and marketing specialists we are interested in people's behaviour – this is the reason why the study and measurement of attitudes is of such importance.

Some key ideas about attitudes

Generally attitudes are considered to be a characteristic of an individual personality, less enduring than temperament, but more enduring than a motive or a mood. It is another conceptual invention or hypothetical construct (like intelligence, personality, motivation) in that attitudes cannot be directly observed – so their study is fraught with many of the problems outlined in Chapter 1.

Think – Can attitudes be inferred from behaviour?
– Can we believe what respondents tell us when we ask attitudinal questions?
– Are attitudes actually predictors of behaviour? etc.

---

1 Attitudes – attitudes exist in relation to specific objects, persons, issues or activities. In the marketing context we may be concerned with any of these categories – the objects may be products we are seeking to sell; the persons may be politicians or pop stars; the issues may be environmental, political or matters of belief; the activities may be anything from selling holidays to not wearing real fur. In effect our attitudes can act as an automatic response to the stimulus – someone mentions a political party and most of us know where we stand with regard to that party.

> **Think** – On what topics do you hold strong attitudes?

2 Attitudes – one of the major ways we recognize attitudes is in the ways in which different people are polarized by the attitudes thay hold – drinkers commonly hold a positive attitude towards alcohol while many religions hold that the consumption of alcohol is wrong.

> **Think** – Which of the attitudes you listed for (1) above were positive and which were expressed as negatives?

3 Attitudes – another important dimension of attitudes is their strength. A person may have a negative attitude towards a particular brand of coffee – but it may not be strong enough to prevent that person from accepting a cup of the brew when visiting a neighbour. We may have attitudes about many things, but only some will be held with strong conviction – others will be held with less confidence. The evidence is that those attitudes we hold with high confidence are the ones which can be most relied on to guide our behaviour, and are the ones which are most difficult to change. Some attitudes are simple 'I like . . .' reactions, whereas others are much more complex. This must be borne in mind when attempting to measure attitudes.

> **Think** – Which of the attitudes you listed do you hold with most confidence?
> – Which do you hold as less significant?.

4 Attitudes – we have developed our attitudes as a result of prior experience. Many attitudes can be traced back to our childhood experiences and so we accept that the family is a major shaper of attitudes which may last a lifetime. However, as marketers we commonly wish to change the attitudes of our consumers, so we will concentrate on environmental factors such as the volume and quality of the information and experience available or required to influence the consumers.

> **Think** – How did you learn these attitudes?
> – How did they arise?

5 Attitudes – many attitudes that we hold are part of our make-up for long periods of time. They are both persistent and difficult to change.

> **Think** – Which attitudes have remained unaltered when you look back at yourself five years ago?

6 Attitudes – despite (5) above, another characteristic of attitudes is that they can and do change over time. Perhaps the biggest problem for the marketer is controlling the timing, nature and direction of any change.

> **Think** – Which attitudes of yours have changed when you look back at yourself five years ago?

Consistency approaches

1 Balance theory (Heider)
This considers the situation where person *A* receives positive or negative information from person *B* about an object. This results in either balanced or imbalanced attitude systems as illustrated in Figure 7.3.

Faced with imbalance the theory suggests that the individual will seek to reduce the tension by

a changing his/her attitude to the person
b changing his/her attitude to the object

and thus establishing a balanced situation.

2 Congruity theory (Osgood and Tannenbaum)
Again this considers positive and negative attitudes but this time it attempts to measure the strength and resultant of the attitudinal forces. Normally ratings are made on a scale running from $+3$ (highly favourable) to -3 (highly unfavourable). Congruity refers to the consistency of attitudes and suggests that we may be able to predict the outcome when a known person gives information about a known object. If we have a discrepancy (as described above in balance theory) then this will result in both attitudes shifting, but the outcome will be dependent on their relative strengths.

In the example shown in Figure 7.4 a negative attitude X_1 towards, say milk, is countered by endorsement of milk by Linford Christie, an Olympic sprint champion, who is valued by the respondent positively (X_2). The outcome, 0, according to this theory lies midway between the two – the attitude to milk improving to neutral, while the resultant attitude towards Linford Christie has declined by the same amount to neutral. Thus, equal strengths of attitudes leads to equal shift.

In the example however, in Figure 7.5, the positive attitude towards the endorser is stronger than the dislike of the object. In this case the theory

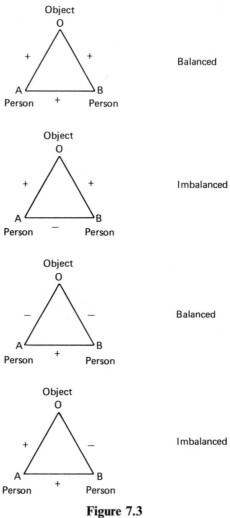

Figure 7.3

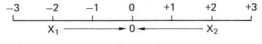

Figure 7.4

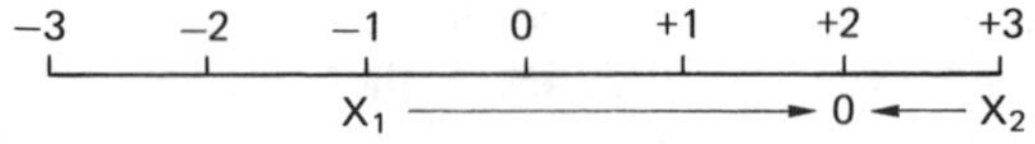

Figure 7.5

predicts the outcome (0) as shown. Thus unequal strengths of attitudes leads to a greater shift towards the more strongly held attitude.

It clearly matters how much the person believes the individual and the information given – it also suggests that changing attitudes has a cost in terms of the attitude to the teller. This assumption may not hold up if the change in attitude results in a change in behaviour which then gives satisfaction (i.e. following on from our earlier example, if I try milk as a result of the endorsement and find it an unexpectedly pleasant experience, I may not hold Linford Christie in less esteem).

3 Cognitive dissonance (Festinger)

This is based on the assumption that attitudes held by an individual tend to be consistent and they are consistent with his/her behaviour. Festinger's approach deals with post-decision (purchase) inconsistencies that arise when positive and negative attitudes to different elements have had to be weighed as part of the decision. Following a decision, information about the positive features of a rejected alternative will generate dissonance – similarly, information about negative features of the chosen alternative will also cause dissonance. The magnitude of this dissonance will be proportional to:

1 the significance of the decision;
2 the attractiveness of the rejected alternative;
3 the number of negative characteristics of the choice made;
4 the number of options considered.

The theory argues that we are uncomfortable with this dissonance and will seek to minimize it by:

1 changing our mind/decision;
2 concentrating on positive features of chosen option;
3 ignoring/devaluing information about negative features;
4 focusing on negative information about the rejected alternatives;
5 changing attitudes;
6 consciously avoiding exposure to potentially dissonant information e.g. by reading only newspapers which reflect our pre-existing attitudes (see also the discussion of selective exposure in Chapter 4);
7 denigrating and devaluing the source of the dissonant information e.g. we may ascribe characteristics of prejudice, ignorance or evil intent to those who hold differing views. Examples abound in the field of politics and we have similar reactions from smokers to the evidence about the dangers of smoking when produced by anti-smoking organizations such as ASH (see also the discussion of projection in Chapter 3).

As our attitudes are very much part of our self concept, it is not surprising that the reactions to cognitive dissonance bear a strong similarity to defence mechanisms as reviewed in our chapter on personality.

4 Fishbein model
This is summarized by the formula

$$A_o = \Sigma \, B_1 \, a_1$$

where A_o = the attitude towards object o,
B_1 = the strength of belief i about o,
a_1 = the evaluation aspects of B,
n = the number of beliefs.

Here evaluations of different aspects can cancel one another out – it is called a compensating model and has a marked similarity to expectancy theories and models of behaviour. Williams (1981) uses the example displayed in Figure 7.6.

Car attribute	Importance B_1	Evaluation a_1	Product B_1, a_1
Speed	1	4	4
Style	2	5	10
Price	3	3	9
Prestige	1	1	1

Total = Σ = 24

Figure 7.6

The success of this approach depends on choosing the relevant attributes to measure – but it can identify the important ones in the eye of the respondent.

The same author put forward what is known as the Extended Fishbein Model:

$$A{-}act = \Sigma \, b_1 \, e_1$$

where A–act = individual's attitude towards performing a specific act,
b_1 = individual's belief that performing act will lead to consequence i;
e_1 = individual's evaluation of consequence i,
n = number of salient consequences involved.

Again the similarity to expectancy theory (Chapter 6) is to be noted. However, the link between attitude and behaviour is not as clear as some theorists would have us believe. Many of us have had experience of persons who have very poor attitudes to, say, bosses or teachers, but whose behaviour does not live up to their words!

Peter and Olson (1990) in reviewing the relationship between measured behavioural intentions and observed behaviour, identify seven factors that reduce or weaken the predictive power:

1 *Intervening time* – the longer the time that elapses between the measure and the actual behaviour, the greater the opportunity for other factors to occur. These may modify or change the original intention so that the observed behaviour no longer matches the stated intention.

2 *Different levels of specificity* – when measuring intention the questions need to be specific and at the same level as the observed behaviour, otherwise the relationship may be damaged. I may hold strong views on the discomfort of wearing ties – but you may observe me on a day when I am going for a job interview and consciously decided that a T-shirt was inappropriate dress for the occasion!

3 *Unforeseen environmental events* – you intend to purchase a particular brand, but your car breaks down and you are unable to go shopping – or, alternatively, when you do get there the shop is sold out and so you make do with a substitute brand.

4 *Unforeseen situational context* – it is possible that the situation that the respondents envisaged when expressing their behavioural intention was not the same as the situation at the time of the behaviour. I may express the intention not to purchase Brand *X* of beer because I view it as rather cheap and less enjoyable than my favourite German lager – however, faced with providing the drinks for a party to which many of my students are coming, the attraction of cheapness may overcome my preference – so I do purchase Brand *X* (in bulk!)

5 *Degree of voluntary control* – some factors may be outside of our control – I intend to take my family out for a picnic this weekend – in the event it may be pouring with rain, I may feel ill, etc.

6 *Stability of intentions* – some intentions are founded on beliefs and attitudes that are both strongly held and stable over long periods of time (e.g. I do not smoke, I do not eat meat, etc.), these give rise to stable intentions and generally more predictable behaviour. Other behaviour may stem from much less strongly held attitudes and less important beliefs (e.g. I like these trousers) and these are much less dependable.

7 *New information* – I may receive information about important consequences of behaviour which leads to changes in my beliefs and attitudes towards the behaviour, and hence my intention. So my original intention no longer accurately predicts my eventual behaviour. Examples could include AIDS education regarding safe sex or changing my intention to buy a particular second-hand car when I heard that it had been stolen.

To this list we can add a number of other possible reasons for attitudes and behaviour not coinciding:

- Lack of need for the object.
- Joint decision making – taking a partner's wishes into account may give rise to compromise purchases which reflect neither party's attitudes!
- Inaccurate/incomplete measures of cognition or effect.

This leads us directly to the problem of assessing attitudes.

Attitude measurement

The assessment of the differences in attitude both within and between people means that we need some form of measurement that is both reliable and valid. As we saw in Chapter 1, reliability is to do with consistency or stability; and validity is concerned with whether we are measuring what we wish to measure (or, indeed, what we think we are measuring).

Thurstone scale

One of the earliest techniques of attitude measurement was developed by L. L. Thurstone (1929). In this approach it is believed that, for any given object, a series of statements can be constructed which range from the extremely favourable to the extremely unfavourable. The statements represent positions along the whole continuum with equal intervals between them. The measure should allow the investigator to discriminate between people in the degree to which they differ on the issue/object.

The process for devising a Thurstone scale is as follows:

1 Collect a large number of statements expressing as many variations of positive and negative feelings about the issue/object. This may be done by literature review, interview or imagination on the part of the experimenter.

2 Give the statements to a large number of judges (making sure that these judges are representative of the population of subjects to be assessed) and ask them to sort each statement into one of eleven piles representing equal steps of evaluation from extremely negative through to extremely positive.

3 Number the piles from one to eleven and the average score assigned by the judges is calculated for each statement. This becomes the 'scale value' of that statement.

4 Discard statements where there is wide discrepancy over the categories into which the judges have placed them.

5 Run a pilot study with subjects to check 'user friendliness' and face validity.

6 Choose a set of approximately twenty statements representing more or less equally spaced values to cover the whole range of the attitude scale.

7 Administer the scale of statements to the subject group with the instruction that they are to mark all statements with which they agree. The individual's attitude score is obtained by calculating the mean value of the items endorsed. For example if a respondent ticked three statements which had scale values of 7.7, 8.0 and 8.3, the person would be allocated an attitude score of 8.0.

Comment – this is relatively ponderous and time-consuming as a process. As there is a degree of avaraging, it is possible for the same score to arise from several different attitudinal patterns. There is a significant problem regarding the apparently equal interval which may only represent the views of the sample of people used as judges. A final problem lies in identifying and choosing the items which discriminate most effectively.

Likert scales

One of the most popular measurement techniques is that credited to Professor Rensis Likert (1932). It is relatively straightforward to understand and is in common usage – a statement is made and the respondents indicated the degree to which they agree/disagree with it. For example we might use the statement 'Obtaining the CIM certificate is the best way to advance a career in marketing'. The subjects are asked which of the five ratings shown in Figure 7.7 they agree with, the numerical value indicating the weight attached to the response. In this case, instead of the weighting being done by the investigator (as with the Thurstone scale), the respondents choose their own degree of agreement with the statement. The total score of the subject is the sum of the values given to all the statements on the issue under consideration.

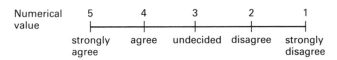

Figure 7.7

The process for devising a Likert scale is as follows:

1 Collect a large pool of statements about the issue/object.

2 For each statement, decide whether it represents a positive or negative attitude towards the issue/object. Discard any statements which appear ambiguous or neutral.

3 Run a pilot study of statements applied to a representative group who are asked to respond on the 1–5 scale as described above.

4 Score the results – strong agreement with favourable items is given a score of 5, strong disagreements a score of 1. The scoring is reversed for unfavourable statements.

5 Calculate the preliminary attitude score by summing across all of the respondent's item scores. For a set of 100 statements the scores will lie between a maximum of 500 and a minimum of 100 (the higher the score, the more positive the attitude).

6 Check each item for internal consistency. This means that the more favourable a person's attitude, the more likely is the endorsement of favourable statements and the less likely is the endorsement of unfavourable statements. The correlation is calculated for each item between its endorsement and the overall attitude score. The relationship may be illustrated as in Figure 7.8.

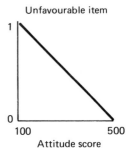

Figure 7.8

7 Choose the twenty or so items with the highest correlations (or the most discriminating) to define the attitude scale.

8 Administer the scale to the subject group and score as described in (d) above.

Comment – this is generally seen as being simpler to construct than the Thurstone scale. It also appears likely to be as (or more) reliable. It has high face validity in that it deals directly with the individual's response to the statement made. Even more than the Thurstone scale, this approach can provide an attitude score which can be arrived at by strikingly different patterns of response.

Semantic differential

This approach is associated with C. E. Osgood and was originally put forward in 1957 in a book jointly written with G. J. Suci and P. H. Tannenbaum. In its original form the authors were investigating the nature of meaning, but it has become widely used in the measurement of attitudes.

Osgood argues that as the basic function of ordinary language is the communication of meaning, ordinary language can be used to discriminate and differentiate between concepts and also to measure their meaning. The respondent is given a number of bipolar adjectives, each with a seven-point scale inserted between the opposites, so that the given topics, objects or issues can be assessed on each scale. This allows the respondent to indicate both the direction and intensity of each judgement.

Try the semantic differential in Figure 7.9 using yourself as the subject.

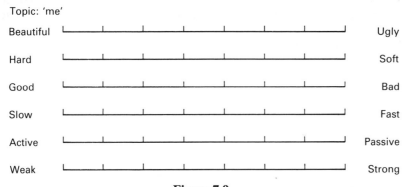

Figure 7.9

The person completing the questionnaire rates each object or concept on each scale – thus producing a profile for each concept.

Try another assessment using the same scales but this time using your 'ideal self' as the subject (see Figure 7.10).

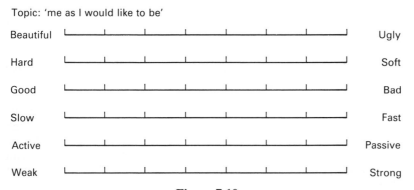

Figure 7.10

Generally it is assumed that concepts are similar in meaning to the extent to which their profiles are similar. The degree to which two profiles are similar is measured by the generalized distance formula

$$D = \Sigma d_i{}^2$$

where D represents the *dis*imilarity between the two concepts, d_i is the difference in the ratings on the 'i'th scale. The squared differences are summed across the N scales being used to rate the two concepts.

Transfer the profile from below on to the scales above and work out the generalized distance for the two concepts.

> **Think** – How does your distance compare with others in your group?
> – On which scales did you have the greatest difference?

Osgood and his fellow workers, in a large number of studies involving both different scales and different concepts, used the technique of factor analysis and identifed three basic dimensions underlying semantic differential ratings. The dimensions are:

- evaluation
- potency, and
- activity.

The *evaluative* dimension is characterized by scales such as:

good – bad
clean – dirty
beautiful – ugly

the *potency* element by scales such as:

large – small
strong – weak
thick – thin

and the *activity* factor by scales such as:

fast – slow
active – passive
hot – cold

The emergence of three dimensions is convenient in that it allows us to imagine the attitude mapped into a three-dimensional space – so most people find the concept of attitude difference or shift relatively straightforward to visualize. This aids the description of difference or change so a person's attitude regarding a product may have shifted to see the product as being, for example, more potent, less active, but much better.

The process for devising a semantic differential scale is as follows:

1 Make a selection of bipolar adjectives ensuring that the two adjectives at the extremes are really opposed (or opposite) to each other.

2 Run a pilot with a representative sample group of subjects, asking them to rate the issue(s)/object(s) on each scale.

3 Score each scale from $+3$ to -3, with positive scores assigned to the positive end of the scale (note: if it is not clear which is the positive end, eliminate that scale).

4 Sum the scores across all evaluative scales and this value, or the average score, is taken as an index of attitude.

5 Test for internal consistency by the same process as described in the Likert scale above (item 6) and only scales with both high correlation and an evaluative element are retained.

6 This set of five to ten items constitutes a semantic differential scale for the measurement of attitudes towards the issue/object in question.

Comment – this is an interesting approach which has some useful factors. The theory suggests that there are three main dimensions – evaluation, potency and activity. This may provide useful information for the marketer in determining the focus of marketing messages aiming to either reinforce or change attitudes. The notion of three dimensions is a happy one as it allows us to imagine an attitude being defined in three dimensional space, which also allows a visual representation for attitude change.

Repertory grid

As we saw in Chapter 4, Kelly's repertory grid technique can be used to map an individual's perceptual space. The same approach can be used to compare attitudes towards products or brands. The grid is administered in the same fashion as described in the 'perception' chapter, but this time using relevant products or brands as the elements.

In the earlier chapter we praised this technique as being personal in attempting to describe an individual's perceptions. This may pose a problem, however, if we are wishing to measure the attitudes of a large number of people – they may all see the world differently!

One way around the problem is to elicit repertory grids from a representative sample of respondents in the manner described in Chapter 4. We can then take the (say) eight most popular constructs to emerge and form a grid which is applied to the respondent group in which we are interested. This has the effect of increasing the generality of the technique (albeit at the expense of diminishing its individuality).

Analysis is still possible in terms of the 'distances' between constructs (useful for designing the marketing message) and the 'distances' between the elements (in this case competing products), so it can be used to identify competitors.

Perhaps more importantly we can begin to focus our marketing message on different groups or clusters which we may have identified, emphasizing the 'positive' points as elicited by the grid. Alternatively we could attempt to design attitude change strategies in order to make our brand more attractive to the other groups of respondents who do not perceive our product positively.

Attitude change

If we accept the proposition that attitudes and behaviour are linked then, as marketers, we will be very concerned with the process of changing attitudes – normally we will be concerned with enhancing positive views of our own product although there can be examples where we may be more interested in downgrading attitudes towards competitors or 'the opposition'.

> **Think** – What examples do you have have of negative attitude change as an objective of the marketer/advertiser?

Earlier in the chapter the inter-relation of the cognitive, affective and conative elements of attitude were discussed. This can be a useful framework for looking at change strategies as it is possible to initiate change through attending to any one of the three components.

Attitude change via cognitions

Here we focus on the beliefs about the attributes of the product. We may aim to:

1 change these beliefs, and/or
2 change the relative importance of existing beliefs, and/or
3 develop new beliefs, and/or
4 change the beliefs regarding the attributes of the 'ideal'.

The UK governement has published a number of reports on diet and health over the last decade and is attempting to change attitudes through what we might call 'cognitive restructuring' of our attitudes towards what we eat. Some years ago it was commonly believed that potatoes and pasta were fattening. This belief has been 'attacked' by the message that carbohydrates are 'energy food' for athletes. Similarly the relative importance of fibre in the diet has been emphasized. New beliefs about sources of protein and other essentials have been developed so that (e.g.) vegetarianism is becoming both more widespread and more acceptable. Lastly our image of the 'ideal' is being manipulated – women have 'suffered' for years from the 'thin is beautiful' message, men are now being pushed to 'fight the flab', wives to feel guilty about having 'chubby hubbies' and athletes such as Linford Christie are promoting semi-skimmed milk.

While we may start with cognitions, the aim is to change the overall attitude. We hope for possible sequences between the stages in Figure 7.11.

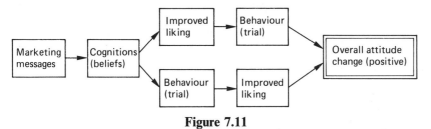

Figure 7.11

> **Think** – Identify some other campaigns which have focused on cognitions as the route to attitude change.
> – Which strategies did they follow?

Attitude change via effects

It is quite feasible to attempt to influence consumers' liking of a product without directly impacting either their beliefs or their behaviour. Here the logic is that increased liking will lead to more positive beliefs which might lead to product purchase. Alternatively, increased liking may lead to purchase. This, in turn, will alter the consumer's experience base and may lead to more positive beliefs about the product. Diagrammatically this can be represented by Figure 7.12.

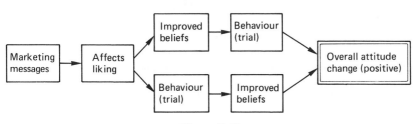

Figure 7.12

Engel, Blackwell and Miniard use the phrase 'transformational' to describe advertising aimed at 'making the experience of using the product richer, warmer, more exciting, and/or more enjoyable than that obtained solely from an objective description of the advertised brand'. The advertisements 'transform' the value derived from product consumption by influencing consumers' perceptions of the product's emotional and symbolic features.

There are a number of approaches possible when aiming for effect change – classical conditioning, effect towards the advertisement, and repetition/exposure.

Classical conditioning. It is possible to use the classical conditioning methods (see Chapter 5) by consistently pairing the brand name with a stimulus that the subject likes. Several current examples use music as the positive stimulus (Hamlet cigars linked with the tranquillity of a Bach aria, Vauxhall cars with an Eric Clapton tune etc). The assumption is that, over a period of time, the positive feelings associated with the established stimuli will transfer to the product (Engel *et al*, 1990, pp. 440–441).

Effect towards the advertisement. Producing an advertisement that is liked in its own right is thought to increase the tendency to like the product. A word of caution needs to struck, however, as there is evidence that 'cult' adverts sometimes fail to make the linkage with the product. Earlier we used the example of the series of advertisements starring Joan Collins and the late Leonard Rossiter which attracted a huge following. Unfortunately follow-up research showed that most viewers were quite uncertain as to whether the product advertised was Martini or Cinzano! The use of humour, celebrities and emotion are all discussed later in the chapter.

Repetition/exposure. There is some evidence to suggest that mere exposure on a regular basis may, in itself, be enough to improve effect or liking although this seems to be most appropriate for low-involvement products.

The implications for the advertiser of adopting an attitude change via affect approach are of some interest:

● classical conditioning approaches give the most appropriate guidelines,
● attitudes towards the advertisement itself seem to be important,
● the advertisements need not contain any factual/cognitive information,
● repetition is critical,
● new measures of advertisement effectiveness may need to be developed.

> **Think** – Identify some other campaigns which have focused on effects as the route to attitude change.
> – Which strategies did they follow?

Attitude change via behaviour

It is quite possible for purchase to precede the development of either cognition or effect, particularly low-cost, low-involvement products – the process is often one of active experimentation on the part of the consumer (I'll try this . . .). In this instance the actions are very much as described under operant conditioning in Chapter 5, so the first problem for the marketer is to induce the individual to purchase or try the product. Free samples, point of sale displays, coupons, price reductions and special promotions are the main techniques used for inducing trial. This time the process may look like that in Figure 7.13.

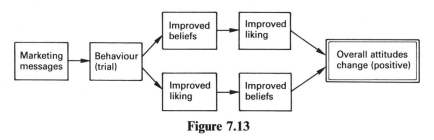

Figure 7.13

> **Think** – Identify some other campaigns which have focused on behaviour as the route to attitude change.
> – What strategies did they follow?

Factors affecting attitude change

There are six broad categories of factor which influence the ease or difficulty of changing attitudes. They are:

1 existing attitudes,
2 source factors,
3 message features,
4 channel of communication,
5 receiver attributes,
6 product characteristics.

We shall examine each of these in turn.

1 Existing attitudes

The process of attitude formation is based primarily on either primary (first hand), or secondary experience (passed on from advertisers, parents, friends, etc.). The presence of pre-existing attitudes makes the process of change rather more difficult due to the commitment of the individual to the existing attitude. Generally the higher the commitment, and the more strongly held the attitude, the harder becomes the task of attitude change.

We saw when we reviewed Osgood and Tannenbaum's congruity theory that where there is a conflict between two attitudes, the resultant attitude tends to have moved more in the direction of the stronger held attitude. This may in part be a reason why it is hard to get people to stop smoking – if they have a lot of self image invested in the activity it will be difficult to get them to change attitude. Festinger's Theory of Cognitive Dissonance also focuses on this same issue and most of the discussion in the preceding section is directly relevant to the change process. Attitudes held due to product experience will also be harder to change than those based on secondary experience (e.g. advertising)

It is interesting to consider the processes involved in political attitude changing as elections draw near. All parties realize that the chances of winning over the voter who is deeply committed to another party are very slight. The committed Tory is unimpressed by Labour's arguments and vice versa. All parties aim to persuade the 'floating voter', the person who does *not* have strongly held attitudes.

Think – Which of your attitudes might be most amenable to change?
– Which might be least?

---

2 Source factors

The source of a message is a very important factor in determining how influential the communication is. It is becoming commonplace to find celebrities endorsing products (often for huge fees) – rock stars such as Michael Jackson and Tina Turner appear in cola commercials, sports stars such as Daley Thomson and John Barnes endorse Lucozade. Sometimes the celebrity explicitly says that the product is great, sometimes implicitly through just appearing (association).

The degree of influence of such appearances appears to be a function of both expertness and trustworthiness – i.e. sports stars should be expert on energy replacement for high levels of performance but, in order to be influential, they should be characters who are trustworthy in the eyes of the consumer (a perception that 'they're only doing it for the money' would tend to discredit the message). Despite this apparently confident and self-evident statement we can be even more impressed by an untrustworthy source arguing against 'own best interest' (e.g. convicted murderer expressing the opinion that the death penalty should be reintroduced).

Credible sources generally aid persuasion – level of knowledge and relevant expertise are both important, but trustworthiness is a key concept – if the source is perceived as being untrustworthy, then expertise/knowledge becomes irrelevant and the message tends to be rejected.

Generally, evidence suggests that the message becomes more persuasive when the source is:

● physically attractive; attractiveness may also be a function of liking the source. A number of studies have suggested that liking the source is an important factor in the persuasiveness of a message – we are more persuaded by those we like than those we dislike;
● a celebrity, or is
● similar to the target audience.

Finding one or two issues of commonality before attempting to change the third has also been found effective on the grounds that the commonality creates some sort of bonding between source and receiver which makes the area of difference harder to sustain. This coincides neatly with Heider's Balance Theory reviewed earlier. This particular approach seems most important when consumers do not engage in high levels of elaboration or mental/cognitive processing activity.

Credibility may also be a function of expectation – several experiments have reported the duping of subjects when the source was introduced authoritatively, and appeared as expected (scientists wear white laboratory coats, doctors also have white coats but with a stethoscope, lecturers often have 'high foreheads' and wear glasses, etc.). Group affiliation may be a follow-on from this point. For change agents to be effective they must be perceived of as being a significant member of the group – the person being influenced should see the change agent as 'one of us'. As we will see groups can exert enormous influence over individuals, both in their behaviour and attitudes.

Think – Which attitudes have you 'modified' in order to be more comfortable within a group or with friends?

---

3 Message features

Messages which are perceived by the receiver as being 'strong' appear to inhibit negative thoughts and encourage positive, and vice versa for weak claims and arguments.

Strength in this context depends on the message being seen as both:

1 relevant to the receiver's situation, and
2 objective i.e. factual as opposed to subjective. Generally we have a problem of interpretation, the price of a product may appear high to one consumer and low to another, so giving the factual price may allow the receivers to make their own judgements. People normally see facts as being open to being checked (even if they do not always check themselves) and evaluated. Facts are also seen as being more believable if they can be verified and under these conditions they create more favourable attitudes.

Early studies found evidence to suggest that significantly greater opinion or attitude change resulted when larger changes were advocated (this may well match with Osgood's Congruity theories above). However there is more recent evidence to suggest that if the change suggested is so extreme as to run counter to the receiver's self-image/concept (and is hence highly involving to the individual) then a move apart may occur. This is in line with what might be expected from our earlier observations on ego-defence mechanisms and perceptual defence.

Claims – Many advertising messages make claims about the product they are promoting. It is interesting to consider briefly the different types of claims that can be made:

1 Search claims ('you'll not find anything cheaper . . .') can be tested before purchase.

2 Experience claims ('using this product will change your life . . .') can only be fully evaluated after purchase.

3 Credence claims ('I believe this is the route to peace and prosperity . . .') may be unevaluatable.

Petty and Cacioppo found that making numerous claims was more important under low elaboration/involvement, but did not matter under high involvement where one 'good' argument could swing the decision/attitude.

1-sided/2-sided. – 2-sided messages put the downside as well as the upside of a product or decision ('you may find cheaper, but you'll not find better . . .') – is perceived as being more truthful than simple one-sided messages. This finding appears to hold good even when the downside argument is relatively weak.

Threat. Karlins and Abelson (1970) conducted an elegant study of attitudes towards tetanus. Different groups were given written descriptions with differing levels of threat/fear inbuilt. Some were told that the disease was 'difficult to control, but relatively easy to cure'; others were told that it was 'easy to contract and difficult to cure'. The high fear group was given coloured photographs and descriptions of death. The effectiveness of inoculation against tetanus was also given. Some were given to understand that injections gave an 'almost perfect' guarantee against tetanus, while others were told that inoculations were generally effective but did not eliminate the possibility of contracting the disease. Some were told that the injection was very painful, others were given no hint of discomfort.

The subjects were later asked about attitudes towards tetanus and inoculation. They were not influenced by evidence of effectiveness or painfulness. They were influenced by fear-arousal. Those who received the high-fear material were more likely both to see the benefits of the vaccine and to take the inoculation.

This study suggests that strong, credible fear messages seem to work! However, Karlins and Abelson also suggested that situational factors may influence the effectiveness of fear as a change agent. They suggest that strong fear appeal is superior to a mild one in changing attitudes when it:

1 poses a threat to the individual's loved ones;

2 is presented by a highly credible source;

3 deals with topics relatively unfamiliar to the individual; and

4 aims at the subjects with a high degree of self-esteem and/or low perceived vulnerability to danger.

Conversely, others have highlighted the importance of subjects' initial concern with the issue. If there is a high initial concern, a fear-arousing communication may overwhelm the individual with anxiety, producing a reduction in the effectiveness of the message perhaps linked with defence mechanisms such as repression and selective perception.

Executional elements. By executional elements advertising specialists refer to the visual image – sounds, colours, pace – used in the advertisement.

It is believed that advertisements that are liked can be effective in changing attitudes and that advertisements that are disliked can lower consumer evaluations of the product. First hand experience casts a few doubts over these assumptions as the writer has found that some advertising campaigns which were perceived as being 'irritating' have worked in as much as brand awareness has certainly been achieved!

This observation might be supported by returning to our comments on the successful marketing of Radion washing powder. Here the brand name has the potential for negative associations – radon (a gas associated with the development of cancer), radium (also linked with cancer), radioactive are all similar sounding words. The manufacturers have done little to suppress such connections – as we have already observed, they have utilized lurid colours on the packaging and posters and linked the product to 'hard' slogans.

Repetition. The importance of repetition has already been mentioned in the chapter on learning and the earlier section of this chapter dealing with effects as the route to attitude change. While repetition is clearly a crucial element in conditioning approaches to attitude change and development, it is not without its drawbacks. Early repetitions can allow better evaluation of the message, but there is evidence to suggest that this reaches a peak and then repetition can become tedious and counter-productive. This does seem to be one of the limitations of using humour in advertisements – few things pall as quickly as the repeated joke!

The distinction appears to be between *repetition* which enhances the impact of the message and *repetitiveness* which is counter-productive. The point at which one turns into the other and tedium sets in, appears to depend on the degree of mental processing that has gone on and the amount of evaluation that has occurred.

4 Channel of communication

Some channels of communication are perceived as being more authoritative than others; reports carried in some newspapers carry more weight than those published in less prestigious journals.

It has been interesting over the years to see the way in which ITN has 'come from behind' so that it is currently not perceived of as being any less authoritative than BBC news. Similarly, some people see the written word as carrying more authority than the spoken word. Television, with its ability to present words, images and written material is hence one of the most potent and versatile of the advertising media.

5 Receiver attributes

Motivation. This has been dealt with extensively in Chapter 6. It may also help to think in terms of utilitarian or hedonic motives with the obvious implications for sending utilitarian or hedonic messages. Needless to say, it is not a simple either/or choice – many products have both characteristics and the advertising for products such as cars and houses reflects both themes of motives.

Arousal. Here we are revisiting some of our earlier work on awareness and attention from Chapter 4. Clearly, people will be unlikely to be much influenced by messages they do not even recognize. Conversely, high levels of arousal or excitement can distort perception considerably. This gives rise to a situation which may be best represented by Figure 7.14.

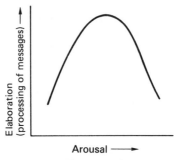

Figure 7.14

This inverted-U highlights the need for enough arousal to make it work and the avoidance of high levels of arousal which may lead to an inability to concentrate on the message. As we might expect, elaboration is highest at moderate levels of arousal. High arousal consumers appear to be more affected by the celebrity of the source.

The advertisement itself can affect the level of arousal – affective messages catch the attention quite well and may, in this way, lead to arousal (or in the case of adverts such as Hamlet cigars, lower arousal). This whole area has some interesting implications for advertisement placement – buying television advertising space during sports events may catch a high number of potential consumers, but the nature of the message may need to be considered if the audience is likely to be in a high state of excitement.

Knowledge. Engel, Blackwell and Miniard argue that knowledgeable consumers are better able to evaluate technical messages (and, in the process, to be more influenced by them). They also suggest that consumer knowledge allows sounder judgement of the strengths and weaknesses of the claims.

Mood. There is some evidence to suggest that the mood in which a consumer receives a message affects the likelihood of change. The suggestion is that being in a 'favourable' mood can help/enhance persuasion while unfavourable moods inhibit persuasion. We also have the notion of arousal (see above). The main messages for the marketer seem to be either the creation of appropriate moods to go with the message (Hamlet cigars using Bach) or alternatively placing your advertisement in an appropriate context (e.g. the choice of magazine, or the placing of a television commercial in the midst of a specific play, soap, sporting event, etc.).

Personality traits. The need for cognition seems to be closely related to the notion of 'elaboration' developed above, and, as might be expected from such ideas the evidence points to persons with high cognition needs (high elaboration) being more influenced by message claims. Individuals with lower cognition needs (low elaboration) are more influenced by peripheral cues. Another dimension of personality that appears to influence attitude change is that of self-monitoring. Persons who are high on such scales are likely to be adept at adjusting to situations and they tend to be more influenced by 'style' or 'image' advertising. Those who are low on the dimension are less likely to change their behaviour and are more influenced by quality messages with higher factual content.

6 Product characteristics

Stage in product life cycle is clearly of relevance where new products focus on awareness and trial. Brand image becomes the focus during growth, maintenance of 'good' attitudes is the objective at maturity. Similarly awareness set analysis (see Chapter 4) may highlight the need to make the consumer aware of the organization/product (e.g. Cornhill Insurance sponsoring Test match cricket). If the product is in the evoked set then maintenance of positive attitudes becomes the target, while placement in the inept set signals that the need for attitude change approaches.

Product experience may well exert more influence than advertising.

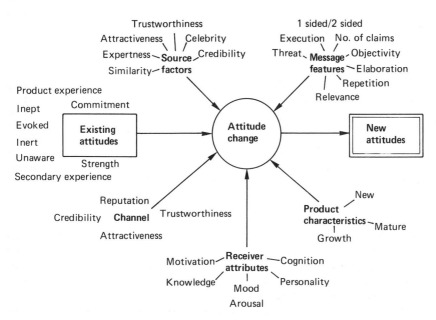

Figure 7.15

Product positioning – the image desired for the product will determine to a great extent the nature of the attitude change attempted and the type of message that is appropriate (e.g. the cut price, good value product will use different messages to the status symbol).

Relative performance (relative to competitors) may define appropriate messages – if your product is superior then use the facts as the message, if not, alternative strategies need to be employed, more fuzzy, subjective, affective advertising copy may need to be used.

Chapter summary exercises

Think – How can the material in this chapter be applied to the marketing of:

> camcorders
> the social policy of a political party
> skis
> holidays
> soft drinks
> instant coffee
> sports shoes (trainers)
> razors
> hair colourant
> toothpaste
> shampoo
> motor cars
> low-fat/low cholesterol/low salt spread
> sanitary protection
> kitchen equipment
> spirits and liqueurs
> low-alcohol wine
> a restaurant
> newspapers
> toilet tissue
> bicycles

Think – How *has* my organization used attitude theory?

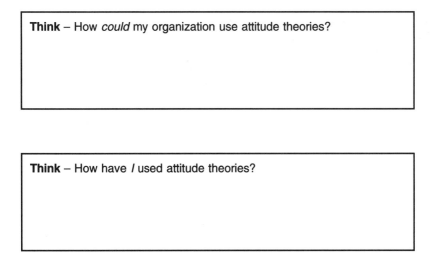

Think – How *could* my organization use attitude theories?

Think – How have *I* used attitude theories?

Some 'typical' examination questions – attitudes

1 Attitude theory

A What is the relationship between attitudes *and* behaviour?

B 'The concept of cognitive dissonance is absolutely crucial to an adequate understanding of consumer behaviour.' Discuss.

C What are the main characteristics of an 'attitude'? How is an attitude formed and in what ways do attitudes typically relate to behaviour?

2 Attitude measurement

D Examine some of the problems associated with attitude measurement, and critically assess no more than three techniques which, in your view, overcome some of the difficulties.

E 'The major problem involved in attempting to predict behaviour on the basis of attitudes held is that attitudes, whilst being important, are not the sole determining factor.'
What in practice are the other influences on behaviour? Given the presence of these other influences, how can attitudes be reliably measured?

F What is the relationship between 'attitudes' and 'behaviour'? What function do attitudes perform in determining an individual's motives, and why is the measurement of attitudes a critical issue for marketers?

3 Attitude change

G A communication system can be analysed in terms of variables such as the source, the message, the channel, and the receiver(s). Using examples of either introducing a new political policy, or changing people towards a healthier diet to illustrate your points, show how marketers utilize this sequence in order to change attitudes and thereby influence consumer behaviour.

H Explain how attitude change might be tackled using either the cognitive element, the affective element or the conative element as the starting point. Illustrate your answer with examples from your experience.

Sources

Allport, G. W. (1989) 'The historical background of modern social psychology', in *Handbook of Social Psychology*, Addison-Wesley.

Bannister, D. and Fransella, F. (1977) *Inquiring Man*, Penguin.

BPP (1991), *Behavioural Aspects of Marketing*, BPP.

Buchanan, D. A. and Huczynski, A. A. (1985) *Organisational Behaviour*, Prentice-Hall.

Engel, J. F., Blackwell, R. D. and Miniard, P. W. (1990), *Consumer Behaviour* (6th edn), Dryden.

Festinger, L. (1959) *A Theory of Cognitive Dissonance*, Harper & Row.

Hawkins, D. I., Best R. J. and Coney, K. A. (1989) *Consumer Behaviour: Implications for Marketing Strategy* (4th edn.), Irwin.

Heider, F. (1958) *The Psychology of Interpersonal Relations*, Wiley.

Kakabadse, A., Ludlow, R. and Vinnicombe, S. (1987) *Working in Organisations*, Penguin.

Karlins, M. and Abelson, H. (1970) *Persuasion*, Crosby Lockwood.

Krech, D. and Crutchfield, R. S. (1948) *Theory and Problems of Social Psychology*, McGraw-Hill.

Oppenheim, A. N. (1966) *Questionnaire Design and Attitude Measurement*, Heinemann.

Osgood, C. E., Suci, G. J. and Tannenbaum, P. H. (1957) *The Measurement of Meaning*, University of Illinois Press.

Peter, J. P. and Olson, J. C. (1990), *Consumer Behaviour and Marketing Strategy* (2nd edn), Irwin.

Petty, R. E. and Cacioppo, J. T, (1987) 'The effects of involvement on responses to argument quantity and quality,' *Journal of Consumer Research*, 14.

Reber, A. S. (1985) *Dictionary of Psychology*, Penguin.

Reeves, T. K. and Harper, D. (1981), *Surveys at Work: a Practitioner's Guide*, McGraw-Hill.

Secord, P. F. and Backman, C. W. (1969) *Social Psychology*, McGraw-Hill.

Williams, K. C. (1981) *Behavioural Aspects of Marketing*, Heinemann.

Part Four

People in Groups

8 'Here we go, here we go, here we go . . .'

Groups and their influence on consumer behaviour

Introduction

Another very important chapter which is concerned with the influence exerted over behaviour by groups and social pressure. It is another subject area that is all around us – we are all part of society and both influence and are inflenced by our social groups. The newspapers regularly carry interesting material – the *Guardian* runs a weekly 'Society' section which often contains relevant and up-to-date material. Keep looking out for 'Is this the end of the family/society/world as we know it?' articles as your course progresses.

At the end of this chapter students should be fully familiar with the following concepts (and the associated language) and *should be able to highlight their relevance to the marketing specialist.*

- Roles, norms, inter-role conflict, intra-role conflict.
- Groups – communication, cohesiveness, conformity,
           – ascribed, acquired, primary, secondary, formal, informal, membership, aspirational, dissociative and reference.
           – processes, formation, development,
           – roles, influence, decision making and leadership.
- Family – importance as socializing agency,
           – importance as a decision making and purchasing unit,
           – traditional family life cycle,
           – 'modernized' family life cycle.

Much of this material is used as a way of segmenting markets – so it is useful to think in terms of differing product types and their interaction with different cultures, groups, ages and so forth. Another useful activity is to establish the habit of analysing advertising messages in terms of their group based content and images.

People in groups

Groups are a basic part of human life. We all come from some sort of family background, we have friends, we work in departments or sections. In Chapter 6 we reviewed Maslow's theories on human motivation and found that he proposed that companionship was a basic human need. So group membership is a common experience for nearly all people and both theory and practice confirm their importance.

Another aspect of group membership is that it usually involves a degree of give-and-take in behavioural terms. We compromise to keep the others happy, or go along with the wishes of the rest when we do not feel strongly about something. In this way groups affect our behaviour.

We will start our review of the subject by considering some of the classic experiments which have highlighted some of the elements of group behaviour.

The Hawthorne Experiments

The famous Hawthorne Experiments were conducted by Professor Elton Mayo at the Western Electric Company in Chicago in the period 1927–32. There were four main studies:

1 The Drawing Office experiment

Here the problem lay in low morale which was blamed on the lighting. Mayo split the department into two – the first group was the experimental group, the second group acted as the control group and their lighting remained unaltered throughout the experiment. When the intensity of the lighting of the experimental group was increased the expected improvement in morale and output occurred. What was unexpected was that the morale and output of the control group rose in exactly the same way. This puzzled Mayo who proceeded to reduce the intensity for the experimental group – output of both groups again rose! His conclusion was that the changed behaviour was nothing to do with the intensity of the lighting, but was a group phenomenon.

2 The Relay Assembly Room experiment

Here a self-selected group of six girls was used. The job consisted of assembling some forty components to produce a small but intricate relay. The production rates of the girls were known and it was thought that the level of production would give a measure of the effectiveness of the changes planned. Throughout this experiment an observer sat with the girls noting all that happened, keeping the girls informed, asking for advice and information and listening to their complaints. Each change was run for a test period of 4-12 weeks. The results are summarized below:

1 Under normal conditions (48 hour week, including Saturdays, no rest pauses) the girls averaged 2400 relays/week each.
2 Put on piecework for 8 weeks – output rose.
3 Two 5 minute rest pauses, a.m. and p.m., introduced for 5 week period – output rose again.
4 Rest pauses increased to 10 minutes – output rose sharply.
5 6 by 5 minute rest pauses introduced – output fell slightly, and the girls complained that it broke their work rhythm.
6 Returned to 2 rest periods, but with hot meal provided free – output rose.
7 Girls finished $\frac{1}{2}$ hour earlier – output went up.
8 Girls finished another $\frac{1}{2}$ hour earlier – output steady.
9 All improvements taken away – returned to original conditions.

This final phase ran for 12 weeks and output was the highest ever recorded at just over 3000 relays/week each! Again the working conditions could not have been the sole determinant of improved performance, and Mayo concluded that this was further evidence of the influence of the group.

3 The Bank Wiring Room experiment

Here Mayo was interested in the section producing telephone equipment. The group were on a production bonus which gave increased earnings for higher output but despite the fact that 7000 units was well within the capability of the group they produced no more and no less than 6000 units per day. The group appeared to have set this arbitrary standard and dealt forcibly (both verbally and physically) with any individual who did not conform to the norm. By interview and observation it was discovered that the workgroup had developed spontaneously into a team with natural leaders (not necessarily coinciding with those put into positions of authority by management) who, within the group, had far more power than the official authorities. This experiment confirmed Mayo's conclusion that the workgroup was, and is, a major determinant of work behaviour (and many of our industrial problems).

4 The interview programme

In this experiment Mayo conducted a non-directive interview programme with the aim of determining what characteristics were common to supervisors of high production groups – the results listed are based on the responses of their subordinates. The characteristics of high producing supervisors were:

1 Under less supervision from their own superiors.
2 Placed less direct emphasis on production as the goal.

3 Encouraged employee participation in decision making.
4 Were more employee-centred.
5 Spent more time on supervision and less on production work.
6 Had greater confidence in their supervisory role.
7 Felt they knew where they stood in relation to the organization.

Although this experiment can be subjected to criticism of its methodology, it is interesting to compare the outcomes with the work of McGregor and Likert in the 1960s which is reviewed in Chapter 11.

The four experiments emphasize the importance of the immediate social group in determining behaviour – in the drawing office and relay assembly experiments the subjects appeared to work harder as the result of some sort of group pressure, while in the bank wiring room the pressure was to limit the rate of work and thus output. So we can conclude that behaviour and attitudes can be influenced directly, and the strength of such pressure is very high – people were actually earning less money than they could have been due to the disciplines exercised by the two informal groups in the bank wiring room.

Mayo's key contribution was to highlight the primary work group as the key to much workplace behaviour. This has important implications for effective management of the organization – and it also emphasizes the prime importance of satisfying the needs of the group.

Additionally, we have the concept of the *'Hawthorne Effect'* where the behaviour of people taking part in an experiment ceases to be typical. This has been examined in some fascinating experiments in the USA – particularly the work of Milgram who found people would do extraordinary things (including apparently causing considerable pain to other human beings) so long as it was part of 'an experiment'.

The power of the group over individual members is considerable, the need to conform and belong being so powerful. Evidence of this power came in a classic experiment conducted by Sherif.

Sherif – the auto-kinetic effect

In 1935 Sherif conducted an experiment in which students were placed in a darkened room. Each student was asked to judge in which direction and how far a spot of light moved. The spot, in fact, remained still and did not move at all – it only appeared to do so (the auto-kinetic effect). Sherif found that under these conditions, each of the subjects developed a range within which they made their estimates.

It also emerged that if an individual made a judgement about the movement of the light in the presence of others, the judgements made were in the same direction and distance of the judgements around them – even if the original estimates, made when alone, were in the opposite direction!

This highlights the great extent to which the individual subject is influenced by the group's judgement and the power of the group to ensure conformity of its members. This experiment and others similar in design have been repeated on many occasions and emphasize the influence that groups can have over an individual's perceptions and behaviour.

Sherif – conflict and co-operation between groups

Sherif carried out a series of experiments in the 1950s which combined field and laboratory methods of investigating group formation and intergroup relations.

The experiments

Boys' camps were chosen as sites for the research on the grounds that (a) they could be controlled and reproduced in the future, and (b) groups formed at summer camp would be informal and made up of boys who were unacquainted prior to the experiment. The subjects selected were similar in background, 'healthy, well-adjusted boys, somewhat above average in intelligence and from stable, white, Protestant, middle-class homes'. The experimental situations were kept lifelike by choosing activities typical of such camps, including canoeing, but usually requiring obstacles to be overcome first.

Data collection methods were disguised or made a natural aspect of the setting. Several methods were used at each step for checking and cross-validation. The experiments were designed in successive stages, each lasting about one week. Stage 1 was focused on group formation, Stage 2 on the development of conflict between the groups and Stage 3 on the resolution and reduction of conflict.

Stage 1: Group formation
Two groups were created and the first stage was characterized by the formation of status and role relationships and norms within the two separate groups. Tasks were given and soon leaders and lieutenants began to emerge. Observer ratings and informal opinions from the boys indicated when the group had established some form of structure. Sociograms ('maps' of who liked and disliked who) were constructed on the basis of these observations. As the groups established themselves, rituals, secret symbols, nicknames and group names were adopted.

Stage 2: Intergroup conflict
Activities where only one group could achieve its goal (and that at the expense of the others) such as tug-of-war, baseball, etc. were introduced. This gave rise to rivalry and animosity between the groups, often to the extent that a subject who once gave another boy in the opposing group a 'best friend' rating, now gave him a negative rating. What became a significant outcome was the clear sign that the effect of the inter-group

conflict was to increase solidarity, co-operativeness and morale *within* each group, while generating a dislike of outsiders.

Stage 3: Reduction of conflict

This stage was devoted to reducing the conflict created in Stage 2. At first, events were organized that involved pleasant contact between the groups, but which did not require interdependence; instead of reducing conflict, these situations provided opportunities for further hostilities.

Events requiring mutual assistance were then introduced. The 'super-ordinate goals' were appealing to both groups but required the co-operation of both teams if success was to be achieved. An example of this type of activitiy was sending a lorry for food, but the lorry 'broke down' when everyone was hungry. The boys got a rope and by working together, managed to get the lorry started.

Eventually the groups became more friendly and positive ratings began to emerge which crossed group lines. 'Best friends' appeared quite often in the 'opposition' group.

Conclusions

1 Conflict is not primarily a result of individual neurotic traits, but arises under given conditions even when the persons involved are well adjusted.

2 Co-operative and democratic group procedures do not transfer directly in inter-group situations. On the contrary, solidarity within groups was highest when group conflict was most pronounced.

3 Interaction between warring groups in pleasant conditions does not necessarily reduce conflict.

4 Interaction between groups in situations requiring co-operation to achieve an overriding (superordinate) goal helps to establish better relations between groups – but single episodes are not sufficient.

5 A number of successive co-operative situations has a cumulative effect in reducing inter-group hostility.

We have seen already how influential groups can be in terms of individual behaviour. If groups are as powerful as these experiments suggest they are of obvious interest to the marketing specialist. If they can change behaviour, it may be possible, through studying their processes, to understand and possibly influence buying behaviour.

It is useful for the marketer to distinguish between different categories of group in order to use them more effectively in the communication process. Behavioural scientists commonly identify a number of different types of group. They include:

1 *Ascribed groups* are groups to which a person automatically belongs – examples include the family, male/female, etc.

2 *Acquired groups* are those to which a person has sought membership e.g. Chartered Institute of Marketing

3 *Primary groups* are usually small with close emotional contact and face-to-face communication – e.g. family, friendship groups.

4 *Secondary groups* are more impersonal in terms of communication and are commonly larger – e.g. societies, colleges, organizations.

5 *Formal groups* have a clearly defined purpose or goal with defined roles – e.g. Behavioural Aspects of Marketing class with teacher/student roles.

6 *Informal groups* usually exist to satisfy the social needs of the members, roles still exist but are rarely allocated formally. Examples would include groups of friends (which may exist quite comfortably *within* a more formal grouping).

7 *Membership groups* are those groups to which an individual belongs whether they are formal or informal i.e. he/she is a member of that group.

8 *Aspirational groups* are those groups to which the individual does not belong, but to which that person wishes to belong.

9 *Dissociative groups* are those the individual wishes not to be associated with (usually because of values and behaviour).

One final term which is used is that of *Reference groups*. These are defined as those which influence behaviour – thus, all of the above categories are reference groups as even dissociative groups fall into this category as people may go to extremes of behaviour to ensure that they are not perceived as 'one of those'!

One aspect which may need to be clarified is the idea that specific groups can fall into more than one category – for instance your family group may well be both ascribed and primary as well as being a membership group.

Think – How would you classify your current work group?
       – your drinking companions?
       – your classmates studying marketing?
       – heavy metal rockers?
       – the Chartered Institute of Marketing?

Once again the issue of perception is critical. Some of you may have classified heavy metal fans as a dissociative group while others may see them as an aspirational group. This was a similar problem to that faced by motor cycle manufacturers who discovered that motorbikes were linked in many people's minds to Hell's Angels – for many, this was a turn-off as they saw Hell's Angels as undesirable and hence they were a dissociative group. To others (only a minority) they were seen as a desirable aspirational group. In order to expand their potential market, many firms advertised in an attempt to change the general perception – 'You meet the nicest people on a Honda' being one of the more memorable and successful slogans.

Think – What are your reference groups?
　　　　– How do they affect your behaviour?
　　　　– What impact does this have on your buying behaviour?
　　　　– How do advertisements 'get at' you in these terms?

Exercise – Discuss the relative importance of these different types of group to the practice of marketing.

The influence of different groups is also a situational variable.

Think – What groups would affect your behaviour and your purchasing if you were
　　　　– arranging your wedding?
　　　　– organizing the end-of-course celebration?
　　　　– about to buy a new suit?
　　　　– fixing a party for your parents' wedding anniversary?
　　　　– deciding on the purchase of a mountain bike?

So, in summary, our behaviour is significantly affected by social groupings. Groups come in a variety of types and forms. The most important groups so far as marketers are concerned are reference groups as these are the ones which affect behaviour and hence purchasing. The basic assumptions which underlie the marketing interest may best be shown in Figure 8.1.

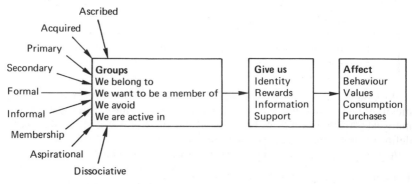

Figure 8.1　Reference groups – a pictorial representation

People in groups – a review of concepts and theories

> **Think** – What groups are you a member of?
> – Make a list of them.
> – Against each one indicate why you joined and your role within the group.

People join, or find themselves in groups for a variety of reasons. Argyle has suggested that some of the reasons are conscious and deliberate, while others are situational or due to circumstances. We may speculate on some of the reasons:

- to achieve a task that cannot be successfully completed alone. This may be an underlying reason for the human race developing tribal systems in the earliest stages of our evolution and continuing with them up to the present time. It could be argued that groups facilitate the satisfaction of Maslow's basic physiological and security needs

- to obtain friendship, companionship and support. We saw in Chapter 6 that Maslow classified the companionship or love need as part of his hierarchy. This companionship need may be satisfied by informal groups which can operate even within formal situations or organizations as we saw in the Hawthorne Experiments

- to obtain status (Maslow again) or to exercise power (as per McClelland's theory of motivation). By definition, status necessitates others as comparators for higher or lower status – and exercising power on one's own in a social vacuum is clearly an unsatisfying nonsense!

- to get what Handy calls 'a psychological home' – a source of warmth and psychological security

- to get power, as in joining a trade union, and lastly,

- because we have no choice – we are born male or female, the great majority of us cannot exercise choice over the families we are born into, we cannot affect the colour of our skin, etc.

> **Think** – How does your list of reasons compare to those reasons given above?

As can be seen from this brief list, our membership of groups is both inevitable and complex, as it encompasses, and contols the satisfaction of, many aspects of human motivation. So let us begin our discussion with a definition of what constitutes a group.

A group is a number of people (more than one) who have:-

1 a common purpose/goal/objective/task; and
2 a sense of 'boundary' and, hence, an identity; and

3 a minimum set of agreed/accepted values and norms governing behaviour within the group; and
4 relatively exclusive interactions within a given context; and
5 a self-perception, by the members, of themselves as a group.

Think – Using the definition above, does a bus queue constitute a group?
– Does your CIM Behavioural Aspects of Marketing class?
– Does a group learning a foreign language in a language laboratory?
– Does the crowd watching a football match?

Groups may be *formal, informal, permanent* or *temporary*.

Informal groups have the prime characteristic of being voluntary – both from the viewpoint of the existing group (do they wish to let the newcomer join?) and from the point of view of the 'applicants' (do they want to join – and how much?). They are dominated by personal rather than role relationships and appear to exist to satisfy the personal and emotional needs of their members.

Think – Can you recognize any informal groups of which you are a member?
– any of which you are *not* a member?

In addition to informal or friendship groups, much of our life is spent in more formal groupings, not least at work. Indeed, we spend a great deal of our waking hours in work situations, most of which constitute operating within formal groups.

Formal groups include departments/sections/classes, etc. and are dominated by task activity and prescribed relationships. It is rare for formal groups to exercise control over membership particularly at the lower end of the organizational hierarchy. Role relationships predominate (e.g. teacher/ student; manager/subordinate). In some cases formal groups may adopt informal characteristics in order to maximize satisfaction for its members, but their very nature means they remain formal.

Think – What examples can you identify of formal groups which choose to behave in an informal manner so that people feel more comfortable?

Organizations are, in fact, made up of a series of formal groups – this has advantages and purpose for both the organization and the individuals as summarized in Figure 8.2.

Organizational purposes	Individual purposes
Distribution of work, control of work, problem solving, decision making, information processing, information and idea collection, testing and ratifying decisions, co-ordination, liaison, increased commitment and involvement, negotiation, conflict resolution inquest, inquiry into the past, etc.	For the individual member a means of: Satisfying needs for friendship, support, companionship (social affiliation needs), establishing self-concept, gaining help and support to achieve a task, sharing/helping in a common activity, satisfying power needs, satisfying security needs, protection.
NB These may well overlap, but generally the need is for clear role, purpose and identity. May be a way to diffuse (or lose) responsibility. May also be better at recognizing problems than solving them.	NB These may well overlap. They may also conflict with organizational purposes – e.g. strikes, 'go slows', working to rule, limiting output, etc.

Figure 8.2

If you become a member of a group in order to satisfy your social affiliation needs – *the price of membership is conformity.*

Element (3) in the definition of groups (p. 216) highlights the point that they develop norms governing behaviour within the group – these may concern:

– the task or activities of the group,
– the non-formal goals such as relaxation or engaging in hobbies,
– internal regulation such as discipline, language or roles,
– opinions, attitudes, beliefs about politics, unions, management,
– outsiders, or anything else the group is interested in,
– physical appearance and dress.

> **Think** – What are the behavioural norms governing the different groups of which you are a member?
> – What does that mean in terms of your different behaviour when you are with different groups?

The idea of group norms governing the behaviour of a number of individuals suggests that individuals modify their behaviour according to the groups they are with. Thus we face the fact that human behaviour may be even less consistent and predictable than may be apparent from our studies so far. This idea of the human being as some sort of social chameleon, changing behaviour in order to match the group situation in which they find themselves, clearly only operates within limits which are likely to be a function of an individual's personality – quiet individuals are unlikely to become raging extroverts, they just become more outgoing when in the company of other shy persons.

Persons who find their behaviour, values or attitudes deviating significantly from the norms of the group are placed in a difficult and uncomfortable position similar to Festinger's Cognitive Dissonance theory discussed in the previous chapter. Robertson and Cooper suggest that an individual in such a position has four options:

1 to leave the group,
2 to conform to the norms,
3 to try to change the norms of the remainder of the group, or
4 to remain a deviant.

They believe that the option chosen will be a function of the individual's personality, the support of others in the group and the strength of feelings about the issue on which deviation occurs.

The idea of modifying behaviour in this way also means that some difficult adjustments may have to be made. Generally conformity means compromise on the part of group members. However we commonly deny that such compromise was either demanded or conceded – but it may well be the underlying reason why people as individuals sometimes behave differently to the same people when in a group.

The degree to which we will conform (and compromise) depends on:

• the strength of our desire for agreement on membership;
• the strength of our wish to avoid 'aggro' or isolation;
• the strength of our belief that the norm reflects our own view (congruence);
• the degree to which we doubt our ability to stand alone;
• our belief in the group's goals.

These factors seem to define and measure our likely dependance on the group – but our need for Handy's 'psychological home' means that they are both universal and influential.

We saw above that groups satisfy both organizational and individual needs but experimental evidence suggests that some commonly held beliefs about groups may not be well founded:

1 Contrary to popular belief, groups do not appear to produce more ideas than individuals – but those they do produce tend to be better thought through, so, in that sense they may produce 'better' ideas.

2 Another surprising finding is that groups often take riskier decisions than the individuals making up the group. This may be due to shared (lost/hidden) responsibility.

3 Highly cohesive groups sometimes make poor decisions. The key work in this area comes from an American researcher called Janis who identified, and put forward explanations for the phenomenon he called 'groupthink'. Here group members will often keep silent rather than 'rock the boat' by giving a view contrary to that being expressed by other group members. Some group members deflect internal debate of the decision by criticizing outsiders or 'the opposition' (similar to Sherif's observations of the

children in the camp experiments). Others act as what Janis calls 'mindguards' (analogous to bodyguards) who attempt to protect the group from dissenting ideas and evidence. It is an irony that such self-imposed censorship is most common in highly cohesive groups. We might speculate that for effective decision-making, too much cohesion may be a bad thing.

In reality the effectiveness of a group may be measured by productivity in terms of the task undertaken and/or the satisfaction of the members with the group experience. It is quite possible to have a very happy, comfortable, non-achieving group, but it does appear that in task achievement group situations, while satisfaction does not always lead to productivity, productivity can often lead to satisfaction.

There are other issues associated with group behaviour. Following Handy's analysis we will consider a number of 'givens' which may be applicable, particularly in a managerial situation.

A The group

1 Size

Here we seem to have two conflicting forces. In the first place there is the argument for larger groups to increase the pool of talent, skill and knowledge available for the group activity. This is balanced by the fact that smaller groups offer a larger share of group attention to the individual member.

Generally, those who participate most are perceived as having the most influence. Therefore, as the group gets larger, influence will tend to devolve to the extroverts (unfortunately this may be unrelated to knowledge, skill or experience).

The foregoing comments identify one critical activity of the chairperson of a committee – that of ensuring that all members get a chance to air their views – in effect the job is to ensure reasonable exposure for all members. Another concept associated with size is that of the cohesiveness of a group (the solidarity effect of being in a group, commonly characterized by the use of 'we', sometimes viewed as the 'glue' holding the group together).

Cohesiveness $\alpha \ \frac{1}{\text{size}}$
α member satisfaction
α how often the group meets
α attractiveness of the group to its members

Thus cohesiveness seems to be a reasonable measure of the power a group holds over its individual members, although, as we have seen above, this does not necessarily lead to effective task performance.

2 Membership

Homogeneous groups tend to be longer lasting, more stable and produce higher levels of member satisfaction. There is, however, a need for variety in the membership to bring in a wider range of ideas and skills. The best rule of thumb would appear to be that we need 'variety with compatability'. The variety enables different tasks and functions to be carried out while the compatability becomes more important as tasks become more complex. Hidden agendas and lack of consensus on role allocation can prove major hinderances and are best overcome where a common objective (or enemy) is clear, together with open communication and trust amongst members.

3 Stage of development

Groups have been observed to develop through several phases in the growth to what is called 'maturity'. The cycle described by Tuckman (1965) has four stages – 'Forming ... Storming ... Norming ... and Performing'. Clearly such a process takes time and in some cases the task may not be deemed important enough to warrant the length of time necessary to develop a fully effective group to deal with it – in other cases the short time-scale may be part of the problem.

4 The task

The actual nature of the task is likely to affect the kind of group that is appropriate – e.g. 'inquests' are different in nature to 'brainstorming' sessions. It has also been found that groups which have a variety of tasks commonly experience difficulty in changing style in mid-stream. Conversely many fewer difficulties are found when the same people sit on different committees – this seems to highlight the importance of the Chair's role in signposting. Other factors which will affect the group are:

- the urgency of the task;
- the importance of the task;
- the clarity of the task; and
- the location of the meeting and of the group members.

This last point often determines who is in charge and who is on 'home ground', and often fixes the patterns of communication which emerge.

The above section, the 'givens', affect the group directly and influence items in the next section which can be more easily amended to affect the efficiency of the groups. These items we will call intervening variables.

B Intervening variables

1 Process and procedure

The original ideas and observations in this area stem from the work of Robert Bales. He suggested that activities fall into two broad categories – 'task functions' and 'maintenance functions' :

Task functions	*Maintenance functions*
Initiating	Encouraging
Information seeking	Supporting
Diagnosing	Compromizing
Opinion seeking	Peace keeping
Evaluating	Clarifying/summarizing
Decision making	Standard setting

1 *Task functions* are activities concerned with task achievement. Clearly much of the function will be determined by the skills of the individual group members in applying good decision-making techniques in the group setting. Another issue is the *actual* decision-making process that is employed (by authority/seniority, by consensus, by majority voting, by minority, by veto, by no response, etc.).

2 *Maintenance functions* are activities concerned with keeping the group operational and efficient – these are the activities which create a group as opposed to a bunch of individuals who happen to be in the same place but not listening to each other. Deutsch called such effective, listening groups 'co-operative' (as opposed to 'competitive') and found them to:

– be more productive;
– produce higher quality;
– have a stronger push to complete the task;
– have greater division of labour and better co-ordination;
– have fewer communication problems;
– be more friendly in the group and experience greater satisfaction.

2 Communication patterns

Such patterns can also affect the efficiency of a group in terms of task achievement. Sociometric analysis of interaction may identify patterns such as described in Figure 8.3.

Experiments show:

1 the wheel is quickest to reach a solution, the circle is slowest

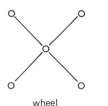
wheel

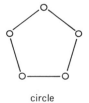
circle

all-channel

Figure 8.3

2 in complex, open-ended problems the all-channel is most likely to reach the best solution – the ability of the centre is the key to the wheel's effectiveness. The wheel is often inflexible if the task changes
3 satisfaction for members is lowest in the circle but is high in the all-channel. The wheel has very high satisfaction expressed by the centre while the 'rim' feels isolated.

The importance of non-verbal communication is often overlooked. On a similar point, the location and/or layout of a group may be important in defining the type/volume/direction of communication and thus its effectiveness in terms of task achievement.

3 Motivation

The motivation of members is obviously likely to be an important factor – in this field our earlier observations on the complexity of motivation still hold good (see Chapter 4). Generally individuals will find satisfaction in the group if they:

- like the other members of the group and are liked by them (companionship);
- approve of the pupeses of the group (task achievement);
- wish to be associated with the standing of the group (status).

Thus Maslow and McClelland seem the dominant theorists (along with Mayo) so far as motivation in groups goes and this will determine the involvement of the individual with group activities.

The 'common enemy' (cf. Sherif and Sherif) is also a major motivator in groups – to improve the effectiveness the leader may find it useful to redefine the task to make it into a common enemy situation.

4 Roles in groups

The concept of role playing in real life is one that is readily observable. Roles tend to be fixed by two (sometimes conflicting) forces:

1 how we see ourselves and
2 what others expect of us.

Earlier studies identified the task roles and socio-emotional (maintenance) roles (see Bales above). This has given rise to the concept sometimes referred to as the 'hypothesis of two complementary leaders'. Wallen has suggested splitting the role into the two elements 'strong fighter' and 'logical thinker' (think about leadership of political parties!).

Handy puts forward some additional roles:

'comedian' – willing butt
'commentator' – observer of proceedings
'deviant' – who may grab the limelight by disagreeing.

Additionally we may also have 'specialists', 'spokespersons' and 'peace-keepers'. Inevitably, most of us play the role of 'follower' most of the time!

Think – Consider groups of which you are a member and identify who plays which roles.
– How were these roles allocated (or did it 'just happen')?
– What roles do *you* play?

Doing this exercise may highlight some interesting insights. Roles are often identifiable even within informal groups – even in something as informal as the Friday night drinking group one can often pick out the joker, the peacekeeper, the spokesperson and so forth. T. T. Patterson has pointed out that some members may hold more than one role and that roles are allocated, not by absolute characteristics, but by a 'best available' process (i.e. the spokesperson role may well be allocated to the least introvert member of the group – even if they are all highly introspective relative to the population at large). Also the allocation of roles in informal groups is commonly done at a subconscious and intuitive level.

Such an analysis can help to explain the problems which sometimes arise when dealing with the group spokesperson. The obvious and common assumption is that such a person is the leader of the group. Role theory could explain the problems that can emerge when this assumption is false and the spokesperson is merely the message carrier – not the one who can make a decision on behalf of the group.

Many textbooks have been written, and many courses run on the subject of 'leadership'. Basically the debate can be simplified and summarized by saying that some people believe that leaders are 'born not made' and that leadership is a function of possessing the appropriate personality traits (sometimes rather rudely referred to as the 'boy scout syndrome') while others believe that leadership is a function of the situation in which the group finds itself.

Think – Which do you think is correct?
– Why?

While there is some attraction in the notion of the born leader – it does seem a rather limited concept for wide application to groups. A major limitation seems to be the question of whether there are enough born leaders to go round, considering the vast number of groups which exist. Additionally, in formal groups the leader is sometimes appointed as manager or section leader by the organization, but they do not always command the respect of the subordinate group. Overall the contingency or situational approach seems to be the most plausible, with leadership roles devolving to those individuals within the group who are perceived to have either the required personality characteristics or relevant skills and knowledge. This approach implies that groups (particularly informal groups) will not have a single, permanent leader, but that different members will take on leadership as and when the remainder of the group see them as leaders. This approach has clear parallels with the concept of opinion leadership discussed in Chapter 9 and Barnard's ideas regarding authority which are mentioned in Chapter 11.

The family

The family may be the single most important type of social grouping so far as marketing is concerned. Its importance stems from two separate, but crucial, processes in which it is a key factor. The first of these is the *consumer socialization process* – by which purchasing behaviours are learned and passed from one generation to another. The second process is that of *the family operating as a consumer decision making and purchasing unit*. However, before we look at these two processes it is worth spending a little time on consideration of the family as a social phenomenon.

The family is defined by the Jarrys as:

'A group of people, related by kinship or similar close ties, in which the adults assume responsibility for the care and upbringing of their natural or adopted children.'

In terms of our earlier analysis the family is a primary group. Human infants undergo an extended period of maturation before they are capable of existing and surviving as independent adults. During this period they require extensive protection and support; and this very dependency helps us to explain the dominant role the family plays in shaping our behaviour, attitudes, values and perceptions of expected roles – the socialization process described in more detail in the next chapter.

Other key terms surrounding the concept of the family is the notion of the *family of orientation* – the family into which one is born and the *family of procreation* – the family which one establishes by marriage. Sociologists also commonly differentiate between the *nuclear family* – biological parents in a stable marital relationship, with their dependent children; and the *extended family* – the nuclear family plus parents, grandparents, in-laws, uncles, aunts and other relatives.

In either case the importance of the family is emphasized by the multiplicity of its functions – it is:

a consumption unit
a purchasing unit
a financial resource
a source of information
a source of physical satisfaction
a source of emotional satisfaction.

The idea of the classic nuclear family demands that only two adults are involved in the activities of parenting, that is they exist as sexual partners, biological parents and social parents, and the mechanism used to knit these different activities together is marriage. However, this is only one form of family grouping and is very much a function of a particular European culture. Sociologists have argued that the development of this family format is the direct result of industrialization. The suggestion is that the mobility associated with the emergence of industrial development has led to the separation and isolation of the nuclear family from the wider kin networks.

Think – Do you still live close to your parents, grandparents and other close relations?
– Do your friends and acquaintances?
– How does this closeness/distance affect family relationships and behaviour?

The concept of the nuclear family gives rise to a very important idea in marketing – that of the *family life cycle* (FLC). This takes the idea of the family as a consuming unit which progresses through a series of stages. It considers aspects of consumer behaviour such as the focus of interest and the probable levels of disposable/discretionary income. It has been a seminal idea in the area of market segmentation.

Traditional family life cycles and buying behaviour

Stage 1 – Single/Bachelor/Young Unmarrieds

Despite earning power often being relatively low, this section of the community are subject to few rigid demands – so they may typically have high disposable income. The likely focus of spending may be a car, furnishing and equipping the first 'home of their own', fashion and recreation, alcohol and eating out, holidays, hi-fi, leisure pursuits and other activities which are likely to centre on obtaining a partner.

Stage 2 – Newly Marrieds

Commonly two incomes with no children to support gives even more disposable income. Again cars, clothing and vacations feature in their buying patterns, but this group also has a very high rate of purchasing durable goods, furniture and appliances in this important 'nest building' stage.

Stage 3 – Full Nest 1

With the arrival of the first child, it is assumed that the mother will cease working. The family income declines sharply at the same time as the young child creates a new focus for family expenditure. Moving into a new home, buying furniture and furnishings for the child, purchase of washing machines, tumble dryers and such reflect changing needs. Similarly, day-to-day expenditure on children's food, toys and activities increases. This stage commonly places the family under financial pressure, reducing savings and often creating dissatisfaction with the financial situation.

Stage 4 – Full Nest 2

At this stage the youngest child is six or over. The general assumption is that the husband's income has increased and the wife may well have restarted work, possibly on a part-time basis to start with. Hence the financial pressures ease. Expenditure tends to be heavily influenced by the children and their needs including some relatively expensive items such as bicycles, fashion clothing, music lessons, etc.

Stage 5 – Full Nest 3

As the children grow older it is assumed that the family will experience a further improvement in finances due to both the wife's improved earnings and the possibility of children getting some part-time or occasional employment. At this stage the family may well replace ageing furniture, buy a better car and/or purchase some luxury items (or items which, until then, had been considered as luxuries – e.g. dishwashers, etc.).

Stage 6 – Empty Nest 1

The couple's joint incomes continue to increase while the children have left home and are no longer financially dependent on the parents. The combination of these two factors give perhaps the highest level of disposable income. Expenditure may focus on higher cost items such as house improvements, luxury goods, holidays and travel.

Stage 7 – Empty Nest 2

Retirement brings a sharp drop in income. Expenditure becomes more health orientated and may involve moving to a smaller house, perhaps in a more agreeable climate.

Stage 8 – Solitary Survivor

One partner has died. If still working the solitary survivor still enjoys a good income and may well move house and spend on holidays, travel, etc., as in empty nest 1.

Stage 9 – Retired Solitary Survivor

Similar to the category above, but with a lower income due to retirement. The emphasis of expenditure may well be similar so long as the individual remains active – but, as the person becomes less independent, more may be spent on purchasing the personal services necessary for survival.

The Family Life Cycle is commonly represented as the steady progression illustrated in Figure 8.4.

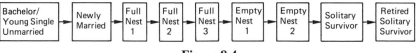

Figure 8.4

> **Think** – Identify current advertising campaigns which appear to be targeted at specific stages in the Family Life Cycle.
> – How many different targeted stages can you think of?

The nuclear family seems to be important in most cultures and is often presented as being both the most common (descriptive), and the most culturally desirable (prescriptive) social formation. However, direct evidence shows that the nuclear family of mother and father plus 2.4 children is becoming much less common as divorce rates rise and the stigma of unmarried motherhood reduces in the eyes of many people.

Additional complications arise from demographic patterns which are emerging. In the UK the birth rate diminished in the 1970s and 1980s leading to smaller family units. Another factor which distorts the 'traditional' view of the family is the growth of the 'two-career family' with a wife who expects to continue her career and take full advantage of legislation enabling a speedy return to work after the birth of children. Such a two income situation implies a possible doubling of income – but, as ever, the marketer is often more interested in disposable or discretionary spending power. For instance, the high earners may be mortgaged to the hilt, the second income may be swallowed up in child-minding costs, or the demands of private education – so the amount which is 'free' for purchasing other products may be less than appears at first sight.

Thus, we may conclude that the family, or at least the 'ideal' nuclear family, is undergoing some significant developments. The emergence of the 'single parent family' calls many of the assumptions of the traditional family life cycle into question – so we may need to look at it again and question its 'normality'.

The situation can become even more complex when we consider the evidence which tells us that a majority of divorced persons remarry. This pattern of divorce followed by re-marriage increases the options dramatically. The possibility of 'inheriting' a partner's older/younger children from an earlier marriage now needs to be considered. The pattern can become even more confused when this couple produce children of their own. The mixed extended families can become very large and difficult to explain. Hence a more realistic representation of the situation might be that presented in Figure 8.5.

Think – What examples can you find of 'non-nuclear' family images in current advertisements?

Reviewing the literature on 'the family' sometimes suggests that the institution is in imminent danger of collapse. Looking at newspapers from ages past may lead us to the conclusion that this is nothing new – people have worried about changes in family roles and relationships for many years. The truth of the matter may be that the family, as a social construct, is continually changing and adapting to meet the perceived needs of the society. Thus there may be no such thing as the 'perfect' family set-up and the idealized notion of the universal nuclear family may be only a dream of politicians and sociologists.

Authors such as Talcott Parsons have lent credence to such a view by charting the evolution of the family from a 'production unit' in early agricultural societies to the more fragmented, and apparently casual and less permanent arrangements which we might recognize in our current society.

Those who decry the current divorce rates and see this as evidence of moral degeneracy and the beginnings of a break-down of society, may be ignoring the fact that the low levels of divorce in (e.g.) the Victorian era, may well have disguised high levels of domestic friction and unhappiness. They may also be underestimating the degree to which a majority of people do, in fact, follow relatively traditional patterns.

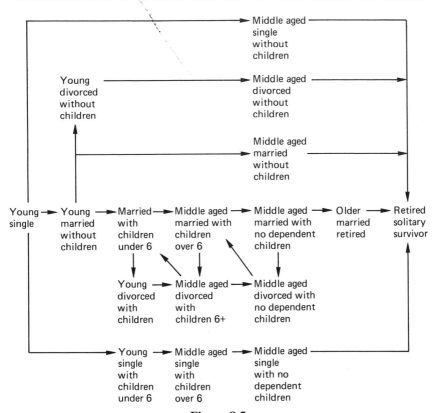

Figure 8.5

A Family Policy Studies Centre report (1985) emphasized this continuity in that they claimed that in the UK:

- nine out of ten people will marry at some time in their lives,
- nine out of ten married couples will have children,
- two in every three marriages are likely to be ended by death rather than divorce, and
- eight out of ten people live in households headed by a married couple.

They did, however, identify some changes, the most significant from our viewpoint being an increasing tendency for people NOT to go through all of the phases of the traditional family life cycle *within one family*. This may not matter too much as the family life cycle is essentially used as a cross-sectional analysis for market segmentation purposes.

In an important article Lawson, following an analysis of the changing demographic patterns in the UK, suggested that the stages themselves have altered in both length and importance. He claims that, in general:

- full nest stages are shorter due to lower birth rates and children being born closer together in time, and,

• bachelor and empty nest stages have grown in length and size.

What is important is that whatever model of the family life cycle is used, it must reflect as accurately as possible the demography of the society.

Lawson presents a 'modernized' family life cycle which, he claims, encompasses over 80 per cent of the population. His data, based on the 1981 census, are set out in Figure 8.6.

Stage	Percentage of households
Bachelor	1.42
Newly married couples	3.11
Full nest 1 (with pre-school children)	11.91
Full nest 1 (lone parent)	1.26
Middle aged no children	1.19
Full nest 2 (school age children)	16.97
Full nest 2 (lone parent)	1.92
Launching families (with non-dependent children)	6.30
Launching families (one parent)	1.45
Empty nest 1 (childless, aged 45–54)	9.45
Empy nest 2 (retired)	9.51
Solitary survivor under 65	2.66
Solitary survivor retired	14.17
Total	81.31

Figure 8.6

The exceptions (the remaining 18.69 per cent) are households with more than one family, those with other residents besides family, young people living in joint households.

In recent years, marketers have found it useful to consider the *household* as another, less limited, way of examining social groupings. The rapid changes in the social norms surrounding marriage and the family have rendered some of the traditional views of the family less valuable as a tool for examining purchasing behaviour. Such a redefinition allows the identification and inclusion of persons sharing a flat or house who may not be married but who, nevertheless, indulge in group purchasing decisions for items such as washing machines and similar household items. As Lawson says in describing the problem of categorizing his missing 18.69 per cent – 'in all these instances the household is likely to be a better unit of analysis for much of consumer behaviour than the family'.

Consumer socialization

Families are a major and significant source of the knowledge, attitudes and skills relevant to their functioning effectively as consumers in the marketplace. The family, being such an important source of emotional and physical satisfaction, exercised considerable influence on the values and behaviours of its members. However, despite the continuing interactive influencing that goes on within any tightly-knit group, one of the key areas of interest for marketers is the way in which children pick up the attitudes, skills and knowledge which may stay with them for life and which influence their behaviour as consumers.

Think – How has family socialization affected your views on such things as
- buying on credit?
- the importance of a 'good' breakfast?
- mail order shopping?
- supermarket shopping?
- doing the football pools and gambling?
- looking smart?
- who does the shopping?
- who does the cooking?
- who does the cleaning?
- who does the ironing?
- who cleans the lavatory?
- What other consumer behaviours can you recognize as being 'learned' from your family?

Almost all of the learning theory reviewed in Chapter 5 is present in the family situation, especially with regard to children:

- children's lives may be seen as a series of trial and error learning situations;
- they are subjected to classical conditioning by their parents;
- the process of growing up and exploring the world leads, inevitably, to operant conditioning;
- some problems are solved by insight;
- other learning is 'stored' and utilized when appropriate situations arise;
- they learn directly from their own experiences;
- they indulge in role play in games, and, also in real life (can you remember the first time your mother sent you to the shops on your own to buy something? – an early role trial);
- they are surrounded by 'role models' (often parents, but also siblings) who supply masses of data for vicarious learning.

Amongst the variety of social learning that occurs within the family setting, the part which interests marketers is the learning about what, when, where, why and how to purchase.

Hawkins, Best and Coney draw a distinction between *directly relevant learning* which is concerned with activities such as how to shop, how to compare and evaluate brands, and how to budget –which includes the development of attitudes about such aspects of marketing as the qualities and desirability of different retail outlets, products, brands, sales staff, clearance sales, mail order and advertising. They contrast this with *indirectly relevant* learning which is concerned with the knowledge, attitudes and values which cause people to want specific goods or services. In other words this is the process of learning about differential evaluations of brands and products. Most of us learn that Rolls Royce produce excellent motor cars without necessarily purchasing one.

> **Think** – How did you learn 'the value of money'?

In terms of directly relevant learning there seems to be a general acceptance that for some staple products, offspring may well purchase the brands that were used when they were growing up. This is obviously of great importance to marketers as it raises the possibility of an inherited lifelong brand loyalty! Examples of product categories which are thought to fall into this category are things such as toothpaste, breakfast cereals, laundry detergent and ketchup.

> **Think** – To what brands do you owe lifelong loyalty?

Another related aspect of consumer socialization is the effect that advertising has on children. Numerous studies have identified that children spend many hours each week watching television, and exposure to advertising messages is a significant part of that experience. While any parent can attest to the value of television as a surrogate childminder it is not without its drawbacks as it may:

- become a source of conflict within the family – 'Mum, I want a new bike': 'You can't have one!';
- become a safety threat by glamourizing unhealthy eating habits (especially high sugar/high fat products) or by giving rise to 'copycat' behaviours such as magic tricks or other stunts;
- raise unrealistic expectations of both products and society;
- influence those vulnerable children who have not learned to distinguish between 'adspeak' and reality. Believing that toys shown on adverts actually move of their own accord would be an example of this;
- establish values which the parents feel are undesirable – particularly those of materialism and those which are determined by stereotypes of gender and ethnic minorities.

An interesting offshoot of this research is that the UK 'watershed' of 9.00 p.m. for 'adult' advertising seems inappropriate when many children watch television way beyond that time.

However, all is not doom and gloom, as the family will often *mediate* the message – parents might point out that sweets or snacks can cause tooth decay and toothache. However, this last comment can only refer to situations where the child watches television in the company of a parent or parent-figure. It will be completely inappropriate in other situations where children are left with the television as 'child minder'. Thus mediation may well be a phenomenon of both class and culture. Perhaps more importantly parents provide powerful *role models* which are likely to be even more significant than the images portrayed on television. The child will observe, at first hand, activities such as shopping, choosing and evaluating. American studies have suggested that male children tend to take up their father's shaving habits with respect to a preference for electric or wet (soap, brush and razor) shaving.

Families as consumer and purchasing units

The family is a group and it has relatively fixed resources. We saw in the Family Life Cycle that the focus of expenditure will tend to change according to the stage of development. This insight only tells half of the story, however, as different members of the family group will have different aspirations which may prove very difficult to satisfy within the budget available. Family holidays can be a prime source of conflict when one parent wants an adventure holiday, the other fancies a relaxing poolside break – and the child wants to visit EuroDisney!

Another example could be the new mountain bike for the teenager which uses discretionary funds that could have bought a weekend break for the parents, new clothing for brothers and sisters, materials for redecorating the kitchen, or a thousand and one other items desired or needed by members of the family group. Thus we may assert with some confidence that a degree of *decision conflict* will be present in many family purchasing decisions.

> **Think** – What other examples of decision conflict within families can you identify?

It is likely that the more expensive the item the greater will be the trade-offs required within the family group. Other factors which may affect the degree of conflict or agreement include the extent to which the item is for individual or family use and the extent of agreement between those family group members who may be expected to share the product.

Advertising messages sometimes seek to minimize this conflict by sending slightly different messages to the different parties. Children may be interested in the taste, image or personality of a breakfast cereal while parents may be concerned with health, nutrition and similar issues. Carefully constructed advertising messages can reduce conflict by reassuring the parent while attracting the child. Recently Shredded Wheat mounted a campaign which 'pushed' sporting hero images at the children while satisfying the parents by emphasizing the product's purity and lack of additives.

> **Think** – What other examples can you find of this kind of conflict reduction?

Roles and processes

It is generally accepted that family consumption decisions encompass a number of different roles. These roles are assumed by members of the family and it is common for individuals to carry out more than one role and, often, more than one person playing the same role! The roles include:

1 *Gatekeeper* – this is the person who controls access to information and ideas. This may be in the sense of:

(a) giving a summary of relevant information – 'I saw a programme on TV which said that X was the best value';
(b) controlling access to information – 'No – you're not watching that!';
(c) mediating advertising messages as described above.

One offshoot of the control function which is often seen in the family setting is the removal of advertising matter before others can see it – or, alternatively, ensuring that the advertisements are left in such positions that they *will* be seen by others.

2 *Influencer* – this person provides information, expertise and/or preferences which are fed to the other members of the group. Sometimes such opinions are sought by other family members, sometimes they are offerred by the individual.

3 *Decider* – this is the person with the authority or power to determine how the family's resources should be allocated. So this is where the decision as to whether a purchase is to be made finally rests. The deciders may well also use their power to influence both the product/brand choice and the evaluative criteria used in the decision process.

4 *Buyer* – this is the person who acts as purchasing agent. In many product groups this means the one who does the shopping, calls the supplier, brings the products home and stores them appropriately.

5 *Preparer* – this is the individual who fits the plugs on electrical appliances, prepares food, and similar functions.

6 *User* – this is the person or persons who consume or use a particular product.

Think – Identify which individuals play (or played) the different roles in your family for activities such as:
    a   producing packed lunches for schoolchildren;
    b   buying a new car;
    c   redecoration of a room;
    d   updating father's wardrobe;
    e   choosing and buying breakfast cereals.

One of the most interesting roles is that of influencer, as this is likely to be a function of the interests, expertise and knowledge of the individual, not just the role of father or mother. As relationships change and become more varied within marriages, it may be that the father is the 'expert' on food and cookery rather than the mother. It seems logical that influence will come with expertise – thus we may have a child who is a technical, electronics fan becoming the influencer (and in some senses the leader) in discussions about the purchase of a CD player or hi-fi system.

The patterns of influence will vary from family to family and from product to product. The complexity of the situation becomes clear with the realization that one individual can be an influencer in one situation, a decider in another, a buyer often or rarely, and a user of many products.

This type of analysis is particularly useful in marketing terms as it may give us an idea of the best direction to direct our persuasive messages. For example, if the decider and buyer are one and the same person, then the marketing effort should logically be directed towards packaging and point-of-sale advertising. However, if they are different persons, more effort will need to be directed to getting the message to wherever the deciders (and their surrounding influencers) might be reached. In some cases the evidence suggests that the user is neither the decision maker nor the buyer. This applies in areas such as pet food where advertisements are aimed at the person who does the purchasing, not the end user. Similarly surveys have suggested that 70 per cent of fragrances used by men are purchased by women (wives or girl friends) and given as presents.

> **Think** – What are the marketing implications of your previous analysis of your own family decision making?

Some media which are widely shared by all the family – television, newspapers and such, offer the chance for marketing messages to be sent to all of the family (and, hence, all of the roles) at the same time. This may give a useful structure for thoughts as to the objectives and content of such messages.

Spousal roles

It seems likely that the husband and wife, in the traditional family set-up, will be the dominant decision makers within the group due to their roles, seniority and earning power. Historically, considerable research has been conducted into which partner makes the decisions about which products.

Writers on marketing decision making such as Davis and Rigaux have classified the decisions into four categories:

1 *Wife dominant*
2 *Husband dominant*
3 *Autonomic* – equal number of decisions made by each partner, but each decision is made independently by one or the other.

Think –   In your family, where on the scale does the decision usually lie
              for the following product groups? Mark an X at the spot.

Food

solely wife	mainly wife	joint	mainly husband	solely husband	could be either

Holidays

solely wife	mainly wife	joint	mainly husband	solely husband	could be either

Television sets

solely wife	mainly wife	joint	mainly husband	solely husband	could be either

Car

solely wife	mainly wife	joint	mainly husband	solely husband	could be either

Children's clothing

solely wife	mainly wife	joint	mainly husband	solely husband	could be either

Husband's leisure clothing

solely wife	mainly wife	joint	mainly husband	solely husband	could be either

Wife's leisure clothing

solely wife	mainly wife	joint	mainly husband	solely husband	could be either

Lawn mower

solely wife	mainly wife	joint	mainly husband	solely husband	could be either

Figure 8.7

4 *Syncratic* – where the decisions are made jointly and equally by the two
   partners.

This is often displayed on a triangular diagram such as Figure 8.8.
    It is quite possible to plot your responses to the earlier 'who makes what
decisions' exercise on such a diagram and it would be of interest to compare
your profile with that of others as there is no right answer. It could be of
even more interest to make comparisons with the responses of your partner
and others in your family group who may have different perceptions of the
decision making processes!

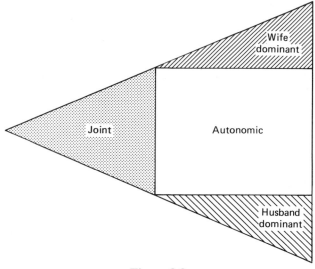

Figure 8.8

Another aspect of the decision making within families is that the responses to the 'who makes what decisions' questions may vary with the decision stage. An example could be the purchase of a car. The initiator/gatekeeper could well be one parent, with perhaps an older child contributing as influencer due to a special interest in motor cars which means the offspring is more up-to-date and technically minded than the parent. This works quite well for the exploratory, information gathering stages of defining the problem and identifying alternative solutions (possible purchases). But as time goes on it is likely that the decision becomes more joint, until the final decision involves an almost equal participation by the two parents.

Once more we may have to draw a distinction between high-involvement, high risk purchases and the more mundane buying activities centred on low-involvement goods. The shift towards joint participation and away from autonomic behaviour tends to be most marked for products and services such as cars, refrigerators, television sets, paint and wallpaper and financial planning and investments. There is evidence to suggest that the family holiday may be the most democratic of a family's purchasing decisions.

Historically it was assumed that some decisions were taken by men while others were taken by women. However this tends to assume fixed roles within the family group for men and women. The stereotypical assumptions allocate women to caring, nurturing and child-rearing activities while the men are seen as macho breadwinners.

Think – What examples can you identify of advertising material which portrays 'non-standard' sexual roles?

While there are some product areas which are gender specific (shaving equipment or sanitary protection) the changing roles and expectations which are so much a feature of our current society must lead us to query the insensitivity of some of the traditional stereotypes which are shown via the media. The impact of feminism, notions of equality within relationships, ideas such as 'new man' and 'independence' all lead to the conclusion that the patterns of influence will vary both from family to family and from product group to product group.

Chapter summary exercises

Think – How can the material in this chapter be applied to the marketing of:

    camcorders
    the social policy of a political party
    skis
    holidays
    soft drinks
    instant coffee
    sports shoes (trainers)
    razors
    hair colourant
    toothpaste
    shampoo
    motor cars
    low-fat/low cholesterol/low salt spread
    sanitary protection
    kitchen equipment
    spirits and liqueurs
    low-alcohol wine
    a restaurant
    newspapers
    toilet tissue
    bicycles

Think – How *has* my organization used knowledge of groups?

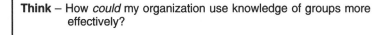

Think – How *could* my organization use knowledge of groups more effectively?

Think – How have *I* used knowledge of groups?

Some 'typical' examination questions – groups

A   A recent article has claimed that the relevance and usefulness of the family life cycle concept to marketing managers has to be questioned. It argues that the model is based on American demographic patterns that have little similarity with the situations found in other countries. Discuss.

B   Examine the relevance of the 'family life cycle' concept to marketing management, with special reference to its applications in the field of market segmentation.

C   There are several kinds of group to which individuals may belong:

- ascribed groups and acquired groups;
- primary groups and secondary groups;
- formal groups and informal groups;
- membership groups, aspirational (reference) groups and non-related groups.

Explain what is meant by each of these terms and show their relevance to the marketing process.

D   Why is the family a crucial concept for marketers?

E   What is a 'group'? Examine the ways in which groups can influence consumer behaviour within such product fields as women's fashions, watches, and instant coffee.

F   'The family is probably the most important group . . . In practice, however, marketers have often failed to consider fully the importance of the family as a decision-making group' (Williams). What is the justification for these propositions and (to the extent that the second one is valid) what might marketers do to redress the balance?

Sources

Argyle, M. (1989) *The Social Psychology of Work* (2nd edn.), Penguin.

BPP (1991) *Behavioural Aspects of Marketing*, BPP.

Buchanan, D. A. and Huczynski, A. A. (1985) *Organisational Behaviour*, Prentice-Hall.

Engel, J. F., Blackwell, R. D. and Miniard, P. W. (1990) *Consumer Behaviour* (6th edn.), Dryden.

Handy, C. B. (1976), *Understanding Organisations*, Penguin.

Hawkins, D. I., Best, R. J. and Coney, K. A. (1989) *Consumer Behaviour: Implications for Marketing Strategy* (4th edn.), Irwin.

Jarry, D. and Jarry, J. (1991) *Dictionary of Sociology*, Collins.

Kakabadse, A., Ludlow, R. and Vinnicombe, S. (1987) *Working in Organisations*, Penguin.

Lawson, R. W. (1988) 'The family life cycle: a demographic analysis', *Journal of Marketing Management*, Vol. 4, No. 1., C.I.M.

Peter, J. P. and Olson, J. C. (1990), *Consumer Behaviour and Marketing Strategy* (2nd edn.), Irwin.

Reber, A. S. (1985) *Dictionary of Psychology*, Penguin.

Robertson, I.T. and Cooper C. L. (1983) *Human Behaviour in Organisations*, Macdonald and Evans.

Tuckman, B. (1965) 'Development sequences in small groups', *Psychological Bulletin*, vol. 63.

Turton, R. (1991) *Behaviour in a Business Context*, Chapman & Hall.

Williams, K. C. (1981) *Behavioural Aspects of Marketing*, Heinemann.

9 So you want to be a social climber

Marketing aspects of sociology

Introduction

In this chapter we examine some of the influences which stem from membership of a wider society. This is a huge field of study – so, once again, we are dealing with 'edited highlights' and attempting to look at them from a marketing perspective.

This is another subject area that is all around us – we are all part of society and both influence and are influenced by it. The newspapers regularly carry interesting material of the 'Is this the end of the society/ world as we know it?'. Keep an eye open as such material often indicates a general area of interest or concern.

At the end of this chapter students should be fully familiar with the following concepts (and the associated language) and *should be able to highlight their relevance to the marketing specialist.*

- Culture
  - characteristics;
  - institutions – folkways, conventions, mores, laws;
  - ideas, values, beliefs;
  - nationality, religion, geographical and age breakdowns;
- Socialization
  - family, school, peer group, mass media;
  - conditioning, imitation, identification, role playing;
- Roles, norms, inter-role conflict, intra-role conflict;
- Status
  - desired, ascribed and achieved;
- Social Class
  - Jicnar definitions;
- Lifestyles
  - psychographics, AIO analysis;
- Communication
  - one-step, two-step and multi-step processes;

– opinion leaders and influentials;
– word-of-mouth;

- Diffusion and Innovation processes.

Once again, much of this material is used as a way of segmenting markets – so it is useful to think in terms of differing product types and their interaction with different cultures, groups, ages. The first 'edited highlight' we shall look at is the broad concept of culture.

Culture

Raymond Williams (1976) maintains that culture is one of the most complicated words in the English language due to its historical development and the fact that it is a word used for important concepts in several different intellectual disciplines. We use the word to describe high art (classical music, theatre, painting and sculpture) and it is often used to contrast these forms with popular taste. It is used by biologists who produce *cultures* of bacteria on petri dishes. Farmers are part of the agri*culture* industry, gardeners practice horti*culture* and so forth.

In the context of this book we consider it as an important area of sociology which is concerned with what we might describe as the 'way of life' adopted by groups of people. It is important to marketers in that it both affects and describes human behaviour. A good way of thinking about culture may be in terms of its usage in words such as agriculture and horticulture as it can be thought of as describing the human environment in which behaviour is developed.

So, for the purposes of studying consumer behaviour it can be defined as:

The values, attitudes, beliefs, ideas, artefacts and other meaningful symbols represented in the pattern of life adopted by people that help them interpret, evaluate and communicate as members of a society.

This is a wide ranging definition for a very wide ranging concept which includes codes of manners, dress, language, rituals, norms of behaviour and systems of belief. It is an all-embracing concept which examines the institutions developed by a society and the ways in which these interact to define and determine acceptable behaviour.

Culture has a number of characteristics:

1 *It is a social characteristic of people* and its purpose is to serve the needs of the people making up the society.

2 *It is learned* by the members of the society by the processes of socialization and it defines the behaviours that are acceptable within the society. As we saw in the last chapter, one of the basic requirements of membership of any group is conformity with its norms and acceptance of its values.

3 *It is cumulative* in the sense that it is passed from generation to generation and often has historical justification. However, this is not to say that culture remains constant.

4 *It is adaptive*. When we look at the diagram below we can see that few of the institutions or elements are absolute – values, religion, politics, laws and so forth can all change in response to the needs of the society. Each and all of these changes influence the culture, customs and rituals of the society.

We could represent culture as in Figure 9.1.

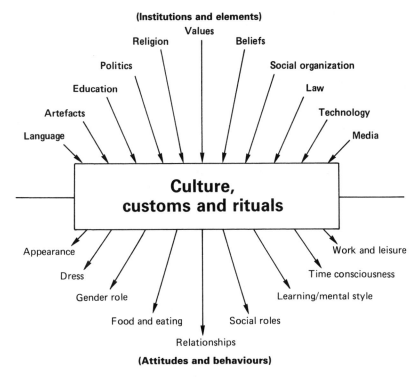

Figure 9.1

In a sense culture is exhibited by the customs and rituals of a society, so it is worth examining these ideas in more detail:-

Customs are the established patterns of behaviour adopted within the society or community. They regulate and regularize social practices and define which behaviours are acceptable. Williams (1981) defined four classes of custom which constitute a continuum of customs from the least to the most serious in as much as the response to non-adherence becomes noticeably more emphatic as we progress from (1) to (4).

1 *Folkways* – these are the everyday customs of the community. Shaking hands would be a typical example; here the general pattern is defined and regarded as being appropriate, it is widely accepted behaviour when meeting people, but significantly, it is not insisted upon and failing to shake hands is not normally punished. If it is noticed, the 'punishment' is likely to be a comment rather than punitive action. This also serves to highlight cultural differences as many continentals are more likely to use a kiss as a greeting.

2 *Conventions* – these are folkways which have become hallowed by time and usage. Thus they are slightly 'stronger' than folkways and are often concerned with behaviours which the society considers polite. Taking a gift of chocolates, flowers or wine when visiting friends for a meal or a party would fit neatly into the convention category (as might the phenomenon of the 'British Sunday Dinner'). Again it is to be noted that the 'penalties' for non-compliance are not severe, but perhaps a little more serious than for flouting folkways.

3 *Mores* are the accepted and strongly prescribed forms of behaviour within the society and cover the more significant social norms. Issues such as murder, theft, incest, monogamy and so forth are covered by mores in the UK. Some societies might include other areas such as honouring your elders. In this category failure to comply results in significant reaction and punishment.

4 *Laws* represent the formalized recognition of mores which the society as a whole deems necessary for its well-being. Laws carry penalties for offenders which are imposed on those caught breaking the law. Most societies have processes for revising and reviewing laws in the light of the beliefs and values obtaining at any given time. Thus they are not absolute, but reflect the society at a given point in time and existing laws can be altered when the society feels it is necessary so to do.

Ritual. This has two meanings in the behavioural sciences. One is the idea of a routine activity characterized by its ordinariness – one may have particular rituals which you follow before going to bed, shaving, getting dressed and so forth. Students commonly go through quite complex rituals to ensure 'good luck' in examinations!

More significant in this context is the ritual which has symbolic significance – such rituals are commonly formal, ceremonial and public. An example might be the degree/diploma/certificate graduation ceremony run by your college. Other examples of ritual behaviour include religious services, weddings, funerals and many sporting events. Sociologists also refer to rituals which constitute the *rites of passage* within a society. These commonly accompany a change of status which is occurring in the course of the life cycle. Examples include the acknowledgement of the arrival of a new child through ceremonies such as christening (or the equivalent in religions other than Christianity); the attainment of adulthood which in the UK is often marked by the 18th birthday party; marriage ceremonies and retirement. These rituals are a means of drawing attention to changes in status and social identity, and also offer a way to manage some of the tensions that such changes may involve, for example, the linking of two families, the acknowledgement of an offspring's independence, or the end of a working life.

These rituals enable the individual to publicly subscribe to the values of the culture; they often involve the conspicuous expenditure of resources and may offer significant marketing opportunities for the sale of appropriate symbols.

> **Think** – What significant rites of passage have you experienced?
> – What expenditure was involved?

The above highlights culture emerging from a number of elements and institutions associated with living within a large group or society. Some of these will repay further examination:

1 Values, beliefs and religion

Sociologists such as Parsons have emphasized 'shared values' as playing a key role in the integration of a society or group. While it can be argued that a similar effect may be obtained via the use of raw power (as in some military dictatorships), most analysts accept that such societies tend to be less stable. So culture is, in part, a reflection of the ethical ideals accepted by the people making up that group and, as such, is concerned with what the society believes *ought* to happen and how it sees itself. This is reflected in the attitudes of individuals, the rules and enforcement processes it employs, and in the customs embraced by the society. Clearly religious beliefs will fall into this category as religion is often the determinant of values, and belief is fundamental to religion. From such beliefs stem ideas which are held as important within UK culture such as the right of free speech, or involvement in decision making via the democratic process. Other societies with different religions, beliefs and values may develop different, but no less valid, cultures.

2 Language and communication

The fact that different cultures speak different languages is an obvious means of distinguishing between large groups of people. Language is itself a fascinating field of study as it has a long history, examination of which emphasizes the fact that language itself is a changing entity. New words get invented, meanings of words change over time, and, as we noted earlier, language is particularly rich in communicating feelings and emotions as well as facts. A specific problem can arise when products (or marketing messages) are expected to cross cultural/language barriers. On occasion, a word in one language may also exist in another, but mean something very different. For instance an Italian walking through a UK shopping centre may see a poster saying 'SALE' in a shop window. This means 'salt' in Italian and thus has the potential to confuse. The problem may be even greater for the visitor from France, to whom the 'sale' sign means 'dirty'! Examples of such confusion in naming products which cross language barriers can give rise to humourous situations (but only if you are not the person responsible for the product). Colgate attempted to use the name 'cue' in France, only to find that it was an obscene slang expression. The Vauxhall Nova tends not to be popular in Spanish speaking areas where 'nova' translates into 'does not go'! Another example is the Toyota MR2 sports car. 'MR2', when said in French emerges as 'MR deux', this, when spoken in French sounds remarkably like another French word 'merde' – needless to say, Toyota changed the name for the French market.

Because of such dangers, consultancies now exist to check out possible product or brand names to ensure that such mistakes do not occur. It is claimed that the up-market ice-cream 'Häagen-Dazs' brand name was invented by such a consultancy, and was adopted specifically because it had no known meaning or association (it also has the advantage of being different and hence noticeable as discussed in the Perception chapter due to the double 'a', the umlaut and the 'z').

Think – What examples can you think of where language is a marketing problem?

---

3 Politics, law, social organization and education

The political system adopted by a nation will be an important determinant of the culture – and will do so in a relatively formal manner. The political system will allocate power and influence to certain groups of individuals and this will, in turn, directly affect 'the way things are done'. Laws logically follow as the formalized statements of acceptable behaviour as discussed above, and will set the limits of tolerated conduct. Social organization will be considered later as notions of social class and status are acknowledged to be important ways of viewing social stratification. Education plays an important part in the whole socialization process, affecting language, values and learned behaviour as well as linking to social class.

4 Artefacts and technology

In the holiday brochure, culture is often linked to historical artefacts. In modern society – the technology directly influences the way in which people live. The explosion in mass communication in some parts of the world has had enormous impact on whole societies and the rate of social change has been accelerated by having live news reports beamed into our living rooms. In a similar way, transport systems within an area will affect the way of life, social interaction and shopping patterns.

Culture will influence many important behaviours and attitudes and some of these behaviours may affect us in the activities associated with marketing. So it is worthwhile looking at some of these areas in a little more detail.

Appearance and dress

Any visit to another country will highlight the different appearance and dress of other peoples. To some extent this may be a reflection of affluence and fashion but cultures may differ significantly in their views on issues such as whether adult males should shave their beards. There are also very different views and standards about the extent to which females may expose skin. Compare the different cultural values which are repesented by women members of some Muslim sects, who dress so that only the eyes are uncovered, with the scantily clad females who appear in photographs from the Cannes Film Festival. Even within a larger society the various micro cultures exert strong influence over their members as witnessed by the pin-striped suit of the stereotypical businessman and the apparel of the football fans turning up for the match. One oddity of culture in the UK is the wearing of ties on important occasions – the tie seems to represent one of the least useful elements of clothing ever devised, and yet it remains essential for many people and would normally be worn for significant encounters such as job interviews.

> **Think** – How might this aspect of culture affect marketing and advertising?

By its very nature appearance becomes highly influential in determining the behaviour of those people within the cultural group and, thus, becomes a field of great interest in marketing terms.

Examples of the influence of culture might be basic items such as clothing or food. In its original form clothing was a means of covering our bodies in order to protect against weather – but fairly rapidly it became a symbol of many other social and personal characteristics. Clothes became a statement about the identity of the person wearing them. The statements could include issues such as gender, modesty, affluence, status, religion, race, age and so forth. From humble initial beginnings clothing has become a complex badge of membership of both society and the groups that make up the society.

Similarly food was initially a means to sustain life – but, again, we have imbued many foods with symbolic meanings. We may eat certain things as special treats, or at specific times (the 'traditional' Christmas dinner would be one example). Food can be an example of family bonding with recipes being handed down from one generation to the next. It can also be a symbol of racial or ethnic identity. In extreme cases certain foods can become religious icons, eaten as part of specific religious ceremonies.

> **Think** – What foods are significant to you?
> – Why?
> – What defines a Sunday Dinner for you?
> – How does this meal differ from other meals in the week?

As we have observed, culture is a wide ranging concept. Part of its significance is that it is the system that provides people with an understanding of acceptable and expected behaviour within the society. This, in turn, will go some way towards providing people with a sense of identity.

Sense of gender roles

Different cultures have different expectations and rules governing the roles of men and women. Traditionally, in the UK, women have been looked on as the homebuilders and nurturers while men have been expected to fulfil the breadwinner role. However, the rise of feminism and the growing value attached to equal opportunities within the society has shifted some of the expectations. A typical example of the use of the expected roles of men and women in advertising material might be the long running Oxo advertisements which showed the wife as the provider of meals for the hungry males of the family. Later versions have portrayed her as rather more independent – but still carrying out the caring role – by the use of Oxo! In contrast, other societies may allocate rather different roles to the genders and enforce those expectations with varying degrees of sanctions.

> **Think** – What other marketing examples can you think of which involve 'usual' gender roles?
> – What examples can you think of which attract attention by using 'unusual' roles?

Food and eating habits

As mentioned above, this is a basic activity which is likely to be affected by culture. It is often regarded as a communal activity where the individuals take meals with their primary groups, so, in addition to fulfilling psychological needs it may be an important mechanism for social bonding. Again, food can have symbolic and ritualistic elements.

> **Think** – What are the ritualistic elements required of:
> – a wedding breakfast?
> – Christmas dinner?
> – a working lunch?

Another aspect of food and culture may arise from the importance of beliefs and religion. Some religious groups will not eat pork, others will not eat beef, still others will not eat meat of any sort, some will not drink alcohol, others will take no stimulants of any kind. Clearly such beliefs will affect buying behaviour with regard to foodstuffs.

Relationships

Relationships may be defined by the culture within which the individuals are operating. Expectations of children by parents (and of parents by children) may vary from society to society.

> **Think** – What obligations do you think children have towards supporting
> their ageing parents?
> – Why?

Mental processing and learning styles

Mental processing and learning styles may vary from culture to culture. Many anthropologists will argue that so-called 'primitive' cultures possess knowledge which more 'advanced' societies have lost. Western societies tend to be dominated by logic and proof in terms of mental processing (witness our discussions in Chapter 2). Other societies may have different approaches – this is often cited as a problem for Western businesspersons visiting Eastern societies.

> **Think** – What examples can you think of where people have adopted
> different mental processes and learning styles?

Time and time consciousness

Another area which can vary markedly from culture to culture is time and time consciousness. Western perspectives of time can seem very short in comparison to other cultures. We go on time management courses, have electronic notebooks that act as alarm clocks for appointments and generally live in a 'hurry, hurry' environment. Yet in contrast we like to holiday in places where the pace of life is slower and this is sold to us strongly in vacation advertisements.

> **Think** – What examples can you identify of different time consciousness?

Occupation

The place and importance of work in our lives can vary dramatically. In the UK asking someone what they are usually results in an answer which involves a job title. We have developed a system where the job a person does fulfils a number of different functions. Our job is:

- the source of income and, hence, economic stability, status and power,
- an important determinant of how we spend our time,

- a source of social contact and friendship,
- a significant factor in the way our place in society is determined,
- a crucial determinant of our own self-image.

It is for these reasons that redundancy or unemployment can be so psychologically damaging for those who experience it.

Cross-cultural issues

Some writers on marketing consider culture as being a single entity and use the notion of macro-culture as an all encompassing method of describing a whole country. They focus specifically on problems of cross-cultural marketing and the problems associated with the selling of goods developed by and for one culture into another. Problems may be experienced when selling British goods in Japan, pork pies to Israel or American technology to Iraq. The difficulties of international marketing are genuine and the culture issue has to be faced by any organization marketing across national or cultural barriers. Ohmae has suggested that, in some cases, it is possible and desirable to promote a standard 'global' product. He suggests that battery-powered products such as cameras, calculators and watches may be 'globalized' successfully via a combination of high technology and economies of scale which allow aggressive cost reduction and the promotion of a global image. At the other end of the scale, premium-priced fashion goods can make up another cluster of products that have been successfully marketed on a global basis. In this instance the success of brands such as Gucci (hand bags, shoes and leather wear) would seem to appeal to an international high-income group that has adopted similar values, tastes and preferences. Generally these are perceived as the rich 'jet set' types who have wealth as a common factor of their micro culture. Due to their high profile in the media, such people may also become aspirational role models for others, less well off. In this way the influence of 'local' cultures gradually becomes eroded. Earlier we commented on the importance of appearance and dress as a cultural sign – in contrast, the globalization of the T-shirt and jeans as a uniform for both the males and females of the younger generations indicates a growing (if limited) universality.

Needless to say, not all products are suited to global treatment and a significant part of international marketing concerns the tailoring of products to suit local markets. Here the choice is commonly between modifying the product to fit the local requirements and modifying the marketing message to make it suitable for the new audience. Examples of *product modification* would be the manufacturers of the board game 'Scrabble' having different numbers of the various letters of the alphabet for different languages reflecting the different frequencies of use within that language, or British cars needing left-hand drive versions for export.

> **Think** – What other examples of product modification can you find?

The alternative is *message modification* to fit the marketing message to the host culture. Here we may be attempting to make a 'standard' product in the original country 'special' in the importing culture. The selling of French water in the UK might be a good example of this.

Think – What other examples of message/image modification can you find?

Originally the concept of culture was applied to whole societies such as nations, but increasingly it has become clear that it is a useful framework to adopt when analysing different sizes of societies and also significant groupings within the set we think of as a society. So it is now applied in a variety of settings:

- *macro-cultures* refer to large groupings such as whole continents (e.g. the idea of European or North American cultures), or
- individual nations (e.g. contrasting English and French cultures),
- *micro-cultures* refer either to significant groupings within a society such as classes (e.g. comparing 'upper' and 'working classes), or
- other micro-cultures such as religious groupings, racial groups specific age groups, or even as 'micro' as followers of a particular football club,
- increasingly the expression is used to describe the style adopted within a business or company and this is referred to as *organizational culture.*

(*Note*: in some older texts, sociologists have used the expression sub-culture. In this volume it is replaced by the phrase micro-culture in an attempt to remove any implication of inferiority associated with the use of the prefix 'sub' which could prove offensive to religious or ethnic groups).

While many of the points that are raised have a degree of validity, there is a danger of oversimplification due to the assumption of national stereotypes as discussed earlier. However, examination of the world in which we live seems not to support such a view. In the UK it seems rash to claim 'sameness' for the different regions of the country; the inner cities and rural areas; protestants, catholics, muslims, sikhs and rastafarians; asian, afro-carribean and anglo-saxon races and so forth. The reality seems to be that society is made up of a series of micro-cultures many of which are significantly different. Far from being a handicap, such a view may help us to segment the society into targetable markets.

It is sometimes suggested that the six prime micro-cultures within our society are based on:

1 *Geography*. This reflects regional differences in patterns of speech (accents), and some stereotyped assumptions about eating, drinking and consumption patterns. Such variations have a strong historical basis as the different communities developed differently due to the economic and geographical factors influencing the area. However, the advent of mass media has had the effect of reducing some of the variance – the

standardization of speech patterns around some notional BBC norm would be an example, although such evening out is opposed by those who wish to keep to the old traditions and maintain separate, distinct cultures.

2 *Ethnicity*. Historically, for obvious economic reasons, ethnic groupings have tended to develop in certain areas. This has the advantage of enabling the original cultures of the immigrants to be maintained. An example of this would be in the author's home town where a significant Polish population has settled mainly within a specific locality. The result of such concentration is that children can be taught the Polish language, the customs and rituals of the 'old country' can be emphasized and maintained, and a number of Polish clubs can exist where the ex-patriates can meet and retain their 'Polishness'. Clearly such a situation suggests that marketing opportunities exist to cater for the needs of this kind of micro-culture. Similar examples from other ethnic groups can be found in most large conurbations. In the past marketers have not targeted ethnic groups for most products – there seems to have been an assumption that mass marketing would, by definition, reach all members of the society. However, we are beginning to see advertising aimed at specific ethnic groups in product areas such as beauty and grooming.

3 *Religion*. For those who subscribe to a religious creed the belief and membership of the religious community is likely to be a major influence on their attitudes, lifestyle and behaviour.

4 *Age*. In the last chapter we looked at the family life cycle (FLC) and discussed the segmentation of markets according to the prime interests and levels of disposable income and the various stages of the FLC could have many of the characteristics of micro-cultures. Perhaps the most significant of these is the so-called 'youth culture'. As a market segment they came to the fore in the 1960s when the combination of the immediate post-war baby boom and increasing affluence led to a sizeable market opportunity. The market was identified by such things as choice of music and clothes. For the first time there was a situation where a very young age group had high disposable income – this led to a massive growth in items such as records and fashion. More recently the emergence of the 'yuppie' has had a major impact on product development, the notion of style, and the identification of a clear market segment. In the UK at the present time, the 'grey' market is becoming increasingly important. Here we have a growing number of older people, some of whom have inherited considerable sums of money following the spectacular rise in property values during the 1980s and so have very great discretionary spending power. There is evidence that this group does not perceive itself as being old and is maintaining high levels of market activity. Given their numbers and relative wealth the 'greys' form a very attractive market segment. The recent growth of television situation comedies which centre on older characters (e.g.'*Til Death Us Do Part, Waiting For God, One Foot In The Grave, The Golden Girls* being the current crop) reflects its influence and potential.

5 *Gender*. As we saw in the last chapter the roles of the sexes are often defined by the family setting and may well determine the location of a number of purchasing decisions. The marketing implications of a micro-culture based on gender rest on the assumption that men or women have beliefs and values which make them different. In this sense we may come back to our basic examples of shaving for men or sanitary protection for women. Beyond these physiological sets we are likely to be concerned with notions of male and female roles within the society. Here we have seen changes over the last decade with the emergence of the career woman and the 'new man', both powerful social images which have developed market segments based on these micro-cultures.

At the simplest level culture is concerned with '*how we do things here*'. So the variations may be viewed as different perceptions of who '*we*' are, and where '*here*' is.

Socialization

We commented in our earlier discussion of culture that it was both learned and passed from one generation to another. This learning process is called *socialization* and we can define it as:

the process by which the culture of a society is transmitted to children and succeeding generations so that they absorb all of its values and symbols and become able to function effectively within it.

It is concerned with the ways in which an individual's behaviour is modified from infancy to conform to the demands of the social system. It involves learning the expectations associated with various roles within the society but, given the nature of human beings, it does not just produce clones – there is another significant element which is about the individuals and the development of their separate identities.

The socialization process is concerned with preparing individuals for the roles that may be required of them and also with the continuation and development of the culture itself. Thus it focuses on relationships between the individual and society. In this sense the study of this concept bridges the disciplines of sociology and psychology. The mechanisms of socialization are basically the same as discussed in our review of learning and learning theory – so we revisit the material from Chapter 5.

Much of our social behaviour is learned via *connectionist* principles. Children are subject to *classical conditioning* in the sense that they will learn family rituals and make the associations between certain stimuli and the linked responses. Much of this learning may continue into adulthood. The author has an unfortunate linkage from his childhood which is that being addressed by his full given forename 'Christopher' still leads to a conditioned response of 'what have I done wrong?'. Similarly the process of growing up will lead to considerable *operant conditioning* where the child experiments with various behaviours and learns which ones lead to reward and positive reinforcement, and which ones lead to punishment. Reflection may lead us on to the conclusion that such conditioning does not only occur in childhood, a significant part of adult life can be viewed in these terms – not least the ways in which our employers may attempt to condition our work behaviours by offering rewards for behaviours *they* define as 'good', and negative reinforcement for those *they* define as undesirable. Further reflection may lead us to conclude that such conditioning is conducted in adult life by others in our lives including our partners, friends, and even governments.

> **Think** – What social conditioning are you aware of in your own
>   development?

Cognitive learning is also highly significant in the socialization process, particularly Tolman's *latent learning*. Here the learning may also be *observational* or *vicarious* as outlined by Bandura. The process of watching other people, absorbing the roles, specific behaviours and making judgements about their appropriateness is likely to result in storing the knowledge for recall at some later point in time.

Imitation is often the immediate outcome of such observational learning and the process of imitating may interact with some of our ideas of operant conditioning and experiential learning – in other words we may imitate behaviour and use the experience of the reaction (positive or negative) to decide whether the behaviour becomes part of our 'normal' repertoire.

Implicit in the idea of imitation is the concept of the *role model* – the individual's perceived ideal which they seek to emulate. *Identification* takes the process even deeper, with the person taking on the perceived attitudes and values of the role model, i.e. attempting to become exactly like the ideal. Once these values and attitudes have been adopted the 'learned' behaviour emerges when the situation is perceived as being appropriate.

> **Think** – Who are your role models?
>   – How have they affected your behaviour?

Role play is another mechanism of learning. It fits most closely with Kolb's *experiential learning* and involves consciously 'trying out' roles. This is a common experience of childhood ('let's play doctors and nurses/ mummies and daddies/cops and robbers, etc.) and is increasingly being used in management training. The practice of playing a role allows experimentation, and repetition leads to the imprinting of particular (but necessarily appropriate) behaviours. This can be a valuable device for developing the skills needed for unaccustomed roles.

> **Think** – Have you ever role-played being the applicant before going for a
> job interview?
> – What did you learn from the experience?

As has been hinted at in the above section, learning and socialization takes place via a number of agencies.

1 Family

Much of the discussion has centred on children learning as this process of passing on from one generation to another has been defined as one of the prime characteristics and aims of culture. The child is particularly susceptible to the learning because of its dependence on the family and its very high involvement with family members and family activities. Our discussion of the family as a primary group in the last chapter highlighted its importance as both a social grouping and a decision making and purchasing unit. Its importance in the socialization process is due to the impact it has in forming the ideas, attitudes or values of the growing individual. The review of personality development in Chapter 3 also emphasized Freud's view that this early stage of life is highly influential in determining the adult personality.

In particular, the child is likely to be exposed to experiences which will fundamentally affect the perception and expectations associated with roles such as 'husband', 'wife', 'mother', 'father'. Embedded in these roles will be values, attitudes, relationships, specific behaviours and decision making patterns. Experience suggests that much of this early learning is carried over into adult life and many problems experienced by people may be diagnosed as a re-enactment of early experiences.

> **Think** – What values, attitudes and behaviours have you carried from
> your childhood?

2 School

Again, this is influential in that it can initiate behaviours, values and attitudes while the individual is both dependent and impressionable. Schools ostensibly teach knowledge and skills to pupils, but few of us would deny that it is a spell in life where cultural values are both introduced and reinforced. The phenomenon of unexpected learning may occur as, for instance, when a pupil is asked to come out in front of the class and work through a long division problem on the board. This experience may not teach the individual anything about mathematics, but a great deal about humiliation (and teachers) may be learned! Similarly, most schools place great emphasis on honesty and ideas such as 'good citizenship', but we also learn that there is a strong, unwritten code that demands that one does not 'tell tales' about other classmates.

> **Think** – What values, attitudes and behaviours have you carried from your schooldays?

3 Peer groups

In the preceding chapter we reviewed the evidence for the influence of our informal social groups. The power of such groups is their ability to control a person's personal and emotional satisfactions. As we saw the 'ultimate deterrent' may be the threat of being isolated or 'sent to Coventry'. As was shown in the bank wiring room section of the Hawthorne experiments, the power of the informal group may well exceed the influence of the formal management system. Outside of the workplace, peer group pressure is often more influential than the expectations of the family. Part of the process of growing up is resolving the potential conflicts between the values, attitudes and behaviours demanded by one's peer group and those expected by the family. This process is commonly a source of tension within families as children progress through adolescence. Both the family and the individual attempting to come to terms with changing status and independence. However, peer groups continue to be important throughout our lives, and may generate significant changes in behaviour particularly if the peer group changes – as may happen when couples form a partnership and each is introduced to the other's group of friends. Thus we see that their influence is a continuing factor in developing values, attitudes and behaviour.

> **Think** – Which of your values, attitudes and behaviours have been influenced by friends, colleagues and peer group?
> – What peer group pressures have you rejected?

4 Mass media

Exposure to the mass media has a significant impact on our view of the world. In earlier chapters the ideas of selective perception and selective exposure were explored and we can see the way in which reading a particular newspaper may reinforce political beliefs and value systems. However, the media are now virtually all pervasive, and few of us can escape images and inputs from television, radio, magazines, and newspapers. Inevitably these will give a particular vision of reality and it seems unrealistic to suppose that people's perceptions will not be affected. Repetition of specific messages gradually 'sink in' to the cultural subconscious – so that the values and assumptions of things such as the 'enterprise culture' of the 1980s influenced the majority of the population. Similarly, single images may live in the mind and affect our perceptions in the longer term. Here the picture of the solitary student standing in front of the advancing tanks in Peking might be an illustration. As students of marketing processes we may also need to consider the cumulative influence of the advertising images that our trade puts before the public. The continual presentation of images of wealth, prosperity, power, gender roles, sexual attractiveness and racial character- istics seems likely to produce expectations in the population at large which at best may be motivating but which may also give rise to frustration, anger, resentment or distress.

Think – How has the mass media affected your values, attitudes and behaviours?

Much of the foregoing discussion has centred on the idea of individuals learning behaviour appropriate to the different roles they play. It is worthwhile to spend a little more time exploring some of the ideas surrounding the notion of a role.

Role

In the last chapter we introduced the concept of the role. We discussed roles within groups and, within the context of the family, the changing nature of gender roles. Looking at the concept in a little more detail we may start with clarifying what is meant by a role.

Engel, Blackwell & Miniard define a *role* as:

What the typical occupant of a given position is expected to do in that position in a particular social context (1990, p. 191).

In other words it is used in very much the same way as it is used by actors. You may have a role which is 'assistant product manager' and there will be behaviours which the person holding that role will be expected to exhibit.

Now it is clear from our discussion of groups in Chapter 8 that we belong to many groups, both formal and informal. Each of these may allocate us one or more roles to play. So you may have roles such as husband or wife, friend, son or daughter, member of a political party, football fan, or churchgoer, in addition to the work roles of 'assistant product manager' and general 'rising star'.

Inevitably a person cannot comfortably exhibit all of the appropriate behaviours at the same time – wearing the tribal warpaint of the football fan is more relevant to match days than formal meetings at work! Indeed, it is interesting to note that several roles within our society demand a specific appearance or uniform – milk and post deliverers, railway guards, bus drivers, clergy. In a less formal sense there may be a 'uniform' for managers or marketing specialists.

> **Think** – Which of the roles that you play involve any form of uniform?

In many situations the 'uniform' is an important role sign, for example being a bride or groom at a wedding (or even a wedding guest). Funerals demand an expected appearance, while attending an exercise class certainly involves considerable expenditure on 'suitable' clothing. This means considerable opportunities for marketing products which could be seen as role signs – briefcases, organizers, 'executive toys' and even motor cars are typical examples of merchandise which may be sold in order to reinforce a person's perceived role.

In examining the expectations surrounding different roles, we are, in effect, attempting to explain the phenomenon described in the last chapter – that of behaviour changing according to the different social groupings in which we find ourselves.

Roles will often define a *relationship* quite specifically – here the role of teacher or tutor would be a good example with the expectations that the teacher will transmit information and the student will accept it. The other individuals who relate to an individual in their specific roles are referred to as their *role set*. The membership of such role sets will change according to the roles being played – e.g. the home role set would consist of family members, the work role set would be made up of colleagues, superiors, subordinates, customers and so forth. Behaviour is likely to change in as much as few families can tolerate a teacher lecturing them over breakfast, while management *students* may even be expected to *manage* when at work.

Once again the core issues appear to centre on the perceptions of the role by both other people and the person carrying it out along with a more generalized expectation of the 'rules' of behaviour associated with the role (i.e. the norms established by society). If all parties share the same perception, things are relatively straightforward, but if there is any degree of mismatch then accommodations will have to be made. Figure 9.2 highlights the similarity of the adjustment process to some of the ideas associated with adult learning discussed in Chapters 3 and 5.

Given that much of role theory depends on the perceptions of the individuals concerned, it is likely that some discrepancies will occur. The problems associated with differing expectations can be classified into:

1 *Role ambiguity* – this is where the expectations are not clearly defined, either for the role player or the associated role set. Thus the problem can centre on:

   (i) the individual's uncertainty of what is expected in the role – examples could include 'finding one's feet' on appointment to a new job, or uncertainty of the full implications of changing marital status or becoming a parent;

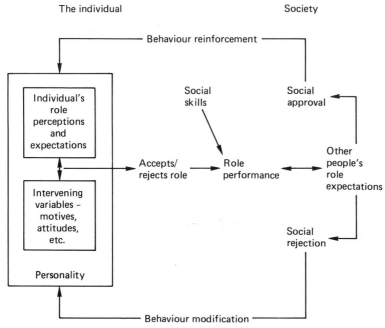

Figure 9.2 The effect of role on the learning of social behaviour (adapted from Williams, *Behavioural Aspects of Marketing*, 1981)

   (ii) the role set's uncertainty of what is expected in the role – examples could include your class 'negotiating' an acceptable style with the tutor, couples working hard in the early days of a relationship to clarify role specializations within the household, or a department faced with a new manager showing uncertainty as to whether the boss will maintain the *status quo* or become a 'new broom'.

2 *Role conflict* – again subdivided into:
   (i) *inter-role conflict* where the conflict occurs *between* roles. An example might be the conflict between the individual being asked to work overtime on a rush job having to decide whether the demands of the employment outweigh missing an offspring's scheduled birthday party. In this case the conflict is between the expectations associated with the 'conscientious employee' role ('of course I will work extra') with the demands of the 'loving parent' role ('of course I'll be back for the party'). Women face particular problems due to expectations that they will fulfil the caring/nurturing roles within families, thus setting up immediate conflicts with employment expectations. Many convenience foods slant their advertising material towards bridging the gap by showing how use of the product will create the space to be a successful career woman *and* feed the family nourishing meals. Such advertising offers a solution to the cognitive dissonance which often arises from inter-role conflict.

(ii) *intra-role conflict* where the conflict arises from different aspects of the same role. For instance in the parental role, the caring and loving elements, at times, may be in conflict with the need to discipline a child.

As we have noted earlier, conflicts or problems often offer marketing opportunities in as much as the solution to the problem (or the resolution of the conflict) may be the true product being sold.

Social class, status and other forms of market segmentation

The foregoing discussion of culture emphasized the importance of the marketer tailoring the product and the message to the culture in which the sale of product or service is to be made. This has clear implications, as outlined, for marketing practice when international and cross-cultural barriers are to be faced.

Another important task for marketing specialists is the segmentation of the society in which they are operating into manageable groups. The aim is to identify groupings, the members of which are sufficiently similar in their values and aspirations for marketing messages to be designed specifically to meet the groups' needs and motives. In this sense segmentation could be considered as identifying a series of micro-cultures, so much of the earlier discussion will apply when operating within a given market.

Two of the most common used terms in segmentation are *class* and *status*.

```
Think  – What class are you?
        – On what basis do you make that judgement?
```

The concept of class is a very complex one which is important in sociology. It has a number of similar and interlinked usages and meanings – some of the key ideas associated with class are:

1 The notion of *hierarchical distinction* which also finds itself expressed in ideas such as *social stratification* – hence the ideas of upper class, middle class, lower class, working class and so forth.

2 The use of census data to provide descriptive categories such as those used by the Registrar General in dividing the population of the United Kingdom.

3 The use of *occupations* to identify what are sometimes referred to as *socio-economic status groups* such as manual and non-manual, or white collar and blue collar occupations.

4 The description of a society in terms of the degree of *social mobility* that is possible. This leads directly to classifications such as *open societies* (social mobility and movement from one class to another being possible) and *closed societies* (social class being defined and fixed at (and by) birth as in caste systems). Ideas of inherited wealth, influence and position, such as is

implied in the existence of the aristocracy in the UK, would indicate a relatively closed system in parts of the society as wealth does not entitle the individual to move into a group such as the aristocracy.

5 The ideas of Marx which centre on ownership and non-ownership of property and resources and which give rise to the classifications of *bourgeoisie* and *proletariat* as the dominant classes in capitalist societies.

6 Weber's use of similar analysis focused on the subdivisions of property that might be the basis of distinctions. Property could thus include ideas such as *knowledge* or *education*.

Think – Which of these ideas were part of your analysis of your own social class?

Within the marketing context the importance of such ideas is that they offer the possibility of segmenting the population into groups which might have similar beliefs, attitudes and values reflected in their behaviour. This would enable suitable marketing messages to be designed and sent specifically to influence the buying behaviour of the group. It could be argued that this is the key reason for examining the society as a whole (and hence this chapter).

We use ideas such as class to help us find groups which are collections of individuals who are of sufficiently similar status to give them the same sort of command over goods and services, and to share belief systems, aspirations and values.

Class is essentially an *objective* means of classifying people according to criteria such as occupation, education, lifestyle, place of residence and income. It implies (and as marketers we seek) an awareness of class consciousness within the group, a degree of uniformity of lifestyle, and social interaction so that processes of group conformity can operate.

Status, on the other hand, is essentially a *subjective* phenomenon which is the result of a judgement of the social position that a person occupies. Here the distinction from class becomes somewhat blurred as the judgement is usually also based on factors such as power, wealth and occupation.

It is possible to identify three forms of status:

1 *Ascribed status* – this is similar to the ideas of ascribed groups described in the previous chapter. This status is something the individual has little control over as it covers the status accorded by society to classifications such as gender (male/female) and race/colour. So far as any individual is concerned this is primarily defined by the 'accident of birth' and is, by and large, permanent. It is an interesting aspect that while ascribed status is outside the control of the individual, it is not necessarily fixed, in as much as it is possible to chart the changes in status of (e.g.) women over a period of time within a given society.

2 *Achieved status* – in contrast, is that which has been acquired by individuals through such things as their occupation, place of residence,

and lifestyle. Once again, this is subjective and open to change as the values of a society alter. It is often assumed that status is linked to spending power, but it is possible to find groups of people who enjoy relatively high status but relatively low income. The clergy, nurses, and even teachers might fall into such a category, but, as with ascribed status, the valuation of occupations (or residential areas) can change. Recent events and publicity seem to have dented the reputation (and status) of groups such as social workers, and the property boom of the 1980s led to disaffection for estate agents.

> **Think** – Which occupations can you think of which are 'on the way up'?
> – Which do you think are 'on the way down'?
> – Why?

3 *Desired status* – this is the social position an individual wishes to attain. Here the analogy is with the aspirational groups discussed in the last chapter. The assumption is that status is actively sought by the individual who seeks to acquire and conform to the desired roles. In this case it is something over which the individual can exercise some control, and is identical to the important notion of ego or status motivation as proposed by Maslow (see Chapter 6).

For marketers the key to influencing consumers in this way depends on the concept of the open society. The idea that individuals can improve their lot and rise in the hierarchy of class and status leads to the strategy of placing the product in such a setting that it appeals to the target segment/class/status group and implies that adoption will lend credence to their aspirations to be seen as a member of the next higher group.

We can examine some popular systems for market segmentation, based on behavioural ideas. The first is shown in Figure 9.3.

The *Registrar General's Scale* uses a five class grouping which is very similar – however, in this case the classes are referred to as I ($=$ A), II ($=$ B), etc. In this system there is a similar distinction between III_1 ($= C_1$) and III_2 ($= C_2$). The Jicnar group D is subdivided into IV ($=$ semi-skilled manual labour) and V ($=$ unskilled). The Registrar General does not have a subsistence/unemployed/pensioner category.

As stated above, the aim is to offer a segment of the population products associated with the class (or group) one higher than themselves. Thus the C_2s are supposed to aspire to the lifestyle of the C_1s, and offering them products with white collar, C_1 characteristics should make it attractive to them.

While these approaches have much to commend them, and many marketing students will be familiar with the systems from studying market research, they do suffer from some significant shortcomings:

1 The definitions of class and status are neither clear nor consistent. Most people believe themselves to be of a different class to that defined for them by such schemes – they may see themselves as being of a higher class, or,

Social Grade	Social Status	Occupations	Examples
A	Upper middle class	Higher managerial/ professional	directors, doctors, lawyers, professors
B	Middle class	Intermediate managerial	managers, teachers, computer programmers
C_1	Lower middle	Junior managerial, supervisory, clerical administrative	foremen, shop assistants, office workers
C_2	Skilled working class	Skilled manual labour	electricians, mechanics, plumbers & other crafts
D	Working class	Semi- and unskilled manual labour	machine operators, assembly, cleaning
E	Subsistence	None	Pensioners, casual workers, unemployed, students

Figure 9.3   Jicnar's social grade definitions

alternatively, may be clinging to a perception of themselves as (e.g.) 'working class' when the objective data suggests otherwise.

Think – Having read the categories of the Jicnar/Registrar General's Scale how accurate was your description of your social class on page 260 above?
 – If it was 'wrong', why?

---

2 The categories are defined by the occupation of the 'head of the household'. Our review of the family life cycle in the preceding chapter highlighted the changes that are taking place in the model of the 'typical' family. The existence of UK law protecting employment rights for women following maternity leave has meant that an increasing number of women are able to return to work earlier that might be suggested by the 'classic' FLC. This emphasizes the importance of the family (or household) as a decision making and purchasing unit, and also the importance of the high proportion of families with two earners. The significance of women's careers (as opposed to the idea that women work for 'pin money') must be accepted.

3 In practice the classes do not necessarily command disposable income in the same order as the grades would suggest. Most of us know C_2s (such as

plumbers, television repair specialists, electricians and the like) who earn a great deal more than the foremen, supervisors and clerical staff with (or for) whom they work. Indeed, many may earn more than the Bs (teachers and middle managers) who are theoretically two categories above them.

4 Improved access to education has made the barriers between classes less distinct. Many graduates now come from working class backgrounds, and, in the light of our comments on socialization and learning processes, it seems naïve to assume they will abandon the values of their early upbringing.

5 Given the lack of job security – now common in the UK – we may face the anomaly that a middle class (B) manager who is made redundant immediately drops to grade E, despite the fact that disposable income could have risen due to redundancy payments. Clearly people do not change their values, attitudes and buying behaviour so dramatically and quickly.

6 There is considerable doubt as to whether it is class which produces the similarity in lifestyles, or lifestyles which produce the phenomenon of class.

Thus, class and status may only be useful for particular products, services or ideas.

One additional observation is that both the Jicnar and Registrar General systems attempt to objectively categorize the population by *class*. However, both use labelling schemes (A–E; I–V) which imply hierarchy and have strong connotations regarding *status* as well. Such inferences were not intended when the systems were created, but have now become deeply embedded in our thinking about class and status.

Another, more concrete, system for segmentation is based on the notion that where people live gives a good predictor of their class and status. It also has the advantage that housing is not mobile and, as residential areas rise or fall in terms of their 'desirability', areas and even specific postcodes can easily be reclassified.

The best known of such systems is ACORN (*A C*lassification *O*f *R*esidential *N*eighbourhoods). The ACORN groups are:

A Agricultural areas,
B Modern family housing, higher incomes,
C Older housing of intermediate status,
D Poor quality older terraces,
E Better-off council estates,
F Less well-off council estates,
G Poorest council estates,
H Multi-racial areas,
I   High status non-family areas,
J   Affluent suburban housing,
K Better-off retirement areas,
U Unclassified.

These broad categories are subdivided to give a total of thirty-eight ACORN types – for instance the B group (modern family housing, higher incomes) is split down into five subsets:

– Cheap modern private housing (B3),
– Recent private housing, young families (B4),
– Modern private housing, older families (B5),
– New detached housing, young families (B6),
– Military bases, mixed owner-occupied (B7).

This type of system is of obvious applicability to direct-mail marketing and is of particular value when analysing catchment areas, especially when organizations are deciding where to site retail stores.

Given the limitations of the more traditional segmentation systems, it is worth commenting on some of the more recent approaches. These stem from some of the ideas covered in previous sections of the book.

Family life cycle segmentation

Our review of the family life cycle gave clear indications of the focus of interest of many family groups at differing stages of the FLC. It is fairly straightforward to translate these stages into market segments for particular products.

Demographic segmentation

Here we return to the notion of things such as the 'Youth' micro-culture and the idea that age grouping is likely to be a determinant of buying behaviour. One of the most obviously segmented markets is that of holidays where companies such as '18–30' and 'Saga Holidays' have specialized in very clearly identified age groups.

Psychographics and lifestyle segmentation

Perhaps the most comprehensive of the newer approaches, and one which seems to have the greatest potential is psychographics and lifestyle segmentation. Lifestyle may be seen as the individual's attempt to achieve their desired self-concept given the constraints of their real world. Psychographics is the main way in which lifestyle analysis has been made available to the marketing specialist. It is an approach which seeks to describe the lifestyle of a segment of consumers and focuses primarily on:

- *Activities:* usually observable and measurable. They could include items such as exposure to various media, visits to cinemas or theatres, shopping at specified shopping centres, holiday patterns, club memberships and so forth.

- *Interests:* defined both in terms of an object, topic, event or subject and the level of excitement and attention that accompanies either short-term or long-term interest in it.
- *Opinions:* the expectations, evaluations and interpretations about objects, topics, events, people or subjects.

For this reason it is sometimes called AIO analysis. However, marketers commonly add some extra dimensions such as:

- *demographics*: factors such as age, income, occupation, gender, education, location;
- *attitudes*: collection of data on orientation to places, ideas and so forth;
- *values*: beliefs as to what is acceptable and/or desirable;
- *personality traits*;
- *usage rates*: consumption within specific product category, e.g. heavy/light users.

Thus it is a potent mixture of factual, 'hard' information identifying aspects such as disposable income, and 'soft', qualitative data coming from motivational research techniques and aiming to ascertain the hidden and perhaps subconscious motivations described in our discussion of Freudian theory above.

It offers a number of attractions to the marketer:

1 it accepts that consumer behaviour is affected by other factors as well as status and class and includes the important variable of individual personality;
2 the notion of lifestyle, by definition, encompasses purchasing decisions;
3 markets can be segmented by lifestyle;
4 appropriate communication channels may be part of the lifestyle and can be relatively well defined and hence exploited;
5 campaigns can present brand personalities designed to appeal to specific lifestyles/AIO groups.

Think – Which approach to market segmentation do you feel is most appropriate for the following products/services?
- Lawnmowers
- Banking Services
- Newspapers
- Suntan lotion
- Satellite dishes and decoders
- Soft drinks
- Washing-up liquid
- Open top sports cars
- Top-of-the-range running shoes
- Denture fixatives

More sophisticated approaches to segmentation

Systems are being developed which incorporate more than one of these 'simple' approaches to segmentation. One of the most impressive and widely used is called MOSAIC and it identifies fifty-eight separate classification types.

In this system the basic classification is done via:

- housing data, similar to the ACORN system described above, but also with input from:
- demographics (interestingly identifying factors such as people who have moved house in the last year and length of time at that address);
- census data focusing on the number and ages of residents;
- census data concerned with ownership, facilities and size of household (giving an indication of lifestyle);
- socio-economic census data – e.g. occupations and car ownership;
- financial data from sources such as lists of county court judgements and finance house/credit card searches.

The possibility of adding more detailed lifestyle/AIO layers to such a model could offer exciting new tools for segmentation to marketers.

Communication systems and patterns of influence

In Chapter 4 we looked at some aspects of communication – in that section the focus was very much on the processes associated with perception. We noted that the perception of the receiver defined whether the communication was successful or not. In Chapter 7 we came back to communication when we looked at the characteristics of influential messages and the way in which they could change attitudes.

Both of these approaches had an implicit assumption that the communication was a single message passed from the sender to the receivers. This is called *one-step communication* and it is shown diagrammatically in Figure 9.4.

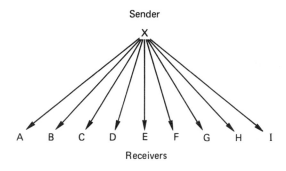

Figure 9.4

This is a common view of marketing communication – the sender transmits a message to each receiver (the targeted potential consumer) and it is then assumed that the individual will respond by purchasing the product or service (or not as the individual decides). This approach gives us yet another way of segmenting the market – the message and the medium can be chosen to appeal to specific target groups. While this is both a very common and common-sense approach to marketing communication it is not without its limitations:

1 Firstly, there may well be grave doubts as to whether the message actually reaches every receiver. There is considerable evidence to suggest that many commercial breaks on television are used by viewers to stretch their legs, make cups of tea, answer the call of nature, look at the newspaper to see what is on other channels and so forth. These are the very times when advertisers have paid large sums of money to communicate with them. In the work situation, organizations such as the Industrial Society have found that company newspapers and newsletters are rarely read in any detail, while newspaper advertisements are commonly skipped in the rush to find the part of the paper which is of direct interest to the reader.

2 Secondly, receivers do not, in reality, respond as independent, isolated individuals – much of the material covered in earlier chapters has emphasized the importance of groups and other social interactions in determining behaviour both in general terms and, more specifically, in purchasing.

So we may conclude that life is not as simple as the one-way model suggests. If you tried the exercise on page 105 try to remember what happened.

Think – Was this one-step communication?

The probable answer to that question is that it was not, as receivers behaving as independent, isolated individuals is quite rare.

One attempt to describe the process more realistically was by Lazarsfeld *et al.* who put forward (in 1948) the idea of *two-step communication*. This may be represented diagrammatically by Figure 9.5.

Here receiver E is seen as an influencer of others. These persons are referred to as *opinion leaders* and they are those individuals who reinforce the marketing messages sent, and to whom other receivers look for information, advice and opinion. As shown in the diagram, it is suggested that, under such a system, the opinion leader will also communicate the message to those receivers who may have missed the original message (*G,H,I* as shown). The early versions of two-step theory assumed most receivers to be relatively passive in terms of information search and exposure to the mass media, and the opinion leaders were active in disseminating the messages.

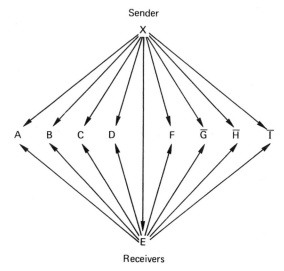

Figure 9.5

The follow-up work on this approach suggested that opinion leaders tended to:

1 be of similar social class as the other receivers (or influenced), but may be of higher social status within that class,
2 be more self confident,
3 be more outgoing and socially active,
4 be more orientated towards innovation,
5 have greater knowledge and interest in the area of influence, and
6 have greater exposure to relevant mass media than non-leaders.

At first sight this looks like the marketing specialist's dream – an individual who will promote the product, on the ground, free! It is not surprising that considerable effort has gone into trying to identify such persons. Several approaches can be taken, for instance, analysis of mailing lists drawn up from coupon replies will identify those who have specific interests and exposure to the mass media; analysis of appropriate organizations' membership lists could show those with the potential to be opinion leaders; while comparison of subscription mailing lists may indicate those who take more than one publication and thus satisfy (6) above. More personalized approaches could include sociometric techniques (asking who they go to for advice) or self-designation (asking people the extent to which their advice is sought).

The potential excitement at the idea of an élite group of opinion leaders who may be 'recruited' to aid the marketing effort had to be tempered when it was found that the sphere of influence of any individual was rather limited. Common sense suggests that it is rare to heed the advice of a single person on a wide range of topics. Experience would indicate that we are more likely to choose our advisor on the basis of *our* perception of their specialism.

Katz, in 1957, suggested that the degree of influence that is possible will depend on:

1 who the opinion leader is – those who are seen as typical of a group may be in a position to exert more infleunce;
2 what the opinion leader knows – the advice of the most expert is likely to carry most weight; and
3 where the opinion leader is located within the group – this could be measured by sociometric techniques as described in Chapter 8.

So gradually the limitations of the two-stage model of communication have become apparent. More recent approaches have tended to describe the process as one of *multi-stage interactions*.

Think – Reflect on your experience of the one-way/two way communication exercise in Chapter 2 : What really happened?

The way the exercise was set up made it *look* like one step – but, if your group was like most others, some strange things probably occurred. A common phenomenon is that some receivers spend a lot time looking at the diagrams being drawn by the people next to them (we sometimes call this behaviour cheating in slightly different contexts!), conversations and sometimes arguments start up over whether receivers have heard the same message, and there is a great deal of communication which goes on between *A, B, C, D, E, F* and *G*. On occasion the sender has trouble getting a word in edgewise, especially during the two-way session. So, in reality, the exercise is often a complex, multi-step communication which could be represented as in Figure 9.6.

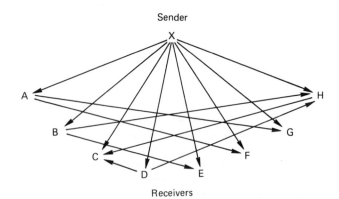

Figure 9.6

One interesting aspect of this is that people commonly pass on the message (sometimes correctly, at other times not) to those who were not paying attention, or who were momentarily distracted. The parallel with marketing messages is clear – consumers talk to one another, and their *word-of-mouth communication* can either help or hinder the intended communication process.

Word-of-mouth communication

This form of communication is particularly significant and important because it occurs in the highly influential reference groups as described in Chapter 8. It is relatively informal, and is difficult to manage because it does not involve the marketer directly. It would seem to be powerful specifically because of this 'neutrality' and the enhanced credibility of the messages.

Engel, Blackwell and Miniard call the transmitters of word-of-mouth communication of this sort *influentials*. In contrast to the original two-step model, these influentials are commonly sought out by the receivers rather than acting as active initiators of the messages. They identify seven conditions, one or more of which need to be present if 'opinion leadership' is likely to occur:

1 The consumer lacks sufficient information to make an adequately informed choice.
2 The product is complex and difficult to evaluate using objective criteria. Hence the experience of others serves as the basis for vicarious learning as described in Chapter 5.
3 The person lacks the ability to evaluate the product or service, no matter how the information is disseminated and presented.
4 Other sources are perceived as having low credibility.
5 An influential person is more accessible than other sources and thus can be consulted more easily.
6 Strong social ties exist between transmitter and receiver.
7 The individual has a high need for social approval.

They also argue that the motivations that drive interpersonal discussions which involve product information fall into one or more of five broad categories:

1 *Product involvement* – here the tendency to initiate conversation is directly proportional to the extent of the interest or involvement in the topic under discussion. The first person within a group of peers to have the new 32-bit, high resolution personal computer with the new software package is likely to tell others as an outlet for the pleasure or excitement generated by its purchase and use.

> **Think** – What examples of your own behaviour can you identify when you
> have behaved in this manner with other people?
> – What examples of other people's behaviour can you identify
> when they have behaved in this manner with you?

2 *Self-Enhancement* – this is when the motivation to initiate the transaction
is to gain attention, show what Engel, Blackwell and Miniard call
'connoisseurship', suggest status, assert superiority or otherwise 'show
off'. It is fairly common for this to include the idea of 'insider
information' in the way people will often tell you how they have just
'found the most marvellous recipe for stuffed mushrooms'.

> **Think** – Have you ever done this?
> – How did the recipients react?
> – Have you ever had this done to you?
> – How did you react to the message?

3 *Concern for others* – the conversation may simply be aimed at helping a
friend or relative to make a better purchase decision. This is particularly
common when social or family ties are strong.

> **Think** – What experience of this sort have you had of giving and taking
> advice from family and friends?
> – Do you think the motivation was genuine altruism?

4 *Message Intrigue* – the need to talk about advertisements or selling
appeals. Jokes are often made using the language and imagery of
advertisements and the recent spate of 'mini-soap' adverts seem to be
aimed at getting people to talk about the advertisement itself.

> **Think** – Can you think of recent examples where this has happened?

5 *Dissonance Reduction* – as we discussed in Chapter 7, cognitive dissonance
(worry or doubts) often follow a significant, high involvement purchase
decision. Dissatisfied or worried customers can be a dangerous source of
negative information if they vent their anger (a defence mechanism) by
criticizing the product.

Perhaps this multi-stage approach differs most significantly from the more
traditional views in its acceptance that a great deal of the communication is
initiated by the person seeking the information, rather than by the influential
opinion leader. Here we return to the crucial notion of the credibility of the
transmitter (discussed at more length in Chapter 7). It is reasonable to think
that messages will be most influential when somebody *seeks* the information
and there is a common assumption that, in comparison with other media,

another consumer has less ulterior or commercial motive for sharing the information.

Another interesting aspect is the evidence that suggests that we pay more attention, and give higher priority, to negative information. This may be because we expect marketers to emphasize positive aspects and we are particularly alert for any counterbalancing messages. There are also suggestions that the dissatisfied customer is more motivated to share 'bad news' than the satisfied consumer is to share 'good news'.

Clearly positive word-of-mouth can be one of the marketer's most potent assets, and, given the comments in the preceding paragraph, negative word-of-mouth is to be avoided if humanly possible. The marketing specialist cannot control these processes directly, but they can be stimulated, channelled and influenced.

The negative messages can be minimized by dealing with complaints as swiftly and efficiently as possible. Disgruntled consumers can spread the word very quickly, so every effort should be made to remove the source of the irritation.

Influentials can be identified and wooed. As discussed earlier, identifying these people is particularly difficult *because one of their key characteristics is their similarity to those they influence.* Thus it is not easy to view them as a distinct market segment. The only times when this might be possible is when the expertise is identifiable and thus certain professional groups can be targeted as being likely opinion leaders (doctors for medical products might be one obvious example, while teachers, sports coaches, vicars might provide others). Another option is to use mass media in the full knowledge that there will be wastage and a degree of inefficiency.

New products – success/failure

It is a common assertion that 90 per cent of new products fail. On the other hand innovation is the lifeblood of the market. In this section we will examine some of the reasons why some ideas/products/services 'take off' and others 'die the death'. One of the key thinkers in this field has been Everett Rogers who defined *diffusion* as the process by which an innovation (any new idea, product or service) is communicated over time among the members of a social system. Out of the mass of research in this area four key elements emerge as being significant to the diffusion process. They are:

1 the innovation itself,
2 the communication processes and channels used,
3 the time at which individuals decide to adopt the product, and
4 the social systems involved.

The field also classifies people into adopter and non-adopter categories and later we will look at the ways in which people may change from non-adopter status to that of adopter – our target!

We will define an *innovation* as any idea or product which is perceived by the potential adopter to be new. This is essentially a subjective definition and, as such, most of our work from Chapter 4 and the study of perception becomes highly significant. While, at first, the use of such a definition looks to be evasive, it does avoid many of the the problems associated with defining newness.

One framework for examining innovation distinguishes between:

1 *Continuous innovation* – the modification of an existing product rather than the establishment of a completely new one. It causes the least disruption to established patterns of behaviour.
2 *Dynamically continuous innovation* – the creation of either a new, or the alteration of an existing product; but one which does not alter significantly the patterns of consumer buying or product use.
3 *Discontinuous innovation* – the introduction of a totally new product that causes consumers to alter their behaviour patterns significantly.

Think – In which category would you place the introduction of:
- a new coloured toothpaste?
- an electric town car?
- toothpaste with added fluoride?
- the microwave oven?
- the launch of a 'new' model of an existing car?
- the Mars ice-cream?
- the introduction of 24 hour cash dispensers at banks?
- the compact disc?
- 'wholefoods'?
- laser printers to replace dot matrix printers for computers?
- 'virtual reality' machines

Another potentially useful way of looking at innovation is to recognize that products may have both *hardware* (physical) elements and *software* (information) elements. The language of the computer is not accidental as it can highlight the importance of the overall package. As with computers, the most advanced hardware is of little use if the instruction manual is inadequate. Similarly it is not uncommon for the emphasis at the product development stage to be on the hardware while the informational and attitudinal elements may be neglected.

It is also widely accepted, following the original work of Rogers, that there are five characteristics which are associated with the success of new products. We will examine them in turn.

1 Relative advantage

This is essentially another perceptual phenomenon – it is the extent to which a consumer perceives the product to have an advantage over the product it supersedes. Clearly the logic suggests that the greater the perceived advantage, the greater the probability of adoption.

2 Compatibility

This refers to the degree to which the product is consistent with existing values and past experiences of the potential consumers. In this part the assumption is that the less a product is compatible with the consumer values, the longer it will take to be adopted. In the previous exercise it might be interesting to think of the relative problems associated with introducing a toothpaste that was yellow, or dark red, or black.

3 Complexity

This is the degree to which the new product is perceived to be difficult to understand and use. The more difficult it is perceived to be, the harder it will be for the product to be accepted. Once more the key is the perception of the consumer – many people perceive the operation of a personal computer as being complex, yet they have mastered the more difficult skill of driving a motor car.

4 Trialability

It is believed that new products are more likely to be adopted when consumers can try them out on an experimental basis. This is relatively simple with low cost items – food product samples are commonly given to shoppers as they enter supermarkets and, in a similar vein, we used the example of free trial sachets of shampoo when we looked at behaviour change as the trigger for attitude change in Chapter 7. However, trialling can be rather more difficult with more expensive, high involvement products. Leasing can be one solution to this problem which can reduce the perceived risk for consumers, and earlier we used the idea of sampling new models of cars when existing models are taken in for service.

5 Observability

This characteristic is a measure of the degree to which adoption of the product, or the results of using the product, is visible to friends, neighbours and colleagues. This seems to affect the diffusion process by allowing potential consumers to see the benefits of the product, and thus increase (or even create) a 'want' for themselves. The process can be given additional impetus if the visible product is seen to be used by celebrities or other role models. Examples of this are designer labels on clothing which are clearly visible, so we have the LaCoste alligator or the Pringle lion (both of which were both visible and worn by sporting celebrities). Some products are, by their very nature, highly visible – persons who buy a new car are unlikely to keep it a secret from their neighbours, most fashion items are clearly observable. Another highly observable innovation which was rapidly adopted was the Sony 'Walkman'. However, some products are very non-observable, few people could tell you the make of dental floss used by even their very best friends.

Think – How do advertisers make us aware of their 'private' products such as toilet paper, toothbrushes, or underwear?

Using the product innovations listed in an earlier exercise (page 274) consider the following:

Think – How well do these products fit the five characteristics of innovation:
  – a new coloured toothpaste?
  – an electric town car?
  – toothpaste with added fluoride?
  – the microwave oven?
  – the launch of a 'new' model of an existing car?
  – the Mars ice-cream?
  – the introduction of 24 hour cash dispensers at banks?
  – the compact disc?
  – 'wholefoods'?
  – laser printers to replace dot matrix printers for computer?
  – 'virtual reality' machines?

And another question for the reader is:-

Think – What successful innovations can you identify which do not possess these characteristics?

And again:-

Think – What new product failures can you identify?
  – How do they fit with the 'required' characteristics?

It may be that some other characteristics have arisen from your analysis of success and failure – there may well be additional factors such as *the time lag* before consumers experience the desired benefits (the prediction would be that the greater the delay in gratification, the less the chance of trying out the product); the *symbolism* of the product for the consumer seems to be another important factor – how else can we explain the dominance of Levi jeans when they are so very similar to most other jeans?

Another issue that deserves some attention is *speed of diffusion*. While the importance of word-of-mouth has been emphasized, it does have a significant drawback in that it is largely outside the marketer's control. The thing that the marketer can control is the *marketing strategy* to be adopted and again this is likely to be a significant determinant of the speed of diffusion. *Promotion* is often used to create a favourable image for the brand by pairing it with suitably positive images. The aim is to boost the symbolism of the product – in many markets where the products are essentially very similar symbolism may be the only relative advantage that an organization has to offer. *Price* can also create brand image as well as an immediate relative advantage. Generally, high prices can denote quality, low prices, low quality. Price can also be used to position a product as 'good value for money'. Once established, economies of scale can sometimes allow a sustained price advantage for a product. Another important element of the marketing mix is *distribution* – good site locations and a large number of outlets obviously will help the diffusion process.

Another factor may well be what Engel, Blackwell and Miniard refer to as *competitive intensity*. Here they are suggesting that some organizations are more highly competitive than others, follow more aggressive strategies and allocate greater resources to the launch of new products. The suggestion is (perhaps not surprisingly) that such organizations' innovations diffuse more quickly.

The *reputation* of the organization can also be a helpful influence – it is often asserted that IBM computers are not as technically advanced as many of their competitors. Their products continue to dominate the market because of the reputation the company holds and the fact that to many people computers mean IBM.

In many fields, diffusion will be helped when there is a *standardized technology*. At the time of writing, doubt is being expressed about the viability of a new television channel in the UK, due to the fact that existing frequencies will need to be changed and millions of video recorders may need to be retuned. The problems of agreeing common international standards for things like the technology for high resolution television have, it is claimed, held up the diffusion process for a period of years.

One final set of factors centre on *interest rates, the state of the economy* and *the notion of consumer confidence*. Such things are often the lifeblood of day-to-day politics, but their impact on consumer behaviour cannot be denied, particularly in the case of high involvement, high cost items. High interest rates will affect the real price paid by the customer, and the level of consumer confidence seem likely to determine an individual's willingness to be committed to expensive, long term payments. When watching the news, it sometimes sounds as if consumers are concerned about the exchange rate and similar economic indicators, whereas the reality is more likely to be both more personal and more immediate. Purchasing behaviour is more likely to be affected by individuals' perceptions as to whether they are likely to receive their performance related bonus – or even whether they will still have a job in six months time.

Think – What experience have you had of putting off a purchase until things had 'picked up'?

Consumers in the diffusion process

An important element of the diffusion process is the consumer and the acceptance that different types of consumers may adopt a new product at different times in the product's life cycle. Rogers' classic work identified five categories of adopter and is often described pictorially in terms of either a normal distribution curve (Figure 9.7) or as an 'S' curve (Figure 9.8).

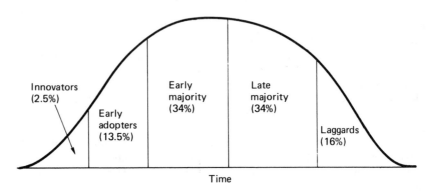

Figure 9.7

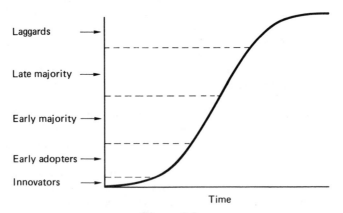

Figure 9.8

– *Innovators* are venturesome individuals who are willing to take risks.
– *Early Adopters* are often viewed as more respectable but are quick to take up new ideas that they have seen 'piloted' by the innovators. They also seem to act as some sort of role models and opinion leaders for the
– *Early Majority* who, typically, may seek to avoid risks and who are relatively deliberate in their purchasing behaviour. While the
– *Late Majority* are sceptical and cautious about new ideas and the
– *Laggards* are very traditional and set in their ways

The time dimension is important as the model suggests that each group learns by observing the previous group's behaviours and then, after the 'vicarious learning', adopts the behaviour itself. If this is correct, the importance of the innovators cannot be overstated. The whole process will stall if someone does not make the first purchase. The characteristics of these consumer groups has been the focus of a great deal of research. The results suggest that innovativeness is often most clearly marked in people who are of high social status, upwardly mobile, educated and/or literate – and young. But, not surprisingly, one of the key determinants is income. High income people not only have the ability to buy more new products, they also have the ability to risk trying new products. This factor is likely to be of extreme importance when dealing with high-cost items, but the linkage when considering low-cost, low involvement goods is less clear.

Some research has indicated personality variables – innovators are more likely to be risk takers. Other research has proposed a possible link between innovation and a cognitive style of problem solving – innovators being persons who tend to produce different ways of organizing, deciding and behaving which may involve significant change and the undertaking of new activities. Communication patterns also appear to link with innovation. Earlier adopters seem to use both mass media and interpersonal sources more than later adopters.

Chapter summary exercises

> **Think** – How can the material in this chapter be applied to the marketing of:
> > camcorders
> > the social policy of a political party
> > skis
> > holidays
> > soft drinks
> > instant coffee
> > sports shoes (trainers)
> > razors
> > hair colourant
> > toothpaste
> > shampoo
> > motor cars
> > low-fat/low cholesterol/low salt spread
> > sanitary protection
> > kitchen equipment
> > spirits and liqueurs
> > low-alcohol wine
> > a restaurant
> > newspapers
> > toilet tissue
> > bicycles

Think – How *has* my organization used sociological ideas?

Think – How *could* my organization use sociological ideas to its advantage?

Think – How have *I* used sociological ideas?

Some 'typical' examination questions – sociology

A What are the merits of 'social class' and 'social status' as the basis of market segmentation purposes? Illustrate your answer with examples of products and/or services for which different forms of segmentation are appropriate.

B Arguing in favour of a global marketing perspective, Ohmae writes that 'On a political map, the boundaries between countries are as clear as ever. But on a competitive map, a map showing the real flows of financial and industrial activity, those boundaries have largely disappeared'. How far do you agree? Why is it that 'globalization' has been more successful with some products/services (such as cameras, watches, calculators and some soft drinks) than with others?

C Several writers have suggested that significant changes in social values are likely to occur in the next decade. To what extent do you agree with such predictions, and in what areas do you expect value changes to be especially noticeable? What could be the significance of such changes to the marketing process?

D What is 'socialization' and what purpose does it serve? Outline the main agencies and mechanisms of socialization, showing how they can be utilized by marketers as a contribution towards the achievement of marketing objectives.

E What do sociologists mean when they refer to the concept of 'culture'? To what extent would you accept the view that cultural differences are becoming less important to marketers as the notion of 'global products' takes hold?

F In what ways, and for what reasons, do cultures differ? If you were Marketing Director of a large multinational, to what extent would you take account of cultural differences when preparing strategies and plans for worldwide sales in any two of the following product areas:
(a) men's toiletries; (b) motor cars; c) soft drinks?

Sources

Bilton, T. *et al.* (1989) *Introducing Sociology*, Macmillan.

BPP (1991) *Behavioural Aspects of Marketing*, BPP.

Engel, J. F., Blackwell, R. D. and Miniard, P. W. (1990) *Consumer Behaviour* (6th edn.), Dryden.

Hawkins, D. I., Best, R. J. and Coney, K. A. (1989) *Consumer Behaviour: Implications for Marketing Strategy* (4th edn.), Irwin.

Jarry, D. and Jarry, J. (1991) *Dictionary of Sociology*, Collins.

Katz, E. (1957) 'The two-step flow of communication: an up-to-date report on an hypothesis', *Public Opinion* Quarterly, 27.

Kotler, P. and Roberto, E. L. (1989) *Social Marketing*, Free Press.

Lazarsfeld, P. F., Berelson, B. R. and Gaudet, H. (1948) *The People's Choice*, Columbia University Press.

Ohmae (1990) *The Borderless World*, Fontana.

Peter, J. P. and Olson, J. C. (1990) *Consumer Behaviour and Marketing Strategy* (2nd edn.), Irwin.

Rogers, E. M. (1962) *Diffusion of Innovations*, Free Press.

Williams, K. C. (1981) *Behavioural Aspects of Marketing*, Heinemann.

Williams, R. (1976) *Keywords*, Fontana.

10 Whatever made you buy that?

Modelling consumer behaviour and decision making

Introduction

This is a topic which some students find rather difficult – others find it stimulating. One early problem that is sometimes encountered is the use of the word 'model', which sounds very academic – in fact, as you will see, we all have our own models which make up our assumptions about people, behaviour and life in general.

The second problem is the diagrammatic complexity of the so-called 'grand models' which cause many people to panic. Those readers who like diagrams and habitually draw things out may well be the ones who find it all relatively straightforward.

The chapter consists of an introduction to models and the modelling approach, examining the characteristics of models and the criteria appropriate for their evaluation. Simple models are considered before moving on to look at comprehensive (or 'grand') models.

In terms of consumer behaviour, the grand models attempt to bring together all of the material covered so far in the course into a coherent whole. So, in addition to developing a new approach, the chapter also acts as an important stage in revising and reinforcing ideas and concepts discussed earlier. The end product, the model of consumer behaviour, being some sort of map of consumer behaviour.

Some students get misled into attempting to memorize the complicated diagrams of the comprehensive models. They would be better advised to concentrate on understanding the general thrust of the approach and linking that with ideas from subjects such as 'Practice of Marketing' or their own direct experience of marketing and selling.

There is much else to consider in the chapter before it is written off. The characteristics of models and the general criteria are useful examination fodder, and an intelligent review of the strengths and weaknesses of the modelling approach could be both valuable and fruitful for those who are not comfortable with diagrams.

Learning objectives

At the end of this chapter the student should be familiar with the following concepts and be able to apply them to different types of purchasing decision.

- Nature of the modelling approach;
- Model characteristics and types;
- Criteria for a 'good' model;
- Classes of variables;
- Simple models:
  - Black Box models,
  - Personal variable models,
  - PV/PPS model;
- Comprehensive models:
  - Engel, Blackwell and Miniard model,
  - Howard–Sheth model,
  - Nicosia model.

Consumer decision making and modelling

The idea of a model of consumer behaviour causes many students to 'switch off'. It may be that some of the models we will look at appear daunting at first sight. More likely is that some people are not comfortable with diagrammatic representations. There is evidence, reviewed briefly when we looked at individual differences in Chapter 2, which suggests that understanding diagrams of this sort is related to perceptual aptitude. As with many other aptitudes (verbal, numerical, mechanical), skills can be developed – so there is hope for us all! An interesting offshoot of the aptitude discussion is that people with an engineering background commonly enjoy diagrams and are often at their happiest with this kind of material. A model in this context is a representation of consumer behaviour. The aim is to provide a simplified portrayal of consumer processes to aid our description, explanation and control of buying behaviour.

One important fact to understand is that models are real, they are not solely the prerogative of the academic. For instance, if you are asked what your reaction would be to raising the price of vending machine drinks at your place of work, you might answer that it depended how large the increase was. If your investigator gives you a series of amounts you may be able to make some guesses as to your likely reaction. So, you might respond that a 10 per cent increase would make little difference, a 50 per cent increase would make you drink less from the machine and think about alternative sources of refreshment, while a 100 per cent increase would mean that you definitely would not use the vending machine. This suggests that you have a model of your own behaviour which is inside your head. It is a model that links consumption (buying behaviour) with price. Such a model is extremely common and we rarely pay a great deal of attention to them in that they are 'implicit' models. In this chapter we are looking at similar approaches which have been formalized and written down. They attempt to clarify the processes underlying consumer behaviour. Thus, in the language of Chapter 1, many of them are no more than hypotheses about consumer behaviour which need considerable research before they can be verified and validated.

Models come in a variety of forms – we shall look at simple models and more complex versions. Some people find it hard to understand why there can be more than one model of consumer behaviour. They argue that if the models are correct, all the representations of a phenomenon should be the same. Perhaps the best explanation comes by analogy.

A map is a representation of a real-life phenomenon. But all maps are not the same. You will probably have seen a road map with towns, motorways and road links clearly marked. Also, you can probably remember your school atlas which contained 'the same' map but with the waterway systems highlighted. Other maps gave the average rainfall and the height above sea level. Some even displayed which parts of the country are made up of limestone, which are sandstone, which bits are granite and so forth. Each of these maps is the same in one sense – a representation of the country – but has been modified and designed to give the reader different information.

Another important fact is that a map or model does not have to be 'accurate' or 'realistic' in order to be useful. One of the most famous visual images in the UK is the map of the London underground system – it appears in most diaries and even crops up on T-shirts. This colour coded map fits neatly on to the paper, the lines are mostly straight and the whole thing is easy to follow and a spectacularly successful piece of design work. The map works excellently so long as you know where you are and which station you wish to get to. It does not work very well if you do not. Additionally, if you were to superimpose the underground map on an ordinary street map of London you would find that the stations and routes do not coincide. In some cases stations on different lines are shown as being well apart from one another when, in 'real life' they are only yards apart. If you have travelled on the underground you will realize that few of the journeys are straight lines. Thus, in order to make a representation, or model of the underground system which was understandable and 'user-friendly', it was necessary to distort and simplify the 'normal' map of London.

Models in the fields of consumer behaviour are somewhat similar to maps. They attempt to give simplified representations of behaviours and influences so that we may better understand them. We have used models throughout this book – but without drawing specific attention to them. This chapter considers them as an approach to consumer behaviour that will hopefully act as a means of drawing many of the threads together into a more coherent whole.

Variables and relationships revisited

Chapter 1 looked at the process of scientific enquiry. You will remember that the scientific method aims to establish the relationships that exist between variables via the

$$idea \rightarrow hypothesis \rightarrow theory \rightarrow law$$

progression which relects the confidence with which the relationships can be shown to have been established. Throughout the book we have examined ideas, hypotheses and theories regarding human behaviour and have used different variables according to the subject under discussion. Some of the categories have been defined in earlier chapters, but we can attempt to review and summarize the different groups of variables.

They can be classified as:

- *Stimulus variables* – the inputs to a situation. Within the contexts we have examined which would come into this category would be perceived needs, social influences (family, class, culture and reference groups), and situational stimuli such as advertising messages.

- *Response variables* – the behavioural outputs from the situation. So, within the marketing context we are looking at purchases, rejection, further search activity and similar manifestations of buyer behaviour.

- *Intervening variables* – the influences which can only be inferred from the exhibited behaviour and which are assumed to mediate the process between the input and output variables. Examples would be perception, attitudes, learning, beliefs and values.

- *Endogenous variables* – these are factors which have a clearly defined effect and which can therefore be built into a model with some confidence. They are similar to the predictable factors discussed in Chapter 1.

- *Exogenous variables* – in contrast, these are factors whose exact influence is hard to define. In this sense they are similar to the unpredictable factors in the control cycle discussion in Chapter 1.

- *Internal variables* – are, as the name implies, factors which are internal to the individual and so we would place motivation, perception, values, attitudes and learning in this category. There is a noticeable overlap with the 'intervening' category described above.

- *External variables* – are the outside influences on behaviour which are sometimes sub-divided into:

    a past experience,
    b present environment, and
    c future expectations.

Classifications of models

Following the boom in modelling approaches at the end of the 1960s the British Market Research Society set up a Study Group on modelling. They developed a number of classifications for different types of model. Some of the catagories defined by this group were:

Micro
Such models focus on a single element of a situation i.e. they have a relatively narrow focus and may centre on an individual or single action

or

Macro
These deal with a wider picture of processes and action – often the whole population, environment, or process.

Data-based
These models are based on logical analysis of the available data and may also be a function of the methods of analysis used.

or

Theory-based
These models are developed by logical extension of existing theories – sometimes of marketing, but often from other disciplines

Behavioural
Based on assumjptions about how people behave e.g. stimulus response theories.

or

Statistical
No built in assumptions about relationships or motivation. Analysis identifies linkages.

Generalized
Such models are designed to apply to a wide range of markets.

or

Ad hoc
Such models are designed to apply to a single market.

Qualitative
These models do not measure any specific variables

or

Quantitative
These measure specific variables and their relative weightings.

Static
These are a 'one-off snapshot' of a particular phenomenon at one specific moment in time.

or

Dynamic
These models attempt to take account of changes which might occur over a period of time.

The group also drew distinctions between the different ways the models might be displayed:

- Verbally– most of us will put our assumptions about consumer behaviour into words, in order to explain them to both ourselves and other people.

- Algebraically – some of our ideas are best transmitted via an algebraic equation – Weber's Law (page 79) or the Fishbein model of attitudes (page 184) would fit into this category.

- Pictorially – almost every diagram in this book can be viewed as a model – a diagram illustrating some point about the topics under discussion.

In addition they identified categories such as *descriptive*, *diagnostic*, and *predictive* models (see also the comparable discussion in Chapter 1 where the aims of scientific investigation were outlined as being description, explanation, prediction and control) and a rather more subjective pair which were called *successful* and *unsuccessful*.

Perhaps the most used set of categories is that of *low*, *medium*, or *high level models*. In this case the level refers to the level of complexity – so a low level model would be a relatively simple representation of the phenomenon while a high level model of the same event would be much more complex and detailed and include many more variables.

Think – Here are some 'models' we have used already in this book. Classify them using the categories outlined above:

1 'attitudes are leading variables to behaviour – i.e. attitude change predates and predicts behaviour...' (Chapter 7)

2

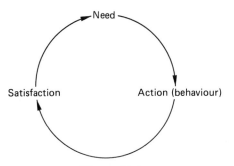

Figure 10.1　　　　　　　(Chapter 6)

3 'intelligence is something to do with an ability to see relationships, and the capacity to use that ability to solve problems'. (Chapter 2)

4 $\dfrac{\Delta I}{I} = k$

Where ΔI is the increment in intensity that is just detectable, I is the intensity of the comparison stimulus and k is a constant. (Chapter 4)

5 Hollander has put forward a model which may help clarify some of the issues and this is shown in the diagram. According to this model the psychological core is a central feature of what we may call personality while accepting the *interactive* nature of behaviour with respect to the person,

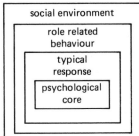

the role, the environment and some concept such as the 'real' self.   (Chapter 3)

6 'reinforcement of successive behaviours which ultimately lead to the desired response'. (Chapter 5)

7 'quiet individuals are unlikely to become raging extroverts, they just become more outgoing when in the company of other shy persons.' (Chapter 8)

8 'The Family Life Cycle is commonly represented as a steady progression':

Figure 10.2

9 Cohesiveness $\alpha \dfrac{1}{\text{size}}$

α member satisfaction
α how often the group meets
α attractiveness of the group to its members
(Chapter 8)

Criteria for the evaluation or construction of models

In the marketing context, the modelling approach has two key objectives:

1 Description, explanation, prediction (and ultimately control) of consumer behaviour, and/or

2 Aiding researchers in their task of developing 'better' hypotheses and theories about the relationships and processes involved in consumer behaviour.

Thus models can be evaluated overall against their ability to satisfy either or both of these objectives.

More specifically, Williams, in 1981, listed eight criteria which should be borne in mind when evaluating a model. He lists them as:

1 *Simplicity* – the aim of models should be to break down complex behaviour into its simpler, more easily understood elements.
2 *Factual basis* – they should be consistent with known facts in order to be descriptive of the reality concerned.
3 *Logic* – to be understandable and plausible, it should be internally consistent and make sense.
4 *Originality* – if the model is to move our understanding forward, it should be original in either the components included, or the relationship between them.

5 *Explanatory power* – it should attempt to explain the 'what', 'why' and 'how' of the behaviour.

6 *Predictive power* – as outlined at the beginning of the book, one of the aims of a model should be to assist the prediction of consumer behaviour.

7 *Heuristic power* – ideally a 'good' model should suggest new or additional areas of research.

8 *Validity* – the model should be verifiable. In other words, one should ideally be able to test the proposed relationships. As we saw in Chapter 1, validity has two sub-sets:

- *external validity* which is concerned with whether the model is generally applicable, or whether it only applies in one specific experimental setting;
- *internal validity* which is centred on whether the relationships described are true and whether the relationships can be verified by use of the scientific method.

As Williams observes 'it would be unrealistic to expect a model of consumer behaviour to meet all these criteria as our knowledge of human behaviour is far from complete and we still lack the techniques to evaluate adequately the relationships postulated in the individual models' (1981, p. 150). Nevertheless, these criteria should prove useful when attempting to evaluate the 'standard' models that will be outlined.

Simple models of consumer behaviour

The comprehensive, or grand models, which we will discuss in the next section, attempt to define and relate all of the variables which affect consumer behaviour. Lower level or simple models, in contrast, fall into three broad categories – black box models, decision process models, and personal variable models.

Black Box models

Black Box models do not consider internal variables. They focus on inputs and outputs without concerning themselves with the intervening mental processes which might determine the outcomes. So an example of a black box model would be a 'map' of the decision environment such as Figure 10.3.

Similarly we could produce a black box model of the buying process which was as simple as Figure 10.4.

Despite their simplicity, black box models can be of value to the marketer as they are based on identifiable, observable and measurable variables. It is possible that input variables can be adjusted and the outputs observed. In this way the economists' theories regarding supply and demand can be

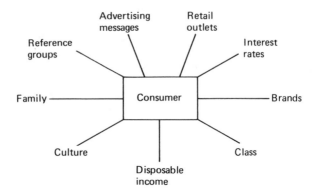

Figure 10.3

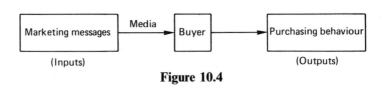

Figure 10.4

tested, or alternatively, ideas about the effects of price reductions on sales can be tried out. It can be argued that if it is found that price reduction increases sales, then marketers can make informed decisions, without necessarily understanding exactly *why* such a reaction results. The emphasis on external stimulus variables is significant as it can allow the marketing specialist insight into the actions that might be taken in order to achieve the desired objectives.

Another advantage is the relatively limited number of variables that are considered. This can be an aid to decision-making as it may prevent the process from becoming bogged down in complexity. The limitations lie in the black box model's inability to explain or predict behaviour in a wide range of situations.

Decision process models

These are fairly common in the field of marketing. They attempt a simple description of the stages consumers progress through in reaching purchasing decisions.

Most are variations on the classic problem solving/decision making process of:

Define problem
↓
Generate alternative solutions
↓
Evaluate alternatives
↓
Decide
↓
Implement
↓
Monitor

Marketing 'editions' of this include the innovation adoption model:

Awareness → Interest → Evaluation → Trial → Adoption

The core of the Engel, Blackwell and Miniard comprehensive model (coming shortly):

Motivation and recognition of need
↓
Information search
↓
Evaluate alternatives
↓
Purchase
↓
Outcomes

and even the promotional 'AIDA' model shows a similar pattern:

Attention → Interest → Desire → Action.

These approaches give a sound basis for marketers seeking to devise strategies that are appropriate for each stage. Inevitably they are not strong on explanation or prediction without considerable elaboration which makes them fall into the comprehensive model category.

Personal variable models

In contrast to black box models, the personal variable models omit external variables. So these models focus on the mental processes of decision-making – internal elements and processes such as perception, motivation, beliefs and values.

One classic example of a personal variable model that we have already met in Chapter 7, is the *Fishbein model*. You may remember the model – it is summarized by the formula:

$$A_o = \Sigma\, B_l\, a_l$$

where A_o = the attitude towards object o,
   B_1 = the strength of belief i about o,
   a_1 = the evaluation aspects of B,
   n = the number of beliefs.

Another personal variable model is the *threshold model*. This operates on the assumption that choices are made by some form of sorting process. A product/brand is thought to be evaluated against a series of criteria or product characteristics. Categories used of the product are 'too much of...'; 'too little of...'; 'enough of...' any characteristic. Thus the name of the model derives from the notion of there being a 'threshold of acceptability' for each attribute. If the product/brand is rated as below this threshold on any of the characteristics, it will be rejected. This approach has proved successful in identifying price levels above which the product will not sell – it may be a fine product but it is perceived as being 'too expensive', and thus rejected.

A perceived value/perceived probability of satisfaction (PV/PPS) model

This is the author's own attempt to synthesize decision process and personal variable models and is based on the view of decision-making as a process in which, when faced with a choice, behaviour is determined by two factors:

1 the value attached to outcomes (perceived value (PV)), and

2 the perception of the probability of each outcome occurring (perceived probability of satisfaction (PPS).

The idea is that we may attach suitable values to each and produce a Subjective Utility (SU) score, using the formula:

$$SU = PV \times PPS$$

One example used by George Wright in his book 'Behavioural Decision Theory' is that of deciding between revising for an examination and going out for a picnic. He points out that the Perceived Value of each option might depend on the weather, so one could allocate a score out of ten for each of the options depending on the weather conditions which might apply. Thus we could produce a table of perceived value which might look like Table 10.1.

Table 10.1 Table of perceived value

Perceived Value	Fine and Sunny	Cloudy but Dry	Wet and Windy
Revising	2	4	8
Picnic	9	6	0

The next stage is to assess the probability of each type of weather. We may ring up the weather bureau to get a forecast for our area and we could allocate probabilities to the various weathers in the light of that information. We could assess the probability of the weather in each category as:

Fine and Sunny	0.3 (3 chances in 10)
Cloudy but Dry	0.6 (3 chances in 5)
Wet & Windy	0.1 (1 chance in 10)

We will remember our statistics classes and the fact that a probability of 1.0 means complete certainty, and that the probability of all the options must add up to 1.0. We can then multiply up the scores for each 'hole' in the matrix to give Subjective Utility scores as shown in Table 10.2.

Table 10.2 Subjective utility scores

Subjective Utility	Fine and Sunny	Cloudy but Dry	Wet and Windy
Revising	0.6	2.4	0.8
Picnic	2.7	3.6	0

So we decide to go for a picnic!

Think – What would you decide if the weather forecast had not been so good and you had assessed the probabilities as:-

Fine and Sunny	0.1 (1 chance in 10)
Cloudy but Dry	0.5 (1 chance in 2)
Wet and Windy	0.4 (2 chances in 5)

There are significant similarities between this approach and other topics we have discussed earlier in the book, most notably Expectancy Theory in Chapter 6 and Fishbein's Compensatory Model of Attitudes discussed above and in Chapter 7.

We can modify this approach to fit it to the marketing situation. The consumers will purchase when they perceive the product and the associated outcome to have both high value and a high probability of satisfaction (or, at least, a PV x PPS score higher than competing products).

The influences could be displayed as shown in Figure 10.5.

Such an approach encompasses most of the material contained in this book and justifies the study of topics such as perceptions, personality, attitudes, learning and social influences. Additionally it is in line with one of the main themes of this book – the overriding importance of perception in the study of human behaviour. It also allows us to analyse purchasing behaviours by setting the two dimensions as axes of a grid as shown in Figure 10.6.

This diagram suggests that consumers are more likely to indulge in extended problem solving behaviours when the perceived value of the

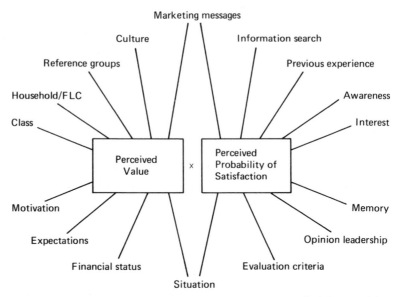

Figure 10.5   The Rice PV/PPS model of consumer decision making

product (or the outcome of its purchase) is high. Conversely, limited problem solving behaviour is associated with low perceived value. When the value is perceived to be low, and the probability of satisfaction is also perceived to be low then the prediction is that a purchase will not occur.

The lower right-hand quadrant is concerned with purchases which are of low perceived value in themselves, but which have a high probability of satisfaction. Here an example might be a situation of running low on petrol while travelling down a motorway. Government quality standards assure the driver that there is little to choose between brands of 4-star petrol, so the car is filled with whichever brand the next service station happens to sell. Many petrol companies attempt to increase the perceived value of their brand by offering air miles, green shield stamps or their equivalent.

This example could be classed as a *distress purchase*, but a similar process would be predicted in *habitual buying* at supermarkets. Low involvement purchases are often made on the basis that there is little or nothing to choose between brands – so it becomes easier for the consumer to make all purchases at one single visit to a superstore, rather than shop separately for each item on the shopping list.

The top left hand quadrant is interesting (high value, low probability) as it may go some way towards explaining otherwise apparently irrational behaviour. An example might be gambling. Millions of people in the UK gamble on the football pools – despite the chances of winning a fortune being infinitesimally small. Here the hypothesis would be that, for many people, the very high value of winning a very large sum of money (with its attendant outcomes of travel, giving up work and being able to afford

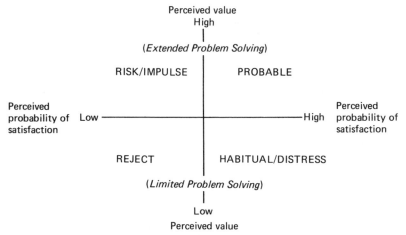

Figure 10.6 Type of purchase analysed in terms of the Rice PV/PPS model

luxuries), more than compensates for the very low probability of that outcome occurring. Thus this can be classed as a *risk* or *impulse purchase*.

The top right-hand quadrant is the marketers dream – high value and high probability of satisfaction – the combination that is most likely to result in *probable purchase*.

Thus, in practical terms this model clearly identifies two key objectives of marketing effort and communication:

1 to raise the perceived value of the outcomes of purchase, and
2 to raise the perceived probability of satisfaction following purchase.

Comprehensive (grand) models of consumer behaviour

In this section of the chapter we will examine three of the most famous of the high level models. These grand models are the more complex formulations of consumer behaviour and they commonly attempt to encompass all the factors and elements which the authors feel to be relevant to the behaviour. Many readers find that the complexity of the final diagram is overwhelming at first sight so we will take one of the models and show how it has been built up out of a series of smaller, simpler models. Thus the final presentation should not come as a shock to the reader. We will start with the Engel, Blackwell and Miniard model, followed by the Howard–Sheth and finally the Nicosia model.

1 The Engel, Blackwell and Miniard model

This is a development of the classic Engel, Kollat and Blackwell model first introduced in 1968 and updated and modified in the 1990 edition of their text. This model takes the process of purchasing as a problem solving/ decision-making exercise. The assumption is that the consumer has a problem which is solved by the purchase of a suitable product. As this is the first of the Grand models we have met it may be helpful to follow the steps the authors follow in order to develop the full model.

They begin by identifying the problem solving and decision-making process they envisage as the basic framework of consumer behaviour. This will enable us to identify different stages of the process through which consumers progress when making purchases and which may help in the formulation of marketing strategy.

The most common, everyday problem solving sequence is:

Define problem → Generate alternative solutions →
Evaluate alternatives → Decide → Implement → Monitor
(the simple model of the decision making process referred to above).

In the marketing context, Engel, Blackwell and Miniard suggest that this becomes:

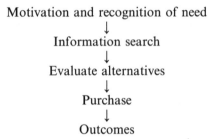

Motivation and recognition of need
↓
Information search
↓
Evaluate alternatives
↓
Purchase
↓
Outcomes

(another simple model)

and this forms the basis of the model which is developed. In order to clarify the building process, we will examine each stage in turn.

Stage 1 – Motivation and need recognition

A problem is something that is not as one would wish. This is a very simple and broad statement, but it has the advantage of emphasizing the personal nature of problem recognition. Person *A*'s problem is not the problem of Person *B*. What worries Person *A* may strike Person *B* as being an absurd thing to be concerned about.

The non-marketing factors which might affect problem recognition could be as represented in Figure 10.8.

In the marketing situation a regular difficulty which is experienced is that problems are often recognized by consumers too late. We only become aware of our insurance policy *after* the storm has damaged the fabric of our house; we only think of the need for carrying a shovel in the boot of the car when we are caught in a snowdrift; we want a garden full of flowers in Spring – but forget to plant the bulbs in Autumn.

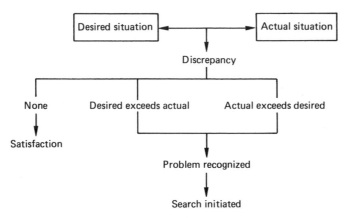

Figure 10.7

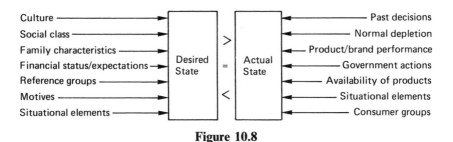

Figure 10.8

Classic advertising campaigns have attempted to bring forward awareness among the consumers with the motoring organizations emphasizing the needs for rescue services.

> **Think** – How could you influence the timing of problem recognition for:
> Home insulation?
> Life insurance?
> Dental floss?
> Car engine tuning?

Engel, Blackwell and Miniard propose *need recognition* as the beginning of the process and they focus on the three key determinants which they identify as:

- information stored in the memory,
- individual differences and
- environmental influences.

As this type of problem solving/decision making is essentially centred on high involvement purchases, need recognition is likely to be linked to ideas such as self-concept and the normative pressure of reference groups, as well as situational factors. This stage of the overall process is summarized in a simple model (see Figure 10.9).

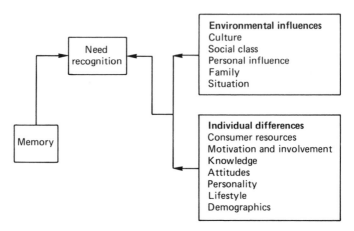

Figure 10.9   Three determinants of need recognition. *Source*: EBM 1990

So already we are using a great deal of the material from earlier parts of this book.

Think – Clarify the factors which might affect need recognition when
          considering the purchase of:
          a new car
          a house/flat/appartment
          a personal computer
          a new cooker
          hi-fi equipment
          a new autumn outfit

Stage 2 – Information search

The next step is the *internal memory search* to establish whether the individual possesses enough information about the available options to make a decision without further action. In low involvement consumer decisions this may often be the case, but *external search* is more usual with high involvement purchases.

It can be seen from Figure 10.10 that opinion leadership and word-of-mouth communication will be significant at this stage, as well as the more formal marketing and advertising messages. Similarly, past learning, stored in the memory system, is shown to be a significant source even in extended problem solving situations.

The information search stage is also affected strongly by individual differences and environmental factors. As we saw in Chapter 2, the traits

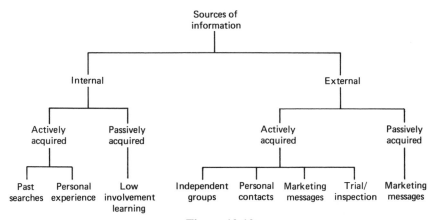

Figure 10.10

and orientation of some individuals means that they have the personality characteristic of caution – such people will tend to conduct extensive and detailed information search. Similarly families and reference groups are likely to make significant contributions to the amount and style of search conducted.

Satisficing – This rather ugly word is sometimes used to describe search activity when a decision is made as to whether further effort is worthwhile. 'Satisficing' is made out of two words – *'satisfy'* and *'suffice'* and implies doing just enough to obtain satisfaction. It indicates a degree of settling for something rather less than perfection.

A typical example might be buying a second-hand car. The consumer makes initial decisions regarding need and defines model, age, condition and price range. Search is conducted via the columns of the local newspaper and a number of possible cars are identified. Contact is made by telephone and a number of appointments are made to view the machines. The first car seen is almost certainly not purchased on the spot as the purchaser needs to feel that comparisons have been made. So additional visits and inspections are conducted. The purchaser, at some point, has to make a decision as to when enough has been seen to make a satisfactory decision. It is likely that a choice is made from three, four or five cars seen – because, at that point, the buyer feels there is enough information to make a reasonable (if not perfect!) choice.

This scenario highlights the fact that many of our decisions are often made on less than complete information. In the case outlined only local cars were looked at; at a given point in time; not all available for sale were examined; cars which might have been ideal were not inspected on the grounds that it was on the wrong side of town or there was no answer to a telephone call. The important point is that the purchaser *feels* that enough information has been gathered. Figure 10.11 describes a simple form of cost/benefit analysis.

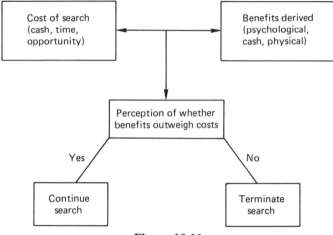

Figure 10.11

In the light of our continuing interest in the differences between high and low involvement purchasing we can speculate that, almost by definition, the perception of the value of continued search is likely to be significantly higher in high involvement decisions.

The external search is dominated by marketing messages and the information so gathered should be fed into the memory system via processes similar to those described in our chapter on Perception:

Exposure → Attention → Comprehension → Acceptance → Retention

This element can be set out as in Engel, Blackwell and Miniard's presentation (Figure 10.12).

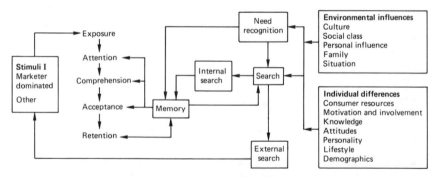

Figure 10.12   Search for information in the decision-making model
Source: EBM 1990

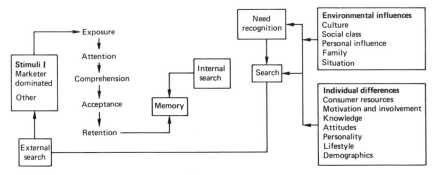

Figure 10.13

This simple model can now be grafted on to our earlier representation to give Figure 10.13.

Think – Clarify the factors which might affect the type of information
search conducted when considering the purchase of:
- a new car
- a house/flat/appartment
- a personal computer
- a new cooker
- hi-fi equipment
- a new autumn outfit

Stage 3 – Alternative evaluation

The evaluation of alternatives is a process which we have all carried out. As we said in Chapter 1, Bloom (1956) claims that 'humans are apparently so constituted that they cannot refrain from evaluating, judging, appraising or valuing almost everything that comes within their purview'. There seems to be a paradox in that we do it all the time and yet two persons' evaluation of the same event or object may not coincide.

Imagine two people settling down to an evening in front of the television – one chooses a documentary because they are interested in the topic, the other chooses a comedy show seeking entertainment. Assuming both shows lived up to expectations both individuals would rate their decision as 'right'.

This highlights the importance of the *criteria* used in the process of evaluation – the obvious criterion for a purchasing decision is 'did it achieve its objective?' – however we now face some sub-issues:

- *What objective?* – as we have seen, it is likely that we have multiple objectives – we want a car that is reliable and well engineered, but we may also want one that will be the envy of our friends; one that is 'sporty' in its image but able to carry a growing young family; and is the 'right' colour.

- *Internal or external outcomes?* – these possibly conflicting objectives can be seen as being internal or external to the decision-making unit – we may satisfy our family but not impress our friends.

- *When should we measure outcomes?* – here we may be looking at the difference between first impressions and longer term satisfaction.

- *Do we look for unexpected outcomes?* – staying with the car example we could find that the choice in retrospect looks less good. Buying a high performance car could bring the expected approbation from our peer group, but also unexpected (and unwelcome) attention from the police and our insurance company.

The criteria we use stem from our values, beliefs, attitudes and intentions. However, it is not unusual for people to seek a single measure that will pin down the payoffs required. But it is reasonable to assume that satisfaction is affected by a number of factors – motivation, values, expectancy, self-image – so logic suggests that we may well need a variety of criteria against which to judge the effectiveness of our purchase: the chances of positive outcomes against all of these criteria may be remote and perhaps unattainable.

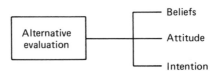

Figure 10.14

The reality, as we saw proposed in Chapter 7, appears to be that people adopt some form of *compensation strategy* in which a perceived weakness in one attribute can be offset by strength in others. Again the evaluation stage can be built into our model as in Figure 10.15.

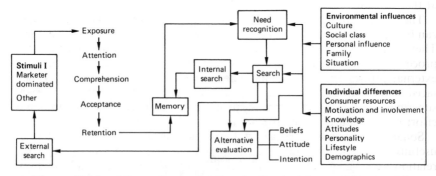

Figure 10.15   Alternative evaluation in the decision-making model.
Source: EBM 1990

Stage 4 – Purchase and outcomes
This stage is relatively simple – a purchase is made and the outcome is satisfaction or dissatisfaction according to the degree to which the product or service meets the criteria for evaluation and hence the expectations of the buyer (see Figure 10.16).

Figure 10.16

However, the model applies primarily to high involvement purchases and so there is a perceived need to make a 'good' choice. Thus a dotted line feeds back from satisfaction, reinforcing product image and strengthening brand loyalty.

Dissatisfaction, on the other hand, is likely to result in post-purchase *cognitive dissonance* as outlined in Chapter 7. This may result in the purchaser registering a complaint with the company – as we observed in the section on attitudes, guarantees and after-sales service go a long way towards calming the dissatisfied customer and preventing bad word-of-mouth messages from circulating. As before this final stage can be added to the diagram, so that the complete Engel, Blackwell and Miniard model achieves its final form (see Figure 10.17).

By following the stages in the build-up of the model, it is hoped than the reader may now feel more confident than if it had been presented as a whole at the very beginning.

The authors draw attention to the fact that a modified form of the model can be used to describe low involvement, limited problem solving behaviour. They suggest that the key difference between EPS and LPS is not that the process is different but it is in the extent to which time and effort is put into external information search and alternative evaluation. In other words, faced with a shopping list containing toilet paper and baked beans in a supermarket, they predict that shoppers will not devote much time and effort to the choices to be made.

Some authorities have criticized the model on the grounds that, while it usefully includes environmental and social factors, it does not define the relationships specifically. Others feel that the separation of information search and alternative evaluation is relatively unrealistic. As with most models, the predictive power is also somewhat limited.

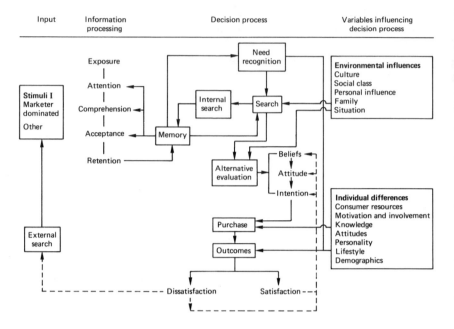

Figure 10.17   A complete model of consumer behaviour showing purchase and outcomes. *Source*: Engel *et al.* 1990

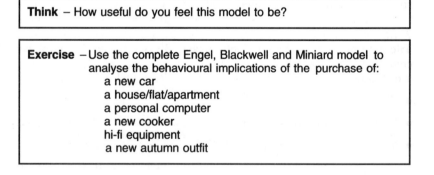

The Howard–Sheth model

The next grand model we will look at is that devised originally by Howard and then revised and published jointly with Sheth. It is another comprehensive model comparable to that of Engel, Blackwell and Miniard. Having described the process by which the previous model was constructed, i.e. building up a series of simple models into the overall Grand model, it is hoped that the reader can now cope with analysing the full model without resorting to the previous level of detail.

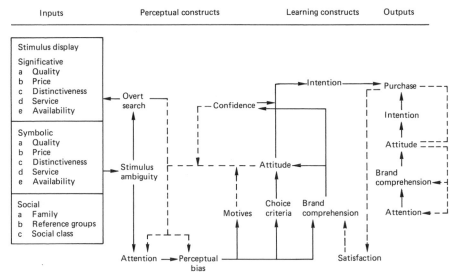

Figure 10.18 The Howard–Sheth model.
Source: Howard and Sheth 1969

The full Howard-Sheth model is as presented in Figure 10.18.

This model is characterized by four major elements – inputs, perceptual constructs, learning constructs and outputs. We can attempt to clarify their roles as follows:

1 Inputs
These cover the sources of information which provide the input, or stimuli concerning the brand or product to the individual. As can be seen they draw a distinction between stimuli which are:

- *Significative* – concerning the physical attributes of the product.

- *Symbolic* – concerning verbal and visual elements of advertising messages.

- *Social* – concerning inputs from the individual's social environment.

2 Perceptual constructs
This part of the model shows four elements:

- *Stimulus ambiguity* – this suggests the consumer may be unclear about the messages being received and may attempt to resolve uncertainty through:

- *Overt search* – similar to the Engel, Blackwell and Miniard section on external search, this may involve interrogation of opinion leaders, purchasing relevant literature or visiting appropriate outlets to obtain more information. Implicit in such activity is

- *Attention* – in the sense of concentration on the material to hand and the whole process is admitted to be subject to

- *Perceptual bias* – as a result of many of the distortions that were discussed in Chapter 2. Thus expectations and situational factors (not included in the model) may have a significant impact.

3 Learning constructs

In this model Howard and Sheth attempt to identify the learning processes which are concerned directly with the product. The perceptual constructs outlined above will, in turn, influence

- *Motivation* – the satisfaction of the consumer's perceived need. In a similar fashion to our earlier discussion, this will influence the

- *Criteria for choice* – here the authors suggest that if criteria do not already exist, a process of extensive problem solving will be required; if criteria are already established, but brands have not been evaluated, limited problem solving will be required; and if the criteria are known and the brand evaluation has already been conducted then routinized buying will suffice.

- *Brand comprehension* – this is concerned with the overall perception of the product which, the marketer hopes, will have been influenced positively by the marketing messages sent. This in turn will influence

- *Attitude* – here the consumer forms attitudes towards product and brand and the influences will be all of the elements discussed in Chapter 7.

- *Confidence* – is another important element of the decision process. The attitudes held and the evaluations carried out will determine the level of confidence the individual may have about the capacity of the product to satisfy the perceived need. The combination of attitude and confidence lead to

- *Intention* – to purchase the product so the final stage becomes the act of

- *Purchase* – The final stages concern post-purchase

- *Satisfaction* – this is very much as described in the Engel, Blackwell and Miniard section, and which will feed back into the consumer's perception of the brand.

4 Outputs

Here Howard and Sheth look on the actual decision-making process as the output which becomes a relatively straightforward sequence of:

Attention → Brand Comprehension → Attitude → Intention → Purchase

The dotted lines in the model represent feedback which influences attitudes. This, in turn, may affect attention and brand comprehension.

Overall the Howard–Sheth model provides an interesting comparison with the Engel, Blackwell and Miniard model described earlier. Here greater emphasis is placed on perception, attitudes and learning processes. The two models are similar in as much as they both propose a rational consumer, but one who is prepared to 'satisfice' where appropriate.

As ever, there have been some criticisms. As with the previous model, the relationship between variables is relatively ill-defined and is the cause of most of the reservations. It has also been pointed out that another limitation is its relative weakness in modelling choices which are made between different families of product – i.e. it is better at describing the choices made between brands than the choices made between unrelated alternatives such as between spending money on a new house or on private education for the children.

Exercise – Use the complete Howard–Sheth model to analyse the behavioural implications of the purchase of:
      a new car
      a house/flat/apartment
      a personal computer
      a new cooker
      hi-fi equipment
      a new autumn outfit

The Nicosia model

This model differs from the previous two in that it specifically includes the perceived attributes of the selling organization. Thus a key feature of the model is the relationship between the firm and the customer. The firm influences the consumer through its promotional and advertising activities and is affected, in its turn, by the customer. It shares with the earlier models the insight that the consumer's buying experience influences future buying behaviour. As can be seen fron Figure 10.19, the model is based on four fields:

1 Field One
This is divided into two sub-fields, the first of which concerns the characteristics of the firm and the second the characteristics of the consumer. The two interact via marketing communication processes and this communication is subject to all the potential distortions of perception and memory. This field would also include social and environmental influences which might affect awareness, motivation and attention, and thus perception. The aim of the communication (so far as the firm is concerned)

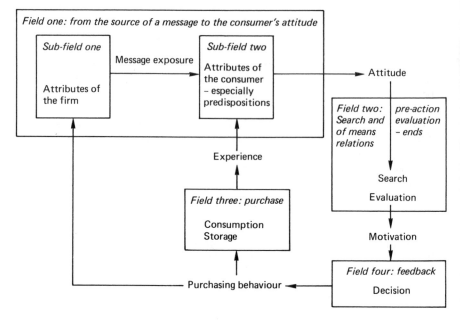

Figure 10.19   The Nicosia model – a summary flow chart.
Source: Nicosia F. M. 1966

is to link with the consumer's existing value system in such a way as to result in a positive attitude towards both the firm and the product.

2 Field Two
This centres on information search and evaluation, very much as outlined in the previous two models we have examined. The importance of the positive attitude is the belief that it will encourage problem-solving behaviour. In the diagram there is an implication that such problem-solving behaviour will result in a positive outcome for the firm, but it is clear that the result of such behaviour could be a decision to reject the product.

3 Field Three
This follows the assumed motivation stemming from field two will lead to the act of purchase – so the output from this stage is shown as purchasing behaviour.

4 Field Four

This is the post-purchase feedback which will affect both the consumer's predispositions and attitudes. The feedback for the consumer is in the form of experience while that for the firm is in the form of sales information that can be used to modify the marketing strategy. So this field implies potential behaviour change for both parties.

The model emphasizes that interactions between the four fields may occur either simultaneously or in sequence; that the process can be initiated at various stages i.e. by the firm via marketing messages or by the consumer. It has the relative advantage of showing the process as interactive; of not considering the consumer in isolation from the firm and its advertising; and additionally it does not assume that attitude leads directly to purchase, but that it triggers a decision-making process.

Criticisms have included the assertions that it is descriptive rather than explanatory or predictive and that areas such as Field One need expansion to do full justice to the rich complexity of the interaction between firm and consumer.

Exercise – Use the complete Nicosia model to analyse the behavioural implications of the purchase of:

    a new car
    a house/flat/apartment
    a personal computer
    a new cooker
    hi-fi equipment
    a new autumn outfit

Chapter summary exercises

Think – How can the material in this chapter be applied to the marketing of:

    camcorders
    the social policy of a political party
    skis
    holidays
    soft drinks
    instant coffee
    sports shoes (trainers)
    razors
    hair colourant
    toothpaste
    shampoo

motor cars
low-fat/low cholesterol/low salt spread
sanitary protection
kitchen equipment
spirits and liqueurs
low-alcohol wine
a restaurant
newspapers
toilet tissue
bicycles

Think – How has my organization used modelling approaches?

Think – How *could* my organization use modelling approaches?

Think – How have *I* used modelling approaches?

Some 'typical' examination questions – Modelling consumer behaviour and decision making

A It has been said that models of consumer behaviour should be characterized by simplicity, their factual basis, logic, originality, explanatory power, predictive power, heuristic power, and validity. What do you think these criteria mean? To what extent are they appropriate? Are there any others which could or should be used in order to evaluate models of consumer behaviour? Which model, in your view, best meets the criteria, and why?

B Answer the following questions in relation to the usefulness, realism and relevance of any models of consumer behaviour with which you are sufficiently familiar:

- Why do marketers use models at all?
- What factors should be taken into consideration when evaluating the value of any given model?
- What are the variables which influence the decision-making of consumers?
- What are the causal relationships involved in the decision-making of consumers?

C It has been argued that the so-called 'grand' models of consumer behaviour (e.g. Howard–Sheth, Engel/Blackwell/Miniard, and Nicosia) are rather cumbersome and difficult to use for practical purposes, while the less sophisticated types of model provide practical tools of marketing analysis. To what extent would you agree with this assessment, and why?

D Compare any two of the following models of consumer behaviour:

- Howard–Sheth
- Engel, Blackwell and Miniard
- Nicosia

Demonstrate the usefulness of your chosen models in respect of a proposed purchase of international airline travel.

E Modelling is based on the principle that a relatively small number of variables account for the vast bulk of consumer behaviour.

a What are these variables?
b What are the general criteria which should be applied when constructing a consumer model?
c Which of the available models, in your view, best fulfils these criteria, and why?

F Evaluate the success of behavioural modelling as a technique for explaining and predicting consumer activity in the marketplace, with particular reference to *one* of the following three: Howard–Sheth, Engel/Blackwell/Miniard, or Nicosia.

Sources

Bloom, B. S. (1956) *Taxonomy of Educational Objectives. Handbook 1 – The Cognitive Domain*, Longman.

BPP (1991) *Behavioural Aspects of Marketing*, BPP

Engel, J. F., Blackwell, R. D. and Miniard, P. W. (1990) *Consumer Behaviour* (6th edn.), Dryden.

Hawkins, D. I., Best, R. J. and Coney, K. A. (1989) *Consumer Behaviour: Implications for Marketing Strategy* (4th edn.), Irwin.

Peter, J. P. and Olson, J. C. (1990) *Consumer Behaviour and Marketing Strategy* (2nd edn), Irwin.

Williams, K. C. (1981) *Behavioural Aspects of Marketing*, Heinemann.

Wright, G. (1984) *Behavioural Decision Theory*, Penguin.

Part Five

People in Organizations

11 If we're all in the same boat – why are we all paddling in different directions?

People and marketing in organizations

Introduction

This chapter is devoted to what is sometimes called 'organization theory'. This is another large area and this chapter attempts to highlight the most significant parts of the field.

Much of earlier work on motivation (Chapter 6) needs to be looked at again from the standpoint of 'what makes *the employee* tick?'. It is also worth looking at the material on the Hawthorne Experiments and the work of Elton Mayo from Chapter 8 as being highly relevant to this area.

At the end of this section the student should be fully familiar with the ideas and contribution of the following theorists and be able to relate their theories to marketing departments:

- Specialization, Co-ordination, Hierarchy, Authority.

- Weber
- Fayol } Classical theorists.
- Taylor

- Mayo
- McGregor } Human Relations theorists.
- Likert

- Systems theory

- Woodward
- Burns and Stalker } Contingency theorists.
- Lawrence and Lorsch

- Management Style.

- Organization culture.

- The Flexible Firm.
- Alternative approaches to job design.

Organization

For the manager, organization is the process of deploying resources, financial, materials, machinery and people in order that the sum total of the resources, and the human activity that links and activates the whole, achieves the objectives for which the organization is set up.

For the employees, it is the state of being employed as part of the group of persons which exists specifically for the achievement of these objectives.

One of the major tasks of management is organizing. This involves deciding on the appropriate resources, deciding who does what, and ensuring that the separate elements knit together effectively.

This process involves the concepts of specialization, co-ordination and the acceptance of hierarchy, all of which are basic to our knowledge of organizations.

Specialization

This is that activity that addresses the 'who does what?' question. It defines the tasks and responsibilities that make up a person's job, and groups them in the distinctive way that allows the definition of that job. It can sometimes group the jobs in such a way as to define a specialism or profession. In this way we start to come to terms with the notion of an occupation – ask any individual what they are, and the odds are that they will reply using an occupation – 'I am a teacher, sales rep, footballer etc.'. The idea of specialization inevitably limits the activities undertaken by a member of the organization, but the extent of the limitation may vary considerably. A senior manager may have a fairly wide brief in terms of job definition. For example, a marketing manager whose task/responsibility for the enterprise is to increase sales and market share has a very open ended brief, whereas machine operators working for the same company have a much tighter specification of their activities.

However, over-specialization can cause difficulties through limiting flexibility, so some organizations consciously develop jobs which encompass a variety of tasks. One large supermarket chain have faced up to the problems of satisfying their need for flexibility by creating a single job description for all junior staff. This eliminates the barriers between the 'normal' specializations of warehouse, shelf-stacking and checkout, by putting all three activities into a single universal job description. Staff can then be deployed with maximum flexibility to whichever tasks have the highest priority at any given time. Some other organizations are moving to defining skills rather than jobs, which again aims to overcome the problems associated with over-specialization.

Even more extreme are the Japanese companies which are moving towards having no job descriptions at all. It is claimed by such organizations that job descriptions are inevitably rigid, self-defeating and a barrier to change. They believe that the work of individuals should be modified as the organization's needs evolve and change. It is perhaps all too easy to dismiss such ideas as being rooted in a different culture. However, given the current levels of unemployment in the UK and the relatively strong position of the employer in the employment contract, such approaches could speedily be adopted.

> **Think** – How specialized is your job?
> – Would it be 'improved' by being more or less specialized?
> – Why?

Co-ordination

The notion of specialization involves the division of the total task of the organization into sub-tasks. Co-ordination involves the re-unification of the sub-tasks into an integrated whole. Thus it is the process of ensuring the individual jobs knit together so that the overall objective of the organization can be achieved. It is perhaps self evident that the size of the co-ordination problem that is faced is also a function of the extent to which the overall task has been subdivided and the degree of interdependence between the sub-tasks. The issue of co-ordination can also be viewed as a problem of control – here we could usefully revisit the ideas set out in Chapter 1. In a world that is less than predictable, organizations will need feedback mechanisms, checks on progress and 'fail safe' planning responses to the unexpected.

There is also a tendency for specialist groups to regard themselves as the centre of their own universe. They may view themselves as being self-sufficient and other departments can become 'the enemy' (look back at the Sherifs' 'Robbers Cave' experiments described in Chapter 8). Such a situation is clearly inefficient so far as the whole organization is concerned – energy is diverted from the main task of organizational success into the fruitless interdepartmental trench warfare experienced in some organizations.

> **Think** – What examples of interdepartmental rivalry have you experienced?
> – What was the effect on the organization overall?
> – How was the problem dealt with?

Much of management is centred on the problem of co-ordination – the structure that is chosen for the organization, the working procedures, the decision-making processes and the management style are all potential elements in the solution.

However, the reality is that many people feel alienated or bored at work and view work as being a 'necessary evil'. They commonly view it as being a means to an end – and their end may not be identical to the end sought by the management. As Watson says:

> Organisations . . . are managed in order to achieve certain goals and policies which are articulated by those who are at the top or 'in charge'. But these goals, as well as the procedures and arrangements which are associated with them are as much the outcomes of the conflicts, negotiations and indeed confusions existing amongst the various individuals and groups which make up the organisation as they are pregiven elements into which people fit. The organisation, then, is an association of people with often widely differing and indeed conflicting interests, preferences and purposes who are willing, within rather tightly defined limits, to carry out tasks which help meet the requirements of those in charge.

This leads us to the notion of hierarchy.

Hierarchy

The underlying assumption of a hierarchy is that people within it are graded in rank order – *B* is higher than *C*, but lower than *A*, etc. Within organizations it also commonly implies that *A* has authority over *B* and so on, which again is usually reflected in positions on an organization chart:

The idea of authority is a complex one, but in its simplest form it could be defined as the right to exercise power. It is possible to have one without the other – e.g. the ineffective supervisor may have authority but little power and the armed robber may have power without authority. As it is so crucial to organizational life it is worth any manager or potential manager reflecting on the answer to the question 'why should anybody do what I tell them?' (it is a salutary question for teachers as well!), so we will look at some of the theories which have been put forward in this area.

Dominance theories

Based largely on the observation of animals, this 'I'm bigger than you . . .' approach leaves us very close to the notion of power – the majority of authorities maintain that the two concepts are different with authority being the legitimate source of influence (the right referred to in the definition) while power implies the naked threat.

Knowledge theories

There is another source of influence which is associated with knowing things that others do not. In the paragraph above the word was used with that specific connotation. It is also used in everday language in the same way – e.g. '*X* is an authority on pre-war steam locomotives'. It must be noted however that this form of authority may be irrelevant if we are not concerned with pre-war steam locomotives! In other words influence depends on the receivers' perceptions and valuation of the knowledge.

Bureaucratic theories

Bureaucratic theories are dominated by the work of Max Weber who suggested that there were three separate types of authority:

1 *Traditional* – often part of our culture, this is the authority that stems from custom and practice – the way it has always been. So we have the hereditary traditions in the UK (often with gender implications) where the eldest son inherits from the father. There are also some traditions which encompass position or ownership – the popular television sit-com *To the Manor Born* was based on the lack of understanding of authority and responsibility implied in these traditions.
2 *Legal/Rational* – is the authority which arises from a process which might be characterized by the British parliamentary system. Debate by representatives leads to a rational rule making process which then covers the population concerned. Examples could include the authority vested in the police as the executive arm of the law making process or the authority of the works rules established after discussion and agreement with the organization's workforce.
3 *Charismatic* – the authority which stems from force of character or personality.

Work-based theories

Work-based theories stem from Etzioni who put forward another three types found specifically within organizations:

1 *Economic* – the rewards, usually in the form of pay/bonuses etc., which can be withheld if the instructions are not obeyed.
2 *Normative* – the pressures of the group – 'we don't do that sort of thing here'.
3 *Coercive* – the threat of the sack if orders are not complied with.

Acceptancy theories

Acceptancy theories are linked to the work of Barnard and suggest that the real power lies with the subordinates on the grounds that they can say 'No' to instructions given by a manager. Barnard claims that four conditions must be met simultaneously for an order to be obeyed. The subordinate must:

1 believe that it is within the general remit of the organization;
2 believe that it is in his overall interest;
3 understand the instruction;
4 be physically and mentally able to comply.

Dependency theories

Dependency theory originated from Douglas McGregor and is best summarized by Figure 11.1.

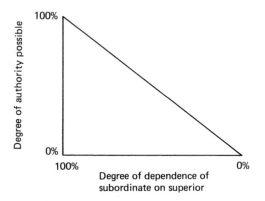

Figure 11.1

This implies that a manager can only exert total authority over someone if the subordinate is totally dependent. Conversely, you can have no authority over a person who is totally independent. This is a global view which can cast some interesting light on managerial behaviours when (e.g.) the labour market is very tight – employees are commonly indulged or when the labour market is very slack – managements commonly become more autocratic.

Think – Which of these theories gives the most satisfactory explanation of the phenomenon we call authority?

Classical theories of organization

Weber proposed a form of organization which dealt with many of these issues and which has been particularly influential in the way we look at organizations. He suggested a form of organization which:

1 allocated activities as 'official duties' of the individual role;
2 had a strict hierarchy of responsibility and jobs, with each jobholder's authority to give commands and take decisions strictly prescribed;
3 allowed promotion only after successfully passing appropriate exams;
4 demanded preparation of written documents (files) to keep records of decisions, precedents, etc.;
5 operated on a system of impersonal written rules;
6 separated 'the job' from 'the jobholder' so that there is no change in organization when someone is promoted or leaves.

Because of (6) above this system is known as *'Bureaucracy'* – organization based on 'office'. This has become a term of abuse in many situations, implying administrative inefficiency, doing everything exactly to the rule book, excessive paperwork and delay. However, it is the dominant system of organizing within large enterprises and has numerous advantages. Firstly it takes care of the specialization issue via (1) above. Hierarchy is welcomed and defined in (2), the combination of (1) and (2) can also encompass the co-ordination needs by defining superiors jobs in such a way as to ensure that they co-ordinate the activities of those reporting to them. (3) helps to eliminate nepotism and the appointment of the incompetent. (5) reduces the dependency of the subordinate on the goodwill of the boss, while (4) and (6) keep the activities consistently centred on the objectives of the organization.

Fayol argued that there existed an 'administrative science' that was independent of the product or service – the duties of administration were planning, organizing, commanding, co-ordinating, controlling.

He put forward a number of guidelines known as Fayol's Principles, they include:

- Authority and responsibility – should be balanced,
- Unity of command – an employee should only receive orders from one superior,
- Unity of direction – the co-ordination of activities to achieve a goal,
- Division of work/specialization,
- Discipline – should be well defined,
- Subordination of the individual interest – to the overall good,
- Centralization is desirable to ensure sound co-ordination of effort,
- Equity, Stability of tenure, Initiative, etc. are all to be encouraged.

While some of these ideas seem difficult to apply in real life, they do address directly many of the key issues of organization.

Taylor and the Scientific Management School advanced the idea of measurement, control and targets. Functional management was suggested and the composite of these three early writers led to the approach sometimes referred to as *Classical Theory*.

Both Weber and Fayol propose structures which are similar and produce the familiar pyramid shaped organization chart which formally defines jobs,

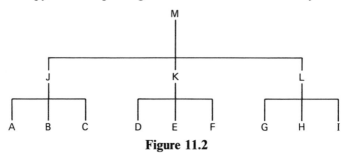

Figure 11.2

responsibilities and relationships.

The characteristics of classical organizational theory are often remembered by the mnemonic OSCAR:

- Objectives – clearly defined,
- Specialization – via clearly delineated jobs and responsibilities,
- Co-ordination – by means of common superiors in the pyramid,
- Authority – determined by position allocated within the hierarchy,
- Responsibility – to balance the unbridled use of that authority.

Other principles associated with classical theory involved continually seeking to maximize efficiency, delegation of responsibility and the appropriate authority, span of control to be limited to what a manager could reasonably cope with and chain of command to be as short as practicable. Another fundamental was that we should group like activities, so the emergence of specialized functions such as marketing, finance, personnel was aided. It also gave rise to the concepts of line (activities are central to the objectives of the organization) and staff departments (providing a support service for the line).

The criticisms of classical theory are numerous. Perhaps the most basic is that it views the organization as a machine, and the people who make up the organization as cogs within that machine. Much of more recent thinking has focused on a more realistic view of the way people behave.

One of the key contributions to the debate are Barnard's criticism of the assumptions of classical theory about authority. As we saw above, he argued that the real power lies with subordinates. If this is correct, much of our thinking about managements' right to order others to do things comes unstuck and alternative relationships would need to be defined.

Simon argued that specialization and unity of command could be irreconcilable – specialism implies having specialized knowledge or skills which others do not possess. Thus the problem arises of how the activities of specialists are to be managed. An example could be the employment of a computer specialist by an organization which recognizes its lack of expertise in that area. The problem may arise of management (who are unversed in the ways of computers) having to manage and evaluate the work and ideas of the specialist. Simon also emphasized the importance of the ways in which work roles were perceived.

Bakke argued that there would inevitably be conflict between the organization wishing to 'socialize' the employee and the individual seeks to 'personalize' the organization. He also developed similar ideas to Simon's on role and suggested that while there was no shortage of persons willing to play the 'benevolent manager' role, there was a growing dearth of persons willing to play the matching 'grateful subordinate' role.

Argyris, in numerous publications, has suggested that conflict was likely to be a problem where people were expected to do jobs in which little control over work is permitted, passivity is expected, they are forced to be subordinate, flexibility is minimized along with skill, *and* they are made dependent. This link to job design will be explored later in the chapter.

Despite these criticisms, classical approaches can be argued to have a good(ish) track record, and could be said to have been the means by which many of us have been able to enjoy the fruits of mass production in the form of readily available and relatively cheap consumer products.

Human relations school of organization (behaviourists)

The founding father of this movement was Elton Mayo (see Chapter 8) plus the influence of the Hawthorne Experiments. The implications of this work for organization theory were considerable, particularly the viewing of an enterprise as a social system. It also emphasized the importance of the human resource within the enterprise and highlighted the impact of influences on work behaviour. The experiments remind managers that informal groups exist at the workplace and that their aims and aspirations may not coincide with those of 'the bosses'.

To some extent the experiments were misinterpreted by managers who read of the ever increasing output in the relay assembly room experiment and assumed that tea-breaks, canteens and letting people go home early were the route to increased productivity. Clearly the messages from the studies are more complex than just 'being nice to people' and involve a fundamental change in the way a workforce is viewed (and treated) by management.

The main criticism of classical theory is usually linked to this concept of a different relationship between employers and employed and may be seen as a continuation of the thinking that is often referred to as the Human Relation School.

Theory X, Theory Y and the notion of managment style

One of the most influential contributors to this approach was Douglas McGregor who introduced his 'Theory X' and 'Theory Y' styles of management. His ideas stem from much of the work already covered in the motivation chapter and are closely associated with Maslow's theories in that field. McGregor suggested that it was possible to identify two polarized management styles which were determined by the assumptions that were made about the behaviour and characteristics of the workforce. Theory X is based on the assumptions of the 'rational economic' theories of behaviour (see Chapter 6). In summary it assumes that:

- The average worker is basically idle, has an inherent dislike of work and will seek to avoid it wherever possible.
- The average employee must be forcefully motivated by direction and threats of punishment to work effectively and give a fair day's work.
- The average worker seeks to avoid responsibility and likes to be directed by superiors.
- The average employee lacks the imagination, ingenuity and interest to solve organizational problems.

McGregor argues strongly that these assumptions are not valid and that Theory X approaches to management should be abandoned. It should be noted that such assumptions could be said to underpin classical organization theory. He uses his dependency theory of authority to explain why classical, autocratic styles had been effective in the past (employees being highly dependent on their work due to lack of protective social security and employment legislation, weak trades unions, etc.) and using the same theory to argue for a different set of assumptions and, hence, a different style of management which he called Theory Y.

The assumptions underlying Theory Y may be summarized:

- People do not have an inherent dislike of work, they are active and expend energy naturally. Depending on the specific situation people may see work as being a source of satisfaction and achievement or it can be seen as an unsatisfying activity.
- People like to exercise self-direction and self-control – and do so regularly in a wide variety of situations to achieve their goals.
- Motivation is an integral part of most people, management do not create it. They like responsibility and will often seek it.
- Many workers have the capacity to solve organizational problems and would welcome the opportunity to do so.

This results in a very different, people oriented management style. He suggests that it can be seen as an agricultural (growing talent) style as opposed to the more traditional mechanical analogies.

It must be stressed that McGregor did *not* suggest that there are Theory X and Theory Y employees – his whole approach is focused on the *assumptions* that managers make about the motivation, capacity and behaviour of their staff. This is not to deny the possibility that managers who behave according to Theory X assumptions may create a self-fulfilling prophecy by 'provoking' what the subordinates might perceive as 'appropriate' reactions. His book *The Human Side of Enterprise* remains a classic and bears reading even after all the years since its initial publication in 1954.

Likert related management style with efficiency and profitability and came to the conclusion that participative styles (System IV) yielded better results that autocratic styles (System I) – he also proposed his 'linking pin' structure which enabled participation in decision making. These latter two figures were, in their way, as generalist and universalist as the classical theorists. The last thirty years have seen the growth of a systems approach to organization, and it is to this that we now turn.

Systems approaches

The systems approach to organization is not so much a theory which describes how to do it, it is more a way of looking at organizations and analysing, explaining and diagnosing solutions to their problems.

It is based on the notion that organizations can be visualized as systems which have inputs, transformational processes, outputs and some form of feedback system which gives information about results and relationships with the environment. This approach has its roots in the physical sciences and has a number of attractive features. Firstly it is essentially a *neutral* approach to the management process – neutral in the sense that there is no underlying assumption, particularly about the people within the systems. Secondly it is a way of analysing that can be used at different levels – individuals, groups, organizations, societal, national, supranational. Thirdly it gives a framework for assessing how well the various parts of an organization interact to achieve the common purpose and provides the important insight that a change in one area of the organization is likely to affect other parts. Finally it emphasizes that an important consideration to be addressed is the way in which the organization interacts with its environment. It is shown diagrammatically in Figure 11.3.

Systems can be viewed as being open or closed. An *open system* interacts continually with its environment as an essential part of its operation – seeking new inputs and learning how its outputs are viewed by the outside world. In contrast, a *closed system* does very little interacting with the environment and, as a result, receives little feedback.

Any organization which is marketing oriented must be towards the open end of the continuum as the interaction with the needs, wants, attitudes and satisfactions of its customers is essential to the marketing process.

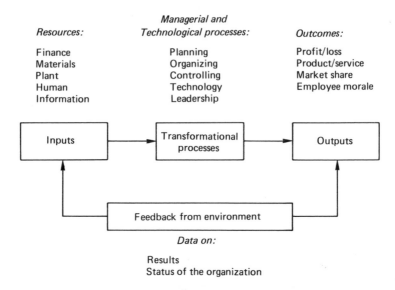

Resources:	Managerial and Technological processes:	Outcomes:
Finance	Planning	Profit/loss
Materials	Organizing	Product/service
Plant	Controlling	Market share
Human	Technology	Employee morale
Information	Leadership	

Figure 11.3

The marketing function within the organizational system

Marketing is one of the key functions within the organization – Drucker, as early as 1955, argued that it is the prime function of any business, as without a market, there can be no business.

Earlier in this chapter you were asked to think about the special qualities which identified the marketing function – you may have identified its close links with the customer as being one of its key characteristics. It is this special relationship which may account for marketing's unique position within the organization. The systems approach and Figure 11.3 may help to illuminate the point. Unlike most other functions, marketing provides vital input in terms of market information. It is a key transformational process especially in its involvement with planning and quality (control) processes. It is a major output in terms of measures such as market share and so forth. But in a systems analysis it is particularly special in that it is one of the prime sources of feedback for the organization as a whole.

Contingency approaches

This is a view of organization which, in effect, argues that there is no single, universal, 'best way' of organizing. What is 'best' will depend on (be contingent upon) a number of factors (contingencies). A number of researchers have identified different elements which affect the choice of appropriate organizational form.

Woodward identified the *production process* (unit, mass, continuous) as being a key variable – with only mass production systems being suited to classical principles and practice.

Burns and Stalker found that the *rate of change of technology* was another key factor – stability lending itself to mechanistic (classical) approaches while rapid change demanded organic, flexible styles for success.

Lawrence and Lorsch developed the idea of a *'differentiated'* organization where the needs of one part of the organization might demand a different approach to another. An example might be Research and Development's need for a long-term perspective contrasted to the production line's emphasis on the immediate.

Harrison and Handy have both highlighted the importance of organization ideologies or cultures.

Child has pointed out the importance of the size variable – the larger the organization, the greater the tendency towards bureaucratic systems.

Almost inevitably there are many different views and a great deal of new language which may prove confusing to the first time reader. One contribution which might help is that of *Tannenbaum and Schmidt* who produced a diagram which represents a continuum of managerial styles. This continuum centres on the decision making processes and draws a distinction between styles in which managers make the decisions on their own, and the more participative processes which welcome subordinate contributions.

Area of managerial prerogative

Area of subordinate involvement
in decision making

Classical	Behaviourist
Autocratic	Participative
Theory X	Theory Y
System I	System IV
Mechanistic	Organic

Think – Where do you think your organization comes on the
Tannenbaum Schmidt continuum?
– Where would you like it to be?
– Why?

Organizational culture

In exactly the same sense as we considered culture in the wider context in Chapter 9, we can look at the culture within an organization. Using our previous analysis each workplace is likely to develop its own micro-culture within the larger society. Organizational theorists have recently identified the importance of organizational culture as an important variable, and one which may allow some useful analysis. The definition of culture in this setting is no different to that which we used earlier – 'a system of shared values, assumptions, beliefs and norms that unite the members of an organization' and, as before, it reflects the common views about 'the way things are done around here'. It is a rather wider concept than that of managerial style which we have already looked at, and can be applied with equal ease to profit and non-profit oriented organizations. It is believed to be important on the assumption that beliefs and values shape behaviour, and that these behaviours can have a significant impact on organizational effectiveness.

In one of the seminal contributions to this view of organizational life, the Peters and Waterman 1982 study of 'successful' organizations (*In Search of Excellence*), the system for describing organizations called the 'McKinsey 7-S Framework' was used. This model includes 'hard' concepts such as strategy and structure as well as 'soft' aspects such as style, systems, staff, skills and shared values. The seven elements of culture are linked in a form of web as in Figure 11.4.

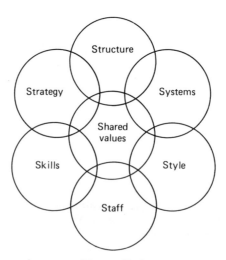

Figure 11.4

Some important concepts surrounding the notion of culture within organizations are:

1 **Direction** – the degree to which a culture supports, rather than interferes with, reaching organizational goals;
2 **Pervasiveness** – the extent to which the culture is widespread or unevenly distributed.
3 **Strength** – the degree to which members accept the values and other aspects of a culture.

Manifestations of organisational culture

As with our earlier discussions of culture, we face the difficulty that culture itself is not directly observable. Again we are forced to infer the nature of the culture from the organization's use of symbols, stories, rites and ceremonials.

Symbols are objects, acts or events that serve as a vehicle to convey meaning. Within organizations such as the Cubs or Guides badges and uniforms are used to denote achievement, acceptance or seniority.

> **Think** – What symbols exist within your organization?

Stories are narratives based on a true event, which are sometimes embellished to emphasize the intended value. Bartol and Martin quote the story of the 3M employee who was sacked following a refusal to stop working on a new product idea, even after a direct instruction from his boss. Despite being fired and removed from the payroll, the individual continued to come to work and continued operating from an unused office. Eventually the employee was rehired, developed the idea into a huge success, and was promoted to vice-president. The story highlights the important value of innovation within the 3M organization – and the part of their culture which says 'if you believe in an idea – stick with it'.

> **Think** – What stories illuminate the culture within your organization?

Rites are relatively elaborate, dramatic and planned activities intended to convey cultural values to participants (and usually an audience), while *ceremonials* are systems of rites performed (usually) in conjunction with a single occasion or event. The school prize day or sports day would be an example from the educational field. Organizations may have rites and rituals covering birthdays (who buys the cakes), courses (end of programme dinners), promotion and so forth. Some may be more formalized as in companies which reward the month's high performers in public.

> **Think** – What rites and rituals apply within your organization?

It is believed that culture can have a positive effect on organizational effectiveness when the culture supports organizational goals, is deeply internalized by members, and is widely shared. We have already used an example from the 3M organization where the consistent and shared emphasis on innovation has helped the company produce a stream of new products as well as making continual improvements in existing ones.

On the other hand it is generally accepted that culture can have a negative impact when it is widely shared and well internalized by staff, but which influences behaviours in directions that do not further (and possibly interfere with) the achievement of organizational goals. In mixed situations, where the culture is unevenly spread and/or weakly held, it is less likely to have much impact either for good or ill.

> **Think** – How positive or negative is the culture within your organization?
> – How would you like to see it changed?
> – Why?
> – How would you go about changing the culture towards that which you want?

Peters and Waterman identified eight characteristics of excellent companies – excellent in the sense of being able to successfully innovate in both product terms and in organizational responsiveness. These characteristics may be summarized:

1 *a bias for action* – the organization gets on with its business, avoiding 'paralysis by analysis', tries out ideas and experiments rather than spending too long discussing how things might work;
2 *close to the customer* – listening regularly and intently to customers to determine their needs and wants. Providing quality in terms of product, service and reliability;
3 *autonomy and entrepreneurship* – developing leaders and innovators by allowing sufficient freedom for them to be creative and experimenting. By allowing (and expecting) mistakes, but learning from them;
4 *productivity through people* – treating the workforce as human beings by providing meaning as well as money for their efforts. Rewarding and supporting individuals making their own quality and productivity improvements;
5 *hands on, value driven* – the management team are close to their operation and have homogeneous business values. This provides Fayol's 'unity of direction' by strong leadership in which values are instilled by actions which reinforce the words;
6 *stick to the knitting* – success via expansion into areas closely related to the core business;
7 *simple form, lean staff* – avoiding complex organization structures, minimizing the layers of staff. Ensuring flexible roles within the structure and able to accept ambiguity and paradox;
8 *simultaneous 'loose–tight' properties* – allowing autonomy to be pushed down to the lowest levels in the organization but ensuring cultural values

are strong and tight. Leaders are 'champions' whose values align closely with the core values and culture of the organization and who can be viewed as role models for vicarious learning within the organization.

> **Think** – How closely does your organization match on Peters and Waterman's eight criteria for excellence?

The Peters and Waterman approach, published in 1982, made a great impact on thinking about organizations. However, their work is not without its critics. It has been pointed out that they employed a case study approach to their research (see Chapter 1) and that they indulged in inductive processes to arrive at their conclusions. Critics argue that although lessons were drawn from so-called 'excellent' companies and common factors were identified, the researchers failed to examine whether less than excellent companies acted any differently. Other criticisms centre on the fact that, only two years after publication, fourteen of the 'excellent' companies had ceased to be 'excellent' against Peters and Waterman's own criteria. The work has also been criticized on the grounds that it assumes that success can be explained solely (or primarily) in terms of organization, and ignores other crucial elements such as customers and competition. All in all this work acts as an 'excellent' example of the problems of the behavioural sciences as outlined in Chapter 1.

Culture can also be used to describe the overall orientation of a company. Bartol and Martin use an opportunity matrix which is set out in Figure 11.5.

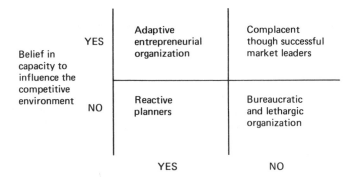

Desired future state – characterized by growth or change

Figure 11.5

This matrix is interesting in as much as it contrasts and opposes entrepreneurial and bureaucratic forms and orientations. This ties in with Stevenson and Gumpert's analysis of the two forms, illustrated in Figure 11.6.

As can be seen, this analysis brings together many of the ideas already discussed in this chapter.

Dimension	Entrepreneurial characteristics	Bureaucratic characteristics
Strategic orientation	Driven by perceptions of opportunity	Driven by controlled resources
Commitment to seize opportunity	Revolutionary change within short period	Evolutionary change over long period
Commitment of resources	Many stages with minimum exposure at each stage	Single stage, with complete commitment based on one decision
Control of resources	Uuse of freelance help and rental of required resources	Employment or ownership of required resources
Management structure	Few levels – emphasis on informal communication patterns	Many levels – emphasis on communication through formal hierarchy

Figure 11.6

> **Think** – Where does your organization come on this entrepreneurial – bureaucratic continuum?
> – Where should it be?

Changing organizational culture

A major task for many organizations is to change to a more appropriate culture. For many, the task will involve the marketing function directly, as it may be seen as a requirement for the whole organization to become more market oriented. As we saw earlier, marketing as a function holds a special place – within the organization, but in direct contact with the outside world. It raises some interesting questions as to what happens to the function if it becomes part of *every* employee's job? Similarly a recent emphasis for many organizations has been the change to a 'total quality culture'. Here the aim is to make quality an integral part of every job.

This kind of culture change is very similar to the problems faced by marketers wishing to change (e.g.) political values or eating habits. Much of the material in this book has been focused on the methods by which it is possible to change attitudes and behaviour. So it should prove relatively easy to couch the problem in terms which will be recognizable to the marketing specialist.

> **Think** – What strategies would you recommend for changing the culture of your own organization?

Most of the issues we have dealt with should come into play – perception, attitude change, learning new behaviours, motivation, coping with group pressures and so forth. A well known model for looking at change processes stems from the work of Kurt Lewin who originally put forward the idea of what he called the 'force field' (see Figure 11.7).

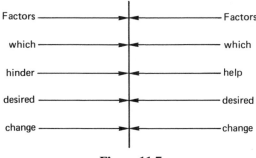

Factors	Factors
which	which
hinder	help
desired	desired
change	change

Figure 11.7

Strategies can be implemented which will reduce the impact of those factors which militate against change and other strategies can be employed which will increase the forces which are promoting the desired change.

> **Think** – How well did your solutions to the last problem fit into this framework?

Within the organizational setting culture change should be somewhat easier than in society at large. It is possible for managers to give direct instructions which will define the new, desired behaviours and values. They can back up such instructions with rules, procedures, rewards, coaching, bonuses and so forth. At the end of the day they may well even take disciplinary action against those who cannot or will not comply.

Perhaps the key factor is to ensure that all the elements of the mix are helping and reinforcing the desired change, i.e. very similar to the notion of direction with which we started this section.

Atkinson's model of 'The Flexible Firm'

This approach is identified with John Atkinson working at the Institute of Manpower Studies and published in 1985. His research identified a model of organization which, it is claimed, provides a more fluid approach to employment patterns to meet the needs of higher productivity, commitment and versatility which rapid change demands.

He identifies three areas of flexibility:

a *Functional flexibility* – where employees can be redeployed quickly and smoothly between tasks and activities. This may mean the redeployment of multi-skilled craftsmen moving between the traditional trade divisions of mechanical and electrical jobs; it may mean moving staff between indirect and direct production jobs; or it could mean a complete change of career from, say, draughtsman to technical sales. As products, production methods and markets change, functional flexibility implies that the same labour force changes with them, in both the short and medium term.

b *Numerical flexibility* – is sought so that the headcount (number of employees) can be quickly and easily increased or decreased in line with even short term changes in the level of demand for labour. It may mean that hire and fire policies can be more easily implemented, or that hiring gives way to looser contractual relationships between manager, organization and employee. The end result sought is that at any point in time the number employed or working exactly matches the number required.

c *Financial flexibility* – is desired for two reasons. Firstly, so that pay and other employment costs reflect the state of supply and demand in the external labour market. There is little new in the notion that employers wish to hire labour as cheaply as possible. The significance lies more in the relativities and differentials between groups than in an across-the-board push to reduce wages, and the implications include a continued shift to plant level bargaining and widening differentials between skilled and unskilled workers. Secondly, and probably of greater importance in the long term, pay flexibility means a shift to new reward systems that facilitate either numerical or functional flexibility – such as assessment based pay schemes in place of 'rate-for-the-job'.

Atkinson suggests that changing the organization of work is the best way of achieving greater flexibility from the workforce, and, as a result, a new model of the 'flexible firm' is beginning to emerge, which makes it much easier to secure all three kinds of flexibility.

The model developed by Atkinson and the IMS is shown in Figure 11.8 and is divided into four categories:

1 Core group
This should contain the key personnel, who are full-time, permanent career employees: for example – managers, designers, technical sales staff, quality control staff, technicians and craftspersons. Their employment security is bought at the cost of accepting functional flexibility, both in the short term (involving cross-trade working, reduced demarcation, and multi-disciplined project teams), as well as in the longer term (career change and re-training). Terms and conditions of employment are designed to promote functional flexibility.

This often involves single status conditions, and the replacement of the 'rate-for-the-job' pay systems with schemes which reward the acquisition and deployment of new skills, and which are at least partly based on performance assessment. However, the central characteristic of this group is that their skills cannot readily be bought in. The firm therefore seeks to bind these key people to the firm and to separate them from the wider labour

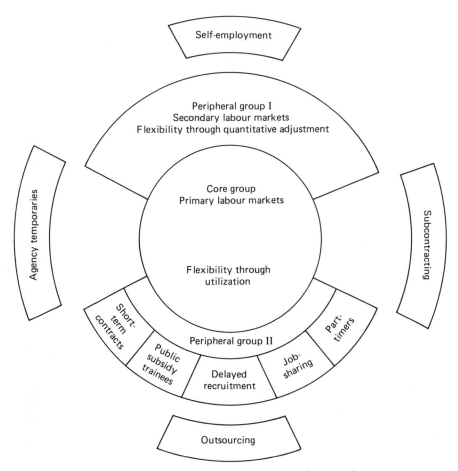

Figure 11.8   Atkinson's model of the flexible firm

market. We may also note that traditional hierarchical division of labour is less appropriate to such a group, which ideally should be both versatile and pragmatic.

2 First peripheral group

These persons are represented by the inner ring of the diagram. They are also full-time employees, but enjoy a lower level of job security and have less access to career opportunities. In effect they are offered a job not a career. For example they may have clerical, supervisory or assembly type occupations. The key characteristic of their jobs is that they can be seen as being 'plug in' rather than firm-specific. As a result the firm looks to the external labour market to fill these jobs, and seeks to achieve numerical and financial flexibility through a more direct and immediate link to the external labour market than for the core group. Functional flexibility is not sought and, because these jobs tend to be less skilled, little training or re-training is needed. Cynics suggest that the lack of career prospects, systematic planning of job content around a narrow range of tasks, and a recruitment strategy directed particularly at women, all tend to encourage a relatively high level of labour turnover. This has the advantage of facilitating easy and rapid numerical adjustment to market uncertainty.

3 Second peripheral group

These persons provide a supplementary flexibility for the first peripheral group in both functional and numerical areas, by employing them on more limited contracts of employment. Part-time working is a good example of this – the jobs having all the characteristics of those in the first peripheral group but with their deployment structured to match changing business needs. 'Twilight shifts', job sharing, short-term contracts, public subsidy trainees, recruiting on temporary contracts all fall into this category. Again the cynic might argue that they all have the same function – to maximize flexibility while minimizing the organization's commitment to the workers' job security and career development.

4 'Outsiders'

These are the sub-contractors, self-employed workers, consultants, agencies and indirectly employed personnel. All of the complications associated with actually employing labour directly are eliminated – and high flexibility can be obtained by 'employing' specialists as the need arises. The downside of such a strategy centres on the more limited ability to control staff and a potential dependency on outside specialists. Generally this category applies to jobs which are not firm-specific – either because they are very specialized (e.g. systems analysis), or very mundane (e.g. office cleaning). This permits not only greater numerical flexibility (with the firm deciding precisely how much of a particular service it requires at any time), but also encourages greater functional flexibility than direct employment. This is claimed to be as a result of the greater commitment of the self-employed to getting the job done and the greater specialization of sub-contractors. Once more the cynic might suggest that it was due to the relative powerlessness of the worker in this context.

> **Think** – How close to the 'flexible firm' model is your organization?
> – Did it develop this way as a conscious decision or did it 'just happen'?
> – To what extent do you think the 'flexible firm' is a new idea, or is it just a description of the ways in which firms have always coped?

Atkinson's ideas have not gone without criticism. Anna Pollert published an article in which she suggested that the ideas were not new, having their roots in productivity bargaining popular in the UK during the 1960s and 1970s. She claims that peripheral employment has not been created by the policies of the larger firms but by shifts in the structure of employment, cost cutting and rationalization.

Other criticisms of this approach focus on whether such ideas are, in fact, new, or whether they are simply the way managers have always reacted – overtime, 'twilight' shifts, temps and contractors were not invented in the 1980s, but have been with us for many years. The definitions of core and periphery workers are rather unsatisfactory and could shift according to levels of unemployment. For example, a shortage of a particular skill or occupation inevitably raises the importance of that group to the organization. In order to protect itself against poaching, the enterprise may decide to bring such employees into the core. There may also be variability regarding the application of these forms of flexibility depending on other factors such as the length of training involved and the cost of various categories of labour, etc. An alternative diagram could be as shown below in Figure 11.9, with flexible strategies being driven by three dimensions:

1　the scarcity/surplus of the particular labour category,
2　the cost of the category of labour (cheap–expensive),
3　the fluctuation in demand for that particular skill or occupation.

Thus our cynic might argue that such an organizational form was not the result of strategic thinking, but a pragmatic reaction to external influences over which the organization has little control.

It must also be noted that the ideas inherent in the model of the flexible firm are not at the stage of widespread implementation as a formal strategy of organizations. Finally, some of the assumptions regarding security of employment of core workers seem misplaced, given the growth in executive unemployment during the recessions in the UK during the 1970s, 1980s and early 1990s. It may be that many professional and executive posts, which have in the past enjoyed a high level of job security, may need to be redefined as more of these job-holders come from agency or fixed-term contract sources.

Despite the academic arguments, it is clear that the notion of flexibility is an important contribution to the field of organization studies and the model gives us a useful language to describe (and perhaps explain) some managerial strategies.

> **Think** – Where do you think marketing staff should be located in the flexible firm?
> – Does this apply to all staff in the function?
> – If not, which staff should be core and which periphery?
> – Why?

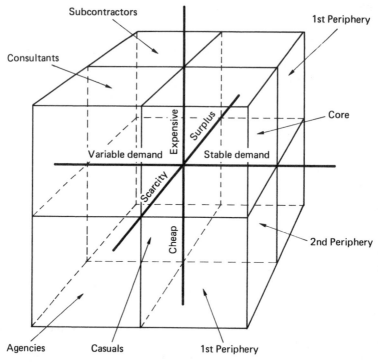

Figure 11.9   Rice's cube – a market forces view of flexibility

Job design

Another important way in which the relationship between individuals and their employing organizations is defined is the way in which jobs are designed and structured. As we saw earlier, the organization's assumptions regarding the motivation of its employees helps to define the style of management which is applied, and the issue of job design is a direct consequence of the same assumptions. There have been several different approaches to job design over the last century; these will be reviewed with the objective of clarifying both the language and the implementation.

1 Job specialization

In one sense this is basic to all organization studies. We earlier saw the emergence of the 'who does what?' question as one of the starting points for organization theory. The idea has become so widely accepted that it could be argued that we accept specialization as a prerequisite for living in our society. As stated above, we commonly define ourselves by our specialisms ('salesperson', 'teacher', etc.) and as we will see in a later chapter much organizational energy is directed towards recruiting, selecting, training and rewarding employees categorized by their specialism. The literature identifies two distinct approaches to specialization:

(a) *Functional specialization*. In this approach the job content is determined by a rational sub-division of the work to be done within the organization. The job is defined by specific tasks, responsibilities, authority and discretion. This results in job holders concentrating on specialized ranges of tasks which their skills, knowledge and abilities enable performance as 'an expert'. This is the basis of undertaking a course such as the CIM Certificate – it presupposes the existence of specialized information necessary to become a functional specialist in the field called 'marketing'.

> **Think** – What are the skills, knowledge and abilities which distinguish the functional specialism of marketing?

(b) *Simplification*. Here the individual job content is reduced as far as possible - minimizing the number of tasks, restricting the possibility of variations of method and timing of operations. The emphasis is on technical efficiency and cost reduction via the minimizing of variety, discretion, skill and training. Under such a system the individual typically repeats a very limited range of tasks over a very short time cycle so that the requirements for expert knowledge or skill is reduced to the lowest practicable level. It represents a highly job-centred philosophy of technical efficiency and cost effectiveness. The usual example given of job design under these principles is that of the car assembly line worker, but the same approach can be, and has been, used for many clerical, administrative and sales jobs.

> **Think** – What jobs within your department most closely fit this 'simplified' model?

2 Job rotation

Moving from one job to another can increase the variety of activities undertaken by a person. From the organization's viewpoint this will have the advantage of increased flexibility - employees can develop expertise in a number of jobs which can be a help in minimizing the disruption caused by absenteeism, sickness, etc. It can allow operation over tea and lunch breaks and even allow continuous operation over holiday periods if required. The individual employee may experience reduced boredom, it may help in sharing out undesirable jobs or conditions. The employee may experience a greater proportion of the whole operation which should increase the sense of identity and achievement. Once more there seems to be two distinct aspects:

(a) *Similarity rotation.* Here the 'different' jobs involve very similar tasks. The act of rotation may, in reality, involve only a change of scenery.

> **Think** – What selling jobs can you identify that have this characteristic?

(b) *Diversity rotation.* In this case the duties are disimilar – so rotation involves some variety of work which as well as possible changes in location. This sometimes happens on production lines where operators exchange work stations. The benefits identified are commonly offset by the inevitably higher training costs.

> **Think** – What marketing jobs can you identify that have this characteristic?

In both cases the issue of whether the rotation is voluntary or pre-planned and controlled by management is likely to be important as is the issue of whether a reduction in boredom is the same as increased job satisfaction.

3 Job enlargement

In many ways this approach to job design is the opposite of simplification as it extends job content by including a wider variety of tasks. In some senses it is similar to job rotation in that it seeks to increase variety, but in this case the tasks are moved to the operator rather than moving the operator to the tasks. The wider range of activities may help in stimulating interest and might lead to satisfaction of esteem needs. Proponents of this system claim that quality should improve although it must be noted that the wider range of tasks will result in a longer time cycle. From the organization's viewpoint it means that fewer persons are involved in the total process which should help with control problems and reduce the level of task interdependence.

> **Think** – How could your job be enlarged?
> – Would you want it to be?
> – Why?

4 Socio-technical systems

This approach stems from the work associated with the Tavistock Institute and is based on the observation that many operating systems are made up of two elements – a technical system and a social system. Traditional approaches by management seek to optimize the technical system and produce a 'best' solution in technical terms. However, the resulting disruption to the social system of the organization may result in an overall performance which is well below the technical 'maximum'. The socio-technical approach suggests that we should attempt joint optimization of the needs of both systems. Three general methods have been identified:

(a) *Social factors* may be consciously structured into the job by actively building in activities and tasks which will involve social contact. At the simplest level it could be asking a normally isolated typist in a typing pool to deliver the finished product to the originator of the work. It is claimed that such contact can foster both formal and informal group activity with other employees, customers, suppliers, etc.

(b) *Teamwork* involves the allocation of work to a group so that the tasks are identified with the group and performance achieved through co-operative working practices. It is particularly appropriate where jobs are highly interdependent within the group. The idea is to foster social satisfactions together with the formation of group norms governing work behaviour and attitudes. Generally this method involves considerable job enlargement together with greater attention to needs which can most appropriately be satisfied within a group setting.

(c) *Autonomous work groups* operate very much as described above but in this case the group exercises autonomy and responsibility for their own work and organization. Thus the advantages are those claimed for teamwork (above) and job enrichment (below). The duties of the group include some responsibilities normally associated with specialists and superiors in the management structure. The members of such a group have a degree of self-determination, relative freedom from controls and authority to make decisions concerning the work activities of members of the group. Typically they may be allowed to regulate the work content of individuals, organize and determine operational methods, conduct planning activities, evaluate quality and performance, participate in goal setting and the determination of standards, etc. The experiments with this form of working conducted at the Kalmar plant of the Volvo organization are the most famous examples of autonomous work groups. While such a system appears to be very successful at satisfying many work needs and yielding high levels of job satisfaction such an approach may not be universally applicable. As noted above, such a system is only suited to situations where the work is truly of a group type and it is to be noted that most of the applications to date have been in mass production settings. Adopting this system also has considerable implications for management, particularly in the area of delegated control functions (the role of the supervisor has been eroded dramatically), while the difficulties of co-ordinating the activities of autonomous groups could also prove problematic.

5 Job enrichment

This is largely based on the work of Herzberg (see Chapter 6) and is an approach to job design which has had considerable publicity over recent years. It extends the content of jobs with the aim of satisfying needs and giving greater intrinsic motivation through job design. In terms of this analysis it is a combination of enlargement, autonomy and responsibility through added planning and control functions. Enlargement may be seen as increasing the job horizontally – giving more tasks of the same type and at the same level, but enrichment can be viewed as a vertical growth in job tasks. It aims to provide increased scope for personal achievement and recognition, more challenging work and a greater opportunity for personal development (all motivators under Herzberg's Two Factor theory). The notion of vertical loading comes from the addition of discretionary elements to the job such as planning, control and quality. The system assumes that the 'hygiene' factors are satisfied and concentrates on the motivators (comparable to Maslow's higher needs and in line with McGregor's Theory Y style of management).

Think – How could your job (or a job known to you) be 'enriched?
        – Would you want it to be?
        – Why?

---

6 Job characteristics

This approach to job enrichment is based on expectancy theory and may best be illustrated by Figure 11.10:

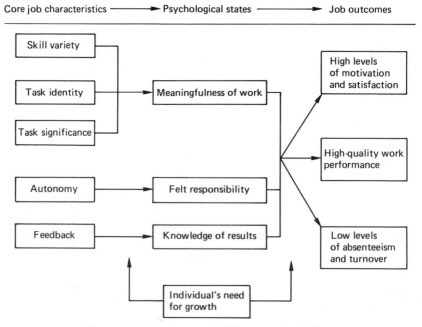

Figure 11.10 *Source*: Hackman and Oldham

The model attempts to define the links between the characteristics of jobs, the individual's experience of those characteristics, and the resulting outcomes (motivation, satisfaction, performance). It also takes account of individuals' desire for personal growth.

The model proposes five *core dimensions* which are defined as follows:

(a) *Skill variety* – the extent to which a job makes use of different skills and abilities;

(b) *Task identity* – the extent to which a job involves a 'whole' and meaningful piece of work;

(c) *Task significance* – the extent to which a job affects the work of other organization members or others in society;

(d) *Autonomy* – the extent to which a job gives the individual freedom, independence and discretion in carrying it out;

(e) *Feedback* – the extent to which information about the level of performance attained is related back to the individual.

The content of a job can be assessed on these five core dimensions by asking the job holder to complete a questionnaire about their experience of the job.

The *motivating potential score* for the job is calculated using the equation:

$$\textbf{MPS} = 1/3 \; \{\text{skill variety} + \text{task identity} + \text{task significance}\} \times (\text{autonomy}) \times (\text{feedback})$$

Note that if autonomy or feedback is zero then the MPS is zero – if any of the other three factors are low or zero the effect is not so marked.

The core dimensions induce three psychological states in the jobholder – these are defined as follows:

- *Experienced meaningfulness* – the extent to which the individual considers the work to be meaningful, valuable and worthwhile;
- *Experienced responsibility* – the extent to which the individual feels accountable for the work outputs;
- *Knowledge of results* – the extent to which the individuals know and understand how well they are performing.

Jobs with a high MPS are more likely to lead to jobholders experiencing these critical psychological states. The expectancy theorists argue that *all three* of these states must be experienced if the personal and work outcomes listed on the right of the diagram are to be achieved. (Note – persons who do not value growth and development – low growth need strength – will not respond in the way suggested by the model).

Having established the individual's perceptions of the job it is possible to diagnose where improvements are needed and this is embodied in the final element of the model – the notion of *implementing concepts*. These are:

- *Combining tasks.* Give more than one part of the work to do. This increases variety and the contribution that the individual makes to the product or service.

- *Forming natural work units.* Give a meaningful sequence of work rather than isolated fragments. This increases the contribution and significance of the job.

- *Establishing client relationships.* Give employees responsibility for making personal contact with others within and outside the organization for whom and with whom they work. This increases variety, gives the person freedom in performing the work and also increases the opportunities for receiving feedback.

- *Vertical loading.* Give employees responsibilities normally allocated to supervisors. These include granting discretion for activities such as: work scheduling, work methods, problem solving, quality control, training others, cost control, work timimg and breaks, deciding priorities, recruitment decisions, etc.

- *Opening feedback channels.* Give employees direct relationships with 'clients' and direct performance summaries. This is aimed at improving the opportunities for feedback of performance results.

Such an approach avoids the oversimplification of many of the 'messiahs' of job design. It incorporates the crucial element of the jobholders' perception of what they are doing and the questionnaire (known as the *Job Diagnostic Survey*) offers us a tool with which we can identify the elements within the job which need changing to improve the performance of the specific jobholder.

The identification of specific actions which might improve or correct the situation is an important addition to the job designer's armoury of techniques. A potential problem is the extent to which an organization is prepared to design individual jobs to fit individual employees. For many enterprises this would pose problems the solutions to which could involve a profound change of philosophy.

7 Theoretically possible alternatives

Torrington and Chapman (1979) identified a number of alternative approaches which might be developed at some future time or which might be appropriate in specific situations.

(a) *Multi-dimensional structuring* – basically this as a 'complex man' attempt at job design which goes beyond the job characteristics approach described above. Its aim will be to encompass all of the complex interacting factors which influence job performance.

(b) *Individualistic* – a pure 'person-centred' approach in which employees might be selected on broader criteria than purely job requirements and then jobs designed to suit their particular characteristics. To date the author's only experience of this approach is the problem of designing a job to suit the characteristics of a managing director's offspring!

(c) *Social planning* – In this approach the selection of employees would be determined by social criteria. Jobs would then be designed to satisfy their abilities, needs and characteristics. In the UK, sheltered workshops for the disabled have been an attempt at this style of job design. It could also be argued that government schemes for the training and employment of young people fall into this category. It would seem, however, that it would need a fairly drastic change in social values overall for this to become used on a large scale.

An overview of job design

The ideas and approaches outlined above can be seen to fit closely to some of the theories of motivation described in Chapter 6. They also link up with some similar and overlapping concepts which are commonly used in organization studies.

1 *Content vs. process theories of motivation* – here the theories are divided between those which concentrate on specific job content motivators (money, social groupings, self-actualization etc.) and those which concentrate on the process of job satisfaction (primarily expectancy theory).

2 *Technical efficiency vs. human relations* – this is the dichotomy addressed by the socio-technical approach.

3 *Locus of control* – should the organization/management control jobs, performance, etc. or can autonomy be tolerated. If it is allowed, how can we 'manage' it?

4 *Job-centred vs. person-centred philosophy* – from whose viewpoint do we look at job design?

The linkage between all of these ideas was summarized elegantly by Torrington and Chapman in Figure 11.11.

At the start of this section we observed that the way an organization designs and structures jobs is a reflection of the assumptions, values and philosophies of its managment. The reality is that managerial perceptions of the importance of its workforce may be driven by rather simpler supply and demand ideas. Simplification as a technique became fashionable during the depression years of the 1930s, while participative approaches such as job enrichment and autonomous work groups came to the fore during the affluent boom years of the 1960s and 70s when labour became a scarce resource. It could be argued that management's preoccupations are driven by economic factors which affect the whole of their perceptions of their world. Thus in times of economic hardship organizations tend to become more autocratic, more job-centred, and less concerned with employees as

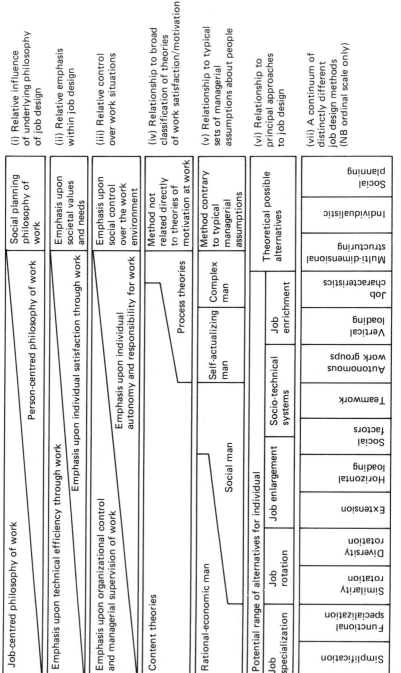

Figure 11.11
Source: Torrington and Chapman

Table 11.1 Additional options for working arrangements

Option	Characteristics	Comments
Overtime	Hours worked over normal contract and paid at 'premium' rates	Uses existing employees – so no additional training needed. Not very cost-effective. Staff may come to expect overtime and may work slowly during normal hours to ensure they get the desired overtime
Shift work	Using plant, equipment and buildings for more than the usual '9 to 5' by incorporating more than one working day, e.g. 2 x 8 hr or 2 x 12 hr shifts	Can offer 24 hour cover if needed. Gives more man-hours per day, greater plant utilization and higher productivity. However, it can be difficult to recruit staff to do 'antisocial hours' and usually involves additional payments to compensate. Can also pose problems of senior management supervision
Flexitime	Enables employees to vary working hours within agreed limits e.g. start work early and finish early. Usually involves the notion of 'core' time when all staff attend	Can contribute to employee motivation by allowing individuals to exercise some control over their own working hours. May pose problems if key staff are not available outside of core time, having gone home early. Can also have some hidden costs such as buildings and telephone exchanges having to be open longer
Annual Hours	Agreement between the organization and the staff for an agreed number of hours during the year	Allows considerable flexibility for working patterns which suit the flow of work e.g. busy/slack periods or seasonal cycles. Such agreements do need to be drawn up and negotiated carefully to ensure acceptance
Part-time	Employing staff for a few hours each week – often on a regular, if temporary, basis	Can be useful to cope with short or sudden surges of work activity. However, part-timers may not be fully committed to the organization
Job sharing	Splitting an existing job so that it is done by two persons each being paid pro rata	Can have advantages of experienced, skilled staff such as female returners but may have problems of coordination, communication and additional administration cost
Teleworking homeworking	Employees work from home on a flexible basis. May involve computer links in the employee's home	Potentially very flexible, retaining existing skills and enlarging the pool of possible employees (e.g. those with small children). Communication and control could be problematic

resource. While in times of labour shortage they come to 'fully appreciate' the importance of their workforce.

Other perspectives on job design

So far this section has looked at job design in terms of what the organization asks the employee to do in terms of the tasks, duties and relationships which make up the job description. As we saw in the Atkinson model of 'the Flexible Firm' it is also possible to design jobs which have differing contractual relationships with the organization. An additional perspective may be obtained by focusing on the options defined by the hours worked by staff. This may best be displayed in tabular form (see Table 11.1).

Some 'typical' examination questions – Organization

A Martin Joseph (*Sociology for Business, 1990*) advances the view that 'Organizations in modern society are rational bodies using logical means to achieve rational ends'. How far do you consider this to be an accurate analysis (a) of what companies do in general, and (b) of the way in which marketing departments behave?

B What is meant by the 'systems' approach to organizational design? How can the 'systems' approach be used to analyse and explain the peculiar position of the marketing function in a typical organization?

C Contrast the systems approach to organizations with *either* classical theory *or* the human relations model. What are the implications of these theories for the role of marketing in a typical large company?

D Why is it vital that marketing ensures a regular two-way flow of information within the organization? How can the marketing function help to achieve such a two-way flow, and what benefits would you expect to follow once suitable systems are in operation?

E Why do sales staff sometimes resist changes introduced by management? What techniques may be employed (by managers) in order to reduce the level of resistance associated with the implementation of change?

F What do you understand by the terms 'mechanistic' and 'organic' (or 'organismic') when applied to organization structures? If invited to set up a marketing department from scratch, would you recommend that it be established on 'mechanistic' or 'organic' lines? Give reasons for your recommendations.

Sources

Atkinson, J. (1984) 'Manpower strategies for flexible organizations', *Personnel Management*, August.

Bartol, K. M. and Martin, D.C. (1991) *Management*, McGraw-Hill.

Handy, C. B. (1976) *Understanding Organisations*, Penguin.

Kakabadse, A., Ludlow, R. and Vinnicombe, S. (1987) *Working in Organisations*, Penguin.

McGregor D. (1960) *The Human Side of Enterprise*, McGraw-Hill.

Peters, T. J. and Waterman, R. H. Jr (1982) *In Search of Excellence,* Harper and Row.

Torrington, D. and Chapman, J. (1979) *Personnel Management*, London: Prentice-Hall.

Torrington D. and Hall L. (1991) *Personnel Management: A New Approach* (2nd edn.), Prentice-Hall.

Turton, R. (1991) *Behaviour in a Business Context*, Chapman & Hall.

Watson T. J. (1986) *Management, Organisation and Employment Strategy*, Routledge & Kegan Paul.

12 Getting past the gatekeeper

Organizations as consumers

Introduction

This is a relatively short chapter as it utilizes much of the material from earlier in the text. In this section the focus is on the specific processes associated with buying within the organizational setting. It is assumed that the reader will be conversant with the material in the previous chapters and will concentrate on applying it to this specific context.

At the end of the chapter the student should be fully familiar with the following ideas and be able to relate them to the industrial/organizational buying situation:

- Similarities and differences between individual, family and organization buying situation.
- Roles in the organizational buying process.
- Different levels of complexity of buying decisions.
- Decision Making Units (DMU's) and the associated roles.
- American Marketing Association 4 cell model.
- Sheth model.

Organizations as buyers

> **Think** – How does your organization make purchasing decisions?

Organizations, like individuals and families, make purchases. In some cases the buying decisions are completely routine – replacing envelope stocks or re-ordering cleaning materials; while other decisions may be new, complex, technical and very expensive. These decisions may need careful problem definition (often by specialists), extensive research, a long and sometimes lengthy evaluation process, negotiated purchase and long periods of post-purchase evaluation. Sometimes a decision is individual, other times it is very formalized with defined guidelines at every stage.

In the words of Hawkins, Best and Coney:

The stereotype of organisational buying behaviour is one of a cold, efficient, economically rational process. Computers rather than humans could easily, and perhaps preferably, fulfil this function. Fortunately, nothing could be further from the truth. In fact, organisational buying behaviour is at least as 'human' as individual or household buying behaviour.

Organisations pay price premiums for well-known brands and for prestige brands. They avoid risk and fail to properly evaluate products and brands both before and after purchase. Individual members of organisations use the purchasing process as a political arena and attempt to increase their personal, departmental or functional power through purchasing. Marketing communications are perceived and misperceived by individual organisation members. Likewise, organisations and individual members of organisations learn correct and incorrect information about the world in which they operate.

Organisational decisions take place in situations with varying degrees of time pressure, importance and newness. They typically involve more people and criteria than do individual or household decisions. Thus, the study of organisational buying behaviour is a rich and fun-filled activity. (Hawkins *et al.*, 1989, pp. 713).

> **Think** – In the previous exercise, thinking of the purchasing activities of
> your own organization, did you conclude that they were a 'cold,
> efficient, economically rational process' or did you analyse the
> situation as one of greater complexity?

The processes involved in group decision making and the specific processes associated with family purchases have already been described in Chapter 8. There are a number of areas of similarity between family decision making and the activities of an organizational decision making unit:

- they are both commonly made by groups of individuals;
- they both have clearly identifiable roles within the process such as: Gatekeeper, Influencer, User, Buyer, Preparer;
- both situations may be characterized by decisions being made within constrained budgets.

There are, however, some significant differences:

- the market is smaller in the sense that there are fewer organizations than members of the general public;
- the market is clearly segmented – a supplier may know all potential customers and a potential buyer may know all potential suppliers, this knowledge can allow marketing efforts to be tightly targeted;
- some organizations, such as Marks & Spencer or British Telecom, have enormous purchasing power;
- organizations are more likely to employ specialists who could have significant impact on the decision process;
- the phenomenon called *reciprocal buying* may exist. Here Company *A* agrees to buy the products of Company *B* on condition that Company *B* reciprocates by purchasing Company *A*'s products;
- much of the purchasing is done on the basis of history and tradition, long term relationships can develop between a supplier and purchaser, this can

lead to repeat orders on the grounds of the supplier being a 'known' quantity in terms of quality, reliability and continuity.

The fact that industrial purchases are made by people, not for their own consumption, but for the good of the organization, should imply that their buying behaviour would be more rational and less emotional than that which applies in the broader field of consumer behaviour. It is also likely that a much wider range of criteria will be used to judge 'good value'. These criteria could include:

Price/Discounts
Technical advantage and advancement
Quality   NB the ranking of these
After sales service and maintenance   factors will vary from
Reliability and continuity of supply   situation to situation
Back-up advisory services
Credit facilities offerred

In addition, the decision could be influenced by other historical relationships between the two organizations – misbilling, difficulty in communication, personal friction or personality clashes in the past can be held in some sort of 'corporate memory' and militate against the errant supplier.

It is useful to draw a distinction between different types of industrial purchasing decision based on the complexity of the behaviours involved and which relate to the complexity of the decisions to be made. We may identify three types which form a continuum. At the simplest end we have:

1 *Routinized buyer behaviour or 'straight re-buy'* where buyers know both their own requirements and the products on offer. The items tend to be regular purchases and the process is usually repeated frequently. In this case, history is likely to be a very significant factor as there is an inertia about such decision making which tends to reward the current supplier – 'better the devil you know'. It is often difficult for another supplier to break into such a market – price cutting is often the only way in.

2 *Limited problem solving or 'modified re-buy'*. In this category would fall the purchase of either a new product or service from an existing or known supplier, or the purchase of an existing product from a new supplier. As the title suggests the process is characterized by limited problem solving behaviours and investigations.

3 *Extensive problem solving or 'new buy'* is the name given to the category of purchase that involves the purchase of new, unfamiliar products or services from previously unknown suppliers. Such processes can be very lengthy as criteria by which the purchase will be judged will need to be developed from scratch.

This categorization is very similar to the distinction that has been made throughout the earlier parts of this book between *low involvement* and *high involvement* purchases by individuals.

Internal processes of the decision making unit (DMU)

In the context of industrial or organizational marketing the Decision Making Unit or DMU is the expression used to describe the group of people who make the buying decision. The DMU can be defined as 'all the people who have influence, whether positive or negative, at one or more stages of the purchasing process'. In many larger organizations this will centre on the Purchasing Department or the role of Buyer, but may extend way beyond the official professional limits.

We will return to the role analysis used in Chapter 8 to highlight the comparisons with family purchasing decisions. One of the main differences between the two situations is the formality of the organizational decisions – the need is identified, requisitions are completed, countersigned by more senior staff and passed to Purchasing before the 'buying' process officially starts.

The roles described briefly in Chapter 8 also exist in this different situation:

1 The *gatekeeper* fulfils the same function as described earlier – that of controlling the flow of information. Such a role may be at a senior level or it may simply be the secretary who controls the Buyer's diary. Many salespersons have found that getting past a receptionist to see the Buyer is as big a challenge as selling the product. However in this situation the gatekeeper could be a specialist who can feed relevant information into the rest of the DMU, and so there may be some overlap with the next role.

2 The *influencers* are particularly important in the technical and the problem solving type of decisions. Who they are and where they are located within the organization are key facts for the supplier to determine. It is likely that the patterns of influence will also be a function of the culture and the orientation of the organization. For instance, in a company which prides itself on its technical advancement and excellence, the engineers are likely to be significant players in any large-scale purchasing decisions. In contrast, engineers may not be so influential in organizations which do not share the value systems and technical orientation. In some organizations the accountants may be the dominant personalities, and it may be found that price becomes the crucial criterion. In yet other circumstances it can be the situation where large-scale purchases will need approval from the whole Board of Directors, thus adding still more influencers to be considered. Some organizations will employ a number of Buyers, the degree of their independence and/or limitation by overall policy will need to be ascertained.

3 The *user* or *preparer*, in the industrial situation, may also be a significant influencer of the decision. Senior managers may heed the experience and opinions of the persons actually doing the job, either via direct communication or by such things as method study reports. Users and preparers may also have very high levels of technical expertise and so their

opinions can influence both the identification of the need and the required specification.

4 The role of the *buyer*, in this context is commonly a job carried out by an individual or a department rather than the activity undertaken by a busy, multi-roled parent. This has the effect of professionalizing the process, and to some extent, removing extraneous elements from the decision. However, the point must be made that the buyer may not make the final decision, indeed, in some cases, the role can become solely administrative.

5 The *decider* is obviously the crucial role, as this is where the whole purchase decision stands or falls. As noted above, the decider can be at a relatively mundane level for routinized decisions, but may involve the Board of Directors for major projects and expenditures.

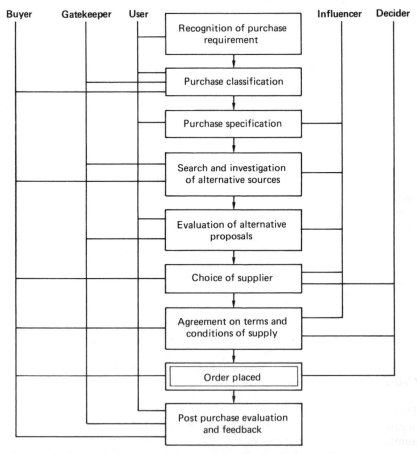

Figure 12.1   A decision process model of industrial purchase behaviour
Source: Behavioural Aspects of Marketing (BPP, 1991)

The foregoing discussion implies that the process is much more complex that just selling the product to the buyer. Hence one of the major problems facing the potential supplier is identifying the individual influencer and decision makers within the target organization. Only when this has been done can the supplier plan the campaign to inform and persuade the key persons within the DMU.

As these people are likely to have different roles, specialisms and professions, a multi-pronged attack may well be necessary involving direct mail and personal contact, as well as the use of technical, trade and professional press and other promotional channels.

The American Marketing Association model

This model, published by the American Marketing Association (AMA), describes the main influences and players in the process. It is usually displayed as in Figure 12.2.

Figure 12.2   Influences on the organization buying process

Cell 1 – The purchasing agent

This is the buyer. This role is located in the quadrant which is within the organization and within the purchasing department. The model identifies a number of factors which affect buying behaviour, these are:

- *Social factors* – here the focus is on the relationships, friendships and antipathies that exist between buyers and suppliers, and the extent to which these relationships impinge on purchasing decisions. Clearly in an ideal world decisions should be taken on purely objective grounds, and such personal feelings should make no difference. It has been suggested, however, that in reality such relationships are highly influential. Hard evidence to support such a contention is difficult to obtain, as any buyer admitting to such influence would be open to accusations of corruption. As the buyer is, in many cases, acting as the purchasing agent on behalf of the DMU as a whole, the relationships which exist between individuals making up the DMU may have a similar, purely interal, effect.

- *Price and cost factors* – while cost is obviously significant in purchasing decisions, its ultimate importance may also be a function of factors such as:

  1   the economic state of the buying organization (it might like to pay more for a 'better' product, but the cash flow situation demands minimum cost);
  2   the level of competition amongst suppliers;
  3   any cost/benefit analyses that might have been conducted;
  4   the purchasing budget; and
  5   the personality and background of the purchasing agent (some writers have made the assertion that an accountancy background makes buyers more cost conscious than does an engineering background).

- *Supply continuity* – this is likely to be a function of both the number of suppliers that are available and the importance of the purchased item to the organization. For items where a shortage could affect the production capacity of the buying organization, it is not uncommon to go for multi-sourcing as a way of insulating the organization against disruption of supplies.

- *Risk avoidance* – it is believed that reducing risk is a common motivation of buyers. This can result in additional investigation of suppliers products and financial stability and is a probable cause of the basically conservative nature of much industrial purchasing and the tendency to stick with 'tried and trusted' suppliers.

Cell 2 – The buying centre

This is the DMU of previous paragraphs. Here the focus is within the firm but between departments – so we are in the field of organizational politics. The key factors in this quadrant are:

- *Organizational structure and policy* – clearly the place of the purchasing department within the organization is of great significance. It will determine the level of influence, reporting relationships and so forth. Policy and history will also determine the extent to which the buyer can take autonomous decisions.

- *Power, status and conflict procedures* – this is, to a large extent, the degree to which the buyer, or the purchasing department, wishes to change or maintain the *status quo*. Internal pressures may come from outside departments to make their own purchasing decisions (a common feature of decentralization and divisionalization). The degree of dissonance will depend on how the existing purchasing department reacts to the proposed changes. Again, the organizational culture will be a significant determinant of how such conflict is resolved.

- *Gatekeeping* – as described above, a key activity is controlling the dissemination of information – the holder of such a position can exert considerable real political influence within the enterprise.

Cell 3 – Professionalism

This is centred purely within the buying department, but examines the influence of professional standards and practice in other organizations. The main factors to be considered in this section are:

- *Specialist journals, conferences and trade shows* – these sources are likely to be the source of a great deal of professional know-how, and keeping up-to-date. Bodies such as the Institute of Purchasing will attempt to set standards for professional conduct and act as a reference group for practitioners. Trade fairs and journals offer opportunities for reaching the potential market.

- *Word of mouth communication* – aspects of this process were discussed in Chapter 9 in the wider context of consumer behaviour. Much of what was written there will apply, but within the smaller context of the purchasing professional. Buyers may exchange information about both products and suppliers – reputations can be made or broken by the professional 'grapevine'.

- *Supply-purchase reciprocity* – the arrangements whereby two organizations may reach an agreement to supply each other.

Cell 4 – The organizational environment

This is the quadrant which is concerned with factors outside of the purchasing department and outside the organization. In this category the influences are such things as:

- *Economic, commercial and competitive factors* – the state of the economy, interest rates, exchange rates and industrial optimism or pessimism are all elements which are likely to affect both the purchasing plans of organizations and the pricing policies of suppliers.

- *Political, social and legal environment* – organizations are part of the wider society and are therefore subject to the laws and influences that make up that society. In this way the purchasing process may be influenced by concerns for things like the physical environment, or the equal opportunity policies of suppliers. We have also had experience of trade sanctions and embargoes which may be applied by governments as part of wider political influencing processes.

- *Technological change* – inventions may change the nature of businesses and their needs.

- *Nature of the supplier* – here it is sometimes assumed that large organizations make inflexible suppliers as their size enables them to adopt a 'take it or leave it' attitude. The other side of this stereotype is that they offer a more reliable and less risky service.

- *Co-operative buying* – this refers to the option of organizations increasing their purchasing power through the formation of consortia. While the advantages of scale are clear, the negative side is the possible need for compromise with other members.

This model is essentially descriptive of the influences on the purchasing decision. An alternative view which concentrates on the purchasing process is the Sheth model of industrial buying, which we will now consider.

The Sheth model of industrial buying

This model highlights the importance of four main factors:

1 the expectations of the individuals making up the DMU,
2 the characteristics of both the product and the buying organization,
3 the nature of the decision making process and
4 situational variables.

To clarify the model we will examine the four elements in turn.

1 Expectations within the organization

These elements are coded (1) and are shaded ■ in Figure 12.3. Sheth emphasizes one of the continuing threads of our studies of consumer behaviour – the importance of *expectations*. Every person in the DMU will bring to their performance their own, unique set of attitudes and orientations – these, Sheth identifies as being conditioned by each individual's *background* (1a). The key elements being:

- *education* – both general and commercial/professional;
- *role orientation* – e.g. engineer, accountant or purchasing specialist;
- *life style* – this is likely to encompass more general values.

Expectations will also be influenced by the *sources of information* and the search process undertaken in order to obtain the data. The sources are listed

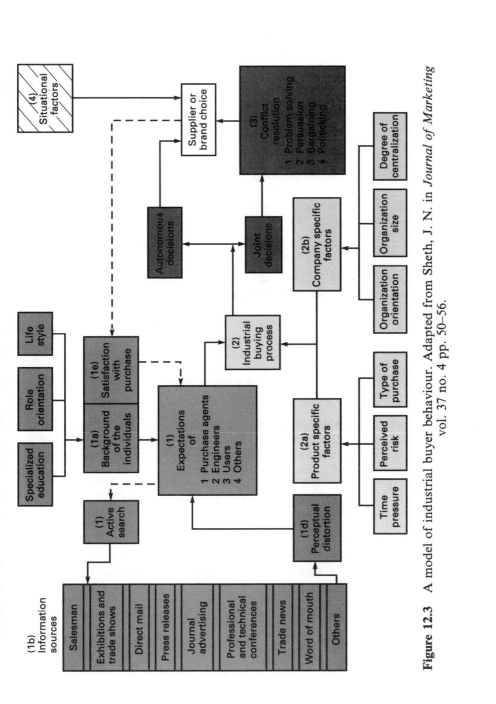

Figure 12.3 A model of industrial buyer behaviour. Adapted from Sheth, J. N. in *Journal of Marketing* vol. 37 no. 4 pp. 50–56.

in the diagram under section (1b). As we have seen in earlier sections of this book, *perceptual distortion* (1d) is always a possibility in any communication process, and industrial purchasing is no exception. Similarly, expectations and the incoming information will be mediated by the individual's *previous experiences* of the product or supplier (1e). The *active search* element (1c) is most commonly conducted by the purchasing specialists as part of their professional employment. This may place them in the influential gatekeeper role, with the capacity to edit and filter in order to structure expectations.

2 Characteristics of the product and the buying organization

These elements are coded (2) and are shaded ☐ in Figure 12.3. In this section Sheth considers the actual *buying process* and contends that it is affected by:

1 *product specific factors* (2a) such as:

- *time pressure* – individually delegated decisions are much quicker than those made by group concensus;
- *perceived risk* – the riskier the perception, the greater the tendency to get more information and involve a larger proportion of the DMU in the decision. This, of course, tends to delay the decision;
- *type of purchase* – routine buying is more likely to be delegated to an individual, while purchases involving extensive problem solving tend to involve all of the DMU in some form of group concensus exercise.

2 *company specific factors* (2b) include:

- *organizational orientation.* Some organizations are production oriented, others towards sales/marketing or technology. This is likely to be a significant determinant of the internal power balance and hence of influence in the DMU;
- *organizational size* – the larger the organization, the greater the likelihood of group decision making. Smaller organizations are more likely to have a single buyer who possesses all the required information;
- *degree of centralization* – highly centralized organizations tend to have a centralized buying function whereas decentralized companies involve a much wider range of employees in the decision process.

3 Nature of the decision-making process

These elements are coded (3) and are shaded ■ in Figure 12.3. Sheth discriminates between autonomous decisions and those taken jointly by the DMU. The autonomous route is relatively straightforward and receives little detailed attention. Given the different goals and orientations of the group, conflict is a likely occurrence. The model devotes a section to examining ways in which such conflict can be resolved. The preferred solution is:

- *problem solving* – here conflict is resolved by a process of more information gathering and the systematic evaluation of alternatives. The disadvantage of this approach is the time such processes take;

- *persuasion* is another option which Sheth suggests is most likely to be effective when the conflict centres on the criteria to be used in the decision. Effort is expended to get dissenters to agree with the majority. Such activities also take up time;

- *bargaining* is another approach which results in a compromise. Such behaviour is fairly common and is generally favoured in the UK culture – 'half a loaf is better than no bread' being a well-known saying. Unfortunately, compromise and bargaining can leave us with the worst of both worlds and irrational decisions which really satisfy nobody;

- *politicking* is the least favoured approach. This is the use of power and influence to obtain trade-offs and manipulate group members in such a way as to get the desired result. The chances of good decisions being made becomes much more remote when the influencing processes centre on pay-off for past favours and coalitions set up to 'defeat' opponents.

4 Situational variables

These elements are coded (4) and are shaded ☒ in Figure 12.3. Under this heading Sheth includes the unforeseen factors that are outside the control of DMU members. Examples could include such events as:

- industrial relations problems;
- major breakdowns;
- cash flow problems;
- bankruptcy;
- changes in tax provisions.

Such factors could affect the purchasing organization themselves, or suppliers.

> **Think** – Which approach – roles, AMA or Sheth do you find most
> convincing to explain your organization's buying behaviour?
> – Why?
> – Which approach would you find most useful if you were planning
> a marketing campaign to sell to organizations?

Some 'typical' examination questions – Organizational buying behaviour

A What are the special features of organizational/industrial buyer behaviour? Illustrate your answer by reference to either the American Marketing Association model or the Sheth model.

B What are the factors influencing organizational buying decisions? How might you use these factors to your advantage if you were trying to sell products such as office stationery or communications equipment to organizations?

C Identify the main differences between individual consumer behaviour and organizational buying behaviour. Explain how these differences might influence the ways in which (a) computers and (b) carpets are marketed to each type.

D What do you understand by the terms 'gatekeeper', 'influencer', 'user', 'buyer', 'decider' when applied to the organizational buying situation. Why is a knowledge of such roles important when marketing to organizations?

Sources

BPP (1991) *Behavioural Aspects of Marketing*, BPP.

Engel, J. F., Blackwell, R. D. and Miniard, P. W. (1990) *Consumer Behaviour* (6th edn.), Dryden.

Hawkins, D. I., Best, R. J. and Coney, K. A. (1989) *Consumer Behaviour: Implications for Marketing Strategy* (4th edn.), Irwin.

Peter, J. P. and Olson, J. C. (1990) *Consumer Behaviour and Marketing Strategy* (2nd edn.), Irwin.

Williams, K. C. (1981) *Behavioural Aspects of Marketing*, Heinemann.

13 If there's nowt so strange as folk – how on earth do we manage them?

Managing people within the organization

Introduction

The second part of this section concerns people, their behaviour and their management at work within the organization. Once again we have the problem that this is another very large field of study – students of the Institute of Personnel Management professional diplomas (comparable to the CIM qualifications) spend all of their time devoted solely to this area.

So this is quite a wide ranging chapter – and as such might be criticized for covering too much. In fact we are attempting a swift review of the prime activities of personnel (or human resource) management. Again, we shall be utilizing the material from earlier parts of the book, but in this case we shall be using the ideas to consider the problems of explaining, predicting and controlling the behaviour of employees rather than customers.

The material on individual differences, abilities, personality and so forth will be used within the context of recruitment and selection. Learning theory comes up again but this time under the heading of training and development. Communication processes apply to communication within the organization rather than between the enterprise and its market. The motivation material needs to be looked at again – this time from the viewpoint of the motivation of the employee.

At the end of this chapter students should be fully familiar with the following concepts and *should be able to relate them to situations within a marketing department*:

- Manpower planning,
- Recruitment and selection,
- Appraisal,
- Training and development,
- Employee motivation,
- Reward systems,

- Communications,
- Responsibility for human resource management.

As in the previous chapter, your own work experiences may prove very useful material for this topic.

Managing within organizations

Work is an important part of most of our lives – but work is also a word that has a lot of different meanings. Engineers may define it as force × distance – but this is very different from working on an essay or working in the library. Academics sometimes draw a distinction between their work (by which they often mean their research or writing activities) and their job (teaching). We say we will go and work in the garden, but we also work out problems as well as work out in the gymnasium.

In the context of this chapter we are looking at work as paid employment – the exchange of effort or labour for some sort of payment or reward. Work is the activity on which most of us spend more waking hours than any other. For most people it is a very important part of their lives and in this chapter we will examine some of the different aspects that affect behaviour at work and our experience of working within organizations.

Career choice

> **Think** – How did you come to choose marketing as a career?

The answers to such a question can be many and varied – some people make conscious decisions while others drift into jobs and then find they like it. Others find themselves in a job and then find it was not a good choice.

> **Think** – How good a choice was marketing for you?
> – How do you make that judgement?

At various points in this book we have argued that the choices made often depend on the criteria used in the decision-making process. Career choice would seem to depend on matching three separate elements of our lives:

1 *Personal characteristics* – as discussed in Chapters 2 and 3, our different profiles of intelligence, aptitudes and personality will be a major determinant of the employement to which we are suited.

2 *Qualifications* – for many occupations qualifications are an essential requirement. Most professions (medical, legal and so forth) demand extensive training and rigorous testing before an individual is allowed to practice.

3 *Motivation and values* – what is it that people *want* to do?

Problems in any of the three areas can cause work difficulties. It is an interesting aspect of career management that promotion may take the individual away from work that they both like and are good at. An example might be that good teachers often get promoted to be administrators – this is the basis of the well-known 'Peter Principle'. This proposes that people will be promoted until they reach a level (or a job) in which they are no longer effective (the Peter Principle calls this the person's 'level of competence'). In the marketing area this could be promoting the successful salesperson into an administrative office job.

> **Think** – Can you identify individuals who have been promoted to their level of incompetence?

As with most of this area the answers are rarely 'right' or 'wrong' in absolute terms, but depend on the individual's perceptions.

Psychological contracts

In this chapter we are focusing on work as an exchange between the seller and buyer of labour. A concept of growing popularity with management writers is that of the psychological contract. This can be viewed as a mutual and interdependent set of expectations between the individual and the organization:

1 those of the individuals who expect benefits from the organization in return for their efforts, and

2 those of the organization which will expect certain required actions in return for their rewards.

While these ideas were developed in the field of work, it can be seen that similar sets of expectations can occur in many social situations. Our discussion of role conflict and families in Chapter 8 would fit neatly into a similar analysis.

> **Think** – What are the sets of expectations for the relationship between you as a student and the organization which provides the input?

In some educational institutions, the above expectations will have been negotiated explicitly and are sometimes referred to as a 'learning contract'.

At the workplace, the concept of the psychological contract goes to the very nub of the relationship between the individual and the organization and it reflects elements of both the individual's personality and background as well as the culture of the organization.

Three main types of contract have been identified:

1   *Coercive contract.* This is the equivalent Likert's 'exploitative' style of management (System 1) where the individuals feel their contribution is extorted in return for inadequate compensation. It is a common perception that parts of the armed services would fall into such a category, although such characteristics can occur in any organization when management cease to listen and begin to impose decisions on a workforce. Such behaviour is most common when economic trading conditions are bad, which also means that the staff have little choice but to stay as there are likely to be few jobs to move to. In such situations staff morale and motivation is usually very low (see also the Equity theory of motivation in Chapter 6).

2   *Calculative contract.* This is characterized by being voluntary on the part of the individual who perceives the contract as being one of doing a set amount of work in return for a set package of rewards. This contract implies that any change in work requirements will result in demands for additional rewards. Such contracts are common, and are the basis of much management activity – productivity bargaining being a classic example of the implied links between behaviour, rewards and motivation.

3   *Co-operative contract.* Here the individual is committed to the organization and the attainment of its objectives – so the behaviour is actively directed towards the achievement of the organization's goals. The motivation stems primarily from achievement and higher order satisfactions and is linked to participative management styles.

While this section produces a few more expressions which are specific to the employment relationship, the underlying approaches have close links with a great deal of the material which we have already covered. Areas of an individual's personality and values from Chapter 3; motivation theories from Chapter 6; management style, organization culture and the exercise of authority from Chapter 11 are all subsumed within the concept of the psychological contract.

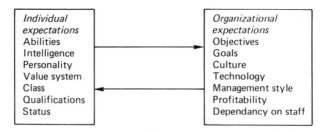

Figure 13.1

It is possible to view the management of people at work as the management of the inevitable tensions implied in Figure 13.1. As we might expect, there is a continuum of formality covering such contracts, at one extreme the expectations are defined, formalized and written; while at the other end the informal, unwritten arrangements are arrived at by force or implicit bargaining.

> **Think** – What is the nature of the 'psychological contract' with your employer?
> – How formalized is it?
> – What is the nature of the 'psychological contract' with your college?
> – How was that arrived at?

Control as a management issue

The problems of controlling a resource as unpredictable and volatile as people are considerable. The notion of the control cycle was introduced in Chapter 1 – and the comments made in that section will bear re-reading. The techniques of managing people within the organization can be viewed as devices to make the management of the organization more straightforward by making the staff more predictable.

Learning approaches to management

Another global view of the management process is that of the manager as teacher. It is possible to view the managerial task as one of teaching staff desired behaviour. Chapter 5 gives us a range of approaches from the punishment of 'wrong' behaviour as in Skinnerian theory, through insight and problem solving approaches (cf Kohler) through to the idea of staff having role models or mentors (cf Bandura).

Using this form of analysis, and considering the behaviours that the manager may wish to encourage (totally standard responses under all conditions, adaptations of responses according to situational factors, problem solving), the manager may adopt a suitable style and create situations for staff to learn appropriate behaviours. The notion of style will also apply to issues such as grievance and discipline where a fundamental difference is likely to arise between those managers who see it as a process of punishment for wrong-doing and those who perceive it as a training, behaviour shaping exercise.

Manpower planning

If we accept the proposition that the people an organization employs are its prime asset – the dynamic which allows all other management activities to exist – then it seems logical that we should plan for the effective and efficient utilization of staff with a care at least equal to the effort we put into developing a marketing plan or controlling our finances. So manpower planning can be seen as the fundamental activity of human resource management.

It is the process by which we seek to obtain and retain the quantity and quality of manpower that the organization requires. It also helps to make the best use of existing manpower resources and helps to identify potential surpluses and deficits of manpower in the future.

In many ways that statement sounds like a definition of personnel management itself so it may be preferable to think of manpower planning as the activity that identifies the personnel problems about which management need to make policy decisions.

In its simplest form the process may be represented so:

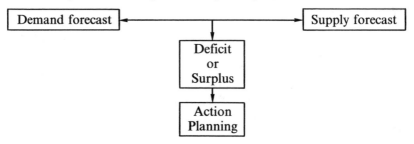

1 Demand forecasting

This is the process of estimating future manpower needs by reference to corporate and functional plans and forecasts of future activity levels.

> **Think** – Imagine that your senior manager tells you that the organization plans to increase activity by 50 per cent over the next year and asks you to prepare a forecast of how many personnel your department would need.
> – How would you tackle the project?

There are a number of different approaches that can be used:

1 *Experienced judgement* – getting managers to think about future workloads and estimate the numbers and types of people needed. This method may seem at first sight to be overly simplistic, but it may be particularly valuable due to the complexity of the data processing that the human brain can handle – I would suggest that it is used as a fall back or check on the results obtained from other methods.

2 *Ratio-trend analysis* – numerical analysis of ratios between activity levels and staff numbers. Example might be a fixed ratio between sales orders and sales clerks – it is also possible to obtain ratios between different types/grades of staff e.g. supervisors/clerks, managers/secretaries, etc.

3 *Time-trend analysis* – this involves the plotting of historical data to establish whether there is a discernable trend or movement. One might find that days lost due to disputes is declining, absenteeism may be

reducing consistently, productivity might be rising, etc. Having established the existence of a trend it may be necessary to use common sense or judgement as to whether it is likely to continue or alter.

4 *Work study techniques* – these might be the basis of some ratio trend analysis in as much as they determine how long operations should take. Thus if targets are given, the number of workers required can then be determined by simple arithmetic.

5 *Working practices* – watch out for predictable changes that will make quantum changes to the assumptions which have been built into the above sums. Examples could include such things as changes in the length of the working week, design alterations affecting work content, introduction of new equipment, additional holidays for staff, etc. (*NB*: these 'step' changes can be overlaid on the calculations and predictions above (1–4).

6 *Econometric modelling* – usually associated with larger organizations, attempts to build all of the above into a single computer program.

2 Supply forecasting

This aims to establish the quantity of manpower likely to be available from inside and outside the organization. The starting point is analysis of:

1 *Existing manpower* – 'broken down by age and sex'(!) and, more importantly, skill, occupation, department, length of service, etc.

2 *Labour wastage* – historical breakdown of labour turnover percentage equals

> No. leavers in period (1 year) × 100/Average No. employees

This is a quick, dirty and popular measure which it might be preferable to replace with wastage rate calculations based on entry cohorts.

3 *Promotions and transfers* – historical data modified by e.g. training plans.

4 *Reasons for leaving* – this may be useful to distinguish between voluntary and involuntary leavers.

5 *Changes in work patterns* – see 1(3) and 1(5) above.

6 *Sources of supply* – these may be national or local and in instances such as the education system the lead time may be usefully long – i.e. graduate supply is linked to undergraduate enrolments. This may be of such importance that protecting supply might be a key manpower strategy.

3 Deficit or surplus

At one level this is a simple comparison of the demand and supply forecasts, but it is important to realize that the whole process will need to be done for each category of skill/occupation. This is an area where global figures are useless – there is no way that a surplus of school leavers/trainees compensates for a shortage of senior marketing research specialists.

Another important issue is that manpower planning is not a once and for all activity – it should be a continuing, roll-over process in which forecasts are updated and reviewed regularly; there is a strong case for building in some contingency plans but this is only possible if your assumptions are clearly identified.

All of the above approach is based on probability in the sense that we make predictions about turnover, promotion, pregnancy, death, etc. without predicting exactly who is going to leave, die, etc. It is common for managerial staff to go for a more personalized form of manpower planning called succession planning.

Here we draw up an organization chart with job holders names entered against each job. Ratings of current performance and suitability for promotion are put against each name (this assumes that you have a decent appraisal scheme on which to base the judgement). You can then enter under (e.g.) 'Managing Director' who will succeed if the current jobholder leaves or has a heart attack. If you like you can put in second and third choices. This is repeated for each of the level below and so on down the chart. This gives clear contingency plans and is also crucial for training needs analysis.

4 Action planning

Having determined the deficit or surplus action plans can be developed:

1 *Recruitment plan* – numbers and types, when and how.
2 *Training plan* – to supply the skills required.
3 *Productivity plan* – to improve productivity may include industrial relations strategy.
4 *Retention plan* – to reduce wastage where appropriate.
5 *Redevelopment plan* – retraining and transferring existing employees.
6 *Redundancy plan* – to cope with surplus, natural wastage, bargaining, etc.

Manpower planning must relate directly to the overall business plan and it is such a crucial activity that it is more important that manpower planning is done, than it be done by the personnel department.

Think – How is manpower planning done within your organization?
– How effective is it?
– How could it be improved?

Recruitment and selection

This is perhaps the most basic of personnel activities – if you get the wrong people in your organization you get problems such as high labour turnover, absenteeism, disputes, low productivity etc. The objective of the system must be to get the *right people in the right jobs*. The emphasis is on the word *right* – 'too good' may pose as many problems as 'not good enough'. We do not have the technology or the knowledge to make truly scientific selection decisions but we can aim to make the process more systematic by adopting the sequence of activities illustrated in Figure 13.2.

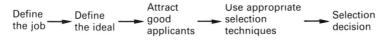

Figure 13.2

1 *Define the job*

Basically we need a detailed, up-to-date job description. This is produced following an activity known as *job analysis*. A job description should contain as a minimum: job title, organizational context and relationships (who jobholder reports to, who reports to jobholder, other relationships, liaison etc.), tasks, duties, responsibilities, working conditions (physical, social, economic), promotion opportunities, training and development opportunities, performance standards, physical and psychological characteristics required to fulfil job.

> **Think** – Do you have a job description?
>   – If so, how accurate is it?
>   – Who prepared it?
>   – When was it last updated?
>   – If you do not have a job description
>   – How do you know what to do?
>   – What other problems have been caused by the absence of a formal statement of your duties?

2 *Define the ideal*

Here it is probably best to to use an established plan to produce your person specification – three such plans are illustrated in Figure 13.3.

Whichever system you use it is important to *work directly from the requirements of the job*. It is also a great help to define clearly those characteristics which are *essential*, those that are *desirable* and any that would *disqualify* an applicant. When describing the ideal be as precise as you can, avoid woolly generalizations such as 'good education', etc. Before

5 Point Plan (Munro Fraser)	7 Point Plan (Alec Rodger)	7 Point Plan (Argyle & Sidney)
1 Initial Impact	1 Physical Make-up	1 Professional Competence
2 Qualifications	2 Attainments	2 Working Conditions
3 Abilities	3 General Intelligence	3 Intellectual Qualities
4 Motivation	4 Special Aptitudes	4 Skill with People
5 Adjustment	5 Interests	5 Motivation
	6 Disposition	6 Adjustment
	7 Circumstances	7 Drive & Determination

Figure 13.3

spending money on advertisements it is worth checking whether the job is necessary, could it be a training post? How does it fit in with the overall manpower plan?

Think – Using one of the plans above, identify the characteristics you would be looking for if you were seeking to select:

a   a sales clerk
b   a sales representative
c   a sales manager
d   a marketing director

---

3 Attract good applicants

Commonly advertising is the way used to get applicants. However, newspapers may be expensive and/or inappropriate. The aim is to get the message to the 'right persons' as cheaply and effectively as possible and stimulate them into applying. The basis of a good advertisement (whether internal or external) is the job description and the person specification. The evidence is that people respond to adverts which contain salary and other key information more readily than they do to those which are woolly, evasive and vague. The more doubts you remove, the more likely the 'right person' is to apply. Generally be as specific and realistic as possible in terms of your requirements so that unsuitable people do not apply (thus saving considerable administrative costs). In this sense a good advertisement can be seen as the first step in selection. Choose the most appropriate media for your message – internal advert, national/local press, professional journals, selection consultants, posters, postcards in the local shop, etc. Always keep a check on the response rates in terms of both quantity and quality – this gives the basis for better decision making on future recruitment.

Think – Using your person specification from the last exercise, design an advertisement for:

a   the sales clerk
b   the sales representative
c   the sales manager
d   the marketing director

---

4 Use appropriate selection methods

These are surprisingly many and varied:

1 *Application forms* are widely used and have the advantage that all applicants present comparable information – they are only as good as the information asked for and it must be noted that school leavers will need a different form to managers, etc.

2 *Intelligence tests* are used by some employers and may be a useful predictor of potential.

3 *Aptitude tests* are perhaps more useful in determining suitability for a specific job.

4 *Personality tests* are becoming very popular for managerial and supervisory jobs.

5 *Typical performance tests* may be easy to set up – in which case use them.

6 *Group selection* methods have many supporters especially for graduates.

7 *References* are widely used but often fail to maximize their usefulness.

8 *Interviews* are used by everyone – the least reliable indicator of all!

9 *Assessment centres* combine most of the above and have the best record.

10 *Medical examination* may determine overall health or check on specific important factors (e.g. colour blindness).

Think – 1 What methods did you experience when you applied for your present post?
– 2 What methods would you use if you were selecting:
  a a sales clerk?
  b a sales representative?
  c a marketing manager?
  d a marketing director?
  e a professional footballer?
  f a spouse?

---

5 Selection decisions

On the basis of the evidence (collected by whatever methods you have chosen) it is possible to rate the applicant on the characteristics used in defining your ideal. Indeed, using a simple rating system one can graphically exhibit the degree of fit with the ideal. Clearly it will be unusual to find perfection! The real problem may be to define the degree of *mismatch* that can be tolerated. On this point it is worth noting that a shortage of product knowledge can be rectified by training (in fact we are describing a realistic system of training needs analysis) but an identified shortage of intelligence is unlikely to be helped by anything short of a brain transplant.

Throughout the system we are describing a choosing process – in any choice a key determinant is the criteria used by the judge. In selection it is important to concentrate on the applicant's capability to perform the job. The whole process is open to bias and this comes from three main sources:

1 items on the *applicant's record* (public school, too many jobs, hobbies);
2 *applicant's behaviour* in the process (we like outgoing, fluent modesty);
3 *applicant's appearance* (tidy, 'pleasant', usually not extreme).

In fact we are describing the like/dislike decision which may be affected by all sorts of psychiatric 'luggage' in our subconscious minds – we like people who are like us, we dislike people who remind us of a hated schoolteacher, etc. The true danger is two-fold – firstly people we like are rated more highly on intelligence, experience, qualifications, adjustment, maturity, motivation, etc. (the 'halo' effect) while those we dislike are ascribed less flattering ratings (the 'horn' effect). Secondly the evidence is that, at interview, we commonly take the decision within the first three minutes – leaving the interviewer free to ask easy questions of the favoured ones and difficult questions of the disliked!

Think – How adequate is this 'systematic' approach?
– How do we go about selection when we are not trying to fill a *specific* job (e.g. in the case of a marketing and/or a graduate trainee)?
– How do we go about it when we are seeking expertise that we do not currently possess – and therefore cannot define the tasks, duties, etc required by the job description?

In general the route to successful selection lies in following the systematic approach. Where humanly possible avoid 'hunch'. Above all, concentrate on the actual evidence and ensure you are only using criteria which relate to the ability to do the job.

Team building

Earlier in the book the importance of human groups was discussed at some length. The Hawthorne Experiments emphasize the fact that organizations are made up of both formal and informal groups which may either help or hinder the achievement of organizational objectives. One of Mayo's conclusions was that the formation of work groups was too important to be left to chance.

We also looked at group decision making and the idea of people fulfilling different roles within the group (spokesperson, expert and so forth). Work done by Belbin has identified a number of roles which appear to be linked to effective performance in work teams.

Belbin's team roles

Co-ordinator

This role is commonly fulfilled by individuals who are stable, dominant and extrovert. This is the person who presides over the team and co-ordinates its efforts to meet external goals and targets. Essentially self-disciplined and may have 'charisma'. The dominance is expressed in a relaxed and assertive way, not oppressively domineering and is usually singularly free of jealousy. The Co-ordinator sees most clearly which members of the team are strong or weak in each area of the team functions and focuses people on what they do best. This is the person who is conscious of the need to use the combined talents of the team as effectively as possible, and may well be the one who establishes the work roles of the others. A good communicator who also listens well. This person sets the groups agenda and clarifies objectives. He or she may well ask a lot of questions of others and is good at summing up and clarifying group decisions.

Shaper

This person is the equivalent of Bales' task leader. Full of nervous energy, anxious, dominant and extrovert this is a person who may often play the leader's role. Sometimes may appear impatient and edgy and may get frustrated if the task is not progressing. Shapers may be less self-confident than they appear – reassurance is often sought via the group's results and the achievement of its agreed tasks. This person is likely to be high on drive. This is nearly always directed to task matters and they may have a tendency to 'steamroller' others within the group. As a result, others may perceive this person as somewhat arrogant and abrasive but this is the one who makes things happen.

Plant

This is the ideas person – the source of original suggestions and proposals who generates the seeds for others to grow until they bear fruit. An unusual mixture of high intelligence, dominance and introversion but, above all, a radical and original thinker. May sometimes upset others with criticism of their ideas – but usually has good counter proposals. There may be some danger that too much time is devoted to ideas that catch the fancy of this person but which do not contribute to the group's task. He or she may also have a tendency to sulk if the original ideas are criticized by others in the group. Despite needing some careful handling this person may well be the provider of the vital spark.

Resource investigator

Stable, dominant and extrovert, the Resource Investigator is relaxed, sociable, gregarious and enthusiastic, with an interest that is easily aroused. The role of this person is to go out of the group and bring back ideas, information and developments. A salesperson, diplomat and liaison officer who is usually a popular person with many contacts. This person trades in ideas but lacks the originality and radical thinking of the Plant – an 'adapter' of ideas rather than an originator. The negative side of the enthusiasm is that it can be short-lived.

Team Worker

Stable and low in dominance, the Team Worker is sensitive to the needs and worries of other team members – in Bales' terms good with the social/ emotional side of the group. Likeable, popular, unassertive and a good internal communicator this person is the 'cement' of the team. Supportive of others' ideas, the Team Worker's natural instinct is to build on it rather than criticize or propose alternatives. While not an obviously important role this person is particularly significant when the group is under pressure or experiencing stress and is a vital counter-balance to the discord that can be caused by the Shaper or the Plant.

Implementer

The practical organizer of the team. Stable and controlled, this is the person who turns decisions and strategies into defined and manageable tasks which the team can get on with. Sincere, trusting, high on integrity and not easily discouraged other than in unstable situations which call for rapid change. Always trying to build stable group structures (because Implementers need them themselves) they are not very sympathetic to what they see as 'airy-fairy' ideas, but are perfectly willing to adapt schedules and proposals to fit in with agreed plans and established systems.

Monitor Evaluator

High in intelligence, this role (in contrast to the Plant) is a bit of a cold fish being a stable introvert whose contribution lies in measured and dispassionate analysis rather than creative ideas. This is the person who will stop the team committing itself to a misguided or unwise project or deadline. By nature a critic, the key to the criticism is logic, not personality. Slow to make up their minds the Monitor Evaluators like to be given time to mull over the issues. This is probably the most objective person in the team but care must be taken not to allow the realism to become a damper on the rest of the team as they can become depressingly negative if they allow their critical powers to override receptiveness to new ideas. The soundest judge in the team.

Finisher

An anxious introvert, the Finisher worries about what might go wrong and is unable to relax until everything has been checked. Not assertive, but with a permanent sense of urgency stemming from the anxiety, this person is often impatient and intolerant of more casual and happy-go-lucky team members. Preoccupied with order, the Finisher is a compulsive meeter of deadlines and fulfiller of schedules. He or she can be a morale-reducing worrier with a depressive effect on other members of the team – but the relentless follow through is critical to team success.

Specialist
In the extreme form these are the persons who contribute expertise but little else. The pure specialist tends to be single-minded, self-starting and dedicated. This is the role which may provide a technical skill which is in short supply. Generally, specialists contribute only on a narrow front – and typically in jargon.

Think – In your particular team at work, what role do you fulfil?
     – Which other roles can you identify?
     – Which roles are not carried out effectively?
     – Using this analysis, how could the overall effectiveness of the group be improved?

The important message from Belbin's work is that no manager or supervisor can fulfil all of these roles as they demand very different personality characteristics. However, a team can encompass all of these needs for effectiveness.

Some people spend a great deal of money and effort attempting to train employees in appropriate team behaviour, but, as such behaviours appear to be a function of personality, the attempts may be of limited value. It would seem to be more realistic to search for appropriate team talents at the selection stage. This would involve additional criteria at the person specification stage, but it may well be an effort well worth making.

The team aspects and roles also need to be taken into account when making internal selections such as occurs in promotion and re-deployment exercises within organizations.

Appraisal

Having recruited a member of staff we will need, at some point, to 'close the circle' by following up on actual performance to check how good the decision was (and how much it cost!). This will also enable corrective training actions to be instituted where necessary, to help make the 'OK' decisions 'good'. In one sense we are all being appraised at work each and every day, by colleagues, bosses, clients, customers and subordinates. The reality is that due to the very nature of the roles we play at work, we commonly receive very little accurate feedback. For example, selectors may conduct truly awful interviews, but the candidate who wants the job will be well advised not to tell them! Lecturers may give poor lectures, but students hoping for good grades are often careful to avoid being critical.

Within the workplace there is a clear need for there to be a formalized system of staff assessment and development as opposed to the inevitable and continuous appraisal that will go on day by day. What appraisal can be used for is perhaps best summarized by Figure 13.4. This highlights the fact that such a system should be much more than just a chance to 'tell them what the

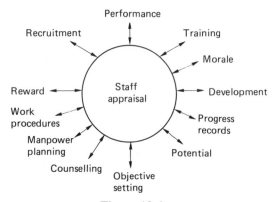

Figure 13.4

organization thinks of them'. As shown in Figure 13.4, appraisal can be used for a variety of purposes and clearly, if used well, it can be a most powerful tool in the management of human resources with implications for many other personnel activities.

Another assumption is that it will be best used as part of an 'open' system – i.e. the whole process can be conducted in secret but if it is then there can be little learning or development of the staff concerned. This in turn implies that full and open consultation will have taken place with the staff concerned before the implementation of any scheme.

There are a number of important issues to consider when designing an appraisal scheme. We will look at them by getting you to do a few more 'think' exercises. The prime issue to consider is why we are undertaking appraisal.

> **Think** – Do we want to
> – improve performance?
> – determine levels of pay?
> – decide on suitability for promotion?
> – allocate penalties for performance below that required?
> – determine training needs?

We may need to think hard about whether it is feasible to attempt to do more than one thing with a single scheme. The evidence is that if pay levels are being determined, most other outcomes become 'unheard' due to our old friend 'selective perception'. The next issue is:

> **Think** – What should be appraised:
> – performance?
> – personality?
> – potential?

It seems clear that the type of scheme we come up with and the information that will need to be collected, will depend on our answer to this first question. This, in turn, gives rise to the next set of questions:

```
Think  – What information do we need to appraise performance?
       – What information do we need to appraise personality?
       – How do we appraise personality?
       – If we do, what does an individual do if they are appraised as
         being 'too introverted'?
       – What do we mean by 'potential?
```

The next important decision to be made is:

```
Think  – Who should appraise:
       – Boss?
       – Boss's boss?
       – Colleagues?
       – the inviduals themselves?
       – Subordinates?
```

One major problem that may arise is that your boss may not know what you do in any detail. This may be particularly true of salespersons who may be away from the office and out of sight of the boss for the majority of their working time. In contrast the job-holders are very aware of what they do. In some companies, notably IBM, the basis for performance review is the individual's own self-assessment. Similar limitations apply when appraising teachers – their bosses rarely sit through a whole class let alone a whole course – so does this mean that students should appraise their teachers?

This gives rise to yet another issue to contemplate:

```
Think  – Are we concerned solely with job objectives/outcomes/ends?
       – Should we also be concerned with the methods/means used to
         achieve them?
```

The issue here may be to question whether sales figures tell the whole story. A salesperson who sells record amounts of double glazing may be doing it by terrorizing old people. Non-achievement of targets may be due to circumstances outside the individual's control.

The final issue to think about is:

```
Think  – How often should we appraise?
```

Leaving too long between appraisals may render any feedback obsolete – while doing it too often may reduce the impact unless it is handled very carefully.

As can be seen, there is no simple format that can be recommended to cover all situations. Each organization needs to address the issues above and design a scheme which meets their objectives.

Exercise – Design the appraisal system you feel would be most
applicable within your organization.
– Think how this would differ from current practice and describe
the steps you might take to introduce it.

Training

Here we are looking at the way people learn to do their jobs effectively and the ways in which the organization might intervene to help this process.

Think – How did you learn the skills required for your present job?
– Which category of learning was it? (e.g. connectionist, classical/
operant conditioning, insight/latent learning, or discovery
learning?)
– How could that learning have been improved?

Much of the learning theory reviewed in Chapter 5 comes into play again. The logic is similar but the objective is slightly different – we are now concerned with people learning how to behave at work, rather than learning to purchase our product/service. Association, Reward and Motivation remain the keywords.

Training is perhaps the activity which has the longest history of all management activities, dating back beyond the industrial revolution to the Guild system of the middle ages. It is to do with developing skills and learning, so we need our theories of how people learn again (from Chapter 5).

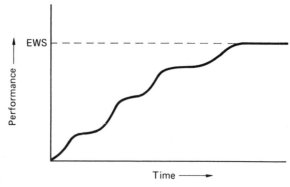

Figure 13.5

The graph in Figure 13.5 illustrates a typical learning curve – note that learning does not take place evenly and/or continuously. As students you will all be aware of the 'plateau' phenomenon! EWS stands for 'experienced worker standard' – the standard of performance we would expect from an experienced worker – this is our target. The aim of training is to steepen the learning curve in order to get the trainee to EWS in the shortest possible time.

The aim is to produce skilled performance. The nature of skill is an interesting concept to consider – speed, quality, consistency are all characteristics of skilled performance – another annoying fact is that skilled performers commonly make the task look easy!

The traditional way of training in the UK is 'sitting next to Nellie' where the trainee is put with an experienced person to 'pick up the job' (something I am sure you have all experienced). This has high face validity (who better to teach than an experienced person?), but the organization tends to lose control over what is learned. It is a slow process and is highly dependent on the quality of the Nellie.

Training, as a management activity, may be viewed as a process with a number of stages.

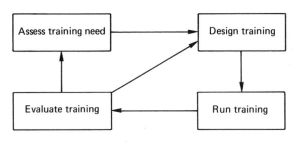

Figure 13.6

Some of these stages are examined in more detail below.

Assessing training needs

Whole books are written on this sub-section alone – but in its simplest form we have four main sources of data:

1 *Manpower plan* – as discussed earlier, manpower planning underpins most personnel activity, and nowhere more clearly than here. If we have identified that an additional x number of y skill will be needed in three years time, then training the required people is an obvious option.

2 *Performance measures* – either work study or an appraisal scheme may identify a training need.

3 *New technology* – plans to introduce new equipment, systems, products or procedures are prime sources for pointing up training needs.

4 *Legislation* – changes in the law may have training implications.

Training design

There are a surprising number and range of learning experiences – lectures, seminars, tutorials, books, journals, games, role-play, simulations, T-groups, CCTV, 'outward bound', instructors, mentors, friends – some are individual, some group, some concentrate on knowledge, some on skills. Each has its own strengths and weaknesses which are often defined by the personality and learning style of the learner (e.g. Kolb's approach to adult learning). Trainers will need to 'pick and mix' to achieve their learning objectives. It may be useful to reflect on our earlier study of learning theory and see if, and how, it can be applied to this situation. In the work situation we are going to be concerned with teaching adults appropriate skills and work behaviours – so Kolb's ideas may be significant in deciding what learning experiences are appropriate for given trainees. We may also find it useful to consider the specific types of behaviours and skills we are seeking to impart. The specific skill of operating a machine or the ability to reproduce consistently and unvaryingly a particular 'sales pitch' might suggest a classical conditioning approach to the learning. Alternatively, management training or a 'sales consultant's' skills appear to be more appropriate to an insight or latent learning style. How did you respond to the question asking which learning experiences had most helped you learn your job?

Evaluating training

To evaluate training is a relatively easy task for operator/craft levels – e.g. assessing the effectiveness of keyboard skills training is largely a matter of measuring speed and accuracy before and after training so that improvement and the effectiveness of the training can be determined. However, evaluating management training is much more difficult – many of the issues that are important were dealt with in Chapter 1. Refer back to your answers to the very first exercise in the book (evaluating the course you are currently undertaking) and the comments that were made at that time regarding criteria, level, timing, expected or unexpected outcomes, who should do the evaluation, for whom, etc. and the point about the difficulty becomes clear. As we said in Chapter 1 'there are significant numbers of choices to be made . . . which will define the confidence with which you can conclude as to the value of the training'. Asking the returning trainee 'was it a good course?' is not enough!

Motivating staff

Earlier in this book theories of motivation were reviewed in some detail, and it was noted that the subject area was important in understanding people's behaviour both as consumers and employees. The summary diagram (page 165) gave an indication of some of the managerial implications of the theories and much of the material in Chapter 6 will bear re-reading in the context of this chapter.

As we observed in the chapter on organization, the process of managing has traditionally meant making some assumptions regarding the motivation and behaviour of people. We then devise management systems based on these premisses in order to exercise control over the workforce.

If we believe that people are driven by the need for money then we will develop reward systems that will offer money as the reward for behaviour approved by the organization. If we made other assumptions we saw how this affects the alternatives available in the field of work design, management style, organization design and organizational culture.

Some of the theories that were looked at earlier can be seen as relatively generalist with applications in both marketing and organization theory, for example Maslow's theory of the Hierarchy of Needs. Some are much more centred on work behaviour, such as Herzberg's Two-factor theory and we can now introduce a couple more work-centred approaches to motivating staff.

The work of Peter Martin and John Nicholls

This pair of British researchers base their ideas on case studies of successful companies. They suggest that motivation emerges from the way in which people are managed and that there are three key elements:

- a sense of *belonging* to the organization created by being informed, involved and sharing in success;
- a sense of *excitement* in the job linked with pride, trust and accountability for results, and
- *confidence* in management leadership – a function of authority, dedication and competence. They present the ideas diagrammatically, as shown in Figure 13.7.

The work of Tom Peters

Peters (of Peters and Waterman *In Search of Excellence*, *A Passion for Excellence*, and *Thriving on Chaos* fame) comes up with another managerial model of motivation. He makes two fundamental assertions:

1 there is no limit to what people can achieve if they are really involved;

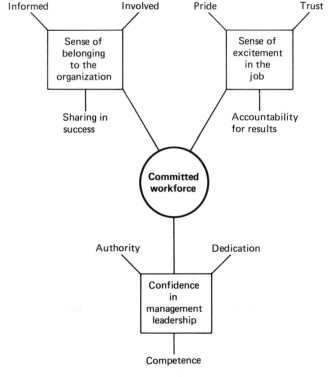

Figure 13.7

2 they work better in 'human scale groupings' (self managed teams).

He identifies the importance of staff involvement and suggests that it can be achieved by:

- everyone being listened to and recognized for achievement;
- recruiting people with the 'right' values and qualities;
- emphasis on training, retraining and upgrading skills;
- incentives based on performance and contribution for all;
- employment guarantees for acceptable performance.

He also recommends the removal of the following inhibitors:

- reduce layers in the organization/eliminated first line supervision;
- middle managers' role to focus on removing barriers to 'production';
- elimination of unnecessary bureaucratic procedures.

Reward systems

Despite the various theories of motivation which we have reviewed – pay remains the concrete expression of what the organization thinks of its employees. Most of us look at advertisements in our professional journals to compare the rates on offer with our own salaries and conditions. Our actual experience of working continually reinforces the importance of pay and rewards in our working lives, so consideration of some of the options is an important element in the effective managment of the workforce. There seem to be a number of issues which are of importance in determining what is a 'good' pay system.

1 Management's objectives for the pay system

Management pay money to employees as wages and salaries – in return they will have things that they wish the pay system to achieve or assist. In asking managers what these objectives are one commonly gets answers that include:

- attracting and retaining good employees;
- incentives or rewards for high productivity;
- incentives or rewards for high quality;
- rewarding flexibility;
- attracting the right employees to more responsible jobs;
- getting people to do less attractive jobs etc.

It will need a pretty impressive system to achieve all that!

Think – as an employee, what do *you* want from your pay system?

---

2 Employees' objectives for the pay system

Asking people the above question gives rise to many responses which often include:

- getting a fair reward for effort;
- getting a fair reward for skill;
- getting a fair reward for performance;
- maintaining/improving purchasing power/lifestyle.

There is an occasional response of 'getting as much as possible for as little effort as possible', but mostly people seem concerned with their version of 'fairness'.

Think – If the employee's income is the employer's cost and the one
seeks to maximize while the other seeks to minimize
– is conflict over pay and rewards inevitable?

---

3 Comparison with the 'outside world'

Here we will need to establish the going rate for the job. The first difficulty is to determine what is the relevant comparitor – some jobs fall into the local market, others may be national while some may actually be subject to international norms, so it is important that you collect your data from the relevant market. Methods and sources include:

- Employment Gazette,
- Employers' Associations,
- Local Press,
- National Press,
- Telephone Surveys.

One potential problem is in getting accurate data – e.g. identical job titles may disguise significant differences in duties and responsibilities, for instance guaranteed overtime or bonuses may be omitted. So it is always important to check out that you are making fair and accurate comparisons. Having established the going rate the employers are then able to make a choice as to where they wish to be in comparison to competitors. In practice they have a choice which ranges from being the front runner and paying the top rate, through being around the mean, to getting away with as little as they can. The decision may be affected by factors such as the degree of unionization, the calibre of labour required, the value of other elements (such as no layoffs), and above all the basic ability of the organization to pay.

4 Internal relativities

The next issue we have to face is the pay of one job relative to the pay of another – here we use some form of *job evaluation*. This is a generic expression which covers a number of different techniques and approaches.

1 *Ranking* – in this method the jobs are considered as a whole. You start with (say) a dozen jobs which are felt to be about right and decide which is the one worth the most money and which is worth the least. Next go for one you feel to be in the middle. You then decide whether the fourth job is in the top or bottom half and so on until all of the jobs are listed in rank order of worth. These dozen jobs are commonly known as the 'benchmark' jobs and others in the organization can be placed relative to this guideline. Once the rank order has been established the jobs can be split into salary or wage bands and other jobs fitted in as appropriate around the benchmark jobs. As a method ranking is simple and easy to understand, however it has the disadvantage of only producing a rank order – i.e. it does not give any indication as to the differential that should exist between two jobs. If you plan to put them into bands anyway then

this is not an insurmountable problem. Another difficulty is that ranking has a tendency to produce results that maintain the *status quo*.

2 *Grading* – again the jobs are considered as a whole but in this technique the grade lines are drawn before you start – so the choice you have to make is about which grade each of the benchmark jobs goes into. Later, other jobs can be fitted in by comparing them to the benchmarks. The advantages and disadvantages of grading schemes are similar to those identified above for ranking.

3 *Points Rating* – here the jobs are measured against pre-determined criteria and awarded points on each. The scales are arranged so that the more points awarded, the more the job is worth. This is known as an analytical technique because the jobs are not considered as a whole but are broken down into their component elements. The greater the total points score the greater the pay. Inevitably life is not so simple and it is common that weightings are attached to different factors which adds another bone of contention to the process. One problem with points rating is that it produces a numerical measure and this carries a spurious air of accuracy – in fact the process is one of subjective judgement and the real accuracy is a lot less than $+/-$ 1 per cent!

These methods go a long way towards defining the size of the difference in pay between different jobs – however, in reality, another major issue is acceptabilty so there is likely to be negotiation which may affect the final outcome. Most of the techniques described are only really useful for comparing jobs in the same 'family' – few will cope with comparing miners to marketers.

5 Pay systems and rewards

There are a variety of pay systems which have different characteristics and which need to be reviewed briefly:

1 *Time Rates* – this is where a wage is defined as £x/hour – i.e. the wage earned is a function of the time worked rather than performance or output. This is common for the payment of salaries and office staff. The characteristics of such a scheme are that the employee gets paid the same amount of money per week irrespective of the amount of work done – so it does not reward exceptional performance. From the employer's side the costs are fixed, but the labour cost component will vary according to the output.

> **Think** – For what types of work do you think this would be a good pay system?

2 *Piece rates or direct bonus* – here the wage is calculated as £y/unit produced or sold. In this case the employer always has the same labour

cost per unit (because for every unit made or sold, £y is paid out in wages/salary). For the employee, earnings increase with output – so such a scheme gives good incentives to high levels of output or sales. One disadvantage to the employee is claimed to be the uneven wage levels from week to week, while the employer may have more difficulty in establishing and maintaining quality standards.

> **Think** – For what types of work do you think this would be a good pay system?

3 *Measured day work* – in this system the organization agrees to pay a sizable bonus to employees on their reaching a previously agreed target of output or sales. The bonus is payable when the target is reached or when failure is not the responsibility of the operator. It can be seen that there is very high incentive to reach the target but none thereafter – thus it can be ideal where the employer needs a fixed output (perhaps to link in with some other part of the company) or where an excess of output would be an embarrassment e.g. in the food trade where the product has a very short shelf-life.

> **Think** – For what types of marketing jobs might this be a good pay system?

4 *Profit sharing* – some companies give staff an annual bonus based on the year's profit – sometimes in cash but increasingly in shares. The increased involvement due to some element of ownership is clearly desirable although cynics agrue that the shareholding is too minute to affect policy or give anything other than a token feeling of being part of the management. The annual cash bonus may be too far removed from the actual actions of the individual and the profit itself may reflect world economics rather than efficiency.

> **Think** – For what types of work do you think this would be a good pay system?

5 *Productivity bonus* – in these schemes the employee is rewarded for effective and efficient effort, thus eliminating some of the implied criticisms of profit sharing. Essentially staff are paid a bonus which is proportional to some such ratio as:

Added value/Total labour cost

It can be seen that the ratio may be improved by either increasing the added value with the existing labour force or producing the same added value with less labour. In this way the productivity rather than profitability is rewarded.

> **Think** – For what types of work do you think this would be a good pay system?

6 *Group bonus* – should only be paid where the work is genuinely a group activity. Paying group bonus to a number of individual pieceworkers on the grounds that they work in the same place and the hope that the speedy will spur the slow to greater efforts seems unrealistic – it seems more likely that the speedy will come down to the level of the slow (cf. Equity Theory in Chapter 6).

> **Think** – For what types of work do you think this would be a good pay system?

7 *Fringe benefits* – are an important and often overlooked element in the reward package. Some may be relatively trivial but others may be very important and valuable. The scope of such benefits is often surprising and ranges from the employee being able to buy company products at a discount to subsidized mortage schemes or free boarding education for children. The company car is a common fringe benefit but in the UK such benefits are increasingly liable to taxation.

Clearly such schemes are not mutually exclusive – many people get a flat salary with a performance bonus as an addition. Thus it may be useful to think in terms of a 'reward package' which could be made up of basic salary, bonus payments and fringe benefits.

> **Think** – What is the make up of your reward package?
> – How fair is it?
> – How could it be improved?
> – Design the ideal mix of rewards for your job.

6 Performance related pay

A significant trend in the late 1980s in the UK was the interest shown in performance related pay systems. In one sense this is nothing new – piecework (see above) is a classic example of paying people according to their output and this was developed by F. W. Taylor in the first decade of the century. Similarly many salespersons have been paid on individual bonus schemes or commission for many years. What has been new about the PRP movement in the 1980s and 1990s has been its extension to apply to many more white collar and administrative/managerial jobs. While it has many attractions in terms of perceived fairness and incentive, there are some interesting issues surrounding the approach. The prime concern must lie with the definition of performance – do we define it in terms of final outputs, or are we concerned with the methods by which such outcomes are achieved? As we queried earlier, do we reward the high performing door-to-door salesperson if we discover that the high sales are obtained by threatening and intimidating old age pensioners?

7 *Cafeteria reward systems*

Chapter 8 introduced the idea of the Family Life Cycle as a means of describing the differing focus of expenditure and interest at various stages of life (we also criticized the original model as being somewhat too simplistic). While such ideas were developed for marketing analysis, the underlying assumptions seem likely to hold good in the wider context and this has resulted in some potentially exciting developments in reward system management.

The basic idea is that a variety of different rewards are drawn up and costed as the menu from which individual employees may pick and choose their own reward packages. Thus at a younger age some employees might choose to have a significant proportion of their reward package in the form of mortgage support, later they may opt for longer holidays or a company car, while at the equivalent of the 'Empty Nest' phase they could elect to have higher pension contributions. The organization still controls the overall size of the package and may impose restrictions on the proportion allowable in some categories, so management can still use such a system to motivate and reward the individual. Such systems are not widely available at the moment (perhaps due to difficulties in clarifying the tax situation), but it does appear to be an attractive alternative to straight salary and has an important motivating element in allowing a degree of self-determination in such a crucial part of the employment contract.

Think – How do you think your ideal mix for *your* reward package will change over time?

Management by objectives (MBO)

One system of managment which became popular in the 1970s was management by objectives. Since then its popularity has waned somewhat, but the underlying principles are the basics of any rational management system. One of its important characteristics is the involvement of staff (jointly with their bosses) in setting down the goals for a specific department, section or job. Despite variations in practice, there is general agreement that the following steps are integral to the MBO process.

1 *Develop overall organizational goals.* Goals at this early stage are likely to be based on the overall mission of the enterprise and will most commonly address targets to be achieved by the organization as a whole. Such goals are usually strategic and are the concern of the top management team.

2 *Establish and agree specific goals (objectives) for individual functions and/ or departments.* At this level the goals are set so that the overall objectives in 1 above can be achieved. Managers will agree targets with the top management for both themselves and their departments.

3 *Establish and agree specific goals (objectives) for sub-units of those departments.* Here the managers will agree with unit heads, the targets for the sub-units concerned.

4 *Establish and agree specific goals (objectives) for individuals.* At this stage the heads of the sub-units agree the targets for individual employees.

5 *Formulate action plans.* Once the goals are set for each of the layers within the organization, there is a need to develop action plans that focus on the methods or activities which are necessary to achieve the targets. Essentially the action plan is a detailed description of what is to be done – with clearly defined targets and timescales. Drawing up an action plan sometimes identifies future dificulties and allows planning to be undertaken to avoid such problems interfering with the achievement of the goals. These plans are usually drawn up by subordinates in conjunction with their bosses.

6 *Implement and maintain self-control.* Fundamental to the original concept of MBO is that once an individual has agreed goals and action plans, a considerable amount of latitude is allowed in carrying out those activities. Here the importance of framing the goals and action plans with quantified targets and timescales is emphasized. The individual knows exactly what is expected, has agreed to the goals, and has the criteria by which measurement will be made. Thus employees should become self-monitoring, self-controlling, and self-motivated.

7 *Review progress periodically.* MBO in no way removes managers' responsibilities for supervising their staff – so reviews become an essential part of the process – to monitor, support, check progress and remove obstacles.

8 *Appraise performance.* At the end of the goal-setting cycle (usually one year) the manager and subordinate are in a strong position to appraise progress and performance by focusing on the extent to which the goals for the individual were achieved. Shortfalls can be analysed and may result in changing systems, modifying future targets, or identifying training needs.

The process may be shown as in Figure 13.8.

MBO has a number of characteristics which make it look very attractive as a managerial approach:

a There is clear co-ordination of goals and plans towards the achievement of the organization's objectives.
b It helps clarify priorities and expectations of staff and managers.
c It should facilitate communication both upwards and downwards within the organization.

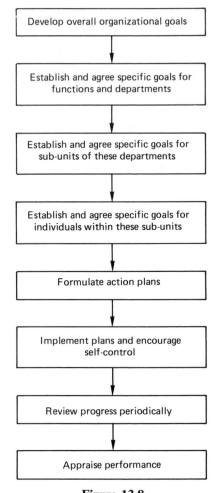

Figure 13.8

d It gives an agreed, factual basis for appraisal of staff.
e The process of involving staff in the setting of their own targets, and allowing them to become self-controlled should improve work motivation without management losing control of the strategic direction of the enterprise.

However, research has shown that it is not always as successful as might be hoped. Again there seems to be a number of reasons for this:

1 It requires considerable training of managers to help them handle the processes effectively.
2 It may require strong and continual commitment from the highest level of management.

3 It can be misused as either a punitive system in which targets are imposed, or as an overly bureaucratic and paper-laden burden for all concerned.
4 It can lead to an over-emphasis on achieving quantified goals and staff may be more concerned with ends and use undesirable means to achieve them.

Think – What objectives/goals/targets might you expect to be set for:
  – a marketing director?
  – a marketing manager?
  – a brand manager?
  – a sales representative?
  – a sales assistant?
  – a sales clerk?

And one more:

Think – If you work to a system like this – how effective is it? If not, how do you know what to do and how well you are doing it?

It is worth noting the similarity between the ideas underlying MBO and the discussion in Chapter 1 on the subject of control. Such systems, by clearly identifying what is expected, allows the practice of *management by exception*. Here managers only become directly involved when significant variance from the target is observed, thus allowing the manager to focus very clearly on managerial tasks.

Communications

A major activity of any management is the communication processes it decides to adopt with its workforce. As we have seen in the previous chapter, these communication processes may be seen as a function of management style – from the 'do as I say' of the autocrat to the 'here is the problem, how can we solve it?' of the participator. Clearly there will be a variety of interpersonal styles within any management team – but this variation can be by design (a contingency approach defining different styles as being appropriate for different managerial tasks and being brought into play at the recruitment and selection stage) or by accident (it just happens that way with little planning or forethought). Similarly, differences may be minimized by consciously seeking managers with an interpersonal style congruent with the organization culture or by training managers in interpersonal skills.

Similarly, the amount of information and the style with which it is communicated, will, to a large extent, define the organization's place on Watson's care versus control continuum. Choices may have to be made about the extent to which a management wishes (or is forced) to deal with and through an organized trades union. The social and political climate of the UK changed markedly from the 1960s to the 1980s both as a result of changing values and of governmental encouragement of the 'enterprise culture'. To a large extent, the wider changes influenced what occurred within companies and organizations. It is possible to use McGregor's 'dependency' approach to authority to explain such shifts given the differing economic circumstances and labour markets obtaining during the period.

The generally weaker trades unions have become less of a communication channel with an increasing tendency for managements to communicate directly with its workforce being identifiable. There is some evidence to suggest that joint consultative committees have come back into fashion with the backing of senior general managers in larger companies.

The marketing specialist have developed considerable expertise in influencing consumers' beliefs, values and behaviour. Huge budgets are spent to 'control' the market. The techniques of communication and persuasion are well developed. It is both interesting and depressing to realize how little of the available knowledge is used by managements in communicating with their own employees.

Think – How could the use of the material in this book be applied to improving communication at your place of work?

Performance management

One significant movement in the past few years has been the development of an overall approach to managing people at work that has been called *performance management*. In one sense it is nothing new, most of the elements have been around the management scene for a while. What is new is the idea of using the various techniques associated with Human Resource Management (perhaps with personnel specialists providing a service function to line managers), using them in an integrated package focused on the improvement of work performance, and keeping the whole process very much centred on the manager–subordinate relationship.

One problem which can be found with most traditional personnel approaches to managing people is the fragmented and sometimes contradictory policies which are adopted. It is not unusual to find companies making statements about how important they see teamwork, while paying individual, competitive bonuses. Other anomolies can emerge when management demand initiative but, in practice, operate very strict rule systems. Still more conflict can arise when line management's values and practices do not coincide with those of the Personnel Department. One important aspect of communication and the management of the human resource within the organization is the need for the personnel policies that are adopted to be internally consistent. Advertisements should be truthful (applicants should not be misled in order to get them to join) appraisal, management style and rewards should all work together to ensure a clear and consistent approach to relationships, expectations and behaviour at work.

The performance management approach is based on the Management by Objectives cycle described above. The employee meets with the manager and agrees the performance targets for the following year. Problem areas are discussed and a plan developed which is specific, measurable and achievable, along with realistic timescales.

One interesting aspect is that the manager has a continuing responsibility for keeping contact with the subordinate in what we could call a *counselling* role – regular, and quite frequent, meetings to review progress and to provide support and guidance.

As part of the overall process, some of our other ideas about managing people will be utilized. Changes in job design could emerge as a possibility, appraisal is regular and focused, training needs might become evident, choices about appropriate reward packages (even the cafeteria approach) could be discussed and implemented. Contact and support by the manager is a key characteristic of such a system and the aim is the alignment of the policies to ensure high levels of job performance.

So we might represent the process in some form such as illustrated in Figure 13.9.

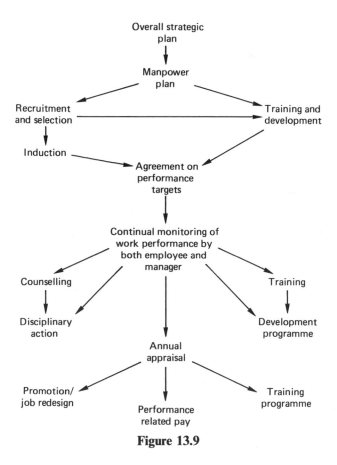

Figure 13.9

> **Think** – How useful would a performance management approach help
> you in your job?
> – How could it be applied more generally to marketing staff?

It is also of interest to look at the problems of managing people at work in terms of the analysis of control systems which were looked at in Chapter 1. There it was observed that manpower planning, recruitment and selection, training, reward systems and rules and discipline could be viewed as mechanisms designed to control that most unpredictable element of the organization, the workforce. The human resource management and performance management approaches to managing people follow this same logic.

Responsibility for human resource management

The last hundred years has seen the growth of human resource specialists – starting with welfare, moving through employment, industrial relations and training phases, to the current Human Resource Management approach. This more recent style is a sharper more business oriented approach than the traditional 'woolly welfare' beginnings of what used to be called personnel management.

However there is still an interesting debate to be conducted about who should fulfil the function. Clearly there is a growing body of expertise and legislation which is important – but it can be argued that the management of people should be done by their own line manager, not by a distant personnel specialist. Some argue that the ultimate aim of personnel management should be to render itself redundant by having trained general managers to standards of excellence in managing people as part of its training function.

Some 'typical' examination questions – Managing within the organization

A What do you understand by the term 'performance management'? Describe the main elements of such an approach to managing people at work and comment on its application within a marketing context.

B Your Managing Director has become increasingly concerned about the low level of commitment and high level of labour turnover in the sales force and he has asked you to investigate. What light could be thrown upon the possible causes of the problem by reference to the following theories of motivation:

   a   McGregor's Theory X and Theory Y?
   b   Herzberg's Two-Factor Theory?
   c   Martin and Nicholls' model?

C It has been argued that there is an implied 'psychological contract' between an organization and its individual employees. What is the basis for this view? How might the 'contract' be formulated for, say, a graduate recruit to the marketing department of a large multinational?

D How useful is performance related pay in the marketing context? Illustrate your answer with examples of its potential application to a number of *different* jobs within the marketing function.

E Outline and justify the appraisal scheme you feel would be appropriate for staff in a marketing department of a large, marketing oriented organization.

Sources

Buchanan D. A. and Huczynski A. A. (1985) *Organisational Behaviour*, Prentice-Hall.

Torrington, D. and Hall, L. (1991) *Personnel Management: A New Approach* (2nd edn.), Prentice-Hall.

Watson, T. J. (1986) *Management, Organisation and Employment Strategy*, Routledge & Kegan Paul.

Part Six

Footnote

14 Crystal balls

Speculations on the future

The future

Forecasting is difficult. The process is so fraught with uncertainty that the only thing you can be sure of is that your forecast will be wrong! The only difference between a good forecast and a bad forecast is that the good is less wrong than the bad.

Nevertheless, we live in the real world, and that world is changing rapidly. In writing this book the author has been only too aware of the changing nature of marketing and advertising – hence the emphasis on the readers looking at their own environment to find examples which illustrate the subject.

In the light of this rapid rate of change it may be worth attempting to make some prophesies about social and behavioural factors which could affect the processes and practice of marketing as well as the general world of work. We may examine some of these possible changes, in no particular order.

Macro issues affecting people at work

The workforce are subject to broader issues in just the same way as the population at large, indeed they *are* the population at large. The 'demographic downturn' will lead to a shortage of school leavers in the mid-1990s. This is likely to create problems for organizations who have traditionally recruited young persons as trainees (the National Health Service being a typical example which will need new sources of trainee nurses if targets are to be met). The knock-on effect of shortages could distort rates of pay and create problems of comparisons and career progression. Organizations may need to seek alternative sources of labour – women returners and the newly retired are the sources most quoted, although government actions such as raising the retirement age could also diminish the impact somewhat.

The legal requirements for equal opportunities for women, ethnic minorities, the handicapped, etc. could also be significantly enhanced by market forces in the changed labour market.

The emergence of a single European market will mean mobility of labour as well as increased markets and competition. The implications for management are considerable with problems of recognition of foreign qualifications, knowledge of other cultures, selection procedures etc. all needing review in the new circumstances. The need for improved language training for all levels of the organization seems imminent, not just overseas representatives and senior management, but also first line supervisors, telephonists, etc.

The development of more flexible working patterns and the advent of new technology may see many more home workers than we currently have – the move towards the flexible firm could go so far as to find very large numbers of persons needing to change their expectations of careers and work relationships. The management skills needed to handle such new situations may need to be identified and training designed for 'the new managers'. Another crucial fact is that the political and social values of a society will permeate all organizations. The political colouring of future governments will determine many of the problems faced by managers.

The development of mass communication systems

We already have satellite television links and there is a growing market for dishes and decoders. It seems likely that the penetration of satellite and cable TV will continue as these channels recognize and realize their economic power in buying up major events (particularly sport) for 'resale' via their particular systems. It could also emerge that the 'media moguls' capitalize on their position and seek economies of scale by standardizing their product over large areas of the globe. The result could be the development of (e.g.) some form of 'Euroculture'. An alternative could be an even more pervasive world-wide American culture.

The speed of world-wide communication suggests that fashions may spread ever more rapidly. The marketing opportunities offered by this increasing ability to reach very large proportions of the population very quickly offers great opportunities for marketers. If this were to happen, the downside would be a tendency for fashions to last even shorter periods of time before they are swamped by the next wave. In such market sectors the diffusion process would be speeded up across the whole range.

A counter prediction could be the likelihood of the development of many more local communication systems which would focus very much on more immediate issues relevant to much more limited geographical areas. The probability is that both scenarios may be true so that, overall, the range of communication media will increase thus offering significant choices and opportunities to the marketer.

Technology

In many ways the future is already with us in the shape of computers, robots, fax machines and so forth. The future looks to expand the utilization of such technology.

This could result in changing patterns of working – the advent of computers and modems means that working from home may be a real possibility for many people. The assumption that this will be particularly attractive to women seems likely to be unfounded if our theories about the value of work as a source of status and social contact are true. The impact on selling jobs could be great, in that representatives may need to visit base only rarely as most contact could be via computer links and teleconferencing facilities.

Another prediction is that the rising importance of electronic communication will render many of our traditional skills obsolete. One which may become markedly less important is book reading. One could easily see the time when material such as included in this text would be transmitted by means other than a book. This raises the interesting possibility that this volume could become a collector's item!

Continuing this train of thought leads on to the impact on the education system. As we learn more about the ways in which people learn, and link this with the advances in technology, it seems likely that we will see the growth of new forms of education – much smaller groups being taught via electronic (TV) media. The implications of such an idea could be quite significant – schools as we know them could be a thing of the past and this, in turn, would have a dramatic effect on the socialization process (remember – school was described as a major element of socialization).

Other developments which could have important implications would centre on the effect of improving technology on the health of the population. Some predictions suggest that we may all live very much longer in the future which would have a significant effect on the already problematic population and demographic profile of society.

The development of exciting new systems currently referred to as 'virtual reality' seem to have the potential to change our lives dramatically. For instance, if it becomes possible to 'experience' luxury overseas holidays without travel, in the privacy of one's own home, the impact on the leisure industry could be spectacular as well as disastrous.

Environmental issues

The rise of the 'green' consumer has been a well documented feature of the late 1980s and early 1990s. Environmental consciousness has made an impact on marketing practice through the emphasis on the use of recycled and bio-degradable packaging, and the development of environmentally friendly products. It would seem probable that this trend will continue with more companies developing products which can be sold under a 'green' banner. To some extent such issues are the concerns of the relatively affluent and developed societies, it could prove difficult to sell the message to societies which can see the luxuries of the developed world, aspire to such benefits for themselves, but do not have the resources to pay the 'green premium'.

Social changes

Within the UK there are suggestions that we will see a change in the political systems – less centralization and more regional structures. The implications for our party political system are significant.

Others predict the decline of class differentiation. What does seem even more probable is that, due to the changes in the demographic profile, a decline in gender role differentiation and dramatic changes in notions of what constitutes 'womens work' will be seen. The signs of a continuing erosion of ideas such as the Welfare State seem clear.

One major imponderable is the state of the economy. Growth in economic terms could have the great benefit of blurring many of the stark changes which seem likely. These seem to centre on the increasing gap between the 'have's' and the 'have not's' which, if the earlier prediction of the decline of the safety net of the Welfare State is true, will mean another way of segmenting the population for marketing purposes. This, in turn, suggests a rapid increase in private medicine, private education and private social services.

At the time of writing the movement towards a more integrated Europe continues. The growth of the EC as a trading and economic unit is highly significant especially in the context of the break-up of the USSR and the similar problems in Yugoslavia. The move of Eastern bloc countries towards the free market system is clearly a marketing opportunity of immense proportions. Paradoxically, the break-up of the USSR could weaken the moves towards a larger unified Europe – as we saw in the Sherif experiments, nothing unites a group more than a common enemy. Once again the future could embrace both the moves towards larger and smaller units by encouraging more relatively small countries to joining together into 'federal' trading coalitions.

Taking an even broader perspective, world wide predictions focus on the increasing expectations of people throughout the world (largely due to the improvements in communications) and the likelihood of a growing lack of tolerance of Northern wealth by the inhabitants of the poorer Southern hemisphere. The indications are that we may well see an increase in political extremism.

Demographics

As already mentioned, the dominant features in the UK are:

1 the impact of the low birthrate in the 1970s on the labour market is the key factor – the reduction in the number of school leavers with all that implies for employment patterns and career paths, and

2 the ageing population – the number of 60+ pensioners is marked.

The predicted advances in medical research and improvements in health care are likely to make the problem even worse.

This could see the end of the 'youth culture' which many say has dominated our society since the 1960s and the associated rise in 'middle-age' numbers and values. There will also be a genuine growth of 'grey power' in terms of both markets and politics.

This also has implications for the 'non-greys'. There could develop a tension between the (relatively) small number of young, economically active souls attempting to care for a population which has become top heavy in terms of pensioners, the retired and, potentially, an overwhelming need for geriatric care. On the other hand nuclear war, AIDS, global warming, holes in the ozone layer may make all of this speculation irrelevant.

As mentioned above, one of the worst problems may be attempting to run a system in the absence of economic growth, with world-wide population explosions, and the expectation of the populace at large as major issues for us all to manage.

Whatever the future holds, whether it be growth, decline or stagnation, the marketing of products, ideas and values will continue to be a major and significant task. The understanding of consumer behaviour will become ever more important.

Solutions to Problems

Pattern to be transmitted under 'one-way' communication conditions:

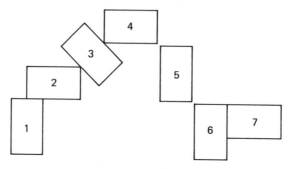

Pattern to be transmitted under 'two-way' communication conditions:

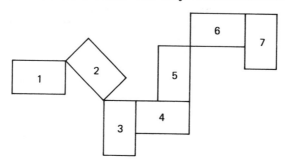

Possible solutions to the problem posed on page 42

(a) If the dots are a little larger then a solution is possible in three lines:

(b) If the line is wide enough then the whole thing can be done in one!

Name index

Subject index